Canada And The States

by

Sir E. W. Watkin

Double 9
BOOKS

Canada And The States
by Sir E. W. Watkin

Copyright © 2023

All Rights reserved.

ISBN: 978-93-61150-14-2

Published by

DOUBLE 9 BOOKS

2/13-B, Ansari Road
Daryaganj, New Delhi – 110002
info@double9books.com
www.double9books.com
Tel. 011-40042856

ABOUT THE AUTHOR

Sir Edward William Watkin, 1st Baronet was a British Member of Parliament and railway entrepreneur. He was an ambitious visionary who oversaw large-scale railway engineering projects to achieve his business goals, eventually rising to become chairman of nine distinct British railway companies. Among his more notable projects were the expansion of the Metropolitan Railway, which is now part of the London Underground; the construction of the Great Central Main Line, a purpose-built high-speed railway line; the creation of a pleasure garden with a partially constructed iron tower at Wembley; and a failed attempt to dig a Channel Tunnel beneath the English Channel to connect his railway empire to the French rail network. Sir Edward William Watkin, 1st Baronet was a British Member of Parliament and railway entrepreneur. He was an ambitious visionary who oversaw large-scale railway engineering projects to achieve his business goals, eventually rising to become chairman of nine distinct British railway companies. Among his more notable projects were the expansion of the Metropolitan Railway, which is now part of the London Underground; the construction of the Great Central Main Line, a purpose-built high-speed railway line; the creation of a pleasure garden with a partially constructed iron tower at Wembley; and a failed attempt to dig a Channel Tunnel beneath the English Channel to connect his railway empire to the French rail network.

CONTENTS

PREFACE

The following pages have been written at the request of many old friends, some of them co-workers in the cause of permanent British rule over the larger part of the Great Northern Continent of America.

In 1851 I visited Canada and the United States as a mere tourist, in search of health. In 1861 I went there on an anxious mission of business; and for some years afterwards I frequently crossed the Atlantic, not only during the great Civil War between the North and South, but, also, subsequent to its close. In 1875 I had to undertake another mission of responsibility to the United States. And, last year, I traversed the Dominion of Canada from Belle Isle to the Pacific. I returned home by San Francisco and the Union Pacific Railways to Chicago; and by Montreal to New York. Thence to Liverpool, in that unsurpassed steamer, the "Etruria," of the grand old Cunard line. I ended my visits to America, as I began them, as a tourist. This passage was my thirtieth crossing of the Atlantic Ocean.

Within the period from 1851 to 1886, history on the North American Continent has been a wonderful romance. Never in the older stories of the world's growth, have momentous changes been effected, and, apparently, consolidated, in so short a time, or in such rapid succession.

Regarding the United States, the slavery of four millions of the negro race is abolished for ever, and the black men vote for Presidents. A great struggle for empire—fought on gigantic measure—has been won for liberty and union. Turning to Canada, the British half of the Continent has been moulded into one great unity, and faggotted together, without the shedding of one drop of brothers' blood—and in so tame and quiet a way, that the great silent forces of Nature have to be cited, to find a parallel.

In this period, the American Continent has been spanned by three main routes of iron-road, uniting the Atlantic and Pacific Oceans: and one of these main routes passes exclusively through British territory—the Dominion of Canada. The problem of a "North-west Passage" has been solved in a new and better way. It is no longer a question of threading dark and dismal seas within the limits of Arctic ice and snow, doubtful to find, and impossible, if found, to navigate. Now, the two oceans are reached by land, and a fortnight suffices for the conveyance of our people from London or Liverpool to or from the great Pacific, on the way to the great East.

Anyone who reads what follows will learn that I am an Imperialist—that I hate little-Englandism. That, so far as my puny forces would go, I struggled for the union of the Canadian Provinces, in order that they might be retained under the sway of the best form of government—a limited monarchy, and under the best government of that form—the beneficent rule of our Queen Victoria. I like to say our Queen: for no sovereign ever identified herself in heart and feeling, in anxiety and personal sacrifice, with a free and grateful people more thoroughly than she has done, all along.

In this period of thirty-six years the British American Provinces have been, more than once, on the slide. The abolition of the old Colonial policy of trade was a great wrench. The cold, neglectful, contemptuous treatment of Colonies in general, and of Canada in particular, by the doctrinaire Whigs and Benthamite-Radicals, and by Tories of the Adderley school, had, up to recent periods, become a painful strain. Denuding Canada of the Imperial red-coat disgusted very many. And the constant whispering, at the door of Canada, by United States influences, combined with the expenditure of United States money on Nova Scotian and other Canadian elections, must be looked to, and stopped, to prevent a slide in the direction of Washington.

On the other hand, the statesmanlike action of Sir Edward Bulwer Lytton, Colonial Minister in 1859, in erecting British Columbia into a Crown Colony, was a break-water against the fell waves of annexation. The decided language of Her Majesty's speech in proroguing Parliament at the end of 1859 was a manifesto of decided encouragement to all loyal people on the American Continent: and, followed as it was by the visit—I might say the triumphal progress—of the Prince of Wales, accompanied by the Colonial Minister, the great Duke of Newcastle, through Canada, in 1860, the loyal idea began to germinate once more. Loyal subjects began to think that no spot of earth over which the British flag had once floated would ever, again, be given up—without a fight for it. Canada for England, and England for Canada!

But, what will our Government at home do with the new "North-west Passage" through Canada? The future of Canada depends upon the decision. What will the decision be? How soon will it be given?

Is this great work, the Canadian Pacific Railway, to be left as a monument, at once, of Canada's loyalty and foresight, and of Canada's betrayal: or is it to be made the new land-route to our Eastern and Australian Empire? If it is to be shunted, then the explorations of the last three hundred years have been in vain. The dreams of some of the greatest statesmen of past times are reduced to dreams, and nothing more. The strength given by this glorious self-contained route, from the old country to all the new countries, is wasted. On the other hand, if those who now govern inherit the great traditions of the past; if they believe in Empire; if they are statesmen—then, a line of Military Posts, of strength and magnitude, beginning at Halifax on the Atlantic, and ending at the Pacific, will give power to the Dominion, and, wherever the red-coat appears, confidence in the old brave country will be restored.

Then the soldier, his arms and our armaments, will have their periodical passages backwards and forwards through the Dominion. Mails for the East, for Australia, and beyond, will pass that way; and the subject of every part of the Empire will, as he passes, feel that he is treading the sacred soil of real liberty and progress.

Which is it to be?

Some years ago, Sir John A. Macdonald said, "I hope to live to see the day—and if I do not, that my son may be spared, to see Canada the right arm of England. To see Canada a powerful auxiliary of the Empire, not, as now, a source of anxiety, and a source of danger."

Does Her Majesty's Government echo this aspiration?

Thinking people will recognize that the United States become, year by year, less English and more Cosmopolitan; less conservative and more socialist; less peaceful and more aggressive. Twice within ten years the Presidential elections have pushed the Republic to the very brink of civil war. But for the forbearance of Mr. Tilden and the Democrats, on one occasion; and the caution of leading Republicans when President Cleveland was chosen, disturbance must have happened.

We have yet to see whether Provincial Government may not, in the Dominion, lead towards Separation, rather than towards Union. While one Custom-house and one general Government is aiding Union, the Province of Quebec accentuates all that is French; the Province of Ontario accentuates all that is British: the problem, here, is how, gradually, to weaken sectional, and how gradually to strengthen Union, ideas. State rights led to a civil war in the United States: Provincial Government fifty years hence may lead to conflicts in Canada.

In the United States there was no solution but war. Surely in Canada we can apply the safety valve of augmenting British aid and influence. Why not try the re-introduction of the red-coat of the Queen's soldier —that soldier to be enlisted and officered, let us hope in the early future, from every portion of the Queen's Dominions—as of the one Imperial army;—an Imperial army paid for by the whole Empire.

Chapter I
Preliminary—One Reason why
I went to the Pacific

A quarter of a century ago, charged with the temporary oversight of the then great Railway of Canada, I first made the acquaintance of Mr. Tilley, Prime Minister of the Province of New Brunswick, whom I met in a plain little room, more plainly furnished, at Frederickton, in New Brunswick. My business was to ask his co-operation in carrying out the physical union of Nova Scotia, New Brunswick, and through them Prince Edward Island and Newfoundland, with Canada by means of what has since been called the "Intercolonial" Railway. That Railway, projected half a century ago, was part of the great scheme of 1851,—of which the Grand Trunk system from Portland, on the Atlantic, to Richmond; and from Riviere du Loup, by Quebec and Richmond, to Montreal, and then on to Kingston, Toronto, Sarnia, and Detroit—had been completed and opened when I, thus, visited Canada, as Commissioner, in the autumn of 1861. I found Mr. Tilley fully alive to the initial importance of the construction of this arterial Railway— initial, in the sense that, without it, discussions in reference to the fiscal, or the political, federation, or the absolute union, under one Parliament, of all the Provinces was vain. I found, also, that Mr. Tilley had, ardently, embraced the great idea—to be realized some day, distant though that day might be—of a great British nation, planted, for ever, under the Crown, and extending from the Atlantic to the Pacific.

Certainly, in 1861, this great idea seemed like a mere dream of the uncertain future. Blocked by wide stretches of half-explored country: dependent upon approaches through United States' territory: each Province enforcing its separate, and differing, tariffs, the one against the other, and others, through its separate Custom House; it was not matter of surprise to find a growing gravitation towards the United States, based, alike, on augmenting trade and augmenting prejudices.

Amongst party politicians at home, there was, at this time, of 1861, little adhesion to the idea of a Colonial Empire; and the reader has only to read the reference, made later on, to a published letter of Sir Charles Adderley to Mr. Disraeli in 1862, to see how the pulse of some of the Conservative party was then beating.

There was, however, one bright gleam of hope. That was to be found in the, still remembered, effects of the visit of the Prince of Wales, accompanied by the Duke of Newcastle, to Canada, and the United States, in 1860.

Entertaining, with no small enthusiasm, and in common, these views of an Anglo-American Empire, Mr. Tilley and I were of the same opinion as to practical modes. We must go "step by step," and the Intercolonial Railway was the first step in the march before us.

In the following pages will be found some record of what followed. Suffice it here to say, that the Railway is made, not on the route I advocated: but it is in course of improvement, so that the shortest iron road from the great harbour of Halifax, in Nova Scotia, to the Pacific may be secured. The vast western country, bigger than Russia in Europe, more or less possessed and ruled over, since the days of Prince Rupert, the first governor, by the "Merchant Adventurers of England trading to Hudson's Bay," has been annexed to Canada, and one country, under one Parliament, is bounded by the two great oceans; and, as a consequence, the "Canadian Pacific Railway" has been made and opened for the commerce of the world.

Mr. Tilley, now Sir Leonard Tilley, is, at the moment, Lieutenant-Governor of New Brunswick, having previously filled the highest offices in the Government of the "Dominion of Canada;" and he has not forgotten the vow he and I exchanged some while after our first acquaintance. That vow was, that we neither of us would die, if we could help it, "until we had looked upon the waters of the Pacific from the windows of a British railway carriage." The Canadian Pacific Railway is completed, completed by the indomitable perseverance of Sir George Stephen, Mr. Van Horne, and their colleagues—sustained as they have been, throughout, by the far-sighted policy and liberal subsidies, granted ungrudgingly, by the Dominion Parliament, under the advice of Sir John A. Macdonald, the Premier. I have, in the past year, fulfilled my vow, by traversing the Canadian Continent from Quebec to Port Moody, Vancouver City, and Victoria, Vancouver's Island, over the 3,100 miles of Railway possessed by the Canadian Pacific Company, and have "looked upon the waters of the Pacific from the windows of a British railway carriage."

My impressions of this grand work will be found in future chapters.

"The Dominion of Canada" now includes the various Provinces of North America, formerly known as Upper and Lower Canada, New Brunswick, Nova Scotia, Prince Edward Island, British Columbia, Vancouver's Island, and the extensive regions of The Hudson's Bay Company, including the new Province of Manitoba, and the North West Territories; in fact, the whole of British North America, except Newfoundland.

This territory stretches from the Atlantic to the Pacific Ocean, and (including Newfoundland) is estimated to contain a total area of some four million square miles.

As matter of mere surface, and probably of cultivable area, also, more than half the Northern Continent of America owes allegiance to the Crown and to Queen Victoria. So may it remain. So it will remain if we retain the Imperial instinct. These noble provinces are confederated into a vast dominion, with one common Law, one Custom House, and one "House of Commons"—by a simple Act of the Imperial Parliament, the Confederation Act of 1867, passed while Lord Beaconsfield was Prime Minister and the Duke of Buckingham Colonial Minister. This union was effected quietly, unostentatiously, and in peace; and (circumstances well favouring) by the exertions, influence, and faithfulness to Imperial traditions, of Cartier, John A. Macdonald, John Ross, Howe, Tilley, Galt, Tupper, Van Koughnet, and other provincial statesmen, who forced the Home Government to action and fired their brother colonists with their own enthusiasm.

At home, all honour is due to a great Colonial Minister—the Duke of Newcastle.

Taking up, some years ago, a tuft of grass growing at the foot of one of the grand marble columns of the Parthenon at the Acropolis at Athens, I found a compass mark in the footing, or foundation—a mere scratch in the stone—made, probably, by some architect's assistant, before the Christian era. I make no claim to more than having made a scratch of some sort on the foundation stone of some pillar, or other, of Confederation. And I throw together these pages with no idea of gaining credit for services, gratuitously rendered, over a period of years and under many difficulties, to a cause which I have always had at heart; but with the desire to record some facts of interest which, hereafter, may, probably, be held worthy of being interleaved in some future history of the union of the great American provinces of the British Empire. I have another motive also: I should wish to contribute some information bearing upon any future account of the life of the late Duke of Newcastle. He is dead: and, so far, no one has attempted to write his biography. That may be reserved for another generation. He was the Colonial Minister under whose rule and guidance the foundations of the great measure of Confederation were, undoubtedly, laid; and to him, more than to any minister since Lord Durham, the credit of preserving, as I hope for ever, the rule of her Majesty, and her successors, over the Western Continent ought to attach. For, while the idea of an union, of more or less extent, was suggested in Lord Durham's time—probably by Charles Buller,—and was now and then fondled by other Governors-General, in Canada, and by Colonial Ministers at home—the real, practical measures which led to the creation of one country extending from the Atlantic to the Pacific were due to the far-sighted policy and persuasive influence of the Duke. The Duke was a statesman singularly averse to claiming credit for his own special public services, while ever ready to attribute credit and bestow praise on those around him.

My first interview with the Duke was in January, 1847. He was then Lord Lincoln, and the Conservative candidate for Manchester; in disgrace with his father. His father was the old fashioned nobleman who desired "to do what he liked with his own," and never would rebuild Nottingham Castle, burnt in 1832 by the Radicals. The son had cast in his lot with Sir Robert Peel and free trade. The father was still one of the narrow- minded class to whom reform of any kind was the spectre of "ruin to the country." They were quite honest in the conviction that the people were "born to be governed, and not to govern." They probably saw in the free importation of foreign food the abrogation of rent.

In 1847 Mr. Bright was the candidate for Manchester, whom we of the old Anti-Corn Law League supported. The interview I refer to was actuated by our desire to avoid an undeserved opposition; Lord Lincoln retired, however, owing mainly to other reasons, including that of the intolerance of a body of Churchmen regarding popular education.

A long period of wretched health compelled me for several years to consume what strength I had left in the ordinary routine of daily business. And it was not until 1852 that any further intercourse of any kind took place between us. In that year I published a little book about the United States and Canada, the record of my first visit to North America, in 1851. And, if I recollect rightly, I travelled with the Duke in the spring of 1852, probably between Rugby and Derby, and found him in possession of a copy of this little book, on which he had, faute de mieux, spent half-a-crown at the book stall at Euston. He recognised me; and it was my fault, and not his, that I saw no more of him till 1857, by which time, no doubt, he had forgotten me. Still our conversation in 1852 about America, and especially as to slavery, and the probability of a separation of North and South, will always dwell in my memory. Lord Lincoln had studied De Tocqueville; but he had not, yet, seen America. He had, therefore, at that time many erroneous views, which could only be corrected by the actual and personal opportunity of seeing and measuring, on the spot, the country, which always really means the people. This opportunity was given to him by the visit of the Prince of Wales to Canada and the United States, in 1860. He accompanied the Prince in his capacity of Colonial Minister.

These casual glimpses of Lord Lincoln were followed by an interview between us in 1857. In the meantime, it is true, he had had my name brought before him during his term of office pending the Crimean War Some one had suggested to the Government to send me out to the Crimea to take charge of the Stores Department, at a time when all was confusion and mess, out there, and I was asked to call on the Minister about it. It seemed to me, however, a duty impossible of execution by a civilian, unless the condition of "full powers" were conceded,—and the matter came to nothing.

In 1856 I was the Manager of the Manchester, Sheffield and Lincolnshire Railway. In that year a reckless engine, travelling between Shireoaks and Worksop, threw out some sparks, which set fire to the underwood of one of the Duke's plantations—for he was then Duke—and he wrote to the Chairman of the Railway, the then Earl of Yarborough, in what appeared to me a very haughty manner. I therefore felt bound to defend my chief, and I took up the quarrel. In a note addressed from the Library of the House of Commons, I asked for an interview, which was somewhat stiffly granted. This was the note which led to our interview:—

"CLUMBER, "1 Decr. 1856.

MY DEAR YARBOROUGH,

"Instead of placing the enclosed extraordinary production in the hands of my Solicitor, I think it best, in the first instance, to send it to you as Chairman of the M. S. & L. Railway, because I cannot believe that either its tone or its substance can have been authorized by the Directors.

"I am sorry to say this is not the first piece of impertinence which I have had to complain of in reference to the damage done to my woods by the engines of the Company, and neither Mr. Foljambe nor I have had any encouragement to treat the matter in the amicable spirit which we were anxious to evince.

"The demands now made by the aggressors upon the party aggrieved is simply preposterous, and, of course, will be treated as it deserves. We shall next have the Company, or rather, as I hope and believe, the Company's Solicitors, demanding us to cut all our corn within 100 yards of the line before it becomes ripe, and consequently inflammable.

"Your Solicitor knows perfectly well that the Company is by law liable for damage done to woods; and, moreover, that such damage is preventible by proper care on the part of its servants.

"I think the Directors ought to order their Solicitor to write to me and others, to whom so impertinent a letter has been addressed, and beg to withdraw it, with an apology for having sent it.

"I am sorry to trouble you with this matter, because I feel that you ought not to be troubled with business in your present state of health; but as you are still the Chairman, I could not with propriety write to any other person.

> "I am, my dear Yarborough,
> "Yours very sincerely,
> "NEWCASTLE.

"THE EARL OF YARBOROUGH, &c., &c."

Accordingly, I went to the mansion in Portman Square. I waited some time; but at last in stalked the Duke, looking very awful indeed—so stern and severe—that I could not help smiling, and saying—"The burnt coppice, your Grace." Upon this he laughed, held out his hand, placed me beside him, and we had a very long discussion, not about the fire, but about the colliery he, then, was sinking—against the advice of many of his friends in Sheffield—at Shireoaks; and when he had done with that, we talked, once more, about Canada, the United States, and the Colonies generally.

After this date, I had to see the Duke on business, more and more frequently. The year after the Duke's return from Canada, in 1861, he happened to read an article I had written in a London paper, hereafter given, about opening up the Northern Continent of America by a Railway across to the Pacific, and he spoke of it as embodying the views which he had before expressed, as his own.

In 1854 Mr. Glyn and Mr. Thomas Baring had urged me to undertake a mission to Canada on the business of the Grand Trunk Railway, which mission I had been compelled to decline; and when, in 1860-1, the affairs of that undertaking became dreadfully entangled, the Committee of Shareholders, who reported upon its affairs, invited me to accept the post of "Superintending Commissioner," with full powers. They desired me to take charge of such legislative and other measures as might retrieve the Company's disasters, so far as that might be possible. Before complying with this proposal, I consulted the Duke, and it was mainly under the influence of his warm concurrence that I accepted the mission offered to me. I accepted it in the hope of being able, not merely to serve the objects of the Shareholders of the Grand Trunk, but that at the same time I might be somewhat useful in aiding those measures of physical union contemplated when the Grand Trunk Railway was projected, and which must precede any confederation of interests, such as that happily crowned in 1867 by the creation of the "Dominion of Canada."

I find that my general views were, some time before, epitomized in the following letter. It is true that Mr. Baring, then President of the Grand

Trunk, did not, at first, accept my views; but he and Mr. Glyn (the late Lord Wolverton) co-operated afterwards in all ways in the direction those views indicated.

"NORTHENDEN, "13_th November_, 1860.

"Some years ago Mr. Glyn (I think with the assent of Mr. Baring) proposed to me to go out to Canada to conduct a negotiation with the Colonial Government in reference to the Grand Trunk Railway. I was compelled then, from pressure of other business, to refuse what at that time would have been, to me, a very agreeable mission. Since then, I have grown older, and somewhat richer; and not being dependent upon the labour of the day, I should be very chary of increasing the somewhat heavy load of responsibility and anxiety which I still have to bear. It is doubtful, therefore, whether I could bring my mind to undertake so arduous, exceptional— perhaps even doubtful—an engagement as that of the 'restoration to life' of the Grand Trunk Railway.

"This line, both as regards its length, the character of its works, and its alliances with third parties, is both too extensive, and too expensive, for the Canada of to-day; and left, as it is, dependent mainly upon the development of population and industry on its own line, and upon the increase of the traffic of the west, it cannot be expected, for years to come, to emancipate itself thoroughly from the load of obligations connected with it.

"Again, the Colonial Government having really, in spite of all the jobbery and political capital alleged to have been perpetrated and made in connexion with this concern, made great sacrifices in its behalf, is not likely, having got the Railway planted on its own soil, to be ready to give much more assistance to this same undertaking.

"That the discipline and traffic of the line could be easily put upon a sound basis, that that traffic could be vigorously developed, that the expenses, except always those of repair and renewal, could be kept down, and that friendly, and perhaps improving and more beneficial, arrangements could be made with the local government—is matter, to me, of little doubt. Any man thoroughly versed in railways and quite up to business, and especially accustomed to the management of men and the conduct of serious negotiation, could easily accomplish this. But after all, unless I am very much deceived, all this will be insufficient, for many years to come, to satisfy the Shareholders; and I should not advise Mr. Glyn or Mr. Baring to tie their reputations to any man, however able or experienced, if it involved a sort of moral guarantee that the result of his appointment should be any very sudden improvement, of a character likely much to raise the *value of the property in the market*, which unfortunately is what the Shareholders very naturally look at, as the test of everything.

"To work the Grand Trunk as a gradually improving property would, I repeat, be easy; but to work it so as to produce *a great success* in a few years can only, in my opinion, be done in one way. That way, to many, would be chimerical; to some, incomprehensible; and possibly I may be looked upon myself as somewhat visionary for even suggesting it. That way, however, to my mind, lies through the extension of railway communication to the Pacific.

"Try for one moment to realize China opened to British commerce: Japan also opened: the new gold fields in our own territory on the extreme west, and California, also within reach: India, our Australian Colonies— all our eastern Empire, in fact, material and moral, and dependent (as at present it too much is) upon an overland communication, through a foreign state.

"Try to realize, again, assuming physical obstacles overcome, a main through Railway, of which the first thousand miles belong to the Grand Trunk Company, from the shores of the Atlantic to those of the Pacific, made just within—as regards the north-western and unexplored district —the corn-growing latitude. The result to this Empire would be beyond calculation; it would be something, in fact, to distinguish the age itself; and the doing of it would make the fortune of the Grand Trunk.

"Assuming also, again I say, that physical obstacles can be overcome, is not the time opportune for making a start? The Prince is just coming home full of glowing notions of the vast territories he has seen: the Duke of Newcastle has been with him—and he is Colonial Minister: there is jealousy and uncertainty on all questions relating to the east, coincident with an enormous development of our eastern relations, making people all anxious, if they could, to get another way across to the Pacific:—the new gold fields on the Frazer River are attracting swarms of emigrants; and the public mind generally is ripe, as it seems to me, for any grand and feasible scheme which could be laid before it.

"To undertake the Grand Trunk with the notion of gradually working out some idea of this kind for it and for Canada, throws an entirely new light upon the whole matter, and as a means to this end doubtless the Canadian Government would co-operate with the Government of this country, and would make large sacrifices for the Grand Trunk in consequence. The enterprise could only be achieved by the co-operation of the two Governments, and by associating with the Railway's enterprise some large land scheme and scheme of emigration."

The visit of the Prince of Wales to Canada and the Maritime Provinces, in 1860, had evoked the old feeling of loyalty to the mother country, damaged as it had been by Republican vicinity, the entire change of commercial relations brought about by free trade, and sectional conflicts. And the Duke, at once startled by the underlying hostility to Great Britain and to British institutions in the United States —which even the hospitalities of the day barely cloaked—and gratified beyond measure by the outbursts of genuine feeling on the part of the colonists, was most anxious, especially while entrusted with the portfolio of the Colonies, to strengthen and bind together all that was loyal north of the United States boundary.

Walking with Mr. Seward in the streets of Albany, after the day's shouts and ceremonies were over, Mr. Seward said to the Duke, "We really do not want to go to war with you; and we know you dare not go to war with us." To which the Duke replied, "Do not remain under such an error. There is no people under Heaven from whom we should endure so much as from yours; to whom we should make such concessions. You may, while we cannot, forget that we are largely of the same blood. But once touch us in our honour and you will very soon find the bricks of New York and Boston falling about your heads." In relating this to me the Duke added, "I startled Seward a good deal; but he put on a look of incredulity nevertheless. And I do not think they believe we should ever fight them; but we certainly should if the provocation were strong." It will be remarked that this conversation between Seward and the Duke was in 1860. That no one, then, expected a revolution from an anti-slave-state election of President. Still less did the people, of either England or the United States, dream of a divergence, consequent on such an election, to end in a struggle, first for political power, and then following, in providential order, for human freedom. A struggle culminating in the entire subjection of the South, in 1865, after four years' war—a struggle costing a million of lives, untold human misery, and a loss in money, or money's worth, of over a thousand millions sterling.

In our many conversations, I had always ventured to enforce upon the Duke that the passion for territory, for space, would be found at the bottom of all discussion with the United States. Give them territory, not their own, and for a time you would appease them, while, still, the very feast would sharpen their hunger. I reminded the Duke that General Cass had said, "I have an awful swallow ('swaller' was his pronunciation) for territory;" and all Americans have that "awful swallow." The dream of possessing a country extending from the Pole to the Isthmus of Panama, if not to Cape Horn, has been the ambition of the Great Republic—and it is a dangerous ambition for the rest of the world. We have seen its effects in all our treaties. We have always been asked *for land*. We gave up Michigan after the war of 1812. We gave up that noble piece, the "Aroostook" country, now part of the State of Maine, under the Ashburton Treaty in 1841. We have, again, been shuffled out of our boundary at St. Juan on the Pacific, under an arbitration which really contained its own award. The Reciprocity Treaty was put an end to, in 1866, by the United States, not because the Great West—who may govern the Union if they please—did not want it, but because the Great West was cajoled by the cunning East into believing that a restriction of intercourse between the United States and the British Provinces would, at last, force the subjects of the Queen to seek admission into the Republic. So it was, and is and will be; and the only way to prevent aggression and war was, is, and will be, to "put our foot down." Not to cherish the "peace-in-our-time" policy, or to indulge in the half-hearted language, to which I shall have hereafter to allude—but to combine and strengthen the sections of our Colonial Empire in the West—to give to their people a greater Empire still, a nobler history, and a prouder lot: a lot to *last*, because based upon institutions which have stood, and will stand, the test of time and trouble. Unfortunately we have had a "little England" party in our country. A Liberal Government, immediately following the Act of Confederation, took every red-coat out of the Dominion of Canada, shipped off, or sold, the very shot and shell to any one, friend or foe, who chose to buy: and the few guns and mortars Canada demanded were charged to her "in account" with the ruth of the miser. If the Duke of Newcastle had been a member of that Cabinet such a miserable policy never could have been put in force; but he was *dead*. I venture to think that the whole people of England, who knew of the transaction, were ashamed of it. Certainly, I saw, a few years ago, that one member of the very Cabinet which did this thing, repudiated the "little England" policy, as opposed to the best traditions of the Liberal party.

The "little England" party of the past have tried, so far in vain, to alienate these our fellow subjects. But, fortunately for the Empire, while some in the mother country have been indifferent as to whether the Provinces went or stayed, many in the Colonies have been earnest in their desire to escape annexation to the States. The feeling of these patriotic men was well described in December, 1862, by Lord Shaftesbury, at a dinner given to Messrs. Howe, Tilley, Howland and Sicotte, delegates from the Provinces of Canada, New Brunswick and Nova Scotia. He said Canada addressed us in the affecting language of Ruth —"Entreat me not to leave thee, nor to refrain from following after thee"—and he asked, "Whether the world had ever seen such a spectacle as great and growing nations, for such they were, with full and unqualified power to act as they pleased, insisting on devoting their honor, strength, and substance to the support of the common mother; and not only to be called, but to be, sons." And Lord Shaftesbury asked, "Whether any imperial ruler had ever preferred," as he said Canada had, "love to dominion, and reverence to power."

Lord Shaftesbury's sentiments are, I believe, an echo of those of the "great England" party; but, I repeat, "little England" sold the shot and shell, nevertheless.

Whatever this man or that may claim to have done towards building up Confederation, I, who was in good measure behind the scenes throughout, repeat that to the late Duke of Newcastle the main credit of the measure of 1867 was due. While failing health and the Duke's premature decease left to Mr. Cardwell and Mr. W. E. Forster—and afterwards to Lord Carnarvon and the Duke of Buckingham—the completion of the work before the English Parliament, it was he who stood in the gap, and formed and moulded, with a patience and persistence admirable to behold, Cabinet opinion both in England and in the Provinces. At the same time George Etienne Cartier, John A. Macdonald, and John Ross, in Canada; Samuel L. Tilley, in New Brunswick, and, notably, Joseph Howe, in Nova Scotia, stood together for Union like a wall of brass. And these should ever be the most prominent amongst the honoured names of the authors of an Union of the Provinces under the British Crown.

The works, I repeat, to be effected were—first, the physical union of the Maritime Provinces with Canada by means of Intercolonial Railways; and, second, to get out of the way of any unification, the heavy weight and obstruction of the Hudson's Bay Company. The; latter was most difficult, for abundant reasons.

This difficult work rested mainly on my shoulders.

It may be well here to place in contrast the condition of the Provinces in 1861 and of the Confederation in 1886. In 1861 each of the five Provinces had its separate Governor, Parliament, Executive, and system of taxation. To all intents and purposes, and notwithstanding the functions of the Governor-General and the unity flowing from the control of the British Crown—these Provinces, isolated for want of the means of rapid transit, were countries as separate in every relation of business, or of the associations of life, as Belgium and Holland, or Switzerland and Italy. The associations of New Brunswick and Nova Scotia were far more intimate with the United States than with Canada; and the whole Maritime Provinces regulated their tariffs, as Canada did in return, from no consideration of developing a trade with each other, or with the Canadas, between whose territory and the ocean these Provinces barred the way. Thus, isolated and divided, it could be no matter of wonder if their separate political discussions narrowed themselves into local, sectional, and selfish controversies; and if, while each possessing in their Legislature men in abundance who deserved the title of sagacious and able statesmen, brilliant orators, far-sighted men of business, their debates often reminded the stranger who listened to them of the squabbles of local town councils. Again, the Great Republic across their borders, with its obvious future, offered with open arms, and especially to the young and ambitious, a noble field, not shut in by winter or divided by separate governments. Thus the gravitation towards aggregation—which seems to be a condition of the progress of modern states—a condition to be intensified as space is diminished by modern discoveries in rapid transit—was, in the case of the Provinces, rather towards the United States than towards each other or the British Empire. Thus there were, in 1860, many causes at work to discourage the idea of Confederation. And it is by no means improbable that the occurrence of the great Civil War destroyed this tendency.

I remember an incident which occurred at a little dinner party which I gave in Montreal, in September, 1861, to the delegates who assembled there, after my visits, in response to the appeal just made to the Governments of Canada, Nova Scotia, and New Brunswick, on the subject of the Intercolonial Railway. It illustrates the personal isolation alluded to above. The Honorable Joseph Howe, then Premier of Nova Scotia, said, "We have been more like foreigners than fellow-subjects; you do not know us, and we do not know you. There are men in this room, who hold the destinies of this half of the Continent in their hands; and yet we never meet, unless by some chance or other, like the visit of the Prince of Wales, we are obliged to meet. I say," he added, "we have done more good by a free talk over this table, to-night, than all the Governors, general and local, could do in a year, if they did nothing' but write despatches. Oh! if you fellows would only now and then dine and drink with us fellows, we would make a great partnership directly." And the great partnership has been made, save only that Newfoundland still remains separate.

In Canada the divisions between the Upper and Lower Provinces were, in 1861, serious, and often acrimonious; for they were religious as well as political. The rapid growth of Upper Canada, overtopping that of the French-speaking and Catholic Lower Province, led to demands to upset the great settlement of 1839, and to substitute for an equal representation, such a redistribution of seats as would have followed the numerical progression of the country. "Representation by population"—shortly called "Rep. by Pop."—was the great cry of the ardent Liberal or "Grit" party, at whose head was George Brown, of the "Toronto Globe"—powerful, obstinate, Scotch, and Protestant, and with Yankee leanings. In fact, the same principles were in difference as those which evolved themselves in blood in the contest between the North and South between 1861 and 1865. The minority desired to preserve the power and independence which an equal share in parliamentary government had given them. The majority, mainly

English and Scotch, and largely Protestant and Presbyterian, chafed under what they deemed to be the yoke of a non-progressive people; a people content to live in modest comfort, to follow old customs, and obey old laws; to defer to clerical authority, and to preserve their separate national identity under the secure protection of a strong Empire. Indeed, it is difficult, in 1886, to realise the heat, or to estimate the danger, of the discussion of this question; and more than one "Grit" politician, whom I could name, would be startled if we reminded him of his opinion in 1861,—that the question would be "settled by a civil war" if it "could not be settled peaceably," but that "settled it must be—and soon."

The cure for this dangerous disease was to provide, for all, a bigger country—a country large enough to breed large ideas. There is a career open in the boundless resources of a varied land for every reasonable ambition, and the young men of Canada, which possesses an excellent educational machinery, may now look forward to as noble, if not more noble, an inheritance than their Republican neighbours—an inheritance where there is room for 100,000,000 of people to live in freedom, comfort, and happiness. While progress will have its periodical checks, and periodical inflations, there is no reason to doubt that before the next century ends the "Dominion," if still part of the Empire, will—in numbers—outstrip the present population of the British Islands.

Now, in 1886, all this past antagonism of "Rep. by Pop." is forgotten. Past and gone. A vast country, rapidly augmenting in population and wealth, free from any serious sectional controversy, free, especially, from any idea of separation, bound together under one governing authority, with one tariff and one system of general taxation, has exhibited a capacity for united action, and for self-government and mutual defence, admirable to behold.

Chapter II
Towards the Pacific—Liverpool to Quebec

Leaving Liverpool at noon of the 2nd September, 1886, warping out of the dock into the river—a long process—we arrived, in the fine screw steamer "Sardinian," of the Allan line, off Moville, at five on the following morning; and we got out of the inlet at five in the afternoon, after receiving mails and passengers. It may be asked, why a delay of twelve hours at Moville? The answer is—the Bar at Liverpool. The genius and pre-vision of the dock and harbour people at Liverpool keep the entrance to that port in a disgraceful condition, year after year—year after year. And the trade of Lancashire, Yorkshire, Cheshire, and Derbyshire, is compelled to depend upon a sand-bar, over which, at low tide, there is eight feet of water only. Such a big ship as "The Sardinian" can cross the bar in two short periods, or twice in the twenty-four hours, over a range, probably, of three or four hours. On my return home I wrote the following letter about this bar to "The Times":—

THE BAR AT LIVERPOOL

"SIR,—You inserted some time ago in 'The Times' a letter from Professor Ramsay detailing the troubles arising to travellers from the other side of the Atlantic, owing to shallow water outside the entrance to Liverpool, and you enforced the necessity of some improvement, in a very able article. Professor Ramsay was at that time returning from the meeting of the British Association, held in the Dominion of Canada.

"Still, while time goes on, and the question becomes more and more urgent, the bar, with its eight feet of water at low tide, remains as it was, save that some navigators contend that it grows worse.

"Yesterday 340 passengers, of whom I was one, by the noble Cunard ship 'The Etruria,' experienced the difficulty in all its varieties of trouble.

"After rushing through very heavy seas and against violent winds for three or four days, we cast anchor a good way outside the bar at 5 o'clock yesterday (Sunday) morning. The weather was too rough for the fine tug-boat, 'The Skirmisher,' to come so far out. So, after swinging about till 10 o'clock, we moved slowly on, crossed the bar about half- past 11, and were off the northernmost dock later on. Here the usual process of hauling the ship round by the aid of the tug took place, and then the further process of putting the baggage on board the tug, in advance of taking the passengers. I was fortunate in being taken off the ship in a special tug-boat by some friends, got to the landing- stage, where the baggage is examined by the Customs, and, a carriage waiting for me, was at the Central Station at Liverpool at one o'clock. But, with all these comfortable arrangements, I had lost at least seven hours, and had missed all morning trains. The other passengers, I fear, did not get through for two or three hours later, and those for London would be lucky if they just caught the 4 o'clock train.

"It would not, I am told, be prudent to take a ship of the size and draught of 'The Etruria' over the bar till two hours before high water on a flowing, and one hour after on an ebbing, tide. Thus, for such a ship—and the tendency is to build larger and larger vessels—the margin, even in moderate weather, is probably three hours out of the twenty-four, or, in other words, exclusion from the port for twenty-one hours out of the twenty-four, more or less.

"Lancashire will soon have to say whether its manufactures and commerce are to be tied to the bar at Liverpool; and, in the new competition of ports, a port open at any time of tide must ultimately draw the trade and traffic.

"Before the Committee of the House of Commons, on Harbour Accommodation, on which Committee I had the honour to sit, it was proved that every country in Europe, having a sea-board, was making and improving deep-water harbours,—except England.

"Take the case of Antwerp, which is already attracting traffic to and from the great British possessions themselves by reason of its great facilities.

"Liverpool is a place where the dogma of absolute perfection is accepted as a religion. But some of us may be pardoned if, in both local and national interests, we must be dissenters.

"That the bar may be made better instead of growing worse is obvious. But the great cure is by cutting through the peninsula of Birkenhead and obtaining a second entrance to the Mersey, always accessible, and obviously alternative. This was the advice of Telford seventy years ago, and 'The Times' has called public attention to a practical way of working out the Telford idea, planned by Mr. Baggallay, C.E., and laid before the Liverpool authorities—in vain.

"I may add that if our ship had called at Holyhead, the London passengers might have left Holyhead on Saturday evening instead of Liverpool on Sunday afternoon, a difference of a day.

"I beg to remain very faithfully yours,
"EDWARD W. WATKIN.

"Northenden, *Oct.* 18, 1886."

Some Liverpool cotton broker wrote to me to say that I had forgotten that there were two tides in the twenty-four hours. Nothing of the kind. There was one word miswritten, and, therefore, misprinted, which I have corrected: but the broad fact remains, and why my compatriots in the broad Lancashire district do not see the danger, I cannot comprehend, unless it be that some of them are up in the "Ship Canal" balloon, and others, the best of them, are indifferent.

Steaming along, after leaving Moville, we passed Tory Island, the scene of many wrecks, and of disasters around. It has a lighthouse, but no telegraphic communication with the shore at all.

I wrote a letter about that to the Editor of the "Standard." Here it is:—

"TORY ISLAND

"SIR,—Newspapers are not to be had here, but as this good ship is only a week out from Liverpool, and five days from out of sight of land to sight of land, I may fairly assume that Parliament is still discussing Irish questions.

"Thus I ask your indulgence to make reference to a question which is decidedly Irish, but is also Imperial, in the sense that it affects the lives of large numbers of persons, especially of the emigrant class, and is interesting to all the navigation and commerce of necessity passing the north-west extremity of Ireland.

"If your readers will refer to the map they will see, outside the north-west corner of the mainland of Ireland, Tory Island. It was on Tory Island that 'The Wasp' and her gallant captain were lost, without hope of rescue, for want of cable communication; and Tory Island itself has excited the interest of the philanthropist on many occasions. On Tory Island there is a lighthouse, with a fixed light, which can be seen sixteen miles. Not long ago, as I learn, a deputation from the Board of Irish Lighthouses went all the way to England to beg the Board of Trade, at Whitehall, to sanction the expenditure of eight hundred pounds, with a view to double the power of the light on Tory Island. Perhaps the Board of Trade, after some interval of time, may see their way to do what any man of business would decide upon in five minutes as obvious and essential. But that is not the point I wish to lay before you. My point is, that while the lighthouse on Tory Island is good for warning ships, and may, as above, be made more effective, no use is made of it in the way of transmitting ship intelligence.

"I ask, therefore, to be allowed to advocate the connection of Tory Island, by telegraph cable, with the mainland of Ireland and its telegraph system. The cost of doing this one way would, as I estimate, be two thousand five hundred pounds; the cost of doing it another way would be about six thousand pounds.

"The first way would be by a cable from the lighthouse on Tory Island, leaving either Portdoon Bay, on the east end of Tory Island, or leaving Camusmore Bay on the south of it, and landing either on the sandy beach at Drumnafinny Point, or at Tramore Bay, where there is a similarly favourable beach. The distance in the former case is six and a half, in the latter seven and a half miles, the distance being slightly affected by the starting point selected. Adopting this route at a cost of two thousand five hundred pounds, which would include about twenty miles of cheap land telegraphs, available for postal and other local purposes, would be the shortest and cheapest mode.

"The second way would be to lay a cable from Tory Island to Malin Head, where the Allan Steamship Company have a signal station. The distance is twenty-nine miles; the cost, as I estimate, about six thousand pounds. I should, however, prefer the former and cheaper plan, as I think it would serve a larger number of purposes and interests.

"From Portdoon Bay, on Tory Island, to Tramore Bay the sea-bottom is composed of sand and shells, very good for cable-laying; and there is a depth of water of from seventeen to nineteen fathoms.

"Tory Island is the turning point—I might say pivot point—for all steam and sailing vessels coming from the South and across the Western Ocean, and using the North of Ireland route for Liverpool, Londonderry, Belfast, Glasgow, and a host of other ports and places. It can be approached with safety at a distance of half-a-mile, near the lighthouse, as the water is deep close to, there being twenty fathoms at a distance of one-third of a mile from the Island.

"The steamers of all the Canadian lines pass this point—the Allan, the Beaver, the Anchor, the Dominion—while all the steam lines beginning and ending at Glasgow, Greenock, and other Scotch ports do the same. Again, all sailing vessels, carrying a great commerce for Liverpool and ports up to Greenock and Glasgow, and round the north of Scotland to Newcastle and the East Coast ports, would be largely served by this proposal. Repeating that this is a question of saving life and of aiding navigation at an infinitesimal cost, I will now proceed to show the various benefits involved.

"First of all it would save five hours, as compared with present plans, in signalling information of the passing to and fro of steamships. As respect all Canadian and many other steamers it would also expedite the mails, by enabling the steam tenders at Loch Foyle to come out and meet the ships outside at Innishowen Head; and this gain of time would often save a tide across the bar at Liverpool, and sometimes a day to the passengers going on by trains. As respects the Scotch steamers going north of Tory Island, it would enable the owners to learn the whereabouts of their vessels fourteen hours sooner than at present. In the case of sailing ships the advantages are far greater. Captain Smith, of this ship, a commander of deserved eminence, informs me that he has known sailing ships to be tacking about at thè entrance of the Channel, between the Mull of Cantyre and the north coast of Ireland, for eighteen days in adverse and dangerous winds, unable to communicate with their owners, who, if informed by telegraph, could at once send tugs to their relief. Again, when eastern winds prevail, in the spring of the year, tugs being sent, owners would get their ships into port many days, or even weeks, sooner than at present.

"But it needs no arguing that to all windbound and to disabled ships the means of thus calling for assistance would be invaluable.

"For the above reason I hope the slight cost involved will not be grudged, especially by our patriots, who have taken the Irish and Scotch emigrants under their special protection. I respectfully invite them and every one else to aid in protecting life and property in this obvious way.

"I am, Sir, your obedient Servant,
"E. W. WATKIN.

"S.S. Sardinian, off Belle Isle,
"*September* 9, 1886."

Our voyage on to Quebec had the usual changes of weather: hot sun, cold winds, snow, hail, icebergs, and gales of wind, and, when nearing Belle Isle, dense fog, inducing our able, but prudent, captain to stop his engines¯ till daylight, when was sighted a wall of ice across our track at no great distance. Captain Smith prefers to take the north side of Belle Isle. There is a lighthouse on the Island, not, I thought, in a very good situation for passing on the north side. But I found that there was no cable communication between Belle Isle and Anticosti. Thus, in case of disaster, the only warning to Quebec would be the non- arrival of the ship, and the delay might make help too late. I ventured to call the attention of a leading member of the Canadian Government to this want of means of sending intelligence of passing ships and ships in distress. In winter this strait is closed by ice, and the lighthouses are closed too. Inside the fine inlet of "Amour Bay," a natural dock, safe and extensive, we saw the masts of a French man-of- war. The French always protect their fishermen; we at home usually let them take care of themselves. This French ship had been in these English waters some time; and on a recent passage there was gun-firing, and the movement of men, to celebrate, as the captain learned, the taking of the Bastille. On the opposite coast is a little cove, in which a British ship got ashore, and was stripped by the local pirates of everything. Captain Smith took off the crew and reported the piracy; but nothing seems to have been done. A British war-ship is never seen in these distant and desolate northern regions. It may well be that the sparse population think all the coasts still belong to France, in addition to the Isles of St. Pierre and Miquelon. This is how our navy is managed. Can it be true that the Marquis of Lorne recommended that an ironclad should be sent to Montreal for a season, as an emblem of British power and sway—and was refused?

After some trouble with fog and wind, preceded by a most remarkable Aurora Borealis, and some delay at night at Rimouska, we reached Quebec, and got alongside at Point Levi, on the afternoon of Saturday, the 11th September; and I had great pleasure in meeting my old friend Mr. Hickson, who came down to meet Mrs. Hickson and his son and daughter, fellow-passengers of mine. I also at once recognized Dr. Rowand, the able medical officer of the Port of Quebec, who I had not set eyes on for twenty-four years. I stayed the night at Russell's Hotel; and next day renewed my acquaintance with the city, finding the "Platform" wonderfully enlarged and improved, the work of Lord Dufferin, a new and magnificent Courthouse being built, and, above all, an immense structure of blue-grey stone, intended for the future Parliament House of the Province of Quebec. The facility of borrowing money in England on mere provincial, or town, security, appears to be a Godsend to architects and builders, and to aid and exalt local ambition for fine, permanent structures. Well, the buildings remain. To find the grand old fortifications of Quebec in charge of a handful of Canadian troops, seemed strange. Such fortresses belong to the Empire; and the Queen's redcoats should hold them all round the world. I was told—I hope it is not true—that the extensive works above Point Levi, opposite Quebec, constructed by British military labour, are practically abandoned to decay and weeds.

Chapter III
To the Pacific—Montreal to Port Moody

On the evening of the 12th September I left Quebec by the train for Montreal, and travelled over the "North Shore" line of 200 miles. One of the secretaries of the Vice-President of the Canadian Pacific, Mr. Van Horn, called upon me to say that accommodation was reserved for me in the train; and that Mr. Van Horn was sending down his own car, which would meet me half way. It was no use protesting against the non- necessity of such luxurious treatment. I was further asked, if I had "got transportion?" which puzzled me. But I found, being interpreted, the question was modern American for "Have you got your through ticket?" I replied, that I had paid my fare right through from Liverpool to Vancouver's Island—as every mere traveller for his own pleasure ought to do; and I was remonstrated with for so unkind a proceeding, as the fact of my having been President of the Grand Trunk was of itself a passport all over Canada.

At Three Rivers, about half way, while reading by very good light— good lamp, excellent oil, very good trimming—there was some shunting of the train, and the usual "bang" of the attachment of a carriage. A moment afterwards Mr. Van Horn's car steward entered, and asked if I was Sir Edward Watkin; and he guessed I must come into Mr. Van Horn's car, sent specially down for me. Where was my baggage? I need not say that I was soon removed from the little, beautifully-fitted, drawing-room into this magnificent car. In passing through, I heard some growls, in French, about stopping the train, and sending a car for one "Anglais." So, on being settled in the new premises, I sent my compliments, stating that I only required one seat, and that I was certain that the car was intended for the general convenience, and would they do me the favour to finish their journey in it? I received very polite replies, stating that every one was very comfortable where he was. One Englishman, however, came in to make my acquaintance, but left me soon. I now became acquainted with Mr. Van Horn's car steward—James French, or, as his admirers call him, "Jim"— and I certainly wish to express my gratitude to him for his intelligence, thoughtfulness, admirable cookery, and general good nature. He took me, a few days later, right across to the Pacific in this same car, which certainly was a complete house on wheels—bedroom, "parlour, kitchen and all." His first practical suggestion was, would I take a little of Mr. Van Horn's "old Bourbon" whisky? It was "very fine, first rate." On my assenting, he asked would I take it "straight," as Mr. Van Horn did, or would I have a little seltzer water? I elected the latter, at the same time observing, that when I neared the Rocky Mountains perhaps I should have improved my ways so much that I could take it "straight" also.

At Montreal, my old friend and aforetime collaborateur, Mr. Joseph Hickson, met me and took me home with him; and in his house, under the kind and generous care of Mrs. Hickson, I spent three delightful days, and renewed acquaintance with many old friends of times long passed. It was on the 28th December, 1861, that Mr. Hickson first went to Canada in the Cunard steamer "Canada" from Liverpool. He was accompanied by Mr. Watkin, our only son, a youth of 15, anxious to see the bigger England. Mr. Watkin afterwards entered the service (Grand Trunk), in the locomotive department, at Montreal, and deservedly gained the respect of his superior officer, who had to delegate to Mr. Watkin, then under 18, the charge of a thousand men. There were, also, Howson, Wright, Wainwright, and Barker; subsequently, Wallis. Mr. John Taylor, who acted as my private secretary in my previous visit, I had left behind, much to his distress at the time, much for his good afterwards. Mr. Barker is now the able manager of the Buenos Ayres Great Southern Railway, a most prosperous undertaking; and poor dear, big, valiant, hard-working Wallis is, alas! no more: struck down two years ago by fever. These old friends, still left in Canada, are leading honorable, useful, and successful lives, respected by the community. To see them again made it seem as if the world had stood still for a quarter of a century. Then, again, there was my old friend and once colleague, the Honble. James Ferrier, a young-minded and vigorous man of 86: who, on my return to Montreal, walked down to the grand new offices of the Grand Trunk, near Point St. Charles—offices very much unlike the old wooden things I left behind, and which were burnt down—to see me and walked back again. Next day I had the advantage of visiting the extensive workshops and vast stock yards of the Canadian Pacific, at Hochelaga, to the eastward of Montreal, and of renewing my acquaintance with the able solicitor of the Company, Mr. Abbot, and with the secretary, an old Manchester man, Mr. Drinkwater. Then on the following day Mr. Peterson, the engineer of this section of the Canadian Pacific Company, drove me out to Lachine, and took me by his boat, manned by the chief and a crew of Indians, to see the finished piers and also the coffer-dams and works of the new bridge over the St. Lawrence, by means of which his Company are to reach the Eastern Railways of the United States, without having to use the great Victoria Bridge at Montreal. This bridge, of 1,000 yards, or 3,000 feet, in length, is a remarkable structure. It was commenced in May and intended to be finished in November. But the foundations of the central pier, in deep and doubtful water, were not begun, though about to begin, and this, as it appeared to me, might delay the work somewhat. The work is a fine specimen of engineering, by which I mean the adoption of the simplest and cheapest mode of doing what is wanted. All the traffic purposes required are here secured in a few months, and for about 200,000_l_. only.

The "Victoria" bridge at Montreal is a very different structure. A long sheet-iron box, 9,184 feet in length, with 26 piers 60 feet above the water level, and costing from first to last 2,000,000_l_. sterling. The burning of coal had begun to affect it; but Mr. Haunaford, the chief engineer of the Grand Trunk, has made some openings in the roof, which do not in any way reduce the strength of the bridge, and at the same time get rid of, at once into the air, the sulphurous vapours arising from coal combustion.

Mr. Peterson told me that their soundings in winter showed that ice thickened and accumulated at the bottom of the river. This would seem, at first sight, impossible. But experiment, Mr. Peterson said, had proved the fact, which was accounted for by scientific people in various and, in some cases, conflicting ways. May it not be that the accumulation is ice from above, loaded with earth or stones, which, sinking to the bottom by gravity, coagulates from the low temperature it produces itself? Mr. Peterson is not merely an engineer, and an excellent one, but an observant man of business. His views upon the all-important question of colonising the unoccupied lands of the Dominion seemed to be wise and far-sighted. He would add to the homestead grants of land, an advance to the settler—a start, in fact —of stock and material, to be repaid when final title to the property, were given.

Taking leave of my old friends, I left Montreal at 8 p.m. on the night of September 15th, in the ordinary "Pacific Express," on which was attached Mr. Van Horn's car, in charge of James French. I went by ordinary train because I was anxious to have an experience of the actual train-working. Mr. Edward Wragge, C.E., of Toronto, an able engineer of great experience, located now at Toronto, has sent me so concise an account of the journey of this train, and of the general engineering features of the line, that, anticipating his kind permission, I venture to copy it:—

"Leaving Montreal in Mr. Van Horn's car, the 'Saskatchewan,' by the 8 p.m. train on the 15th September, we passed Ottawa at 11.35 p.m.

"During the night we ran over that portion of the Canadian Pacific Railway which was formerly called the Canada Central Railway, and reached Callander (344 miles from Montreal), the official eastern terminus of the Canadian Pacific Railway, at 8.30 a.m. 13 miles from this, at Thorncliff is the junction with the Northern and Pacific Junction Railway, which forms the connection with Toronto and Western Ontario, being distant from Toronto 227 miles. At North Bay, which is a divisional terminus, the line touches Lake Nipissing, where there is a flourishing settlement, the land being of a fair quality. The line is laid with steel rails, about 56 lbs. to the lineal yard, and with ties about 2,640 to the mile. For the first 60 or 70 miles from Callander the line is ballasted entirely by sand, and, with the exception of a few settlements, is entirely without fencing. Most of the bridges are of timber; but there are one or two of the larger ones of iron or steel, with masonry abutments.

"At Sudbury is the junction with the Algama Branch, not yet opened for traffic. This is 443 miles from Montreal. After leaving Sudbury the character of the country changes, and is alternately swampy and wild rocky land. Numerous large trestles are necessary, which will eventually be filled in with culverts and earthwork. The schedule running time of the trains along this portion of the line is 24 miles per hour, including stoppages.

"At 8 p.m. Chapleau, another divisional terminus, was reached, and the schedule running time during the night from that point to Heron Bay, reached at 5.15 a.m. the following morning, is 20 miles an hour. At Heron Bay (802 miles from Montreal) the north shore of Lake Superior is first touched, and the line runs along it to Port Arthur, a distance of 993 miles from Montreal. The scenery here is very wild and picturesque. At one time the line runs along the face of the rock, with the lake from 50 to 100 feet below, the road-bed being benched out on the cliff, and at another time is away back among barren hills and rocks, crossing several large streams (with either bridges of iron and masonry or timber trestle work), which streams flow into the lake at the north end of deep indentations or arms of the lake. The line through this district is winding, having many sharp curves and steep grades. There are several short tunnels, all of them through rock, and not lined. The schedule time for trains on this portion of the line is 16 miles per hour. We were detained some little time near Jack Fish, owing to a slight land slide coming down in one of the cuttings.

"The Nepigon River is crossed at a high level with a steel trussed bridge, masonry piers and abutments, and there is an old Hudson's Bay settlement on the river a short distance above the bridge. Between Nepigon and Port Arthur the line runs through a country much more accessible for railways, and the schedule time here is at the rate of 24 miles an hour. We reached Port Arthur at 4 p.m. on the 17th. This is a flourishing town, situated at the head of Thunder Bay, a large bay on the north shore of Lake Superior, and has a population of four or five thousand at the present time. From the north shore of Lake Nipissing to this point, however, a distance of over 600 miles, the country may be said to be almost without inhabitants, except those connected with the working of the railway, squatters, and Hudson's Bay trappers and traders. The weather was chilly during the evening of this day, and a heavy sleet storm arose before arriving at Port Arthur. At night a fire had to be lighted in the car, as there was a sharp frost. During the night the train was detained for some little time east of Rat Portage, in consequence of a trestle having given way while being pulled in, and the train arrived at Rat Portage at 7.30 a.m., four hours, behind time.

"From Port Arthur the line westward is run upon the 24 o'clock system, commencing from midnight; 1 p.m. being 13 o'clock, 2 p.m. being 14 o'clock, and so on. The train arrived at Winnipeg at 12.45 on the 18th (1,423 miles from Montreal), and time was allowed to drive round the town, the train leaving again for the west at 13.30 o'clock. From Winnipeg westward the line runs through a prairie country, which extends without intermission to Calgary, a distance of 838 miles, and 2,261 from Montreal. At Winnipeg the Company have good machine shops, round houses, &c., and a large yard, and has acquired 132 acres of land for these purposes of working and repair and renewal.

"The country for three or four hundred miles from Winnipeg west is more or less settled; in some parts farms are quite numerous, and the land good and well cultivated. At Portage la Prairie the Manitoba and North- Western Line leaves the Canadian Pacific. It is being rapidly pushed forward, and 120 miles of it have already been completed through the 'Fertile belt.' It should have been mentioned that the line between Port Arthur and Winnipeg, a length of 430 miles, was constructed by the Government of Canada and given to the Canadian Pacific Railway Company free as a portion of their system. This part of the line is laid with 57 lbs. steel rails, and is well ballasted. The line is also ballasted east of Port Arthur, though in some places the ballast is of poor quality, and in others there is not sufficient of it. West of Winnipeg, however, there is no ballast across the prairie, except where the excavations through which the line goes afford ballast, it being simply surfaced up from side ditches with whatever the material may happen to be; but it is in good condition for a line of such a character, and the schedule time is 24 miles an hour, including stoppages.

"The train ran through Qu'Appelle, Regina, and Moose Jaw during the night of the 18th, and reached Dunmore (650 miles from Winnipeg) at 15.30 o'clock on the 19th. At this point there is a branch, 3-feet gauge line, 110 miles in length, to the Lethbridge mines, belonging to Sir Alexander Galt & Company. His son, Mr. Galt, met us at Dunmore, and invited us to go and inspect the mines, but as it would have made a delay of at least one day, the idea had regretfully to be abandoned. The train reached Bassano (750 miles from Winnipeg) at 19 o'clock, our time, having made up 3 hours and 20 minutes since leaving Winnipeg, which was the time late leaving there. The train was then exactly 97 hours since leaving Montreal, having travelled 2,180 miles, an average speed, including all stoppages and delays, of 22-1/2 miles an hour.

"During the night of the 19th and the early morning of the 20th, the train ran through Calgary, at the foothills of the Atlantic slope of the Rocky Mountains; and at 5.30 on the 20th arrived at the summit of the Rocky Mountains. As it was just daylight we were enabled to see the scenery at that point and Kicking Horse Pass. From the summit of the Rocky Mountains, for some nine miles, the line is considered to be merely a temporary one, though permanently and strongly constructed, there being a grade for two or three miles of it of 4-1/2 feet per hundred, say 1 in 22-1/2. There are several catch sidings on this grade, running upwards on the slopes of the mountains, for trains or cars to be turned into, in the event of a break loose or run away, and a man is always in attendance at the switches leading to these sidings. All this day the train ran through mountains, the Rocky Mountains, the Selkirk Range, and Eagle Pass. With the exception of the steep grade mentioned, the ruling ones are 116 feet to the mile, and there are numerous sharp curves, usually to save short tunnels. The line, however, is in some parts well ballasted, and work is still going on in this direction. The rails are of steel, 70 lbs. to the yard, and the locomotives, of the "Consolidation" pattern, with eight driving wheels, are able, Mr. Marpole, the able divisional superintendent, stated, to take a train of 12 loaded cars over the ruling grades, two of them being required for the same load on the steep grade already mentioned at Kicking Horse Pass. Mr. Marpole stopped the train at the Stony Creek Bridge, a large timber structure 296 feet high, and said to be the highest wooden bridge in America. The scenery through the Selkirks is magnificent, the mountain peaks being six and seven thousand feet above the level of the railway, many of them even at this season of the year covered with snow, and there being several large glaciers.

"During last year, before the line was opened for traffic, observations were taken with the view of ascertaining what trouble might be anticipated from avalanches, the avalanch paths through the Selkirks being very numerous. Several large avalanches occurred, the largest covering the track for a length of 1,300 feet, with a depth in one place of 50 feet of snow, and containing, as was estimated, a quarter of a million cubic yards of snow and earth. The result of these observations caused the Company to construct during this season four- and-a-half miles of snow sheds, at a cost of $900,000, or $200,000 a mile.

"The sheds are constructed as follows:—On the high side of the mountain slope a timber crib filled with stones is constructed. Along the entire length of the shed, and on the opposite side of the track, a timber trestle is erected, strong timber beams are laid from the top of the cribwork to the top of the trestle, 4 feet apart and at an angle representing the slope of the mountain, as nearly as possible. These are covered over with 4-inch planking, and the beams are strutted on either side from the trestle and from the crib. The covering is placed at such a height as to give 21 feet headway from the under side of the beam to the centre of the track. The longest of these sheds is 3,700 feet, and is near the Glacier Hotel.

"Over the Selkirk Range the schedule time for trains from Donald to Revelstoke, that is, from the first to the second crossing of the Columbia River, a distance of 79 miles, is only eleven miles an hour; but this time table was made before there was much ballast on this portion of the line, and better time can now be made. On the 21st September the Fraser River was crossed early in the morning over a steel cantilever bridge, and the line runs down the gorge of the Fraser River to Port Moody, reached at noon. The train had thus been travelling from 8 p.m. on the 15th September to 12 noon on the 21st, apparently a total of 136 hours; but, allowing for the gain of three hours in time, an actual total of 139 hours. During this time the train travelled 2,892 miles, or an average speed made throughout the journey, including all stoppages, of 20-1/2 miles per hour, and this is the regular schedule time for passenger trains at the present time.

"Port Moody is the present terminus of the Canadian Pacific Railway, but the line has been partially graded for 12 miles further to Vancouver. Owing, however, to the hostile attitude of some landowners, the Company have not been able to complete this work, as the contention has been made that, although the Company have power to build branches, an extension of the main line is not a branch, and the Company will have to obtain legislation before this can be done. Vancouver at the present time is said to have a population of about 3,000. It is situated at Burrard Inlet, a mile or so inside what are called the First Narrows, but the neck of land on which it is situate is only about a mile across; and in the future, when the town grows, English Bay, which is outside the Narrows, can easily be made the harbour in preference to the present one, as it is fairly well sheltered, and affords good anchorage.

"The trip down Burrard Inlet, the Straits of Georgia, and through the San Juan Archipelago to Victoria, a distance of about 90 miles from Port Moody, occupied 9-1/2 hours, and Victoria was reached at 10.30 on the night of the 21st September."

To this memorandum I may add a few words. First, in praise of the excellent rolling stock; secondly, of the good discipline and smartness of the service; and, thirdly, of the wonderful energy, boldness, and success of the whole engineering features of this grand work of modern times. I should be ungrateful if I did not thank the chief officers of the Canadian Pacific, whose acquaintance I had great pleasure in making, for their exceeding kindness, for the full information they afforded to me, and for showing me many cheap, short, and ready plans of construction, which might well be adopted in Europe. These gentlemen have looked at difficulties merely in respect to the most summary way of surmounting them; and, certainly, the great and bold works around the head of Lake Superior, the many river and ravine crossings of unusual span and height, and, especially, the works of the 600 miles of mountain country between Calgary and the last summit of British Columbia, so successfully traversed, would make the reputation of a dozen Great George Streets.

Chapter IV
Canadian Pacific Railways

The pioneer suggestion of a railway across British territory to the Pacific has been claimed by many. To my mind, all valuable credit attaches to those who have completed the work. The christening of "La Chine"—the town seven miles from Montreal, where the canals which go round the rapids end, and the St. Lawrence and the Ottawa rivers join their differently coloured streams—contained the prophecy of a future great high road to the then mysterious East, to China, to Japan, to Australia; and it is to the Sieur de la Salle, who, 200 years ago, bought lands above the rapids from the Sulpician Fathers of Montreal, and began his many attempts to reach the lands of the "setting sun," that we owe the name; while the resolution of Sir Charles Tupper, carried in the Dominion Parliament, finally embodied in an Act which received the Royal assent on the 17th February, 1881, and was opposed throughout by the "Grit" party, was really the practical start. It would be inadequate to write of the Great Canadian Pacific Railway without some reference to the history of railways in Canada itself.

In the interesting book, "Rambles on Railways," published in 1868, it is remarked that great as has been the progress of Canada, in no respect has the growth of the country shown itself in a more marked manner than in the development of its railway system. It was in 1848, or almost immediately after the completion of the magnificent canal system of Canada proper, and by which vessels of 800 tons could pass from the ocean to Lake Ontario, and *vice versa* (ships now pass from Chicago to Liverpool of over 1,500 tons burthen), that the Canadians discovered it was necessary, notwithstanding their unrivalled inland navigation, to combine with it an equally good railway communication; and accordingly, in 1849, an Act was passed by the Canadian Government pledging a six per cent. guarantee on one-half the cost of all railways made under its provisions. In 1852, however, the Government, fearing the effect of an indiscriminate guarantee, repealed the law of 1849, and passed an Act guaranteeing one-half of the cost of one main Trunk line of railway throughout the Province, and it was under this Act that the Grand Trunk Railway was projected.

These terms were subsequently modified, by granting a fixed sum of 3,000_l_. per mile of railway forming part of the main Trunk line. It is true that prior to these dates railways existed in Canada. There was, for example, the horse railway from La Prairie, nine miles above Montreal, to St. John's on the Richelieu River, opened in July, 1836, and first worked with locomotives in 1837; there was also a horse railway between Queenstown and Chippewa, passing Niagara, opened in 1839, and over which I travelled in 1851; but with these exceptions, and the Lachine Railway, a line running from Montreal for seven miles to the westward, the railway system of Canada cannot be said to have commenced until after the passing of the Railway Act in 1849, and even then, it was not for about a year that any progress was made. Soon after that date, however, the works of several lines were pushed forward, and in 1854 the section between Montreal and Quebec was opened, the first train having carried Lord Elgin, who was then *en route* to England to confer with the home authorities respecting the future Reciprocity Treaty with the United States Government. So, whilst in 1852, Canada could only boast of about 30 miles of railway, she has now over 10,000 miles. The population of the Dominion is estimated roughly at 5,000,000, so that this mileage gives something over two miles of railway for every thousand inhabitants, a greater railway mileage system per head of population than, perhaps, is possessed by any other country in the world.

The old Grand Trunk proprietors feel that their early pioneer services to Canada, and their heavy sacrifices, have rather been ignored in competition, than recognized, by the Canadian Pacific not being an extension of the Grand Trunk system. Had I remained in office as President of the Grand Trunk, undoubtedly I should have laboured hard to bring about such a consummation, which undoubtedly would have economised capital and hastened the completion of the great Inter- oceanic work. But the London agents of Canada, who were, and are, responsible for launching the Grand Trunk and for its many issues of capital to British shareholders, have undoubtedly aided the competition and rivalry complained of; for in July, 1885, they floated—when other great financial houses were unable— 3,000,000_l_. sterling, not for the Pacific line itself, but to complete other extensions of the Pacific Company's system of a directly competitive character with the Grand Trunk, and which could never have been finished but for this British money, so raised. While I do not enter into the controversy, it still seems to me that blame lies nearer home than in Canada, if blame be deserved at all. Great financiers seem sometimes ready to devour their own industrial children.

The Canadian Pacific Railway from Quebec to Port Moody is a mixture of the new and the old. The first section, from Quebec to Montreal, is an old friend, the North Shore Railway, once possessed by the Grand Trunk Company, and sold back to the Canadian Government for purposes of extending the Pacific route to tide-water at Quebec, and making one, throughout, management. From Montreal to Ottawa, and beyond, is another section of older-made line. The piece from Port Arthur to Winnipeg is an older railway, made by the Canadian Government. Again, on the Pacific there is the British Columbia Government Railway. All the rest, round the head of Lake Superior up to Port Arthur, from Winnipeg across the Great Prairies to Calgary, and on to, and across, the Rocky Mountains, the crossings of the Selkirk and other Columbian Ranges, is new Railway — with works daring and wonderful.

Pioneer railways are not like works at home. The lines are single, with crossing places every five, ten, or twenty miles; ballast is not always used, the lines on prairies being laid for long stretches on the earth formation; rivers, chasms, canons and cataracts are crossed by timber trestle bridges. The rails, of steel, are flat bottomed, fastened by spikes, 60 lbs. to the yard, except through the mountains, where they are 70 lbs.

Begun as pioneer works, they undergo, as traffic progresses, many improvements. Ballast is laid down. Iron or steel bridges are substituted for timber. The gorges spanned by trestles are, one by one, filled up, by the use of the steam digger to fill, and the ballast plough to push out, the stuff from the flat bottomed wagons on each side and through the interstices of, the trestles. Sometimes the timber is left in; sometimes it is drawn out and used elsewhere. This trestle bridge plan of expediting the completion, and cheapening the construction, of new railways, wants more study, at home. Whenever there are gorges and valleys to pass in a timbered country, the facility they give of getting "through" is enormous. The Canadian Pacific would not be open now, but for this facility.

All these lines across the Continent have very similar features. They each have prairies to pass, with long straight lines and horizons which seem ever vanishing and never reached; mountain ranges of vast altitudes to cross, alkaline lands, hitherto uncultivable, hot sulphur springs, prairie-dogs, gophyrs, and other animals not usually seen. The buffalo has retired from the neighbourhood of these iron-roads and of the "fire-wagons," as the Indians call the locomotives. Here and there on all the prairies on all the lines, heaps of whitened bones, of buffalo, elk, and stag, are piled up at stations, to be taken away for agricultural purposes. The railways resemble each other in their ambitious extensions. The Canadian Pacific Railway, from Quebec to Port Moody, is above 3,000 miles in length, but the total mileage of the Company is already 4,600 miles, and no one knows where it is to stop, while Messrs. Baring and Glyn will, and can, raise money from English people; the Union Pacific possesses 4,500 miles in the United States; the Southern Pacific nearly 5,000; and the newest of the three, the Northern Pacific, has about 3,000 miles, and is "marching on" to a junction with Grand Trunk extensions at the southern end of Lake Superior, in order to complete a second Atlantic and Pacific route, through favoured Canada. Each of these great lines has found the necessity of supplementing the through, with as much local traffic, as it can command. Some of this is new, such as the coal traffic from Sir Alexander Galt's mines, situated on a branch line of 110 miles, running out of the Canadian Pacific at Dunmore, and the mineral traffic in the territory of Wyoming on the Union Pacific. But, again, some of it is the result of competition. Let us hope that the development of both Canada and the United States may quickly give trade enough for all. It seems to me, however, that the Ocean to Ocean traffic, alone, cannot, at present at least, find a good return for so many railways.

Canada has been unusually generous to the promoters of the Canadian Pacific Railway. A free gift of five millions sterling: a free gift of 713 miles of, completed, railway: a free gift of twenty-five millions of acres of land: all materials admitted free of duty: the lands given to be free of taxation for twenty years: the Company's, property to be free of taxation: the Company to have absolute control in fixing its rates and charges until it should pay 10 per cent. dividend on its Ordinary Stock: and for twenty years no competitive Railway to be sanctioned;—summarize the liberality of the Dominion of Canada, in her efforts to bind together her Ocean coasts. The work is essentially an Imperial work. What is the duty of the Empire?

Chapter V
A British Railway from the Atlantic to the Pacific

My letter of the 15th November, 1860, to a friend of Mr. Thomas Baring, then President of the Grand Trunk Railway of Canada, gives concisely my general notions of opening up the British portion of the Great Continent of America. A while later a leading article written by me appeared in the "Illustrated London News" of the 16th February, 1861. The article was headed, "A British Railway from the Atlantic to the Pacific." I will here quote a portion of it:—

"'I hope,' said her Majesty, on proroguing Parliament in 1858, 'that the new Colony on the Pacific (British Columbia) may be but one step in the career of steady progress by which my dominions in North America may be ultimately peopled in an unbroken chain, from the Atlantic to the Pacific, by a loyal and industrious population.' The aspiration, so strikingly expressed, found a fervent echo in the national heart, and it continues to engage the earnest attention of England; for it speaks of a great outspread of solid prosperity and of rational liberty, of the diffusion of our civilization, and of the extension of our moral empire.

"Since the Royal Speech, Governments have done something, and events have done more, to ripen public opinion into action. The Governments at home and in Canada have organized and explored. The more perfect discoveries of our new gold fields on the Pacific, the Indian Mutiny, the completion of great works in Canada, the treaties with Japan and with China, the visit of the Prince of Wales to the American Continent, and, at the moment, the sad dissensions in the United States, combine to interest us in the question, and to make us ask, 'How is this hope to be realized; not a century hence, but in our time?'

"Our augmenting interests in the East, demand, for reasons both of Empire and of trade, access to Asia less dangerous than by Cape Horn, less circuitous even than by Panama, less dependent than by Suez and the Red Sea. Our emigration, imperilled by the dissensions of the United

States, must fall back upon colonization. And, commercially, the countries of the East must supply the raw materials and provide the markets, which probable contests between the free man and the slave may diminish, or may close, elsewhere. Again, a great nation like ours cannot stand still. It must either march on triumphantly in the van, or fall hopelessly into the rear. The measure of its accomplishment must, century by century, rise higher and higher in the competition of nations. Its great works in this generation can alone perpetuate its greatness in the next.

"Let us look at the map: there we see, coloured as 'British America,' a tract washed by the great Atlantic on the East, and by the Pacific Ocean on the West, and containing 4,000,000 square miles, or one-ninth of the whole terrestrial surface of the globe. Part of this vast domain, upon the East, is Upper and Lower Canada; part, upon the West, is the new Colony of British Columbia, with Vancouver's Island (the Madeira of the Pacific); while the largest portion is held, as one great preserve, by the fur-trading Hudson's Bay Company, who, in right of a charter given by Charles II., in 1670, kill vermin for skins, and monopolise the trade with the Native Indians over a surface many times as big again as Great Britain and Ireland. Still, all this land is ours, for it owes allegiance to the sceptre of Victoria. Between the magnificent harbour of Halifax, on the Atlantic, open throughout the year for ships of the largest class, to the Straits of Fuca, opposite Vancouver's Island, with its noble Esquimault inlet, intervene some 3,200 miles of road line. For 1,400 or 1,500 miles of this distance, the Nova Scotian, the Habitan, and the Upper Canadian have spread, more or less in lines and patches over the ground, until the population of 60,000 of 1759 amounts to 2,500,000 in 1860. The remainder is peopled only by the Indian and the hunter, save that at the southern end of Lake Winnipeg there still exists the hardy and struggling Red River Settlement, now called 'Fort Garry:' and dotted all-over the Continent, as lights of progress, are trading posts of the Hudson's Bay Company.

"The combination of recent discoveries places it at least beyond all doubt that the best, though, perhaps, not the only, thoroughly efficient route for a great highway for peoples and for commerce, between the Atlantic and the Pacific, is to be found through this British territory. Beyond that, it is alleged that while few, if any, practicable passes for a wagon-road, still less for a railway, can be found through the Rocky Mountains across the United States' territory, north-west of the Missouri, there have been discovered already no less than three eligible openings in the British ranges of these mountains, once considered as inaccessible to man. While Captain

Palliser prefers the 'Kananaskakis,' Captain Blakiston and Governor Douglas, the 'Kootanie,' and Dr. Hector the 'Vermilion' Pass, all agree that each is perfectly practicable, if not easy, and that even better openings may probably yet be found as exploration progresses. Again, while British Columbia, on the Pacific, possesses a fine climate, an open country, and every natural advantage of soil and mineral, it has been also discovered that the doubtful region from the Rocky Mountains eastward up to the Lake of the Woods, contains, with here and there some exceptions, a 'continuous belt' of the finest land.

"Professor Hind says:—

"'It is a physical reality of the highest importance to the interests of British North America that this continuous belt can be settled and cultivated from a few miles west of the Lake of the Woods, to the passes of the Rocky Mountains; and any line of communication, whether by wagon, road, or railroad, passing through it, will eventually enjoy the great advantage of being fed by an agricultural population from one extremity to the other.'

"Although the lakes and the St. Lawrence give an unbroken navigation of 2,000 miles, right to the sea, for ships of 300 tons burden, yet if there is to be a continuous line, along which, and all the year round, the travel and the traffic of the Western and Eastern worlds can pass without interruption, railway communication with Halifax must be perfected, and a new line of iron road, passing through Ottawa, the Red River Settlement, and this 'continuous belt,' must be constructed. This new line is a work of above 2,300 miles, and would cost probably 20,000,000_l_., if not 25,000,000_l_., sterling.

"The sum, though so large, is still little more than we voluntarily paid to extinguish slavery in our West Indian dominions; it does not much exceed the amount which a Royal Commission, some little time ago, proposed to expend in erecting fortifications and sea-works to defend our shores. It is but six per cent, of the amount we have laid out on completing our own railway system in this little country at home. It is equal to but two and a-half per cent. of our National Debt, and the annual interest upon it is much less than the British Pension List.

"We say, then, 'Establish an unbroken line of road and railway from the Atlantic to the Pacific through British territory.'

"Such a great highway would give shorter distances by both sea and land, with an immense saving of time.

"As regards the great bugbear of the general traveller—sea distance— it would, to and from Liverpool, save, as compared with the Panama route, a tossing, wearying navigation of 6,000 miles to Japan, of 5,000 miles to Canton, and of 3,000 miles to Sydney. For Japan, for China, for the whole Asiatic Archipelago, and for Australia, such a route must become the great highway to and from Europe; and whatever nation possesses that highway, must wield of necessity the commercial sceptre of the world.

"In the United States, the project of a Railway to the Pacific to cross the Rocky Mountains has ebbed and flowed in public opinion, and has been made the battle-cry of parties for years past, but nothing has yet been done. Such a project, in order to answer its purpose, requires something more than a practicable surface, or convenient mountain passes. Fine harbours on both Oceans, facilities for colonization on the route, and the authority of one single Power over the whole of the wild regions traversed, are all essential to success. As regards the United States, these conditions are wanting. While there are harbours enough on the Atlantic, though none equal to Halifax, there is no available harbour at all fit for the great Pacific trade, from Acapulco to our harbour of Esquimault, on Vancouver's Island, except San Francisco—and that is in the wrong place, and is, in many states of the wind, unsafe and inconvenient. The country north-west of the Missouri is found to be sterile, and at least one-third of the whole United States territory, and situated in this region, is now known as the 'Great American Desert.' Again, the conflicting interests of separate and sovereign States present an almost insuperable bar to agreement as to route, or as to future 'operations' or control. It is true that Mr. Seward, possibly as the exponent of the policy of the new President, promises to support *two* Pacific Railways—one for the South, another for the North. But these promises are little better than political baits, and were they carried out into Acts of Congress, financial disturbance would delay, if not prevent, their final realization; and, even if realized, they would not serve the great wants of the East and the West, still less would they satisfy England and Europe. We, therefore, cannot look for the early execution of this gigantic work at the hands of the United States.

"Such a work, however, is too costly and too difficult for the grasp of unaided private enterprise. To accomplish it out of hand, the whole help of both the Local and Imperial Parliaments must be given. That help once offered, by guarantee or by grant, private enterprise would flock to the undertaking, and people would go to colonise on the broad tracts laid open to their industry."

My subsequent and semi-official inquiries induced me to modify many of the conclusions of the article quoted above. On the essential question of the pass in the Rocky Mountains, in British territory, most adapted by Nature for the passage of a road or a railway, all the evidence which I collected tended to show that the passage by the "Tete-jaune Cache," or "Yellow-head," Pass, was the best. The Canadian Pacific Company have adopted the "Kicking Horse" Pass, much to the southward of the "Yellow-head" Pass. Again, it became clear to me that the whole Rocky Mountain range was rather a series of high mountain peaks, standing on the summit of gradual slopes, rising almost imperceptibly from the plains and prairies on the eastern side, and dropping suddenly, in most cases, towards the sea-level on the western or Pacific side, than a great wall barring the country for hundreds of miles, as some had dreamed. Every inquiry from trappers, traders, Indian voyageurs, missionary priests of the Jesuits, and from all sorts and conditions of men and women, made difficulty after difficulty disappear. The great work began to appear to me comparatively easy of execution between Fort Garry, or the lower town of Selkirk and British Columbia; the cost less; and, owing to facilities of transport, especially in winter, the time of execution much shorter than had been previously assumed. In addition, an examination into the physical conditions of the various routes proposed through the United States, convinced me that here again the difficulties were less, and facilities for construction greater, than I and others had first imagined. In fact, I came rightly to the conclusion that the more southerly the United States route, and the more northerly the British route—while always, in the latter case, keeping within cultivable range—the better. Still, at this time there was much to find out. As respects real knowledge of the country to be traversed, the factors of the Hudson's Bay Company knew every fact worth divulging, but they were afraid to speak; while the Catholic missionaries, accustomed to travel on foot in̄ their sacred cause over the most distant regions, possessed a mine of personal knowledge, never, so far as I could learn, closed to the Government of Canada or to any authorized inquirer.

Prior to my sailing to New York, *en route* for Canada, to fulfil my mission for the Grand Trunk, in 1861, I had a long interview with the Duke of Newcastle, as Colonial Minister. He had seen, and we had often previously discussed, the questions raised in the article above quoted, and which he had carefully read. The interview took place on the 17th July, 1861. Every point connected with the British Provinces in America, as affected by the then declared warlike separation of the northern and southern portions of the United States, was carefully discussed. The Duke had the case at his fingers ends. His visit to America with the Prince of

Wales, already alluded to more than once, had rendered him familiar with the Northern Continent, and its many interests, in a way which a personal study on the spot can alone bring about; and he declared his conviction that the impression made upon the mind of the Prince was so deep and grateful, that in anything great and out of the ordinary rut of our rule at home, he would always find an earnest advocate and helper in the Prince, to whom he said he "felt endeared with the affection of a father to a son." I called the Duke's special attention to the position and attitude of the Hudson's Bay authorities. How they were always crying down their territory as unfit for settlement; repelling all attempts from the other side to open up the land by roads, and use steamers on such grand rivers as, for instance, the Assiniboin and the Saskatchewan. He said Sir Frederick Rogers, the chief permanent official at the Colonial Office, whose wife's settlement was in Hudson's Bay shares, and who, in consequence, was expected to be well informed, had expressed to him grave doubts of the vast territory in question being ever settled, unless in small spots here and there. The Duke fully recognized, however, the difficulty I had put my finger upon. I never spent an hour with a man who more impressed me with his full knowledge of a great imperial question, and his earnest determination to carry it out successfully and speedily. The Intercolonial Railway, to connect Halifax on the Atlantic with the Grand Trunk Railway at Riviere du Loup, 106 miles below Quebec, he described as "the preliminary necessity." The completion of an iron-road, onwards to the Pacific, was, "to his mind, a grand conception." The union of all the provinces and territories into "one great British America," was the necessary, the logical, result of completing the Intercolonial Railway and laying broad foundations for the completion, as a condition of such union, of a railway to the Pacific. He authorized me to say; in Canada, that the Colonial Office would pay part of the cost of surveys; that these works must be carried out in the greatest interests of the nation, and that he would give his cordial help. This he did throughout.

In bidding me good-bye, and with the greatest kindness of manner, he added: "Well, my dear Watkin, go out and inquire. Master these questions, and, as soon as you return, come to me, and impart to me the information you have gained for me." Just as I was leaving, he added, "By the way, I have heard that the State of Maine wants to be annexed to our territory." I made no reply, but I doubted the correctness of the Duke's information. Still, with civil war just commencing, who could tell? "Sir," said old Gordon Bennett to me one day, while walking in his garden, beyond New York, "here everything is new, and nothing is settled." Failing health, brought on by grievous troubles, compelled the Duke to retire from office in the course of 1864, and on the 18th of October of that year he died; on the 18th October, 1865, he was followed by his friend, staunch and true, Lord Palmerston, who left his work and the world, with equal suddenness, on that day.

But from that 17th July, 1861, I regarded myself as the Duke's unofficial, unpaid, never-tiring agent in these great enterprises, and, undoubtedly, in these three years, ending by his retirement and death, the seeds were sown.

Chapter VI
Port Moody—Victoria—San Francisco to Chicago

At "Port Moody," and even at the new "Vancouver City," I felt some disappointment that the original idea of crossing amongst the islands to the north-east of Vancouver's Island, traversing that island, and making the Grand Pacific terminus at the fine harbour of Esquimalt, had not been realized. Halifax to Esquimalt was our old, well-worn plan. The "Tete Jaune" was our favoured pass. This plan, I believe, met the views both of Sir James Douglas and the Honorable Mr. Trutch. But I consoled myself with the reflection, that if we had not gained the best, we had secured the next best, grand scheme—a scheme which, as time goes on, will be extended and improved, as the original Pacific Railways of the United States have been.

The sea service between "Port Moody" and "Victoria," Vancouver's Island, is well performed; and Victoria itself is an English town, with better paved streets, better electric lighting, and better in many other ways that might be named, than many bigger American and English towns I know of. I spent four delightful days in and about it, including an experimental trip, through the kindness of Mr. Dunsmuir —the proprietor of the Wellington Collieries, a few miles north of Nanaimo—over the new railway from Victoria to Nanaimo, constructed, with Government aid, by himself and Mr. Crocker, of San Francisco. I had the pleasure of making the acquaintance of Sir Mathew Begbie, the Chief Justice of British Columbia, to whose undaunted courage Vancouver's Island and British Columbia owed law and order in the dangerous and difficult times of the gold discoveries.

Upon the question of relative distances, engineering, and generally what I saw between Port Moody and Chicago, I again take advantage of Mr. Edward Wragge's excellent notes.

"*Table of Distances between Liverpool and China and Japan, via the Canadian Pacific Railway, through Canadian territory, and via New York and San Francisco, through United States territory:*—

ROUTE THROUGH CANADIAN TERRITORY

"Summer Route MILES.

Liverpool to Quebec, *via* Belle Isle 2,661
Quebec to Montreal 172
Montreal to Port Moody 2,892
Port Moody to Vancouver 12
Vancouver to Victoria 78
Vancouver to Yokohama 4,334
Vancouver to Hongkong 5,936

"Winter Route MILES.

Liverpool to Halifax 2,530
Halifax to Quebec 678
Other points as in summer.

Summer route, Liverpool to Yokohama 10,071
Winter route, " " 10,618

ROUTE THROUGH UNITED STATES TERRITORY

Liverpool to New York 3,046
New York to Chicago, *via* N.Y.C.
and M.C. Railways 961
Chicago to San Francisco 2,357
San Francisco to Yokohama 4,526
San Francisco to Hongkong 6,128
Liverpool to Yokohama 10,890

"For distance to Hongkong, add 1,602 miles to the distance to Yokohama.

"*Note,* —Distances by rail are statute miles. Distances by sea, geographical miles.

ESQUIMALT AND NANAIMO RAILWAY AND COAL MINES AT WEST WELLINGTON AND NANAIMO

"The Esquimalt and Nanaimo Railway runs from West Victoria, near Esquimalt, to Nanaimo, which latter place is a small mining town in the Island of Vancouver, lying on the east coast, on the shore of the Straits of Georgia, nearly opposite Burrard Inlet, from which it is distant about 28 miles.

"The line is well constructed with a good and substantial road-bed; steel rails, weighing 54 lbs. per yard (except a few miles near Nanaimo, where they are 50 lbs. per yard); well ballasted, and well tied; the bridges and trestles are all of timber, of which material there is about 1,000,000 cubic feet employed altogether. The steepest grade is 80 feet per mile rising towards Nanaimo, and 79 feet per mile rising towards Esquimalt; these grades are rendered necessary to enable the line to overcome the summit lying between the two places, and which is 900 feet above the level of the sea. Running, as the line does, through a rugged country, there are a good many sharp curves rendered necessary. The distance from Esquimalt to Victoria is 75 miles. The line was not quite completed when we went over it; and the buildings, turn-tables, &c. were not yet erected, although some of them were under construction.

"The traffic on the line will be light, the country being sparsely settled. It will consist to some extent of coal; but there is water competition for the carriage of this article of merchandize; and the station at Victoria is too far from the town at present for much of it to come by rail for consumption in the town. There is a wharf in the harbour of Esquimalt, at which coal can be delivered to men-of-war lying there. Mr. Dunsmuir, of Victoria, is the chief proprietor of the railway, and he has associated with him Mr. Cracker, President of the Southern Pacific Railway, and others.

"The Government of Canada gave a bonus of $750,000 (say 150,000_l_.) in aid of the construction of the railway, and a belt of land, with the minerals under it, of 10 miles in width on each side of the line.

"During the afternoon of the 23rd of September we visited the West Wellington Coal Mines, 4 or 5 miles beyond Nanaimo, and to which the railway is to be extended, work on the extension having just been commenced. The mines are owned by Messrs. Dunsmuir & Sons, and at the present time they are working at five shafts, the output for the month of August being 17,000 tons. We went down the shaft of No. 5 pit, which was 240 feet deep, and found the seam was very thick, from 10 to 11 feet, but not very solid block coal, having apparently been crushed. The mines are all connected with wharves on the coast at Departure Bay by a three-feet gauge railway; the lines around the mines were all in fair order. The line is worked by small locomotives, six wheels coupled and no truck, of the Baldwin Locomotive Company's manufacture, the load handled by them being 15 cars, each containing 3-1/2 tons of coal, and averaging in dead weight 1-3/4 tons each. The grade down to the port is very steep, and the heaviest work for the engines is in taking the empties back again.

"The coal is mined by white miners, who employ each of them a Chinese labourer; they employ gunpowder for blasting purposes, chiefly Curtis &

Harvey's make, and use naked lights of oil. The miners are found in all tools except their auger drills, which they all use, and which cost some $30 each. Each miner has an allowance of one ton of coal per month for his own use. There was a little drip at the foot of the shaft we went down, but otherwise the mine was quite dry. The mode of unloading the cars at the wharf was rather primitive, but at the same time simple and ingenious. When the car has been weighed it is run forward by five Chinamen to the end of the wharf, the front end of the car being hinged at the top, with a catch opened by a lever, a short piece of track sufficiently long for the car to stand upon is built projecting beyond the wharf and over the hold of the vessel, this piece of track is laid on a framework, which is hinged to the wharf in front so as to tip up from behind, to it is attached a long wooden pole as a lever, round the end of which is a rope, made fast to the wharf by a belaying pin; as soon as the car is on the tipping track, the lever on the front end of the car is knocked up so as to allow the coal to fall out, and the end of the long wooden pole is allowed to rise slowly by the rope being loosened, the coal then shoots out of the car. When empty the Chinamen weigh down on the pole and bring the track, with the car on it, back to its former position, making the rope fast to the belaying pin, and the car is run back to make way for another. We were told that in this way five Chinese have put 1,000 tons of coal on board a vessel in a working day.

"On the following morning we visited the mine at Nanaimo, of the Vancouver Coal Company, and Mr. S. Robins, the superintendent, showed us over his works, and accompanied us down the shaft into the mine. The shaft is 600 feet deep, and the heading and workings are under the sea to a distance of 400 or 500 yards. The coal is hard and of good quality, making a good gas coal (which the West Wellington coal does not do). There have been one or two faults met with lately in the seam, which is 7 feet thick; but Mr. Robins thinks they have been overcome. There is only one shaft working, and the output in the 24 hours of the day previous had been 434 tons. The coal comes to the surface in two 'boxes' at a time, each containing about 35 cwt. This Company has good railway tracks of 4 feet 8-1/2 inches gauge, with English locomotives, &c. The machinery and appliances at this mine were all better and more costly than at the West Wellington mines, and the cars were hopper bottomed, and discharged their contents directly into the hold of the vessels by simply opening the hopper bottom. The staff of men employed at the present time amounts to 350, and the miners are white men, with Chinese labourers. The work at this mine and West Wellington is all done by piecework.

ESQUIMALT HARBOUR AND DOCK

"The harbour at Esquimalt is quite land-locked, and can be very easily protected from an enemy approaching by sea, the heights around being easily fortified, as there are many in good positions for commanding the entrance, both at a distance from it, and also in the immediate vicinity; there is plenty of depth of water at low tide to enter the harbour. A fort on the Race Rocks, where there is a lighthouse, and which are some 2 miles or so from the coast, would, if supplied with heavy guns capable of long range, command the whole of the San Juan de Fuca Straits, the distance from Race Rock to the American shore not exceeding 8 miles.

"The harbour contains an area of about 400 or 500 acres, in which there is sufficient depth of water for large vessels to lie at all states of the tide.

"The line of railway from Nanaimo to Esquimalt touches the harbour, and has a wharf at which coal from Nanaimo and West Wellington mines may be delivered at any time.

"The graving dock, which has been some eleven years in progress, or rather which was commenced eleven years ago, but which practically has been constructed within the past two years, has a length of 430 feet on the ways, and could easily have been made, in the first instance, 600 feet in length for a comparatively small additional cost. The cost will have been, when completed, about $700,000, and it is now waiting only for the entrance caisson, which is being made at the Dominion Bridge Company's Works, near Montreal.

"The masonry of the dock is of a hard sandstone, the character of the workmanship being very good, and the dock very dry and free from leakage; it has been constructed, so as to save excavation, in a small creek, but this has caused an additional thickness for the walls, and a considerable quantity of filling behind them. It would appear that it could have been built for very much less money had a site been selected among the numerous rocky situations in the harbour, where the rock would only have required facing with masonry instead of the work having been done as it has.

"The naval-yard is a fair size; the workshop is small, however, and apparently little or no materials for the repair of vessels are kept on hand. It will be a necessity for this to be remedied if the graving dock is to be of any use for ships of the navy. We saw two torpedo boats, and some Whitehead torpedoes, the boats were built in Great Britain for Chili, and purchased from the Chilians two years ago.

SAN FRANCISCO TO CHICAGO

"Left San Francisco on 29th September, 1886, at 7.30, by steam ferry to Oakland, 4 miles across the harbour; left Oakland by train at 8.10 a.m.; 32 miles from Oakland we reached Port Costa, where the train was ferried across an estuary of the sea to Benicia; for 20 miles from there the line (the Central Pacific division of the Southern Pacific Railway Company) runs, across a flat, marshy country, then into a cultivated country with the western foothills of the Sierra Nevada rising around it, the country being very dry and parched, having had no rain since March: the farm-houses have the Eucalyptus, or Australian blue gum, planted around them; and about 75 miles from San Francisco we entered the vineyard country, which continues to and past Sacramento. Reached Sacramento, which is 90 miles from San Francisco, and only 30 feet above the level of the sea, at 12 o'clock; the schedule time from Oakland, including the ferry at Port Costa, being 25 miles an hour. At Sacramento we crossed the Sacramento and American Rivers, the former by a Howe truss bridge, one of the spans being a swing-bridge, and having a total length of 700 or 800 feet; the latter by a Howe truss bridge, and fully a mile of trestle work.

"From Sacramento the line begins to rise so as to cross the Sierra Nevada Range; the country is rolling, and with the 'live oak' trees scattered over it among the grass presents quite a park-like appearance. The grades as we ascend are very steep, 116 feet to the mile, this line being well ballasted. In the valleys the line was laid originally with steel rails of 50 lbs. weight, and 3,080 ties to the mile, in the mountains with 60 lbs. rails, but no renewals are made with less than a 60 lbs. rail. From Rocklin to Newcastle the vineyards and orchards are very numerous, and again at Colfax, at which latter place we got some very fine grapes grown at an elevation of 2,400 feet above the sea. In the afternoon we passed the mining country, where the whole features of the country have been changed by the use of the 'Monitor' for hydraulic mining, by means of which the sides of the mountains have been washed down to the valleys, filling them and the streams up, and doing much damage to the flats below: this system of directing a stream of water through a six-inch nozzle against the cliff to wash out the gold has now been discontinued, and is illegal, owing to the damage caused by it. The snow sheds commence at Blue Canon, 4,693 feet above the sea, and 170 miles from San Francisco. They are simply rough wooden sheds to protect the line from drifting and falling snow, there being no avalanches to contend with on this route.

"Some of the views on the Sierra Nevada are very fine, notably that at 'Cape Horn.' There is very little timber until Blue Canon is reached, but from there to Truckee and beyond the timber is good, and about equal to that on the Rocky Mountains of the Canadian Pacific Railway. There are several saw mills in this vicinity. After leaving Emigrant Gap we ran through a continuous snow shed for 39 miles, which was very unpleasant, both by reason of the smoke in the cars, and the noise, as well as the loss of the view. We reached Reno about 10 p.m., an hour and a half late. The schedule time over the mountain, up grade, is 17 miles an hour, and from Oakland to Reno, 246 miles, 20 miles an hour. Reno is 4,497 feet above the sea. The summit of the Sierras, which is 196 miles from San Francisco, is 7,017 feet above the sea. We remained all night at Reno. While there we saw in the morning a locomotive engine, with cylinders 22 x 30 and eight driving wheels coupled, said by the driver to weigh 165,000 lbs., start for the ascent of the mountain, up grades of 116 feet to the mile, with 22 cars and a van.

"The country round Reno is table land with high mountains around it. The only crop grown is 'alfalfa,' a species of clover. Three crops a year are taken off the land, and it fetches, as fodder, from $8.00 to $16.00 per ton, according to the season.

"At Wadsworth we saw a very nice reading-room and library for the employes of the railway. This is quite a model station, kept green and bright with lawns and flowers. It is a division terminus, and has a machine shop, round house, &c. The country from Reno to Salt Lake is dry, and almost a desert, sandy, and with sage bush in tufts; the journey through it was hot and terribly dusty. The view of Brigham and other villages, with farms at the foot of the hills on approaching Ogden, was a great relief after the monotony of the last day's run.

"At Ogden we were transferred from the Central Pacific to the Union Pacific train, and upon leaving there passed, after a few miles, through Weber Canon, and afterwards Echo Canon; the scenery was very picturesque, and, at this season of the year, was rendered more so by the beautiful autumn tints which were afforded by the foliage of the bushes which grow up the mountain sides for more than half their height. At Evanston we left the mountains and got on the high table land, over which we ran all day, having it cool and pleasant, a great contrast to the heat of the previous day. During the night of the 1st October we had it quite cold, our altitude being at no time less than 6,000 feet above the sea.

"On the morning of the 2nd October we reached Laramie, where we saw the works of the Union Pacific Railway Company for Burnettizing their ties. The ties are placed on trucks, run into a cylinder, steamed, treated with a solution of chloride of zinc, with glue mixed with it, and afterwards with a solution of tannic acid. When dried they retain only about 1 1/4 lb. of the material with which they have been treated. Mr. Octave Chanute, of Kansas City, Missouri, United States, erected the works for the Union Pacific Company, and has an interest in the patents under which the process is carried out, which is a modification of Sir William Burnett's process. At 8.55 we crossed the highest point on the Rocky Mountains, 8,235 feet above the sea, on table land, no peaks being more than a few hundred feet above us. The rock here is all red granite, and some of it disintegrated, which is used for ballast. There are many snow sheds on the high land here, but none very long. We ran rapidly down from 'Sherman,' the summit, to 6,000 feet level, and more gradually afterwards, running all day through the plains, over which, although very dry, numerous herds of cattle and horses were pasturing, and we reached Omaha at 7.50 a.m. on the 3rd October.

"At Omaha we crossed the Missouri River. The bridge here, of iron, founded on iron cylinder piers, is for a single track only, and is being taken down bit by bit, and a double track iron bridge on masonry piers substituted..

"From Council Bluffs, the station on the Iowa side of the Missouri River, we left by the Chicago and North Western Railway, which is a well constructed, well equipped, and first class American Railway. The line runs through a good agricultural country, the chief crop being Indian corn, and was doing a good business. We met many freight trains during the day, and saw several trains of cattle going east also. We reached Chicago on time at 6.50 a.m. on the morning of the 4th October."

Chapter VII
Negociations as to the Intercolonial Railway; and North-West Transit and Telegraph, 1861 to 1864

It was in September, 1861, that I visited Frederickton and Halifax on the question of the Intercolonial Railway, travelling by way of Riviere du Loup, Lake Temiscouata, Little Falls, Woodstock, round by St. Andrews, Canterbury, Frederickton, St. John, Shediac, and Truro to Halifax. Later in the autumn, representatives from New Brunswick and Nova Scotia visited Quebec and Montreal, and it was generally agreed that deputations from Canada and from the two Maritime Provinces should proceed to England. These deputations were, from Canada the Hon. Mr. Van Koughnet, from New Brunswick the Hon. Mr. Tilley, and from Nova Scotia the Hon. Joseph Howe. It was impossible to choose a more influential delegation: men earnest in the cause they came to advocate; politicians of tried metal; men of great influence in the colonies they represented.

I arrived in England from Canada in the beginning of November, 1861, and at once telegraphed to the Duke, and on my way to London, at his request, I visited him at Clumber, and made my report of progress, which appeared to be highly satisfactory. The only difficulty, as to the Intercolonial, appeared to rest in Mr. Gladstone's "peculiar views about subsidies, grants, and guarantees out of the funds, or on the security, of the State." But the Duke said, he must "labour to show the Chancellor of the Exchequer that this was no new proposal; that, in fact, the Provinces had been led to believe that if they would find the money, the State would guarantee the interest under proper precaution, as the State had guaranteed the capital for the Canadian canals, every shilling expended on which had been honourably repaid." In fact, "this work was not a mere local work, but satisfied military and other Imperial conditions." The end of this, and many other, interviews, at the Colonial Office and at the Duke's residences, was complete concurrence in the following programme:—(1) the Intercolonial guarantee must be carried by the Duke; (2) measures must be taken to start Pacific transit, in the first instance, and as a pioneer work, by roads and telegraphs; (3) Confederation must be pushed on; and (4) that the difficulties arising from the position of the Hudson's Bay Company must be gravely considered with a view to some solution.

Mr. Van Koughnet, accompanied by Mrs. Van Koughnet, was, unfortunately, wrecked off Anticosti, in the Allan steamer "North Briton." Happily every one, after a time of great peril, was landed in safety, while losing personal baggage and almost everything else. At a critical moment Sir Allen McNab, who was on board the ship, also on his way to England, when the vessel was expected to go down, said to Van Koughnet, "Come with me and bring your wife, and we will go down together, away from this crowd of frightened people"—alluding to the mass of steerage passengers jostling about in panic.

On the 11th November Mr. Howe and Mrs. Howe, and Mr. Tilley arrived: and I took the delegates to the Duke's house in London on the 14th. The Duke received these delegates with very great cordiality. He had made, already, an appointment with Lord Palmerston, the Prime Minister, and had spoken to Mr. Gladstone. So, armed with a letter from the Duke, we went on to Cambridge House. We were shown into a room overlooking the court-yard, and had not long to wait for the veteran minister. He came, as usual, with his grey—not white—hair brushed up at the sides, his surtout buttoned up to his satin neck-tie, or, more correctly, "breast- plate," which had a jewelled pin in the midst of its amplitude. He said, the Duke had told him our business, which was very important, not only for the interests we represented, but for the Empire, and especially so at a time when the "fires were alight" across the British border.

Mr. Howe very ably and concisely stated the case. No subsidy wanted, simply a guarantee on perfect security. Precedent for such guarantees, which had always been punctually and fully met. Previous promises of previous Governments—sanction of such statesmen as Lord Grey, Lord Derby, and Bulwer Lytton. Peculiar need of the work at this time; and so on.

Palmerston listened attentively, did not interrupt; did not while Howe, and afterwards Tilley, were speaking, stop either, by asking a single question; but when they had concluded, he repeated and summed up the case in far fewer words than had been used to state it: and in a manner which gave a new force to it all. He then spoke of the various treaties with the United States. He spoke of the giving up of the fine Aroostook district, now part of the State of Maine, and with some heat said, that "the Ashburton Treaty was the most foolish treaty ever made." He replied to the argument about the past commitment of other Governments, by describing it as "not possessing much attraction for an existing Government." Here Howe made him laugh much, by saying, "At least, my Lord, it might have an influence with your conscientious Chancellor of the Exchequer."

After a good many questions and answers affecting the state of the Provinces, the facilities and difficulties of moving troops in winter, the conveyance of the mails, future closer relations of commerce between the Provinces, and, especially, the state of things in the United States,—he asked us to "Go and see Gladstone." We "might say he had suggested it."

Then he shook hands, with a swinging jollity, with each of us, saw us to the door, and, finally, wished us "success." There might have been no "Trent" affair pending, to look at him.

Some delay took place before we could see Mr. Gladstone. But we finally accomplished the interview with him at his fine house in Carlton House Terrace, on the 23rd November. After waiting some while, following, as we did, about a dozen previous waiters on the Chancellor, we were shown into Mr. Gladstone's working room, or den. The room was very untidy. Placards, papers, letters, newspapers, magazines, and blue boots on the table, chairs, bookshelves, and the floor. It looked, altogether, as if the window had been left open, and the contents of a miscellaneous newspaper, book, and parliamentary paper shop had been blown into the apartment. Mr. Gladstone, himself, looked bored and worried. Though perfectly civil, he had the expression of a man on his guard against a canvasser or a dun. He might be thinking of the "Trent" affair. We stated our errand, and as I had, as arranged, to say something, I used the argument of probable saving in the Atlantic mail subsidies, by the creation of land routes, &c. He brushed that aside by the sharp remark, "Those subsidies are unsound, and they will not be renewed." He then spoke of the objectionable features of all these "helps to other people who might help themselves." He did not seem to mind the argument, that assuming this work to be of Imperial as well as of Provincial importance, unless aid,—costless to England, or, at the highest, a very remote risk, and not in any sense a subsidy,—were given, the work could not proceed at all. He struck me to be a man who thought spending money, or taking risks, however slight, a kind of crime. That, in fact, it was better to trust to Providence in important questions, and keep the national pocket tightly buttoned. We got little out of him, save an insight into the difficulty to be overcome. And yet he had been a party to the Crimean War. On the final discussion, in the House, on the vote for the Intercolonial guarantee, on the 28th March, 1867, Mr. Gladstone concluded his speech by declaring, "I believe the present guarantee does depend upon motives of policy belonging to a very high order, and intimately and inseparably associated with most just, most enlightened views of the true interests of the Empire." Thus we had sown the seed not in vain, and the counsel of the Duke was not forgotten.

Mr. Van Koughnet arrived on the 26th November. On the 27th I took him to see the Duke, and we had a long conference.

Finally, it was decided to send in a memorial to the Duke to lay before the Cabinet. Howe prepared it. It was most ably drawn, like all the State papers of that distinguished man, and it was sent in to the Colonial Office on the 2nd December, 1861. Thus, all had been done that could then be done by the delegation. We had to rely upon the Duke. Our difficulty was with Mr. Gladstone.

In the time of waiting, Howe, Tilley, and I, attended meetings at Bristol, Manchester, Liverpool, Oldham, Ashton, and other places, endeavouring, with no small success, to make the Intercolonial Railway a public question.

But the delays; the "pillar to post"; the want of knowledge of permanent officials, whose geography, even, I found very defective, made our efforts irksome, and now and then, apparently, hopeless.

But an event had startled England, like a thunderclap in a summer sky. On the 8th of November, 1861, Captain Wilkes, of the United States ship "San Jacinta," took the Southern States envoys—Messrs. Slidel and Mason—and two others, forcibly from the deck of a British mail ship, "The Trent." The country was all on fire. Palmerston showed fight, and the Guards and other troops, and arms and stores to the value of more than a million sterling, were sent out to Canada. The delegates were sent for to the War Office, and, as desired, I accompanied them. At the time all seemed to hang in the balance. The powers had joined England in protest, and our ambassador was instructed by despatch, per ship —for the submarine wires were not at work—to leave Washington in seven days if satisfaction were not given.

At the War Office we met Mr. Cornewall Lewis, Minister for War, a man erudite and accomplished, who had lived on public employments nearly all his life, but who hardly knew the difference between the two ends of a ramrod. He asked, in long sentences, the questions which Palmerston had put shortly and in the pith; all sorts of queries as to winter transport in the Provinces, the disposition for fight of the people, and so on. Then it was demanded, What we had to suggest? Van Koughnet, who writhed under the tone adopted, bluntly said, "Why, to fight it out, of course; we in Canada will have to bear the first brunt. But we cannot fight with jack-knives; and there are no arms in the country. You have failed to keep any store at all." This led to a deliberate note being taken by the Under Secretary, the present Marquis of Ripon. Other details followed, and then, finally, we were asked if we had anything more to propose? To which I answered "Yes; send out a man who may be truly regarded as a general." This was received with silence and open mouths. The fact was, the soldier in command in Canada was General Fenwick Williams, a most gallant man, who, in a siege, would eat his boots before he would give in: but was not the man who could so manoeuvre small bodies of men as to keep in check, in forests and on plains, large masses of the enemy. When we left, Captain Gallon came running after us, and said, "I am so glad you said that, we all feel as you do here" — (the War Office).

Although the Government of the United States retreated from an undefendable position, wisely and with dignity, by surrendering their prisoners, who, delivered over to a British man-of-war, landed in England on the 29th January, 1862, — still it was decided to keep the troops in the Provinces, to reinforce them, to add to the armaments, and to adequately arm strategic points alongside the American frontier. And, as President of the Grand Trunk, I was asked to go out to Canada to aid and direct transport across the country.

In the meantime — whether the cause was the "Trent" affair, or pre-occupation on the part of the Duke, or neglect of permanent officials, or their bad habit at that time of regarding Colonists as inferior persons — our delegates and their wives felt hurt at the social neglect which they experienced. And I agreed in the truth of their complaints so much, that I formally addressed the Duke on the 31st December. He acknowledged the neglect, apologised for it, and thereafter, until the day of their departure, the delegates, and Mrs. Howe and Mrs. Van Koughnet, were received in high circles, and were especially invited to Clumber.

To sum up, I left England for Canada, in "The Asia," on the 1st February, 1862, landing at New York, where my son and Messrs. Brydges and Hickson met me — and after a deal of hard work on the part of every officer and man on the Grand Trunk, and no small anxiety, labour, responsibility, and exposure to storms and climate, inflicted upon myself, Mr. Brydges, Mr. Hickson, and the whole staff, Quartermaster- General Mackenzie sent us a handsome acknowledgment of our semi- military services. But the authorities at home did not condescend to recognize our existence or our labours.

The late Sir Philip Rose gave me the greatest assistance with Mr. Disraeli, Sir E. Bulwer Lytton, and all the great party whose confidence he possessed. The following letter, addressed to him by Sir E. Bulwer Lytton, will be read with great interest: —

"BUXTON, DERBYSHIRE,
"*April* 27, 1862.

MY DEAR SIR,

"I am much flattered by your wish, and that of our Colonial friends; but I fear that I must decline the important and honourable task to which you invite me: partly from a valid personal reason; partly on political grounds.

With regard to the first, I am here for a course of the Baths, in hopes to get rid of a troublesome lumbago, which has harassed me all the winter, and appears to have been epidemical from the number of victims it has cramped and racked this wet season. And I fear I shall not be able to get away till the middle of May, unless it be for some special vote. But apart from this consideration, I doubt whether it would be prudent for any member of Lord Derby's late Government, with the support of those leaders who might very soon form another administration, to urge upon Parliament any new pecuniary burthen, nay, any new loan, in the face of a deficit. Would not this really play into Gladstone's hands, and furnish him with a plausible retaliation in case of attack on the side in which he is most vulnerable, viz., the dealing with a deficit as if it were a surplus? And again, would it be quite prudent in the coming Conservative Chancellor of the Exchequer and his future colleagues to commit themselves to a measure they might find it inconvenient to carry out when in power?

"These are doubts that occur to me; and would be well weighed by Mr. Disraeli—who might, perhaps, agree with me, that, on the whole, it would be better that this very important question should be brought before the House by some one not in the late Cabinet—some great merchant, perhaps—some one, in short, who could not be supposed to compromise or commit the future administrative policy of the party.

"I remain, however, of the same opinion, that aid to intercolonial communication can be defended on Imperial grounds—and would in itself, if not opposed on purely fiscal reasons, be a wise as well as generous policy.

"I regret much that my absence from town prevents, my seeing Mr. Watkin and profiting by the information, he could give me. I fear he will have left London before I return to it. But I should be very glad if he would write to me and acquaint me with the exact state of the case at present—and the exact wishes and requests of the Colonists.

"Is it a renewal of the former proposition or what? 'The whole question of intercolonial communication' is a vast one. But I suppose practically it would limit itself before Parliament to the Railway before submitted to us—according to the pamphlet you sent me.

"Believe me,
"Yours very truly and obliged,
"E. B. LYTTON."

The following letter was addressed to me:—

"BUXTON, "*May* 3,1862.

DEAR SIR,

"Allow me to thank you cordially for a letter, which cannot but be extremely gratifying to my feelings. Certainly my first object when I had the honour to preside at the Colonial Office was to attach all parts of that vast Empire which our Colonies comprise to the Mother Country, by all the ties of mutual interests and reciprocal affection.

"The importance of the Railway line between Halifax and Quebec must be transparent to every clear-sighted politician. And had I remained in office, I should have urged upon my colleagues—I do not doubt successfully—the justice and expediency, both for Imperial interests, commercial and military, and for the vindication of the Imperial good faith which seems to me indisputably pledged to it, some efficient aid, or guarantees the completion of the line. I should willingly have undertaken the responsibility of recommending that aid to Parliament; and I do not think the House of Commons would have refused it when proposed with the authority of Government. In that case the Railway by this time would have been nearly, if not wholly, completed.

"Traffic begets traffic; railways lead on to railways; and a line once formed to Quebec, it would not be long before the resources of British Columbia would, if properly directed and developed, suffice to commence the Railway that must ultimately connect the Atlantic and Pacific. That once accomplished, the destinies of British North America seem to me assured.

"I shall rejoice to hear that the present Government make a proposal which the Provinces accept. Some time, I conclude, must elapse before their decision can be known; and in that case the question can scarcely come before Parliament this Session. A mode of aid accepted by the Colonies would have my most favourable consideration; and, I cannot doubt, my hearty support, whatever might be the administration that proposed it.

"Yours truly obliged,
E. B. LYTTON."

The Canadian Parliament met, early in March, 1862, at Quebec; in bitter winter and snow storms. We took down all the members who chose to go, by a special through train, in charge of Mr. Brydges,—desiring to show them that, poor and unfortunate as the Grand Trunk might be, we could carry "M.P.Ps." safely and quickly, as we had carried soldiers, and guns, and stores, to the satisfaction of the military authorities. The train made a famous journey. In a few days I followed in company with the Honourable John Ross, and was several days on the road—in constant fight with snowdrifts—in getting to Point Levi. Then came the canoe crossing of the St. Lawrence, an enterprise startling, no doubt, as a first experience, though safe, if tedious. We were put in a canoe, really a disembowelled tree, and this was dragged, like a sledge, by a horse down to the margin of the river, where it was launched amongst floating ice, going up, down, and across the stream and its eddies. Our canoe men coming to a big piece of ice, perhaps 20 feet square, jumped out, dragged our canoe over the obstruction, and then launched it again. When getting jammed between the floating ice, they got on the sides of our boat, and working it up and down, like pumping the old fire engine, they liberated us. Sometimes we went up stream, sometimes down—all points of the compass—but, after an hour's struggle, we gained the wharf at Quebec, safe and sound. But a while after I certainly was exercised. It was important that Mr. Brydges should go back to Montreal, and my son went with him. I watched their crossing the river from the "Platform," in a clear, grey, winter afternoon. They were two hours in crossing the river, a mile or two in width, in a straight line. At one time, I almost despaired, for they had drifted down almost into the Bay; but, by the pluck and hard work of their men, they kept, in this tacking backwards and forwards, and up and down, gradually making their way, till they landed, a long way below the right point, however, and we exchanged handkerchief signals—and all was well.

In the interval between this and my last visit, Lord Monck had been appointed Governor-General in place of Sir Edmund Head, retiring. In talking with the Duke about this appointment, he said, "I offered the position to five men previously, and they refused it." I replied, "Did your Grace offer it to Lord Lawrence, now at home?" The Duke put down his pen, turned from one side of his chair to the other, looked down and looked up, and at last said, "Upon my honour, I never thought of that. What a good appointment it would have been!" Be that as it may, Lord Monck made an excellent Governor in very difficult times. Canada, and the great cause of Confederation, owe him a deep debt of gratitude.

I found unexpected difficulties about Grand Trunk affairs. The Government were afraid of their own shadows. Instead of bringing in the Grand Trunk Relief Bill as a Government measure, as we had expected, they, in spite of remonstrance from Mr. Gait, confided it to a private member, and such was the, unexplained, opposition that I verily believe had the Cartier-Macdonald Government remained in power the Bill, though entirely in the nature of a private Bill, affecting the public in every sense of indirect advantage, would have been thrown out. The newspapers throughout the two Provinces, with half-a dozen honorable exceptions, were vile and vicious, as trans-Atlantic newspapers especially can be. I was full of unexpected anxiety. The Government tactics were Fabian; and on the 5th

April they decided to adjourn the House to the 23rd. So I went home in the "China" from New York on the 9th April with my son; saw the Duke of Newcastle, discussed the situation; saw the opening of the Great Exhibition of 1862 on the 1st May, and a few days afterwards sailed, with Lady Watkin, in the old Cunarder, the "Niagara;" arriving at Boston after a long and difficult passage, and then travelling on to Quebec. But, on the 20th May, an event occurred—caused, it seemed to me, as a looker on, through want of tact—which ended in the resignation of the Government. The circumstances were these. Under pressure from home, administered through the new. Governor-General, the Ministry had brought forward measures of defence. They proposed to raise and equip, at the cost of Canada, 50,000 men. They proceeded, if my memory serves me, by the introduction of a Bill, and that Bill was rejected by a very small majority (61 to 54), composed of Sandfield Macdonald and a few others, described as "Ishmaelites." Upon that vote Mr. Cartier at once resigned, as I thought in too much haste. I met him as he walked away from the Parliament House in the afternoon, and expressed regret. He said, with set teeth, clenched fist, and sparkling eyes, "Ah! Well, I have saved the honour of my country against those 'Grits' and 'Rouges;' traitres, traitres." Mr. J. A. Macdonald, afterwards, took the matter very quietly, merely remarking that the slightest tact might have prevented the occurrence. So I thought.

The question was, Who was to succeed? In the ordinary course Mr. Foley, the assumed leader of the Opposition, would have been sent for. It was the opinion of the Honorable John Ross that he ought to have been. But the Governor, considering, I suppose, that the scanty majority was led by Sandfield Macdonald, sent for him. All sides believed that it would be a ministry of a month. But this astute descendant of Highlanders managed to stay in for nearly two years: two years of no good: two years of plausible postponement of all that the Duke had been so loyally working for in the interest of Canada. Personally, I had no reason to complain as regarded Grand Trunk legislation. Sandfield Macdonald promised to carry our Bill, and he honourably fulfilled his promise. The Bill passed; Lady Watkin and I sailed from Boston for England on the 7th June.

But the refusal of the Canadian Parliament to vote money for defence had created a very bad impression in England. England had made large sacrifices in filling Canada with troops and stores, at a critical time—and it was naturally said, in many quarters, "Are these people cowards? Are they longing for another rule?" Sir E. Bulwer Lytton, when Mr. Rose and I called upon him at his lodgings, in St. James's Place, during my short stay in London, said, "I do not see what we can do. Had Canada helped us at all, we could have succeeded. Now every one will say, What is the use of helping such people?" And Mr. Disraeli said, in the House, answering a statement that the vote of the Canadian Parliament did not represent the feeling of the people: "I decline to assume that the vote of a popular assembly is not the vote of those they represent." All this was awkward. But I resolved I would never give in. So I went to Canada again in the autumn of 1862.

Mr. Joseph Howe came from Halifax to Canada to meet me. He did all he could to induce Sandfield Macdonald to settle the long out-standing postal claim on Canada of the Grand Trunk; but in vain. He never would settle it, just and honest as it was. Mr. Howe tried to induce the Government to take up the Intercolonial question where we had left it in the previous autumn: and in this he so far succeeded that it was agreed a delegation from Canada should meet delegations from Nova Scotia and New Brunswick before the end of this year—1862—in London. Messrs. Howland and Sicotte were the Canadian delegates; Mr. Howe for Nova Scotia, and Mr. Tilley for New Brunswick. We set to work to carry both the Intercolonial guarantee, and the Pacific transit scheme, the moment these gentlemen arrived in England.

Meeting Messrs. Rowland and Sicotte at their hotel, in Jermyn Street, on the 2nd December, 1862, and discussing matters all round, they certainly led me, unsuspectingly, to believe they had the same desire to carry the Intercolonial as that entertained by Messrs. Howe and Tilley; and further, that if a road and telegraph project could be carried on the broad lines laid down in so many discussions, their arrangements on both questions would be cordially welcomed and approved by their colleagues. I very soon found out, however, that they were "riding to orders," and those orders, no doubt, being interpreted, were: "Refuse nothing, discuss everything, but do nothing."

On the 8th December we met the Canadian delegates at the bank of Messrs. Glyn, in Lombard Street, and we drew up a proposal, which these gentlemen corrected. We adopted their corrections and sent in the paper, as an agreed paper, to the Duke.

Two days afterwards, for better assurance, we received the following memorandum:—

"With a view of better enabling the gentlemen whom they met yesterday at 67, Lombard Street, to take immediate measures to form a Company for the object of carrying out the construction of a telegraph line, and of a road to establish frequent and easy communication between Canada and the Pacific, and to facilitate the carrying of mails, passengers, and traffic, the undersigned have the honour to state, that they are of opinion that the Canadian Government will agree to give a guarantee of interest at the rate of four per cent, upon one-third of the sum expended, provided the whole sum does not exceed five hundred thousand pounds, and provided also that the same guarantee of interest will be secured upon the other two-thirds of the expenditure by Imperial or Columbian contributions.

"If a Company composed of men of the standing and wealth of those they had the pleasure to meet is formed for the above purposes, under such conditions as will secure the interests of all parties interested, and the accomplishment of the objects they have in view, such an organization will be highly favourable to the settlements of an immense territory, and, if properly administered, may prove to be also of great advantage to the trade of England.

"London, 10 Decr. 1862.
            "L. V. SICOTTE,
            "W. P. HOWLAND.

    "To MM.
Glyn,
Benson,
Chapman,
Newmarsh,
Watkin,
    &c. &c. &c."

A few days afterwards these Canadian delegates started an objection. The Imperial Government merely gave land and did not take one-third of the proposed guarantee, and the following further memorandum was sent to me:—

"Although little disposed to believe that Her Majesty's Government will not accede to the proposal of co-operation they have made in relation to the opening of communication from Canada to the Pacific, the undersigned have the honour to state, in answer to the letter of Mr. Watkin of the 17th instant, that in their opinion the Government of Canada will grant to a Company organised as proposed in the papers already exchanged, a guarantee of interest, even on one-half of the capital stated in these documents, should the Imperial Government refuse to contribute any portion of this guaranteed sum of interest.

"In answer to another demand made in the same letter, the undersigned must state that the guarantee of the Canadian Government of this payment of interest ought to secure the moneys required at the rate of four per cent, and that they will not advise and press with their colleagues a higher rate of interest as the basis of the arrangement.

"London, 20 December, 1862.
            "L. V. SICOTTE,
            "W. P. ROWLAND.

"ED. WATKIN, Esq., London."

So much, and so far, for the Pacific affair. But in the Intercolonial discussion there was an undercurrent. The only points left for discussion with the Duke and Mr. Gladstone were the question of survey, which was easily settled, and the question of a sinking fund for the loan to be made on the credit of Great Britain. At first Mr. Gladstone insisted on such a short term of repayment, and therefore so heavy a put-by, that his terms took away the pecuniary value of the guarantee itself: that is to say, that what the Colonies would have annually to pay, would have amounted to more than the annual sum for which they could have borrowed the money themselves. I suggested a longer term, and also, that the interest on the annual put-by, to accumulate, should be altered so as to alleviate the burden. In answer to a letter written with the assistance of Messrs. Howe and Tilley, I received the following from the Duke:—

"CLUMBER, "8 *Decr.* 1862.

MY DEAR SIR,

"I am sorry to say your letter confirms the impression I have entertained from my first interview with the Canadian delegates—an impression strengthened by each subsequent meeting—that Mr. Sicotte is a traitor to the cause he has come over to advocate. I am unable to make out whether he is playing false on his own account or by order of his colleagues; but I cannot say I have any reason to associate Mr. Howland with the want of faith in any dealings with me.

"You can have no idea how I have been compelled to forbear and to fence with Mr. S. to prevent his breaking off upon every possible occasion and upon any almost impossible pretext. His whole aim has been to find some excuse for throwing up the railroad and saying it was the act of the Imperial Government. As for Mr. Gladstone being 'all powerful,' he knows that in the financial details alone Mr. G. interferes, and I presume Mr. Rowland would tell him that this is the duty of a Finance Minister.

"Nothing struck me more than Mr. S.'s objection to *your* being present at our meetings. When you did 'drop in' I felt obliged to say nothing about it till your card was brought, and on that occasion I particularly remarked that his usual obstructiveness was suspended.

"The *one* point now in dispute between the delegates and the Treasury is really of no importance to either party. I hope and expect that Mr. G. will give way; but I suspect if he does Mr. S. will be (by no means for the first time) much disappointed.

"Have you seen a remarkable letter in the 'Standard' of the 6th, signed 'A British Canadian,' commenting upon Mr. Sicotte going over to Paris and dictating to the editor of 'La France' an article upon a despatch of mine to Canada on the subject of the Militia? The article in 'La France' can *only* come from *a* member of the present Canadian Government.

"Do not at present get up any new deputation or go to Lord Palmerston. Considering Mr. G.'s strong opposition to the whole scheme on principle, I cannot say I think he has shown any desire to thwart by obstacles in details a measure upon which his views have been overruled, and it would be ungracious to show distrust where none at present has been merited. I may differ with him on some points; but he has certainly conceded more to me than I to him, and I could be no party to attempting to supersede his proper functions of the financial watch-dog!

"I am anxious not to be brought up to town *unnecessarily*, for I am conscious that I want *comparative* rest, and that my health is not very fit for the commencement of a Session; but whenever you are passing between London and Manchester I shall always be happy to see you, and glad if you can stay a day or two—only invite yourself.

"Yours very sincerely,
"NEWCASTLE."

The next day I had the following:—

"CLUMBER, "9 *Decr*. 1862.

MY DEAR SIR,

"It is no easy matter to give any advice as to what should be done, especially as I do not know whether Mr. Gladstone is still in London, though I rather imagine he has left for Hawarden.

"If Mr. Sicotte were anywhere but here (where he never ought to have been), I should advise Messrs. Howe and Tilley to see Mr. Gladstone, perhaps with you; but I can neither recommend them to see him *with* or *without* Mr. Sicotte, so long as he is here.

"As I wrote to you yesterday, the business ought to have been closed three days ago, for though I think. Mr. Gladstone's stipulation wrong, it ought not to have been allowed to interfere with a final arrangement.

"I agree with you that the new phrase about an 'uncovered loan' is not very intelligible, but I put the same interpretation upon it that you do.

"I am not without hope that whilst I am writing some 'leeway' may have been recovered through Sir F. Rogers and Mr. Anderson, but, as the best thing I can do, I propose this:

"I *ought* to go down to Surrey, to attend Mrs. Hope's funeral on Thursday morning, but being far from well, I was inclined to excuse myself from so long a railway journey, which I find injurious, but my decision is altered by your difficulty. I will be at Thomas' Hotel to- morrow night at 10 o'clock, if you can meet me at that time, and if you like to appoint Howe and Tilley a quarter of an hour later, I will see them and discuss what we ought to do.

"I feel very confident we can yet set matters right, if we can only prevent Mr. Sicotte upsetting the coach.

"I cannot see you on Thursday, as, being in London, I must go by the 9 a.m. train to attend the funeral at Deep Dene, and I may be late in returning to town in the evening.

"I am, yours sincerely,
"NEWCASTLE."

Memorandum from my diary of 10th December, 1862.

"To the Duke (*of Newcastle*), at 10 p.m.—(Thomas Hotel), by request. Saw Howe (*representing Nova Scotia*), and Tilley (*representing New Brunswick*) after. Very satisfactory. Duke said Gladstone had expressed strong approval of Pacific, &c. affair—and had added, 'that it was one of the grandest affairs ever conceived, and he hoped it would be completed in Duke's time—and it should have his hearty support.' Good."

Messrs. Sicotte and Rowland suddenly went home, and we appeared to be at a dead lock. After several letters and suggestions, the Duke sent me this letter:—

"CLUMBER, "6 *Jany.* 1863.

MY DEAR SIR,

"I have received several letters from you without sending any answer; but I must confess I am so disheartened about the result of all the trouble I have taken with the 'delegates,' that I do not know how to proceed, or, rather, I do not see the possibility of proceeding at all.

"At the last interview I had with the Canadian delegates, everything was considered settled to their satisfaction, except the one point of a sinking fund, and even that was admitted by all but Mr. Sicotte to be met by Mr. Gladstone's consent, that the money should be invested in Colonial securities. Thus matters stood until the *day* the Canadians embarked, when (avoiding an interview with Sir F. Rogers, and everybody else) they sent me in a paper, couched in terms offensive to the British Government, and complaining of every single provision in the conditions—evidently got up to carry out Mr. Sicotte's pre- arranged plan of upsetting the whole scheme, and throwing the blame on the Imperial Government.

"Unless this miserable creature and his colleagues are turned out of office on the first day of the Session, it is manifest that the measure will be *sold* for party purposes; and in that case I shall be unwilling to play into their hands, by giving them the N. W. Transit Scheme.

"I cannot be in town till after the 19th. I will see you then, if you wish it, or any day next week if, on your way to or from Manchester, it were convenient to you to dine and sleep here. I shall most likely be alone.

"I do not understand your alarm about a clause in the Treasury Minute. I know of no provision which impedes legislation this Session, except that requiring a previous survey, which I more than once discussed with you, and which I thought you agreed could easily be met.

"When you are in London Sir F. Rogers can show you Messrs. Sicotte and Rowland's extraordinary paper, if you wish to see it.

"I am, my dear Sir,
"Yours sincerely,
"NEWCASTLE."

Sir Frederick Rogers showed me the "extraordinary paper" of Messrs. Sicotte and Howland, and yet Mr. Howland, on his return, favoured me with the following letter:—

"QUEBEC, "3_rd April_, 1863.

MY DEAR SIR,

"The pressure of public business has prevented me from sending an earlier reply to your valued favour of the 26th February. In reference to the tariff of charges of your Company, you must be aware that it is not legal, unless approved by the Governor and Council. I am not aware of the circumstances stated by you, but presume, that if the Provincial Secretary called for your tariff, it was because it had not received the sanction of the Government; however, I feel safe in saying, that in the exercise of that power the Government would not be actuated by any feeling other than that of performing a public duty.

"Mr. Sicotte and myself were treated with the greatest consideration and kindness by His Grace the Duke of Newcastle, and I deeply regret that the action which we felt it necessary to take, in the performance of a public duty, should have produced any unpleasant feeling on the part of his Grace: however important the Intercolonial railroad may be, the opening up of the N. W. Territory would increase its value, and, in fact, afford much stronger grounds for its construction than exists at present, and the immediate result of opening up that territory would, in my opinion, be productive of much greater good to the people of England and Canada than would result from the construction of the Intercolonial railroad.

"I send by post the report of Mr. Taylor to the United States Government, upon the N. W. Territory of B.A., by which you will perceive, that they attach much greater importance to the future of that country than the people of England or Canada have hitherto shown. The description given of the climate appears to have been compiled from reliable data, and affords the clearest information upon that point that has as yet come before the public: I regret not having another copy to send His Grace the Duke of Newcastle; if he has not received one, will you be kind enough to send him this.

"Mr. Sandford Fleming (who is an engineer of high character and ability) is now here, as a delegate from the people of Red River, in charge of a memorial on their behalf to the Governments of Canada and England: this memorial is accompanied with a very clear statement of the condition and prospects of the country, and a report upon the proposed communication to be made through it. I am now getting the documents printed, and when done I will send you a copy, and one will be forwarded by His Excellency to the Duke.

"Mr. Fleming and myself are preparing some suggestions for you, in reference to the purchase of the rights of the Hudson's Bay Company, with a view to show in what manner it could be carried out, and afford security that the country should be opened for settlement, and at the same time afford an inducement to the parties who might become the purchasers. It would truly be a great project, and if the Company would come down in their pretensions to what their possessory rights are really worth, it could be carried out, and result in great good to the country, and offer great inducement to those who might engage in it.

"I am much pressed with work, and somewhat better in health.

"Yours faithfully,
"WM. P. HOWLAND.

"EDW. WATKIN, Esq.,
"21, Old Broad Street, London."

And if further proof were wanting that these gentlemen deserved the previously-quoted strictures of the Duke, always bearing in mind the trouble, responsibility and expense incurred, mainly at their instance, upon the Pacific project, the following gives it:—

"No. 1107. SECRETARY'S OFFICE, QUEBEC, "1_st Augt_. 1863.

SIR,

"I have the honour to inform you that your letter of the 27th ultimo, addressed to the Hon. John S. Macdonald, has been transferred to this Department.

"I am now directed to state, in reply to the inquiry therein made, that the details of the scheme for the promotion of telegraphic and postal communication across the Continent of British North America have not, as yet, been placed before the Provincial Government in such a definite shape as to enable them to determine the course which it may be advisable to take in relation to that important undertaking.

"The Government will, however, be prepared, whenever a sufficiently matured scheme shall be submitted for their consideration, to give the subject their most earnest attention.

"I have the honour to be, Sir,
"Your most obedient Servant,
"E. A. MEREDITH,
"*Assistant Secretary.*"

"EDWD. W. WATKIN, Esq.,
"*Montreal*"

Two days after the Duke's last letter, came the following:—

"KELHAM, NEWARK, "8 *Jany.* 1863.

MY DEAR MR. WATKIN,

"Since your letter of the 6th (received to-day), you will partly have learnt why I could not answer some of your private letters, but as regards the official letter respecting the Western project, I think you will see that I cannot answer it without consulting my colleagues. *I* cannot *grant* a subsidy, and on the other hand I should be unwilling to *refuse* it. The proposal that part of the subsidy should be Imperial necessarily entails delay. I do not think I can possibly send an answer till after the next Cabinet.

"I shall be sorry to miss Mr. J. A. Macdonald. The only chance of seeing him would be if he could dine and sleep a night at Clumber on his way to Liverpool. Unfortunately I must be all day on the 16th at Newark on County business. Could he come on the afternoon, of 15th without inconvenience?

"I am, yours very sincerely,
"NEWCASTLE."

And farther letters in the order given.

"CLUMBER, "15 *Jany*. 1863.

MY DEAR MR. WATKIN,

"I have written officially to the Admiralty respecting the formation of a Naval Station at Esquimault, but I will now write privately to the Duke of Somerset and ask for an early answer.

"Mr. Macdonald came last night, and I was delighted to see him a new and healthy man. I had an interesting conversation with him, but fully expecting he would stay till to-morrow reserved several things for to-day. It was not till breakfast was over that I knew he was returning in five minutes. As, however, his return to Canada is postponed for a week, I shall see him in London.

"I am, yours very sincerely,
"NEWCASTLE."

"CLUMBER,
"26 *Jan*.

"Your letter received just as I am starting for London. I remain there, and can see Mr. Cameron in town any day. I was in London last week, and saw Mr. Macdonald. Mr. Cameron was Mr. Malcolm Cameron, a man whose worth was undoubted.

"Yours, &c.,
"N."

"DOWNING STREET,
"20 *Feby*. 1863.

MY DEAR MR. WATKIN,

"It has not been till to-day that I could have given you any answer respecting the proposed subsidy to the N. W. Transit.

"I think a short verbal communication would be more satisfactory than explanation by letter.

"Can you call here to-morrow about 2.30, or, if more convenient, at Thomas' Hotel—between 11 and 1.

"Yours very sincerely,
"NEWCASTLE."

"DOWNING STREET,
"27 *March*, 1863.

MY DEAR SIR,

"I do not on the first blush of your proposal see any great difficulty in agreeing to it,—if indeed the Imperial Government is in absolute possession of the tract of country you speak of.

"I have requested Sir F. Rogers to look into this and see you if you like to call upon him when you come to town.

"I leave London to-morrow morning for, I hope, a fortnight.

"I am, yours sincerely,
"NEWCASTLE."

This letter of the 27th March, 1863, was in reply to a letter from me:—

"ROSE HILL, NORTHEN,
"March 27th, 1863.

MY LORD DUKE,

"In looking over the maps very carefully prior to sending in the documents proposed to be transmitted through your Grace, I find that it is very probable—from the desirability of carrying a telegraph through a wooded country, and avoiding the plains, where buffaloes often move about in square miles of extent—that we may go through the Imperial territory for a more or less considerable distance. It therefore strikes me, that what I have before suggested, as to the desirability of Imperial assistance, may not be reconciled with Mr. Gladstone's desire to avoid an Imperial contribution of money. I therefore suggest to your Grace, that the Imperial Government should agree to give a grant of land of some reasonable extent, also that portion of the territory lying between the Hudson's Bay territory and British Columbia which belongs to the Crown, provided a telegraphic and road communication passes through any portion of that territory.

"If this meets your Grace's views, would it not be better that the fact of the Imperial Government having made this concession should be recited in the preamble of the proposed Bill which we are to send to Canada, and that thus invited to the scheme by a contribution of land, power to purchase or control should be directly given by a clause to the Crown? If your Grace will give me your views upon this at once, I will have the documents prepared accordingly, and transmitted without delay.

"'Minesota' has given about two millions of acres in aid of works to extend their rail and water communications in the direction of Red River.

"I have to thank your Grace for sending me Mr. Foley's report, and, also, copy of the Minutes of Council as to the Intercolonial and the western project.

"The territory I allude to is hunted over by the Hudson's Bay Company, and forms, mainly, a portion of what they call the Athabasca district."

It was matter of deep regret to me that the Government of the day would not accept any share of the pecuniary responsibility of adding to the compactness of the Empire, by connecting the two oceans by telegraph and by road. The despatch which I copy—dated Downing Street, 5 March, 1863—distinctly says, in its third paragraph, "Her Majesty's Government are of opinion that they cannot apply to Parliament to sanction any share in the proposed subsidy by this country."

"DOWNING STREET, "5_th March_, 1863.

SIR,

"I am directed by the Duke of Newcastle to acknowledge the receipt of your letter of the 27th of December, and to express his Grace's regret that so long, though quite unavoidable, a delay should have occurred in replying to it.

"I am now desired to make to you the following communication:—

"Her Majesty's Government are of opinion that they cannot apply to Parliament to sanction any share in the proposed subsidy by this country; and though they take great interest in the project contemplated with so much public spirit by the gentlemen represented by you for carrying a telegraphic and postal communication from the confines of Canada to the Pacific, they do not concur in the opinion of the Canadian delegates that the work is of such special 'Imperial importance' as to induce them to introduce for the first time the principle of subsidizing or guaranteeing telegraphic lines on land.

"Her Majesty's Government are further of opinion that without a submarine Transatlantic telegraph the proposed line in America will be of comparatively small value to the Imperial Government, and that whenever a scheme of the former kind is renewed, it is almost certain that this country must be called upon to bear a much larger charge for it than that which it is now proposed to devolve upon the British Colonies in respect of the land-telegraph and communication.

"As Canada has offered to bear one-half of the proposed guarantee, the Duke of Newcastle is prepared to recommend, and his Grace has no doubt of ready acquiescence, that British Columbia and Vancouver Island shall pay the sum of L10,000 per annum, as their share of L20,000 (being at the rate of L4 per cent, on a capital of L500,000), to commence when the line is in working order.

"It will, however, be necessary, before any proposal is made officially to the Colonies, that the Duke of Newcastle should receive further details. It is requisite that his Grace should be informed what provision will be proposed as to the duration of this subsidy; what conditions as to the right of purchasing the line, and to what authorities that right should belong; and on what terms the whole arrangement may be revised in the event of the Hudson's Bay Company coming to any agreement for the sale of their territory.

"There will doubtless be other provisions which the Colonies will expect.

"I am, Sir, your obedient Servant,
"T. F. ELLIOT.

"E. W. WATKIN, Esq."

I close this narrative of the Pacific Transit Scheme with the despatch of the 1st May, 1863, which summarises the proposals made and generally concurred in. These long discussions were not abortive, for they led up to the great question of the buying out of the Hudson's Bay Company, without which neither successful Confederation, nor its child the Canadian Pacific Railway, would have been achieved in this generation.

"DOWNING STREET, "1_st May_, 1863.

SIR,

"I am directed by the Duke of Newcastle to state that he has had much satisfaction in receiving your letter of the 28th ultimo, enclosing the heads of a proposal for establishing telegraphic and postal communication between Lake Superior and New Westminster, through the agency of the Atlantic and Pacific Transit and Telegraph Company. These proposals call for some observations from his Grace.

"New Westminster is named as the Pacific terminus of the road and telegraph. His Grace takes for granted that if the Imperial Government and that of British Columbia should find on further inquiry that some other point on the coast would supply a more convenient terminus, the Company would be ready to adopt it.

"*Article* 1.—His Grace sees no objection to the grant of land contemplated in this Article, but the 'rights' stipulated for are so indeterminate that without further explanation they could scarcely be promised in the shape in which they are asked. He anticipates, however, no practical difficulty on this head.

"*Nos.* 1 *and* 2.—The Duke of Newcastle, on the part of British Columbia and Vancouver Island, sees no objection to the maximum rate of guarantee proposed by the Company, provided that the liability of the Colonies is clearly limited to 12,500_l_. per annum. Nor does he think it unfair that the Government guarantee should cover periods of temporary interruption from causes of an exceptional character, and over which the Company has no control.

"But he thinks it indispensable that the Colonies should be sufficiently secured against having to pay, for any lengthened period, an annual sum of 12,500_l_. without receiving the corresponding benefit, that is to say, the benefit of direct telegraphic communication between the seat of government in Canada and the coast of the Pacific.

"It must, therefore, be understood that the commencement of the undertaking must depend on the willingness of the Canadian Government and Legislature to complete telegraphic communication from the seat of government to the point on Lake Superior at which the Company will take it up. Nor could his Grace strongly urge on the Colonies of Vancouver Island and British Columbia the large annual guarantee which this project contemplates, unless there were good reason to expect that the kindred enterprise of connecting Halifax and Montreal by railway would be promptly and vigorously proceeded with. It will also be requisite to secure by formal agreements that the guarantee shall cease, and the grants of land for railway purposes revert to the grantors, in case of the permanent abandonment of the undertaking, of which abandonment some unambiguous test should be prescribed, such as the suspension of through communication for a stated period.

"The Duke of Newcastle does not object to five years as the maximum period for the completion of the undertaking—and he thinks it fair to exclude from that period, or from the period of suspension above mentioned, any time during which any part of the line should be in occupation of a foreign enemy. But injuries from the outbreaks of Indian tribes and other casualties, which are inherent in the nature of the undertaking, must be taken as part of the risks which fall on the conductors of the enterprise, by whose resource and foresight alone they can be averted.

"His Grace apprehends that the Crown land contemplated in Article 3, is the territory lying between the eastern boundary of British Columbia and the territory purporting to be granted to the Hudson Bay Company by their charter. His Grace must clearly explain that Her Majesty's Government do not undertake, in performance of this article of the agreement, to go to the expense of settling any questions of disputed boundary, but only to grant land to which the Crown title is clear.

"With regard to the 7th Article, the Duke of Newcastle could not hold out to the Company the prospect of protection by any military or police force in the uninhabited districts through which their line would pass —but he would consider favourably any proposal for investing the officers of the Company with such magisterial or other powers as might conduce to the preservation of order and the security of the Company's operations.

"With reference to the 9th and concluding Article, the Duke of Newcastle would not willingly undertake the responsible functions proposed to him, but he will agree to do so if by those means he can in any degree facilitate the project, and if he finds that the Colonies concur in the proposal.

"Subject to these observations, and to such questions of detail as further consideration may elicit, the Duke of Newcastle cordially approves of the Company's proposals, and is prepared to sanction the grants of land contemplated in the 3rd Article. He intends to communicate the scheme, with a copy of this letter, to the Governor- General of Canada, and the Governor of Vancouver Island, recommending the project to their attentive consideration.

> "I am, Sir, your obedient Servant,
> "C. FORTESCUE.

"E. W. WATKIN, Esq."

Chapter VIII
Negociations for Purchase of the Hudson's Bay Property

In response to our demand for a large tract of land through the "Fertile belt" of the Hudson's Bay territory, the Governor answered, almost in terror, to the Duke of Newcastle:—"What! sequester our very tap-root! Take away the fertile lands where our buffaloes feed! Let in all kinds of people to squat and settle, and frighten away the fur- bearing animals they don't hunt and kill! Impossible. Destruction— extinction—of our time-honoured industry. If these gentlemen are so patriotic, why don't they buy us out?" To this outburst the Duke quietly replied: "What is your price?" Mr. Berens, the Governor, answered: "Well, about a million and a half."

Finding that our demands for land alongside the proposed road and telegraph were not acceptable to the Governor and Court of the Hudson's Bay Company, we had nothing for it but either to drop the Pacific transit proposal, after many months of labour and trouble, or to take the bold course of accepting the challenge of those gentlemen, and negociating for the purchase of all their property and rights. Before making a decided move, however, I had many anxious discussions with the Duke as to who the real purchaser should be. My strong, and often urged, advice was, that whoever the medium of purchase might be, Great Britain should take to the bargain. I showed that at the price named there could be no risk of loss; and I developed alternative methods of dealing with the question:—That the fur trade could be separated from the land and rights, and that a new joint stock company could be organized to take over the trading posts, the fleet of ships, the stock of goods, and the other assets, rights, and privileges affecting trade, and that such a company would probably pay a rental— redeemable over a term of years, were that needful to meet Mr. Gladstone's notions—of 3 or 3-1/2 per cent, on 800,000_l_., leaving only 700,000_l_. as the value of a territory bigger than Russia in Europe. Such a company would have to raise additional capital of its own to modernize its business, to improve the means of intercourse between its posts, and to cheapen and expedite the transport to and fro of its merchandise. I carefully described the nature of these changes and all that they involved. The Duke seemed to favour this idea. Then I pointed out that, if desired, a land company could be organized in England, Canada, and the United States, which, on a similar principle of rental and redemption, might take over the lands—leaving a reserve of probably a fourth of the whole as the, unpaid for, property of the Government—at the price of 700,000_l_. If these proposals succeeded, then all the country would have to do was to lend 1,500,000_l_. on such security as could be offered, ample, in each case, in my opinion. But I said it must be a condition, if these plans were adopted, to erect the Hudson's Bay territory into a Crown Colony, like British Columbia, and to govern it on the responsibility of the Empire. I showed that this did not involve any large sum annually; and that, as in the case of British Columbia, the loss would be turned into a profit by sales of the one-fourth of the land to be given, in return for the responsibilities, taken, to our country. Again, the cost of government might be recouped by a moderate system of duties in and out of the territory, to be agreed with Canada and British Columbia on the one hand, and the United States on the other. This, in outline, was one plan. The next was, to sell a portion of the territory to the United States at the price, which I knew could be obtained, of a million. A third plan which I suggested was, to open up portions of the "Fertile belt" to colonization from the United States. To offer homes, in a bracing, healthy country—with fertile lands and long waterways—to the multitudes of men and women in Ohio, Kentucky, Maryland, and many other States, who desired to flee from war and conflict; whose yearning was for settled government and peace. These men and women had still resources, friends, and credit, and if our country opened its arms to them, they would flock to the old red flag, and bring their energies to bear on the industrial conquest of these vast regions to the West.

But—if any man went, morally, down on his knees to another, I did to the Duke, to beg, beseech, implore,—that this great bargain, this purchase of purchases, of a Continent, should be made for our country, and should be untainted by even the suspicion of a mercantile adventure. In the end, I thought I had converted the Duke, well disposed always, to the wisdom of such a policy. Following this line, we discussed many details. He "would not sell," but he would "exchange;" and, studying the map, we put our fingers upon the Aroostook wedge, in the State of Maine—upon a piece of territory at the head of Lake Superior, and upon islands between British Columbia and Vancouver's Island—which might be the equivalent of rectification of boundary on many portions to the Westward along the 49th parallel of latitude.

Further, at one of our many interviews a name for the new Crown Colony, if established, was mentioned—"Hysperia." Dr. Mackay had suggested it to me. The general answer of the Duke was—"Were I a minister of Russia I should buy the land. It is the right thing to do for many, for all, reasons; but ministers here must subordinate their views to the Cabinet." Still, he went so far, that I believed if the Hudson's Bay property were once bought, the Duke would manage to take the purchase over for the country. I was too sanguine. I had not measured the passive resistance of the inside of the Colonial Office to everything that inside had not initiated; though the fact that day by day objections, urged to the Duke from inside, were put to me, by him, and, I believe, always satisfactorily answered, might have warned me. I hope to live to find three conditions established at the Colonial Office:— (1) That no one, from the head down to the office boy, shall enter the doors without having passed in general and in British Empire, geography. (2) That no one shall be promoted who has not visited some one British Colony or Province; and (3) That no one shall be eligible for the highest offices who has not visited and studied, personally, every portion of the distant British Empire.

With confident hope I went to work. It is true that Mr. Thomas Baring warned me. He said: "If the Duke wants these great efforts made he must make them on behalf of the Government: he must not leave private persons to take the risk of Imperial work." And, in this state of mind, Mr. Baring refused, afterwards, to be one of the promoters of the Pacific scheme, a refusal which led Mr. Glyn to hesitate to sign the legal papers without his friend and colleague. It was an anxious time for me; for on my head rested the main responsibility. One circumstance somewhat sustained me. On "the 10th December, 1862, at Thomas' Hotel, the Duke had read to me a private letter from Mr. Gladstone to him, containing these words. Words of which I was allowed to make a note" Your Pacific scheme would be one of the grandest affairs ever achieved, and I hope it will be completed in your time. It shall have my hearty support." Alas! however, Mr. Baring was right.

The first official interview with the Governor and Court of the Hudson's Bay Company was at the "Hudson's Bay House," Fenchurch Street, on the 1st December, 1862. The room was the "Court" room, dark and dirty. A faded green cloth, old chairs almost black, and a fine portrait of Prince Rupert. We met the Governor, Berens, Eden Colville, and Lyell only. On our part there were Mr. G. G. Glyn (the present Lord Wolverton), Captain Glyn (the late Admiral Henry Glyn), and Messrs. Newmarch, Benson, Blake, and myself. Mr. Berens, an old man and obstinate, bearing a name to be found in the earliest lists of Hudson's Bay shareholders, was somewhat insulting in his manner. We took it patiently. He seemed to be astounded at our assurance. "What! interfere with his Fertile belt, tap root, &c.!" Subsiding, we had a reasonable discussion, and were finally informed that they would give us land for the actual site of a road and a telegraph through their territory, but nothing more. But they would sell all they had, as we "were, no doubt, rich enough to buy," for "about" 1,500,000_l_., as they had told the Duke.

The offer of the mere site of a road and ground for telegraph poles was of no use. So, just as we were leaving, I said, "We are quite ready to consider your offer to sell; and, to expedite matters, will you allow us to see your accounts, charters, &c." They promised to consult their Court. And, gradually, it got to this, that I was put in communication with old Mr. Roberts, aged 85, their accountant, and with their solicitor, the able and honorable Mr. Maynard, of the old firm of Crowder and Maynard, Coleman Street, City.

I had many interviews; and on the 17th March, 1863, I met the Governor, Mr. Ellice, jun. (son of Edward Ellice-the "old bear"), Mr. Matheson and Mr. Maynard. They showed me a number of schedules, which they called "accounts." Next day I had a long private interview with Mr. Maynard, but "could not see the 'balance-sheet.'" The same day I saw the Duke with Messrs. Glyn and Benson. Next day (19th) I spent the forenoon with Mr. Roberts, the accountant, and his son and assistant, at the Hudson's Bay House. Mr. Roberts told me many odd things; one was that the Company had had a freehold farm on the site of the present city of San Francisco of 1,000 acres, and sold it just before the gold discoveries for 1,000_l_., because two factors quarrelled over it. I learnt a great deal of the inside of the affair, and got some glimpses of the competing "North West" Company, amalgamated by Mr. Edward Ellice, its chief mover, many years agone with the Hudson's Bay Company. Pointing to some boxes in his private room one day, Mr. Maynard said: "There are years of Chancery in those boxes, if anyone else had them." And he more than once quoted a phrase of the "old bear": "My fortune came late in life."

On the 8th May I went to see the Duke. He was very ill; but his interest in the Hudson's Bay purchase was unabated. I saw him again on the 15th, and wrote a letter to the Hudson's Bay Company. On the 19th Mr. Maynard told me that the Hudson's Bay Court were meeting that day to reply to my letter. The reply came on the 21st, and was "nearly what we wished."

Owing to the Duke's illness, and to some secret difficulty which he never enlightened me upon, I was given to understand, after a short, but anxious delay, that any purchase must be carried out by private resources; but all sorts of moral support would be at our service. What good was moral support in providing a million and a half? What was to be done? There were only two ways: one, to make a list of fifteen persons who would each take a "line" of a hundred thousand pounds for himself and such friends as he chose to associate with him; the other, to hand the proposed purchase over to the just founded International Financial Association, who were looking out for some important project to lay before the public.

Leaving out Mr. Baring and Mr. Glyn (senr.) we had a strong body of earnest friends, substantial men, and we could, no doubt, have underwritten the amount. My proportion was got ready; and my personal friends would have doubled that proportion, or more, if I had wanted it. I strongly recommended this course. But the Hudson's Bay Company would give no credit. We must take up the shares as presented and pay for them over the counter. Thus, the latter alternative was, after some anxious days, adopted. Mr. Richard Potter was the able negociator in completing this great transaction, began and carried on as above. The shares were taken over and paid for by the International Financial Society, who issued new stock to the public to an amount which covered a large provision of new capital for extension of business by the Company, and a profit to themselves and their friends who had taken the risk of so new and onerous an engagement.

I may finish this section by stating that, as respects the new Hudson's Bay shareholders, their 20_l_. shares have been reduced by returns of capital to 13_l_., and having, nevertheless, in the "boom" of lands in the West, been sold at 37_l_. as the price of the 13_l_.; they are now about 24_l_. Thus, every one who has held his property, and will continue to hold it, has, and will have, a safe and unusually profitable investment. These shareholders, besides the large reserves near their posts, which I shall enumerate later on, have a claim to one-twentieth of the land where settlements are surveyed and made. This gives a great future to the investor. On the other hand, Canada—in place of the Mother Country, to whom the whole ought to have belonged, for the purposes previously set forth—has obtained this vast and priceless dominion for a payment of only 300,000_l_., on the award of Earl Granville; and the Pacific Railway, by reason of that great possession, has been completed and opened.

But there is much to record between the period of purchase and the sale to Canada.

I here give to the reader some letters of the Duke's relating to these negotiations generally:—

"DOWNING STREET,
"14 *Augt.* 1862.

MY DEAR SIR,

"I am glad to tell you that since I received your letter of Saturday last, the Hudson's Bay Company has replied to my communication, and has promised to *grant* land to a company formed under such auspices as those with whom I placed them in communication. The question now is—what *breadth* of land they will give, for of course they propose to include the whole *length* of the line through their territory. A copy of the reply shall be sent to Mr. Baring, and I hope you and he will be able to bring this concession to some practical issue.

"I was quite aware of the willingness of the Company to *sell* their *whole* rights for some such sum as 1,500,000_l_. I ascertained the fact two months ago, and alluded to it in the House of Lords in my reply to a motion by Lord Donoughmore. I cannot, however, view the proposal in so favourable a light as you do. There would be no immediate or *direct* return to show for this large outlay, for of course the trade monopoly must cease, and the sale of land would for some time bring in little or nothing—certainly not enough to pay for the government of the country.

"I do not think Canada *can*, or if she can *ought* to, take any large share in such a payment. Some of her politicians would no doubt support the proposal with views of their own,—but it would be a serious, and for some time unremunerative, addition to their very embarrassing debt.

"I certainly should not like to *sell* any portion of the territory to the United States—*exchange* (if the territory were once acquired) would be a different thing,—but that would not help towards the liquidation of the purchase-money.

"I admire your *larger views*, and have some tolerably large ones in this matter of my own, but I fear purchase of this great territory is just now impracticable.

"I am, yours sincerely,
"NEWCASTLE.

"Edwd. Watkin, Esq."

This letter was written in the educational period. The doubts came from the officials of the Colonial Office. I removed them.

"Downing Street,
"17 *Novr.* 1862.

"My dear Mr. Watkin,

"I send you the 'route' from the Pacific to Canada, which I promised.

"I cannot vouch for it; but it comes from an unusually well-informed quarter, and I incline to think it is much nearer accuracy than such information as represents the obstacles to be almost insuperable.

"I am, yours very truly,

"NEWCASTLE."

"Memorandum of a Route from Vancouver Island to Canada.

Stations Conveyance Time

"Victoria, Vancouver Island Yale, on Fraser River, or Douglas, on Harrison Lake Steamer 2 days Lytton, on Fraser River, or Lillovet Stage coach 2 days Alexander, on Fraser River Do. 4 days Fort George, on Fraser River Steamer 2 days Tete Jaune Cache do. Do. 5 days between 53 degrees and 54 degrees N L — — —- 15 days =======

The stage road from Douglas to Lillovet is described as complete, and that from Lillovet to Alexandria as in progress, as also the machinery of a stern-wheel steamboat for the water communication between Alexandria and Tete Jaune Cache.

The last-named place [Sidenote: Tete Jaune Cache.] is situated between 53 degrees and 54 degrees N.L., and is at the western extremity of the most practicable pass of the Rocky Mountains. The distance from this to Jasper House, [Sidenote: Jasper House, between 53 degrees and 54 degrees N.L., and distant 120 miles from Tete Jaune Cache.] at the eastern extremity of the pass, is 120 miles by trail, admitting, it is said, of conversion at small cost into an easy carriage road.

The distance from Jasper House to the next post, Edmonton, [Sidenote: Edmonton, 200 miles by road from Jasper House, and 90 miles by road from Assiniboin.] on the Saskatchewan, is 200 miles by road through a level wooded country, or the Elk and Athabasca Rivers may be descended by water to Fort Assiniboin, whence to Edmonton is only 90 miles.

The road communication between Tete Jaune Cache and Edmonton is represented as the only necessary work beyond Alexandria, and may be opened for 50,000_l_.

Two courses are suggested from Edmonton to the Red River, one by water along the Saskatchewan and Lake Winnipeg, another by road from Carleton, on the Saskatchewan, through the Prairie.

No remarks are offered upon the character of the route between the Red River and Lake Superior, except that it is said to present no serious difficulties.

"13_th Nov_. 1862.

R.E."

MY DEAR SIR,

"I have had a long interview of two hours today with Mr. Berens, Mr. Colville, and Mr. Maynard; but I am sorry to find that matters have by no means progressed so far as I was led to expect.

"I think I ought now to see Mr. Baring, Mr. Glyn, and yourself as soon as possible.

"Can they and you come here on Thursday at any hour not earlier than 2.30 nor later than 4? If that will interrupt other business, I could propose 11.30 on Friday at Thomas' Hotel.

"Yours sincerely,
"NEWCASTLE."

"CLUMBER,
"7 *April,* 1863.

MY DEAR SIR,

"I have received from Sir F. Rogers the draft print of your Bill, and his remarks upon it.

"I still think it quite possible to meet your views respecting the lower portion of the Athabasca territory; but the *mode* of doing it does not appear to me so simple or clear.

"I should much desire to consult the Land Commissioners before the matter is settled; and I do not see that the delay of ten days or a fortnight from this date could endanger the measure, for Lord Monck wrote to me by last mail that the Parliament had as yet not begun business.

"If you agree to this, I will send the papers and my remarks to the Land Commissioners at once, and see you (after getting their report) on Wednesday next, or any day after it, except Friday.

"Pray let me hear by return.

"Yours very sincerely,
"NEWCASTLE."

"DOWNING STREET,
"6 *May,* 1863.

MY DEAR MR. WATKIN,

"I hope and believe that the despatches in their final shape, as they went out to N. Columbia on Friday last, and to Canada on Saturday, were quite what you and the proposed 'N. W. Transit Company' would wish.

"I added words which (without dictation) will be understood as implying 'No Intercolonial, no Transit.'

"If you happen to be in this neighbourhood any day between 3 and 4.30, I shall be glad to see you, though I have nothing at all pressing to say.

"Yours very sincerely,
"NEWCASTLE."

Chapter IX
The Right Honorable Edward Ellice, M.P

I have alluded to this remarkable man under the soubriquet attached to him for a generation—"the old Bear." I assume that when his son, who for many years represented the Scotch constituency of the St. Andrews Burghs, grew up, the father became the "old" and the son the "young" Bear. Mr. Ellice was the son of Mr. Alexander Ellice, an eminent merchant in the City of London. Born, if the "Annual Register" be accurate, in 1789, he died at the end of 1863. It is strange that he began life by uniting the Canadian fur trade with that of the Hudson's Bay Company, and just lived long enough to witness the sale and transfer of the interests he had, by a bold and masterly policy, combined in 1820. Leaving Canada, Mr. Ellice joined the Whig party, and was returned to Parliament for Coventry in 1818; and, with the exception of the period from 1826 to 1830, he retained his seat till the day of his death. Marrying the youngest sister of Earl Grey, of the Reform Bill—the widow of Captain Bettesworth, R.N.—who died in 1832, leaving him an only son; and, in 1843, the widow of Mr. Coke, of Norfolk, he became intimately connected with the Whig aristocracy.

In Mr. Ellice's evidence before the Parliamentary Committee of 1857, on the Hudson's Bay Company, I find that, in answer to a question put by Mr. Christy, M.P., as to the probability of a "settlement being made within what you consider to be the Southern territories of the Hudson's Bay Company?"—he replied, "None, in the lifetime of the youngest man now alive." Events have proved his error. Mr. Ellice was a man of commanding stature and presence, but, to my mind, had always the demeanour of a colonist who had had to wrestle with the hardships of nature, and his cast of countenance was Jewish. According to his own account, he went out to Canada in 1803, when he must have been a mere youth, and then personally associated himself with the fur trade, a trade which attracted the attention of almost the whole Canadian society. It was, in fact, at that time, the great trade of the country. The traders had inherited the skill and organization of the old French voyageurs, who, working from Quebec and Montreal as bases of their operations, were the doughty competitors of the Hudson's Bay Company, many of whose posts were only separated by distances of a hundred miles from those of the French. When Canada became the possession of our country, in the last century, Scotch and English capital and energy reinforced the trade; and, as time went on, a powerful organization, called the "North-West Company," arose, and extended its operations right across to the Pacific.

At the end of the last century, or the beginning of this, Mr. Ellice's father, as Mr. Ellice stated, "had supplied a great part of the capital by which the whole north-west trade was conducted." Profitable trading brought division of interests; and, in addition to smaller swarms from the parent hive, a new organization, called the "X. Y. Company," or "Sir Alexander Mackenzie and Company," carried on trade in competition with the original "North-West Company of Canada." Mr. Ellice became connected with this "X. Y. Company" in 1805. The leading spirit of the North-West Company was Mr. McGillivray: and Mr. McGillivray and Mr. Ellice were, as a rule, cordial allies. Two leading firms engaged in the fur trade were McTavish, Fraser & Co., and Inglis, Ellice & Co.

Competition raged amongst these Canadian interests, and between them and the Hudson's Bay Company, whose affairs were administered from England. The business was carried on, therefore, with great extravagance. The Indians were tempted and corrupted by strong drink. Frequent collisions took place between the Indians and the whites, and everything grew worse till 1811. In 1811 Lord Selkirk joined the Hudson's Bay Company. He became not only a stockholder in the Company, but took great interest in the trade; and he was the proprietor of a large tract of territory on the Red River, acquired from the Hudson's Bay Company under a deed dated 12th June, 1811. In this territory, he made settlements for the purposes of agriculture.

The conflict of interests between the Canadian fur traders and the Hudson's Bay Company became more and more violent, and ended in bloodshed. Finally Lord Selkirk, in virtue of his assumed powers as a magistrate, seized Mr. McGillivray, of the North-West Company, at Fort William, at the head of Lake Superior, and the whole of his property. The confusion and outrage became so great that Canada became alarmed, and a Mr. Coltman was sent up as Commissioner. Mr. Coltman reported, and made a recommendation that, to restore peace and order, some attempt should be made to unite the interests of the various fur traders in the country. In the meantime the Hudson's Bay Company ceased to pay dividends, and the other companies were almost bankrupt. At this moment Mr. Ellice, by great tact, and force of will, succeeded in uniting all the conflicting combinations; and from that time onwards the fur trade has been carried on under the Charter of the Hudson's Bay Company, extended by licenses, from time to time renewed, of exclusive trade in the North-West and in the Pacific States, including Vancouver's Island. Out of these fusions arose the Puget Sound Company, created to utilise, cultivate, and colonise the Pacific territories, over which licenses to trade had been given to the Hudson's Bay Company.

The vigorous action of the united interests soon told upon the trade and discipline of the vast area hunted and traded over. The Indians were brought back to tea and water in place of rum and brandy; and peace was restored, everywhere, between the white man and the red. The epidemics of small pox, which had at times decimated whole tribes of Indians, were got rid of by the introduction of vaccination. Settlement, if only on a small scale, was encouraged by the security of life and property. The enlargement of their action, as issuers of notes and as bankers aided the trade and the colonists; and so good was a Hudson's Bay Company's note that it was taken everywhere over the northern continent, when the "Shin Plasters" of banks in the United States and Canada were refused. When, for a short time, in 1865 and 1866, I held the office of shareholders' auditor of the Hudson's Bay Company, I cancelled many of these notes, which had become defaced, mainly owing to the fingering of Indians and others, who left behind on the thick yellow paper coatings of "Pemmican," —the pounded flesh and fat of the buffalo, done up in skins like sausages—a food eminently nutritious and lasting long, but fearfully odorous and nasty.

Mr. Ellice supplied much of the political energy inside the old Reform party, displayed in the Reform Bill struggle of 1830-1832. He became one of the Secretaries of the Treasury; and, in 1831, had to organize the eventful election of that year. His great powers and never-failing energy, devoted in early life to the fur trade and its conflicts, became of infinite value to the country, in many momentous struggles, at home, for liberty and progress. It amused me much when, by chance, meeting Mr. Ellice, after we had bought and paid for his Hudson's Bay property, to see the kind of astonished stare with which he regarded me. I think the purchase of the Hudson's Bay Company was a mystery to him. I remember meeting him at the Royal Academy a few months before his death. He stopped opposite to me, as if to study my features. He did not speak a word, nor did I. He seemed in a state of abstraction, like that of a man endeavouring to recollect a long history of difficulty, and to realize how strangely it had all ended,—by the negociation I had brought to a head.

Chapter X
The Select Committee, on Hudson's Bay Affairs, of 1857

This Committee was appointed "to consider the state of those British possessions in North America which are under the administration of the Hudson's Bay Company, or over which they possess a licence to trade." Lord John Russell, Mr. Gladstone, the present Lord Derby, Mr. Roebuck, Mr. Labouchere, Mr. Lowe, and Mr. Edward Ellice, were of the nineteen members of which the Committee originally consisted. Later on, the names of Mr. Alexander Matheson and Viscount Goderich were substituted for those of Mr. Adderley and Mr. Bell; and Mr. Christy was added to the Committee. The evidence before the Committee much resembled that taken by the Committee of 1749. There were the same disaffected, and discharged, officials; the same disappointed merchants and rivals; the same desire, in varied quarters, as before, to depreciate and despoil a somewhat prosperous undertaking. The rival views were those of the majority of the Committee, on the one hand, and of Mr. Gladstone, on the other. The claims of Canada to annex territory useful, in her opinion, to her inhabitants, was solidly urged. But the Honorable John Ross, then President of the Grand Trunk Railway of Canada, who was the first witness examined, said, "It is complained that the Hudson's Bay Company occupy that territory and prevent the extension of settlement and civilization in that part of the Continent of America. I do not think they ought to be permitted to do that; but I think it would be a very great calamity if their control and power in that part of America were entirely to cease. My reason for forming that opinion is this: during all the time that I have been able to observe their proceedings there, there has been peace within the whole territory. The operations of the Company seem to have been carried on, at all events, in such a way as to prevent the Indian tribes within their borders from molesting the Canadian frontier; while, on the other hand, those who have turned their attention to that quarter of the world must have seen that, from Oregon to Florida, for these last thirty years or more, there has been a constant Indian war going on between the natives of American territory, on the one side, and the Indian tribes on the other. Now, I fear very much that if the occupation of the Hudson's Bay

Company, in what is called the Hudson's Bay territory, were to cease, our fate in Canada might be just as it is with Americans in the border settlements of their territory."

Mr. Ross advocated a railway to the Pacific, and he showed good practical reasons for it. Failing a railway, he claimed a "good, broad open road." On the question of renewed competition in the fur trade, he added, "I believe there are certain gentlemen at Toronto very anxious to get up a second North-West Company, and I dare say it would result in something like the same difficulties which the last North-West Company created. I should be sorry to see them succeed. I think it would do a great deal of harm, creating further difficulties in Canada, which I do not desire to see created."

"Certain gentlemen at Toronto" have ever been ready to despoil any old and successful undertaking.

Mr. Gladstone's resolutions, as proposed at the end of the evidence, were negatived by the casting vote of the chairman, Mr. Labouchere, the numbers being 7 and 7. Mr. Gladstone proposed that the country capable of colonization should be withdrawn from the jurisdiction of the Hudson's Bay Company; while the country incapable of colonization should remain under that jurisdiction. And, having thus disposed of any chartered, or other, rights of the Company, his last, or 10th, resolution, said, "That inasmuch as the Company has tendered concessions which may prove sufficient to meet the necessities of the case, the Committee has come to no decision upon the question how far it may be, as some think, just and even necessary, or on the other hand, unwise or even unjust, to raise any judicial issue with the view of ascertaining the legal rights of the Company."

The Committee's report recommended that the Red River and Saskatchewan districts of the Hudson's Bay Company might be "ceded to Canada on equitable principles," the details being left to her Majesty's Government. The Committee advised the termination of the government of Vancouver's Island by the Hudson's Bay Company; a recommendation followed, a year later, by the establishment of a Crown Colony. But they strongly advised, in the interests of law and order, and of the Indian population, as well as for the preservation of the fur trade, that the Hudson's Bay Company "should continue to enjoy the privileges of exclusive trade which they now possess."

Chapter XI
Re-organization of Hudson's Bay Company

Thus, after a long and continuous period of inquiry and investigation— a grave game of chess with the Hudson's Bay Company—many anxieties and a great pecuniary risk, surmounted without the expected help of our Government, the battle was won. What now remained was to take care that the Imperial objects, for which some of us had struggled, were not sacrificed, to indifference in high places at home, or to possible conflicts between the two Provinces in Canada; and to secure an energetic management of the business of the fur trade and of land development by the executive of the Company, whose 144 posts covered the continent from Labrador to Sitka, Vancouver's Island, and San Francisco.

It seemed to me that this latter business was of vital and pressing importance. The Hudson's Bay factors, and traders were, in various grades and degrees, partners in the annual trade or "outfit," under the provisions of the "deed poll." This "deed poll" was the charter under which the hardy officials worked and saved. Their charter had been altered or varied over the long period since the date of the Royal concession, in the twenty-second year of the reign of Charles the Second. The deed poll in existence in 1863 provided that the profits of the fur trade (less interest on capital employed in the trade, which belonged to the stockholders who provided it) were to be divided into 100 parts, of which 60 parts belonged to the stockholders, and 40 to the "wintering partners." The "wintering partners" were the "chief factors" and the "chief traders." These 40 parts were again subdivided into 85 shares; and each "chief factor" was entitled to two of such shares, and each "chief trader" to one share. The clerks were paid by salary, and only a person who had served as a clerk could be promoted to a "chief tradership," and only a "chief trader" to a "chief factorship." Thus all had a direct or remote partnership interest. On retirement, an officer held his full interest for one year and half his interest for the succeeding six years.

I had much apprehension that if the unexpected sale and transfer of the share property, under terms and conditions in every sense unique, were not frankly and explicitly explained, and under authority, alarm and misconception would arise; while the news of the transfer would find its way to distant regions in a distorted fashion, and through unfriendly sources, long before the explanation and answer could arrive. My fear, owing to bad management in London, was somewhat realized, and I found that I had not rushed across the Atlantic, to perform every service in my power to the undertaking, in June, 1863, one moment too soon.

Then, having studied the "deed poll," I felt that, unless we made the factors and traders partners in the whole enterprise—fur trade, banking, telegraphs, lands, navigation of rivers—on generous terms, we could not expect to elicit either their energies or their adhesion to a new order of things.

Further, I saw no way to secure supervision and control over the Fertile belt, and all around it, except by the construction, to begin with, of a main line of telegraph from St. Paul to the Hudson's Bay territory, and thence by Fort Garry to the extreme western post on the east side of the Rocky Mountains. Such main line to be supplemented by other subsidiary lines as rapidly as possible. The "wire," to my mind, was the best "master's eye" under the circumstances. But, apart from business re-organization, it was most essential to explain everything to the Government of Canada; and to ascertain the views of political parties, and of industrial interests, as, also, of religious bodies, as to future government. In dealing with these questions, I had to assume an authority which was to have been confided to a delegation, to consist of Captain Henry Glyn, Colonel Synge, and myself.

On leaving England promptly—the main work being done—Mr. Richard Potter undertook for me all the details which, if at home, I should have managed, and he especially took up the discussions at the Colonial Office, which I had personally carried on, with the Duke, for the previous period.

Thus it was that the new Board was constituted, and the arrangements for taking over were made in England without my taking any, further, part. Sir Edmund Head was appointed Governor at the suggestion—almost the personal request—of the Duke of Newcastle: some members of the old Board were retained for the, expected, value of their experience, and amongst the new members were Mr. Richard Potter and Sir Curtis Miranda Lampson, a rival fur trader of eminence and knowledge, and an American. A seat at the Board was left vacant for me.

It may be interesting here to quote what the Duke of Newcastle said, in explaining, in the House of Lords, the recent transactions with the Hudson's Bay Company.

TIMES, *July* 3, 1863. [HOUSE OF LORDS.]

"The DUKE OF NEWCASTLE, in moving the second reading of the British Columbia Boundaries Bill, said that he should give some further information as to an extension of the means of communication across that great interval of country between British Columbia and Canada. After referring to the system of government which then existed both in Vancouver's Island and British Columbia, and to the revenues of both colonies for the previous few years—that of British Columbia being most remarkable, having nearly doubled itself in two years (the imports in 1861 being $1,400,000, and in 1862 $2,200,000)—the noble Duke proceeded to say, that the greatest impediment to the future prosperity of the Colony was a want of communication with the outer world. He had stated on a previous occasion that he hoped to be able to state this year to the House that arrangements had been made to complete the communications between the Colony and the east of British North America, and he thought he could now inform their Lordships that such arrangements would be carried out. He had desired a gentleman of great experience, knowledge, and energy, who was constantly travelling between Canada and this country, to inquire whether it would be possible to effect a communication across the Continent. This gentleman—Mr. Watkin—had returned with considerable information, and he had suggested to him to place himself in communication with persons in the commercial world who might be willing to undertake the carrying out of such a communication. He had put himself in communication with Mr. Baring and others, and he believed they had arrived at the conclusion that if arrangements could be made with the Hudson Bay Company the undertaking should have their best attention. In order that these important communications might be made certain, guarantees were to be given by Canada on the one hand, and British Columbia and Vancouver Island on the other. A complete Intercolonial railway system had long been looked forward to by those interested in our North American Provinces, and it would be impossible to overrate the importance to this country of an inter-oceanic railway between the Atlantic and Pacific. By such a communication, and the electric telegraph, so great a revolution would be effected in the commerce of the world as had been brought about by the discovery of the Cape of Good Hope. It was unnecessary to point out to their Lordships of what importance it would be in the case of war on the other side of the Atlantic. There was another matter on which he wished to say a few words. Some eight or nine days ago it was stated in a portion of the press that the Hudson Bay Company had sold their property. That statement was not altogether accurate, and certainly it was premature, for he had been informed within two hours before he came down to the House that the whole arrangement had only been completed that afternoon. He had not received any official communication on the subject, but some of the gentlemen concerned had been kind enough to inform him of the facts. He had stated on a former occasion that the Hudson Bay Company had wished to sell. Certain parties in the City had, in the first instance, entered into communication with them for the purpose either of purchasing or obtaining permission for a transit through the Company's possessions. After some negociation the alternative of permission for a transit was agreed upon. That conclusion having been arrived at he did not know what it was that raised the whole question of sale again, but some fortnight or three weeks ago fresh negociations were opened. Parties in the City proposed to the Hudson Bay Company to give them by way of purchase a sum of 1,500,000_l_. What had taken place was this: The Hudson Bay Company very prudently required that the money should be paid down, and that the whole sum of 1,500,000_l_. should be ready on a given day, which he believed was yesterday. Of course the intending purchasers could not carry out that transaction in the course of a week, and they, therefore, applied to the International Financial Association to assist them. The Association agreed to do so, and the money either had been paid or would be on a day arranged upon. A prospectus would be issued tomorrow morning, and the shares would be thrown upon the market, to be taken up in the ordinary way upon the formation of companies. These shares would not remain in the hands of the Association, but would pass to the Proprietors, as if they had bought their shares direct from the Hudson Bay Company. Of course the Company would only enjoy the rights which those shares carried, and no more. They would, in fact, be a continuation of the Company; but their efforts would be directed to the promotion of the settlement of the country: the development of the postal and transit communication being one of the objects to which they would apply themselves. Of course, the old Governor and his colleagues, having sold their shares, ceased to be the governing body, and a new council, consisting of most respectable persons, had been formed that afternoon. Among them were two of the Committee of the old Company, with one of whom, Mr. Colville, he had had much personal communication, and could speak in the highest terms as a man of business and good sense. There were, also, seven or eight most influential and responsible people, and the name of the Governor, Sir Edmund Head, who had been elected to-day, would be a guarantee of the intentions of the new Company, for no one would believe that he had entered into this undertaking for mere speculative purposes, or that the Company would be conducted solely with a view to screw the last penny out of this territory. While the council, as practical men of business, would be bound to promote the prosperity of their shareholders, he was sure they would be actuated by statesmanlike views. No negociation with the Colonial Office had taken place; and as this was a mere ordinary transfer, no leave on their part was necessary. But arrangements must be entered into with the Colonial Office for the settlement of the country; and at some future time it would be, no doubt, his duty to inform their Lordships what these arrangements were."

The Prospectus, as issued in London, for the new organization, at the end of June, 1863, contained this paragraph:—

"With the view of providing the means of telegraphic and postal communication between Canada and British Columbia, across the Company's territory, and thereby of connecting the Atlantic and Pacific Oceans by an exclusively British route, negociations have been pending for some time past between certain parties and Her Majesty's Government and the representatives of the Government of Canada, and preliminary arrangements for the accomplishment of these objects have been made through Her Majesty's Government (subject to the final sanction of the Colonies), based upon a 5 per cent. guarantee from the Governments of Canada, British Columbia, and Vancouver Island. In further aid of these Imperial objects, Her Majesty's Government have signified their intention to make grants of land in portions of the Crown territory traversed by the proposed telegraphic line.

"One of the first objects of the Company will be to examine the facilities and consider the best means for carrying out this most important work; and there can be little doubt that it will be successfully executed either by the Hudson's Bay Company itself, or with their aid and sanction.

"For this, as well as for the other proposed objects, Mr. Edward Watkin, who is now in Canada, will be commissioned, with other gentlemen specially qualified for the duty, to visit the Red River and southern districts, to consult the officers of the Company there, and to report as to the best and safest means of giving effect to the contemplated operations."

A letter of instructions, from the new Governor, dated London, 6th July, 1863, received by me about the 22nd July, after I had made no small advance in the real business, stated:—

SIR,

"I am authorized by the Committee of the Hudson's Bay Company to request you to proceed on their behalf to the Red River Settlement, for the purpose of reporting to them on the state and condition of this Settlement, the condition of the adjoining territory, the prospect of settlement therein, and the possibility of commencing operations for an electric telegraph line across the southern district of Rupert's Land.

"The Committee have full confidence in your discretion and judgment, but they have deemed it right to associate with you in this inquiry Governor

Dallas, of the Red River Settlement, with whom they request you to communicate at once.

"The Committee are aware that it is now so late in the season as to preclude you from doing more than procure such information as may enable them to commence fresh inquiries at the opening of next season.

"I have the honour to be, Sir,
"Your obedient Servant,
"EDMUND HEAD, Governor.

"EDWARD WATKIN, Esq."

I found soon after my arrival in Canada that Governor Dallas was coming down from Red River, and would meet me at Montreal. He was a very able man; cool, clear, cautious, but when once he had had time to calculate all the consequences, firm and decided. He had been for years on the Pacific coast; and, thanks to his prudence, the landing, in 1859, of General Harney, and a detachment of United States troops on the Island of St. Juan, between Vancouver's Island and the mainland, on the Pacific, had been controlled and checkmated, by the proposal of a joint occupation until negotiations had settled the question of right. This right was, afterwards, given away by our Government under the form of an arbitration before the Emperor of Germany. Governor Dallas' opinion of the transaction will be gathered from his letters to me of the 29th and 30th October, 1872, hereafter copied.

The Governor and I became fast friends, and our friendship, cordial on both sides, continued until his death, a very few years ago. The only fault of Governor Dallas was a want of self-assertion. Brought out by the Mathesons—hardy Scots of the North—as he was, he made a reasonable fortune in China: and coming home, intending to retire, he was persuaded to accept the Governorship of the Hudson's Bay Company on the death of Sir George Simpson. Meeting at Montreal, our first act of "business" was to voyage in the Governor's canoe from Lachine through the rapids to Montreal; a voyage, to me, as almost a novice, save for my New Brunswick canoeing, of rather startling adventure; but the eleven stalwart Indians, almost all six feet high, who manned the boat, made the trip interesting, as it was to me in the nature of a new experience. These men had been with Governor Dallas nearly 4,000 miles by river, lake, and portage; and he told me he never knew them to be late, however early the start had to be made; never unready; always cheerful and obliging; and that a cross word had never, in his hearing, been uttered by any one of them. These men made Caughna Wauga, opposite Lachine, their home, and there were their families.

After the most careful study and discussion of the questions above alluded to, and others, the discussion extending over a month, we agreed to various memoranda. The one affecting the re-organization of management was as follows:—

"The first measure necessary towards the re-organization of the Hudson's Bay service, will be the abolition, or modification of the deed poll, under which the fur trade is at present carried on. The difficulty involved in this proceeding is, an interference in the vested rights of the wintering partners (chief factors and chief traders). That might be overcome by some equitable scheme for the extinction of those rights, which would serve the double purpose of rendering practicable a reorganization of the service, and a reduction in the number of superior officers, at present too large. This reduction would give the opportunity of dispensing with such men as are inefficient, and of retaining those only likely to be useful. The Company are under no covenants in reference to the clerks.

"The arrangements of the deed poll are, in outline, as follows:—The profits of the fur trade (less the interest charge, which goes exclusively to the stockholders) are divided into one hundred parts; of those, sixty are appropriated to the stockholders, and forty to the wintering partners. These last are subdivided into eighty-five shares, of which two are held by each chief factor, and one by each chief trader.

"Clerks are paid by salary. Only a clerk can be promoted to a chief tradership (1-1/85 share), and only a trader to a chief factorship (2- 1/85 shares). The promotions are made by the Company on the nomination of the chief factors, though this rule has not always been adhered to. On retirement an officer holds his full interest for the first year, and half this interest for the succeeding six years. The deed poll authorizes the Company to put an officer on the retired list, without reasons assigned, after he has served four years, but they cannot deprive him of his retired interest except for proved misconduct; but neither of these regulations has ever been put in force. It is possible the wintering partners might raise a question whether, under the existing deed poll, the Company could make any great changes in their business, or embark in new undertakings, if likely to affect injuriously the incomes of the officers on the active list, or the interests of those on retirement.

"One mode of removing this obstacle would be to ascertain the value of a retired interest, and to give a money compensation to each officer on his entering into an agreement to consent to the abrogation of the deed poll. This would involve an outlay of money, but would also be productive of a considerable subsequent annual saving.

"The eighty-five shares belonging to the wintering partners are, at this date, held as follows:—

```
15 chief factors 30 shares
37  "  traders 37  "
10 retired chief factors 13  "
10  "   "   traders 5  "
        —-
        85  "
        ===
```

"As regards the shares held on retirement, some of the interests have nearly run out, and none of the parties have any voice in the business.

"The value of a 1-85th share has been, on the average of the last thirteen outfits, which have been wound up (1846-1858), about 408_l_. At that rate a chief factor's retired interest would amount to 3,264_l_., and a chief trader's to 1,632_l_., less discount, supposing payment to be made at once, instead of its being spread over nine or ten years. On the other hand, the invariable custom of the service has been to allow every officer one or more year's furlough on retiring, which has come to be considered almost a right; when more than one year has been granted, it has been by special favour. Adding one year's furlough, a factor's retired allowance would be 4,080_l_., and a trader's 2,040_l_. The discount being taken off, to render them equal to cash, would make a factor's allowance about 3,000_l_., and a trader's 1,500_l_.

"The cost of commutation, on the above scale, would be—

```
15 chief factors, at 3,000_l_ L45,000
37  "  traders, at 1,500_l_  55,500
18 shares held on retirement, about 14,000
            — — — —
            L114,500
            ========
```

"Without allowing a year's furlough, the above amount would be reduced about one-sixth.

"The outlay would only be called for in the case of such officers as are already retired, and of such as under a new agreement might not be re-engaged. The retired interest of the officers who might enter into a new engagement would be provided for in the revised deed poll.

"As a set-off for the outlay on commutations would be a large reduction in the pay of officers, to be hereafter noticed, and the Company would also receive actual value for their money; and on buying out the wintering partners they would become possessed of their 4/10th share of the profits of the trade.

"Under the present organization the pay of officers in the service is about as follows: —

> Governor-in-Chief L 2,000
> 16 chief factors 12,000
> 35 chief traders 14,000
> Clerks, about 10,000
>
> — — —-
>
> L38,000
> =======

"The following would probably prove a more efficient staff: —

> Governor-in-Chief L 2,000
> Lieutenant-Governor 1,250
> 4 councillors, at 800_l_ 3,200
> 25 chief traders, at 300_l_ 7,500
> 100 clerks, at various salaries, about 10,000
>
> — — —-
>
> L23,950
> =======

"The saving of 14,000_l_. per annum would soon reimburse the Company's outlay in buying up the present interests of the factors and traders.

"The system of making the pay of officers (of the upper grade) dependent on the success of the business, has worked well, and might be advantageously continued, in a modified form, to be hereafter noticed.

"The duties of the officers of the proposed reduced staff would be adapted to the existing distribution of the territory into departments and districts, which are as follows: —

"There are four main divisions—the Northern, Southern, Western, and Montreal Departments, roughly bounded as follows:—the 'Western' embraces all the country west of the Rocky Mountains; the 'Northern' is composed of the country east of the mountains, as far as Lake Winnipeg and Lac la Pluie, and from the American frontier to the Arctic Sea; the 'Southern' embraces the southern and eastern shores of Hudson's Bay; and the 'Montreal' extends from Lake Superior down the Gulf of St. Lawrence to Labrador. These departments are divided into districts, and in each district are several posts. The limits of districts are fixed by local peculiarities; but commonly embrace some large river, on which the various stations are planted—such, for example, as the McKenzie and the Saskatchewan. There are twenty-three districts on the east side of the mountains; to the west such subdivision of the business is now scarcely practicable, and is being abandoned. To proceed to the duties of the officers.

"The Governor-in-Chief would fulfil his present large functions, and be the medium of communication between the Company and their officers in the country.

"Under the present system the Governor is supposed to maintain a personal supervision of the whole service. This is practically impossible, the country being too large to enable him to travel over more than a limited section of it in each season. To relieve him of that heavy duty, and at the same time to maintain a real and close personal inspection, one of the four councillors might be stationed in each department, of which, in the absence of the Governor, he would be the chief officer, and held responsible for all local details, and the various posts in which he should periodically inspect and report upon. Once, or oftener, in each year, a meeting of the Governor and the four councillors should be held, at any time or place most convenient—say, Fort Garry, Montreal, or elsewhere. Aided by such a council, the Governor would be accurately informed as to details in every part of the country, and able to deal satisfactorily with all local questions.

"The duty of the Lieutenant-Governor would be to relieve the Governor-in-Chief of some share of his labours, and to act in his absence as President of Council.

"The chief traders would, as a general rule, be placed at the head of districts, and the clerks in charge of posts.

"The very efficient class of officers known as 'postmasters' would remain as at present. They are usually men who have risen from the ranks from merit; and, being good interpreters, and Indian traders, are commonly placed in charge of small posts. Their scale of pay is rather less than that of clerks, and they are rarely advanced to any higher rank; indeed, their ambition is satisfied when they are made postmasters.

"Reverting to the mode of paying officers, and making their incomes to some extent dependent on the success of the business, it might answer to give them an interest as stockholders. Instead of paying a chief trader 300_l_. per annum, he might have 250_l_., and a sum of 1,000_l_. of stock placed to his credit, of which he would receive the dividends only, the stock itself reverting to the Company when his connection with them terminated.

"A councillor might have 700_l_. pay and the dividends on 2,000_l_. stock. It would also be a great encouragement to the officers, and secure prolonged service, to give them an annual increase of stock—say, 200_l_. to be added for every year's service. Thus, if a man did not get as early promotion as he expected, he would still benefit by length of service.

"The principle of retired interests might be maintained, by allowing the officers to receive the dividends on the stock they held at retirement for— say, seven or ten years, before it reverted to the Company.

"To carry out these arrangements, it would be necessary to set aside in trust about 150,000_l_. stock. But the Company would lose nothing by it, as they would save in salaries what they gave in dividends.

"At the outset only 35,000_l_. of the stock would be called for, with an increase of 5,400_l_. per annum. Even allowing for a considerable retired list, it is doubtful if the whole 150,000_l_. would ever be appropriated; and of course the dividends on whatever portion was not appropriated would revert to the Company.

"In the revision of the deed poll, it would be essential to retain the clauses which secure to the Company the right to place officers on the retired list, and to dismiss them for misconduct.

"The mode of keeping the accounts, both in London and in the country, is one of much importance, requiring early consideration. At present there are no accounts, properly speaking, kept at the posts; and very great delay occurs in ascertaining the results of the business from London. It is essential to introduce some system of analysed post accounts, which should keep the Governor and his Council fully informed of the state of the business at every post, and by which they might judge of the management of the officers in charge. There is now no practical check on extravagance or dishonesty, except that arising from the upright principles of the officers in the service. The adoption of a system of local audit appears the best remedy for many of the existing evils.

"The Company's agent at New York (Mr. Wm. McNaughton), who is a valuable officer, has not at present sufficient employment to make his position worth occupying. As there is a valuable market in New York to which it would, at certain times, be advantageous to send buffalo robes, wolves' and some other furs, which could be done without interference with the market in England, it is important to render the New York agency more efficient.

"(Signed) A. G. DALLAS.

"(Signed) EDWARD W. WATKIN.

"*7th August*, 1863."

This memorandum was sent home to Governor Sir Edmund Head, with other papers.

On the serious questions of the future relations of the vast territory to Canada and the Mother Country; how it could best be settled; how it should be governed; what arrangement as to boundaries, and so on—I had many and serious conferences with public men. And in answer to many questions as to my own views, I drew up the following memorandum, as a *resume* of the whole subject. It is now nearly twenty-four years old. I have read it again and again. I am not ashamed of it. I see nothing to retract; little to alter:—

"The present state of government in the Red River Settlement is attributable alike to the habitual attempt, encouraged, perhaps very naturally, in England and in Canada, to discredit the traditions, and question the title of the Hudson's Bay Company, and to the false economy which has stripped the Governor of a military force, with which, in the last resort, to support the decisions of the legal tribunals. No other organized Government of white men in the world, since William Penn, has endeavoured to rule any population, still less a promiscuous people composed of whites, half-breeds. Indians, and borderers, without a soldiery of some sort, and the inevitable result of the experiment has, in this case, been an unpunished case of prison- breaking, not sympathised in, it is true, by the majority of the settlers, but still tending to bring law and government into contempt, and greatly to discourage the governing body held responsible for keeping order in the territory.

"At the same time it must be conceded, that, while government by a merchant organization has eminently succeeded, up to an obvious point of time and circumstances, in the cases both of the East India and Hudson's Bay Companies, and is still applicable to the control and management of distant districts, it contains within itself the seeds of its own ultimate dissolution. In fact, the self-interest, however enlightened, which brings a dividend to stockholders, is opposed to the high impartiality and absence of individualism which should characterize a true Government. Individuals and corporations may trade and grow rich,—Government may not; they may embark in constant speculation, while it cannot; they must either insensibly measure their dealings by consequences, as affecting *gain*, or be suspected of doing so, while the interest of Government is not individual, but collective; its duty being, to give facility to the acquirer, security to the possessor, and justice and equal protection to all.

"Therefore, although the Government of Red River has had few faults and many excellences, and has been marked by a generous policy, in many instances it has been, and is, open to suspicion; because the commercial power which buys furs, trades with Indians and whites alike, and is, in fact, the great merchant, storekeeper, and forwarder of the country; appoints a Governor and assistants, places judges upon the bench, selects magistrates, and administers the law, even amongst its possible rivals and trade competitors. Such a state of things is unsound in principle, and ought only to be continued until a stronger and permanent Government can be organized; at the same time it can only be continued in safety, on the opening up of the country, by arming the Governor with a military force of reasonable amount.

"That the Hudson's Bay Company *can* govern the country efficiently, on this obvious condition of all other Governments, is clear enough; and the peaceable relations between the Indians and the whites, and between the various tribes themselves, throughout the whole of this enormous territory, as well as the general state of health and occupation of the aborigines, prove how perfect and wise has been the management of the country. But government of Indians, who can be employed and traded with, and who at last become more or less dependent upon the Company's organization, as in this case, is one thing,— government of a large and expanding colony of free white men is quite another.

"It is a question whether the government of the Indians can or ought to be changed, for a long period to come, so completely is the Indian life now associated with the operations of the Company. Of course, the settlement of a new or an extended colony, involves the extinguishment of Indian rights within the area proposed; and while the outside district not set apart, would still be roamed over by the Indians, and be valuable for the fur trade, its limits must, from time to time, be narrowed by further additions to the circle of civilization and free government. Thus, the Hudson's Bay Company, if dispossessed of the government of Red River, and the proposed new Colony, would still manage and govern where it traded, and would still preserve sobriety, order, and peace amongst the Indian tribes of its territory thus limited.

"It may happen that the Hudson's Bay Company may be compelled to govern everywhere, by the refusal of the Home or Canadian Government to encounter the responsibility and expense, which at first might be serious, and which, as regards cost, must be greater in their hands than in those of a Company using portions, of its business organization for purposes of administration. It is well to look these probabilities fairly in the face.

"Such a necessity may arise from the indisposition of certain schools of politicians at home to incur Colonial expense, and the responsibility of defending a new nation flanking the United States; it may happen, owing to the refusal of Lower Canada to widen out the borders, and thus increase the political power of Upper Canada; or it may be objected in Canada generally, that the finances of the country will not, at present, prudently authorize the maintenance of a new Canadian military force; and again, the Indian war in Minnesota, which may spread itself, may raise up fears of Indian wars in the new country to be settled.

"Should the Hudson's Bay Company be compelled, then, to continue to govern the whole territory, the first essential, as before said, is a military force. That force may consist partly of regular troops, partly of mounted irregulars or militia, and it need not, in their hands, be large. The population is suited to military pursuits, and the half- breeds mounted would make an excellent irregular cavalry. And the next essential would be a convention and treaty with the United States, as to boundary and transit through the United States and Hudson's Bay territory respectively, for purposes of travel, and commerce, and of postage, and the telegraph.

"Then the limits of colonization must be defined, and it must be maturely considered at the outset, and decided as to how far, and in what form, and how soon, the principle of self-government shall be introduced. It is assumed that a thriving and expanding colony of white men neither can nor ought to be taxed and governed without their own consent, obtained in some form or other; and that it would be both unwise and unjust to attempt a permanently autocratic government. This is a most serious question, and the Act 31st George III., under which Canada was governed until 1841, would appear to solve the difficulty. The general scheme of government of that Act might operate so soon as the new Colony had a population of (say) 50,000, and its provisions might be elaborated into a constitution, to be voted by the Colony in general assembly, so soon as the population reached (say) 300,000.

"The grand basis of all successful settlement—the land—presents fewer difficulties than might have been imagined, because the admirable model of the land system of the United States is before us, and no better can be devised to enable a country to grow up side by side with the Republic. Reliable surveys and plans, cheap and unclogged titles to the land in fee, a limited upset price of not exceeding $1-25/100 an acre; division of the land saleable into regular sections; the issue of land warrants and regulations as to location, which will prevent, as far as may be, monopolies of land in the hands of speculators—are all essential conditions, and whatever power governs, they must be equally observed.

"Again,—reserves of land, on a liberal scale, must be made to support schools and churches, and to assist roads and other public works conducted by the Government.

"But let it be hoped that this necessity of continued government by the Hudson's Bay Company may be avoided by the wise and far-sighted action of the Home Government and of Canada. No beneficial decision can be arrived at without the concurrence of both powers, for each have rights and ideas in some respects differing, and Canada especially has the deepest concern in the future organization of the North-west. In selecting a governing power for such a country, the strength and influence of that power are the grand essentials. Even with equal enlightenment, these essentials could not be overlooked. A weak Government would invite attack, deter investment, and check general confidence.

"Apart from the government by the Hudson's Bay Company, there appear to be these alternatives: —

"1. Government by Canada annexing to her territory a tract of country extending to the limits of British Columbia, under some reasonable arrangement with the Hudson's Bay Company, fairly protective of their rights, and which arrangement ought not to be difficult to draw out, when once the principle of the settlement of the country, and the land system, and extent of land reserves, are agreed upon.

"2. Government by the Crown, as a separate Crown Colony, totally independent of Canada.

"3. Government by the Crown as a separate Crown Colony, with federation, more or less extensive, with Canada, and the establishment of a customs union between the new and old communities.

"It must always be observed that a decision as to the fate of this territory must be immediately made. It cannot wait political necessities elsewhere, or be postponed to suit individual wishes. The fertile country between Lake Winnipeg and the Rocky Mountains will be now settled, since that is now a fixed policy, and its plan of government must be in advance of, and not lag behind, that settlement. The electric wire, the letter post, and the steamboat, which two years more will see at work, will totally change the face of things; and as Minnesota has now 250,000 inhabitants, where, in 1850 there was hardly a white man, so this vast district may, when once it can be communicated with from without, with reasonable facility, be flooded with emigrants, not forgetting a very probable rush of English, Irish, and Scotch farmers, and settlers from the United States, who here will find a refuge from conscription and civil war.

"The discoveries of gold, and the disturbed state of the border Indians in Minnesota, are both unanswerable reasons of necessity for the immediate establishment of a permanent form of Government, and fixed laws and arrangements for the settlement and development of the country.

"1. The government of the North-west, as an 'annexe' to Canada, possesses advantages of contiguity and similarity of ideas on the part of Canadians and the probable settlers. Canada, it will be said, has a good and responsible Government, and why not now extend its machinery to the 1,300 miles between the height of land and the Rocky Mountains?

"But will Canada accept the expense and responsibility, and, more especially, is it just now politically possible? Were Canada politically and practically one united country, the answer would be perhaps not difficult. But Canada, for the present, is really two countries, or two halves of one country, united under the same form of government, each half jealous of the mutual balance, and neither half disposed to aggrandize the power or exaggerate the size of the other.

"Would Lower Canada, then, submit to see Upper Canada become, at one bound, so immensely her superior? And would Upper Canadian statesmen, however personally anxious to absorb the North-west, risk the consequences of such a discussion as would arise? Would it be possible, in fact, to found a Government based upon the platform of accepting the responsibility of settling, defending, and governing the North-west? If not, then, however desirable, the next best alternative must be chosen.

"Assuming that at some period, near or distant, the British North American Provinces, between the Atlantic and the Pacific, unite in a federal or legislative union, and thus become too great and too strong for attack, that next best alternative would point to such arrangements, as respects the North-west, as would lead on to and promote this union, and not stand in its way. Thus, disputes about race and customs should, if possible, be avoided by anticipation, and the constitution and power of the new Colony should foreshadow its connection with the countries to the east and to the west. Future isolation should be forbidden, while present independence should be accorded.

"2. The above assumption tends to throw doubt upon the desirability of establishing a Crown Colony, separate in all respects from Canada, and able to shut out or let in Canadian produce and manufactures at its pleasure. This is a danger to be foreseen and avoided.

"The new Colony, placed between Canada and the Pacific, must be essentially British, in the sense of its forming one secure link in a chain of British nations, or, in the interests of Canada, it had better never be organized. The power and *prestige* of the Crown is essential to this end, and a separate Colony, even, would have many advantages *per se*. It would also save Canada the cost of a new Government at a time when financial pressure and political majorities would be in the way. A Crown Colony could not be looked upon with jealousy in Canada, while government by the Hudson's Bay Company would be so regarded.

"3. But a Crown Colony with such a federation as would not alter the political balance of Upper and Lower Canada, and with a system of free trade with Canada, would appear to solve the whole difficulty; and if so, the scope of the federative principle would be matter to be settled between Canadian statesmen and the Colonial Office. The interchange between the North-west and Canada appears to be an absolute necessity in the interest of the latter. As Government, however, would require taxation, the new Colony must, in all probability, have its Custom- house; and it should be considered whether the Custom-house of Canada would not serve, as far as the eastern frontier is concerned, for the new Colony. If so, why should not duties, on a scale to be agreed upon under constitutional powers to agree, be levied on imported foreign goods, by Canada, and the duties be divided between the two powers in agreed proportions? Were this done, at least in the beginning, expense would be saved to the new Colony, a revenue would be easily collected for it, through existing machinery, and Canada would obtain the revenue and trade. Of course the scale of duties must be moderate, so as not to excite dissatisfaction, by establishing dear prices, and it would be the interest of Canada to make them so, for the more she stimulated the growth of the new customer, the better for the trade. On the other hand, the new Colony would be insured a market and an outlet for its own productions, and would be content, therefore, to accept a reasonably high scale of duties, levied for revenue purposes only, on its articles of foreign consumption."

I discussed the question involved at length with the Honorable George Brown and with his brother Gordon, at Toronto. I felt the importance of having the views, and, if possible, the concurrence of the leader of the "Grit" party. He led me to think that he concurred with me; and I sent him a copy of this document. He kept it some time, and then re- directed it to me without remark. Afterwards, I received a verbal message to the effect that "It would not do at all." I became convinced that nothing "would do at all" with a small band of men—who, at that time, had objects of their own—in Upper Canada. Some of them—few in number, I am happy to know, and impecunious—appeared to consider the old corporation of the Hudson's Bay in the light of Blucher, when driving through the streets of London, "Mein Gott! what a plunder." Some of them tried their best to confiscate the property; and once or twice, by weakness and vacillation in London, they almost gained the day.

Governor Dallas and I also carefully considered the telegraph question; the route, the cost, and the best agencies to complete its very early construction.

The two agreements, which, as matter of history, I here copy, were intended to bring about the complete connection of the Hudson's Bay territories direct with England and with the United States.

"Memorandum of Agreement between Mr. Edward W. Watkin and Mr. O. S. Wood (subject to the approval of the Montreal Telegraph Company and the United States Telegraph Companies, affected by this Agreement, and also by the Governor and Committee of the Hudson's Bay Company) for completing telegraphic communication between the Atlantic and Pacific.

"1. The Montreal Telegraph Company to construct a new line of telegraph between Father Point and Halifax, *via* Dalhousie and Mirimichi, to be completed on or before the 1st October, 1865; and also a line from the telegraph at Arnprior to the Hudson's Bay post at the Sault St. Marie, to be completed on or before the 1st October, 1865, with all necessary instruments, stations, staff, and appliances for a first- class through and local telegraph line.

"2. The Hudson's Bay Company (directly or through parties to be appointed by them, as they may elect) to construct a telegraph line from Fort Langley to Jasper House, thence to Fort Garry, and on to the United States boundary, near Pembina, to be completed on or before the 15th October, 1865; and also a telegraph from Fort Garry to the Hudson's Bay post at Fort William, at the head of Lake Superior; and also to make arrangements with other parties to erect a telegraph from Fort William to the Sault St. Marie, with all necessary instruments, stations, staff, and appliances for a first-class through and local telegraph line: provided always that the construction of the telegraph between Fort Garry and Sault St. Marie is dependent upon arrangements with the Canadian Government, and that it is understood that, failing or pending these arrangements, the route to be adopted shall be *via* Detroit, St. Paul, and Pembina to Fort Garry.

"3. The telegraph from Fort Langley to Halifax to be worked for all through business as one through system, and the through rates to be divided *pro rata* the mileage, except that for the lines west of the Sault St. Marie (to be erected by the Hudson's Bay Company as above) an additional mileage proportion of thirty-three per cent. over the actual distance shall be allowed, until those lines pay ten per cent per annum on the outlay, after paying all operating and other expenses, including repairs and renewals, and this allowance shall be a condition with the United States lines between Canada and the Hudson's Bay boundary.

"4. Arrangements to be made by the Montreal Telegraph Company, with parties in the United States, for the construction of a telegraph from St. Paul to the connecting point near Pembina.

"5. The Sault St. Marie and Sarnia to be respectively the boundaries of the Montreal Telegraph Company and of the Hudson's Bay Company and their representatives, for the purposes of this Agreement.

"6. This Agreement to be for twenty-five years.

"(Signed) EDWD. W. WATKIN.
"(Signed) O. S. WOOD.

"Montreal, *August* 10_th_, 1863."

"Agreement between Mr. Edward W. Watkin and Mr. O. S. Wood, for the construction of the telegraph between Fort Garry and Jasper House, and, if hereafter agreed, between Fort Langley and Jasper House, and Fort Garry and the United States boundary near Pembina (subject to the approval of the Governor and Committee of the Hudson's Bay Company in England).

"1. Mr. Wood to construct a telegraph, and all needful works and stations, from Fort Garry to Jasper House, at the cost of the Hudson's Bay Company, and to put the same in full operating order, and also instruct, and where necessary provide, the staff for the operation and repair of the line.

"2. Mr. Wood to proceed with Governor Dallas to St. Paul, with as little delay as possible, and on to Fort Garry, if necessary; and to make all arrangements required for transporting the telegraph wire, insulators, fittings, instruments, and other materials to Fort Garry; for distributing all materials from Fort Garry; for cutting, preparing, and distributing the poles; and generally for commencing and for completing the work (including a system of posts at proper distances apart) in an efficient manner, and at the earliest period.

"3. Mr. Wood to receive the cordial aid and cooperation of the staff of the Hudson's Bay Company in carrying out this work, under the orders, instructions, and control of Governor Dallas.

"4. Mr. Wood's travelling and other necessary expenses, and the salaries and other necessary expenses of his assistants, to be paid, and, in consideration of his services, he is to receive the sum of ten thousand (10,000) dollars, as a fixed payment; one-third to be paid on the storage of the materials as above at Fort Garry, one-third upon the completion of two hundred (200) miles of the telegraph, and one-third on the completion and operation of the whole line between Fort Garry and Jasper House; and further, should the whole be completed prior to the 15th October, 1864, Mr. Wood is to receive a bonus of two thousand (2,000) dollars, so soon as the line has been one month in operation; and should the whole cost of the work not exceed thirty thousand (30,000) pounds sterling, Mr. Wood to receive a further bonus of fifteen per cent. on all savings upon that sum, payable when the line has been in operation twelve (12) months.

"5. Should the telegraph lines between Fort Langley and Jasper House, and Fort Garry and the United States boundary near Pembina be ordered to be constructed, and the Hudson's Bay Company desire it, Mr. Wood to undertake the construction, on proportionate terms.

"(Signed) EDWD. W. WATKIN.
"(Signed) O. S. WOOD.

"Montreal, *August* 10_th_, 1863."

"MEMORANDUM *by Mr. Wood as to supply of Materials.*

"MONTREAL, "*August* 10_th_, 1863.

DEAR SIR,

"We shall want 40,000 insulators—they will cost from $6 to $8 per 100; 35,000 red cedar top pins will cost $3 per 100; 40 sets of telegraph instruments at $60 per set; main and local batteries, $500.

"As some of these articles ought immediately to be prepared, since their preparation takes a little time, I will at once, in accordance with our understanding of this morning, order a small quantity, and the remainder when I receive your confirmation of the whole arrangement. In the meantime I shall go to New York personally, to arrange the exact form and description of insulator, it being very desirable to have this article of the most perfect description.

"Yours faithfully,
"(Signed) O. S. WOOD.

"EDWD. W. WATKIN, Esq."

My official letter to Sir Edmund Head from Montreal, 24th July, 1863, summarized all my proceedings up to its date.

"MONTREAL,
"*July* 24_th_, 1863.

SIR,

"I have the honour to acknowledge your official letter of the 6th July, requesting me to proceed to the Red River Settlement, for the purpose of reporting upon the state and condition of that Settlement, of the condition of the adjoining territory, the prospects of settlement therein, and the possibility of commencing operations for an electric telegraph line across the southern district of Rupert's Land; and associating with me in this inquiry Governor Dallas, of the Red River Settlement, with whom you request me to communicate at once.

"I observe that the Committee consider the lateness of the season will preclude me from doing more than procure such information as will enable them to commence further inquiries at the opening of the next season.

"In consequence of verbal communications received before leaving England, and suggestions unofficially received from members of the new Committee, I have deemed it my duty, though unofficially, to communicate with the Canadian Government, and with those gentlemen likely to form the Government of Canada, should any change of ministry take place on the opening of Parliament, so as, as far as possible (unauthorized as I was), to prevent antagonism to the operations of the new organization pending official communication and explanations from the Governor and Committee.

"No one can be better aware of the state and views of parties in Canada than yourself. The leader of the present Government expresses a strong opinion in favour of the settlement of a separate Crown Colony in the Hudson's Bay district, and this also is the view taken by Mr. Cartier and Mr. J. A. Macdonald, and is strongly concurred in by Mr. Cazeau, the Vicar-General, who, as you are aware, leads the Catholic party in Lower Canada. On the other hand, the feeling of Mr. Geo. Brown and the 'Grits,' as heretofore expressed, has been in favour of annexing the Hudson's Bay territory to Canada, thereby securing that preponderance which would practically settle the question of the future government of the whole country.

"The views of the Duke of Newcastle, and also, so far as I understand them, the views of yourself and your colleagues, being in favour of the establishment of a separate colony unconnected with Canada, I consider the discussions which have taken place have now put the question in its right position here; but at the same time I shall endeavour to see Mr. George Brown, and give such explanations, unofficially, as may at all events prevent his considering that he has not been consulted in this important transaction.

"I have also placed myself in communication with many of those who have advocated the settlement of the North-west, including Professor Hind, who has explored much of the district; and, at my request, Professor Hind has written a memorandum, and letter upon the gold discoveries in the Hudson's Bay territory, which I now enclose.

"I have no doubt that Governor Dallas's own letters will more than corroborate what is stated in this memorandum, and I need not suggest that the most anxious and immediate attention of yourself and the Committee be directed to these discoveries, and to their political and other necessities and consequences.

"Having possessed myself of so much information in reference to the subjects referred to Governor Dallas and myself, I think we shall be able to fulfil the wishes of the Governor and Committee, Governor Dallas being here, accompanied by Mr. Hopkins, without the necessity of my proceeding on this occasion to the Red River; though, should further discussion with the Governor lead to our joint impression that such a visit would be advantageous, I shall not hesitate to undertake the journey.

"In advance of some memorandum to be prepared for you by Governor Dallas and myself, and which I shall beg him to be good enough to draft, I would mention that I have suggested that the Governor issue a circular to the employes of the Company, stating briefly the nature of the recent changes of proprietorship in the Company, and thereby having the tendency to remove any misconceptions which might arise, and which, I regret to learn, have in some few quarters appeared amongst the factors and other officers of the Company, who, as partners in the trade, have considered themselves entitled to be consulted by the late Governor and Council on the subject of the transfer.

"Governor Dallas informs me that the outfit of 1862-3 will show very much improved results; and I have little doubt that the wise and energetic measures which he has initiated since his tenure of office will bring abundant benefits in every direction. The result in the western district, which, if I recollect rightly, exhibited a loss, and which, in the past year, with all exclusive privileges taken away, gives a profit of no less than $166,000, is a convincing proof of what may be effected by improved business organization and thorough energy and firmness. It has, however, been matter of considerable anxiety to me to learn that it is Governor Dallas's desire to return to England next year.

"As regards the future management of the fur trade, Governor Dallas is of opinion that a considerable reduction may be made in the number of the employes; and that by a judicious weeding out of those who, in all large establishments managed from a distance, either were originally, or have become, inefficient, not only will expenses be saved, but a much larger trade be carried on.

"In any considerable change of personnel, the partnership rights of the factors will have to be considered; and one of the gravest and most difficult subjects of consideration will be, how to reconcile the rights of these gentlemen in a share of profit with that reorganization which the commercial interests of the Company evidently require.

"These changes can only be made after discussion with the factors and chief officers; and in some cases it may be desirable to buy out individual interests on a more or less extended scale.

"The 40 per cent. of the net profit of the Company allowed to the factors, in addition to the salaries of considerable amount, is a heavy drain, and involves other considerations opposed to rigid discipline, which need not be further touched upon here, but which are sufficiently obvious. This re-organization can only be effected by giving to the Governor very large and exceptional powers, and without delay. If these powers are given, I am quite confident that the results will be such as abundantly to satisfy the Committee. Hitherto, as it appears to me, far too little discretion has been permitted; and the practice of sending all the accounts home to England, and dealing with them in such a manner that the Governor could not tell from time to time how the financial results of expenses and profits were progressing, has produced its inevitable consequences. In future, I feel convinced, it will be found matter of the utmost consequence to concentrate the accounts at Fort Garry, and to send copies of the vouchers, journals, and ledgers from Fort Garry to England, instead of adopting the reverse practice, and endeavouring, as hitherto, to make the accounts travel as long a distance and be made up over as remote a time as possible. With proper telegraphic and postal communication between the principal posts of the Company and Fort Garry and Montreal, there is no reason why the accounts should ever be two years in arrear in future.

"As regards the settlement of the country, and, involved in that important question, the state and prospects of the Red River, the discoveries of gold above alluded to involve very serious considerations.

"Assuming a rush of miners to different portions of the territory, the machinery of Government for the preservation of order cannot be for a moment neglected, or its construction be delayed. This involves, again, the question of the establishment of a new colony. Is that colony to be governed by the Hudson's Bay Company, who are essentially a trading and landowning corporation, or is it to be governed in the name of her Majesty, the Hudson's Bay Company, so far as the limits of the Crown Colony are concerned, becoming merely traders and landowners, and ceasing to govern as at present?

"All the difficulties at Red River—which, after all, have been much exaggerated, and can be very easily dealt with—would be disposed of at once were a Governor, appointed by the Crown, to be sent out; and it does not follow that representative institutions need at first be granted, though ultimately they would become matter of necessity. The great object of the Governor and Committee—and Governor Dallas and myself perfectly agree in the view—should be to induce the Colonial Government to found a Crown Colony under arrangement with the Hudson's Bay Company with the least possible delay.

"Such a Government would not only relieve the Hudson's Bay Company of an immense responsibility, but it would render titles to land sold by them, and claims to interest in the minerals, far more certain, marketable, and profitable than at present.

"The commercial re-organization of the Company is a matter perfectly easy in the hands of Governor Dallas, empowered to act in accordance with his own best judgment; but this question of the government of the country is, after all, the grand difficulty, and, if successfully negotiated, the grand hope of success as regards the future settlement of this vast district.

"As to the suitability of an immense portion of the district west of Fort Garry for eligible settlement, Governor Dallas—who has now made journeys of 1,800 miles in the last year—has no doubt whatever; and I trust that the old traditional phantoms of inhospitable deserts will be finally dismissed from the minds of the new Governor and Committee, especially when they have before them the many letters and reports in evidence of the true state of affairs, which must be in possession of the Company in Fenchurch Street.

"As regards telegraphic communication, I have made every inquiry necessary upon the subject, and Governor Dallas agrees with my views of the importance of connecting the Hudson's Bay posts by telegraphic communication.

"Subject to further discussion, I may indicate my opinion that the route suggested by Governor Dallas through the Hudson's Bay territory, viz., from Jasper House by Edmonton, Carlton, and Fort Pitt to Fort Garry, would be the proper route for a telegraph.

"This portion, as it seems to me, should be constructed at once, and by the Hudson's Bay Company.

"Were it to be constructed in Canada, it would not cost more than 15,000_l_. sterling. It may cost less, though in some cases it may cost more, through your territory; though I am inclined to think that it may be constructed for 20,000_l_. as an outside sum, and that it is impossible that the cost of this portion of the work should exceed 30,000_l_. in any event.

"This outlay being sanctioned, the connection with the American telegraph through Minnesota would be a matter of negociation; and the extension of telegraphic communication to Fort William on the one side, and to Fort Langley on the other, would depend upon the subsidies to be obtained from Canada, and from British Columbia and Vancouver Island.

"I have the assurance of the present leader of the Canadian Government, that the offer to give a subsidy, made last year, will be officially renewed, and I shall endeavour to get this promise put into writing, and send it to you home.

"British Columbia, I assume, would do what the Colonial Office requested, but, in any case, we ought not to commit ourselves to a through communication through Canada and British Columbia without a clear understanding as to the subsidies. At the same time, if you, the Hudson's Bay Company, have command of one thousand miles of telegraph, enabling you to transmit information through your own channels with a new expedition, you will practically have command of the future discussion of this large question.

"I have obtained estimates, and made calculations of the cost of these telegraphic operations, and I have selected a very eligible gentleman, Mr. Wood, the Manager of the Montreal Telegraph Company, who, I am quite sure, will carry out the operation, with the assistance of the employes of the Hudson's Bay Company, and under the orders of Governor Dallas, with perfect success.

I should recommend that immediate steps be taken; and there is no reason, in my opinion, why all the materials should not be on the ground by the end of the coming winter, since much of it can be taken by canoe, and the remainder may be taken across the snow in the winter; and why may not the whole telegraph from Jasper House to Fort Carry be completed by September in next year?

"The present attitude of the Sioux Indians in the State of Minnesota deserves serious attention. Little Crow has waited upon Governor Dallas, and the Governor has written to General Sibley.

"I have suggested whether a visit to Washington would not be desirable, and that the opportunity of assisting the American Government to make peace with these troublesome Indians should be improved, by attempting to get a settlement of your Oregon claims.

"I have the honour to be, Sir,

"Your most obedient Servant,

"(Signed) EDWARD W. WATKIN.

"Sir EDMUND WALKER HEAD, Bart., &c. &c.,

"Governor, Hudson's Bay Company."

Finding, however, that the Governor and his Committee were not prepared to act with the energy and preciseness I had desired, I closed my, unpaid, mission by the following letter of 26th August, 1863, from my house, Norfolk Street, Park Lane.

"NORFOLK STREET, PARK LANE, "*August* 26, 1863.

MY DEAR SIR,

"I have to thank you for sending me copies of the official letter from the Secretary of the 13th instant, in reply to my report and private letter of the 24th July, and of your private notes of the 13th and 18th instant, the latter noticing my letter of the 4th instant.

"I desire at once to say that the heads of arrangement which I have written down with the Montreal Telegraph Company and with Mr. Wood, for your consideration, were of course entirely subject to the sanction of the Governor and Committee of the Hudson's Bay Company. And, in accordance with what I understood to be your views, when to-day you were good enough to leave the Deputy-Governor in order to see me in the board room by appointment, I shall consider it my duty to cancel all that has passed, in such a manner as, I trust, will be perfectly satisfactory to your colleagues. There will then remain nothing beyond a responsibility for a few essential materials, as to which time was an object, amounting to not more than a few hundred pounds at the utmost, which I shall take entirely upon myself, under the circumstances of doubt and difficulty as to the opinions of the shareholders of the Hudson's Bay Company which you represented to me. And with a desire to avoid similar complaints, I do not propose to make any charge whatever for my own expenses, or, if I may be excused the word, services, in connection with the mission I have had to undertake. That mission, however, cannot go without explanation, for I am anxious to avoid all misconception now, or hereafter, and I desire, therefore, by a frank statement, at once to court contradiction, should it be merited.

"Having had much to do with the discussions which led to the transfer of the Hudson's Bay Company's property, I had expressed my willingness, inconvenient as it must be to me, to act as a member of a proposed commission of three, including Captain Glyn, R.N., and Captain Synge, R.E., whose duty would be to investigate the position of the undertaking at its head establishment,—to report upon the re-organization of its business, the development of its mineral resources, the settlement of portions of its territory as a new colony, and the opening up of the country by the telegraph and by means of transit. Captain Glyn and Captain Synge had both been consulted, and the Duke of Newcastle had been applied to to obtain leave for Captain Synge at the War Office. I had been led to believe that my services were considered of some value, and I left England on the 20th June, expecting that Captain Glyn and Captain Synge would follow me in a week, and that we should at once proceed to Red River, and send home a first, but full, report by the beginning of October. I understood also that such a report was desired, to clear away any objections to the operations of the re-organized Company which might be factiously raised. And when, after my arrival in Canada, I received the prospectus with your name as Governor of the Company at its head, I found a condition of that document to be that I was to examine and report and advise generally, in concert with other gentlemen, specially qualified for the duty, not only upon the question of telegraphic and postal communication, but also as to the other objects proposed in the scheme officially laid before the public.

"Before leaving England, I repeatedly pressed the necessity of communicating with the Governor and 'wintering partners' of the Company in America, so that they should not hear of the transfer of the property for the first time from the newspapers; and I expected to be specially authorized to give the needful information and assurances. I was no party, I beg to say, to this mention of my name in the prospectus; but my friends and business connections who may have taken shares on the faith of my name, will naturally hold me responsible accordingly. Still, anxious to witness the success of a project which, energetically managed, is so intrinsically sound, I refrained from writing to you to decline the responsibility, hoping that the original plan of delegation, though delayed, would be carried out. That plan, I must observe, involved not a mere commission of engineers to explore the route for a telegraph to Jasper House, as assumed in the Secretary's letter of the 13th inst., but far wider objects, the realization of which would, I venture to think, have given satisfaction at home, and have dissipated many misconceptions, now existing, inimical to the interests of the new proprietary.

"Your letter to me of the 6th July did not reach me till the 20th, and in the meantime the newspaper notices in England led to many official and unofficial inquiries from me, involving difficulty of answer. I found, in fact, that the staff of the Hudson's Bay Company was quite at fault, and that public men in Canada misunderstood the objects of the new organization, for want of information very simple in its nature, but which—except so far as the prospectus authorized me—I had no right to supply.

"Several of the Hudson's Bay Company's chief factors and traders had, it appeared, addressed a memorial to the then Governor and Committee, some months ago, upon the rumoured sale of the property, and had been, as stated to me, informed that no transfer was likely to take place, or would in fact be undertaken without previous consultation; and yet these gentlemen learnt for the first time from the public papers that new arrangements had been made. It was not unnatural, therefore, considering the relations of these gentlemen with the Company, that they should feel much annoyed; nor was it, perhaps, surprising that an influential member of the body should have predicted a general resignation of the factors 'from Labrador to Sitka,' followed by a confederation amongst them, in order to carry on the fur trade in competition with the Hudson's Bay Company, they possessing, as was said, 'the skill, the will, and the capital to do it.'

"The appearance of Mr. Lampson's name as Deputy-Governor, in the absence of any prior explanation, aggravated the first feeling of distrust; for it was said that he and his connections had been, and then were, the Company's great, and often successful, rivals in the fur trade, carrying on a vigorous competition at all accessible points.

"The arrival of Governor Dallas at Montreal some days before my receipt of your letter of the 6th July, enabled these misconceptions to be dealt with; and the issue of a circular by the Governor, together with many personal explanations, and some firmness on the part of Mr. Dallas, will, I trust, very soon remove the want of confidence and dissatisfaction on the part of the staff, which at first looked threatening. These explanations, of course, took time, and rendered the Governor's presence in Canada necessary.

"Governor Dallas and myself made various opportunities of meeting members of the present and of the late Government of Canada, and of talking over the subject of the North-west, and of its organization and government; and I feel convinced that these unofficial discussions were of considerable use, and may help to prevent antagonism and territorial claims on the part of Canada, which, in my opinion, might be very embarrassing, and ought to be foreseen and avoided. Possibly the following article in the Government organ, written by order, and handed to me by the Honorable W. P. Howland, will best exhibit, without further troubling you, the friendly spirit of the Canadian Government before I left for England:—

"(From the *Quebec Mercury*.)

"'The recent announcements concerning the transfer of the title and territory of the Hudson's Bay Company to a new corporation have naturally awakened considerable interest in Canada. So far, however, no specific intimation of the opinions of the new Company has been given. It is understood that they will not confine themselves to a mere following in the footsteps of their predecessors, but that colonization, telegraphy, the opening up of common roads, and eventually of railroad communication, enter into the scheme which, whether as regards the interests at stake or the capital involved, may be said to be colossal in its character. It is no doubt anticipated by the new Company that the Canadian Government and people will cheerfully aid them in an enterprise which evidently concerns us so closely. Speaking in general terms, we presume that it may be conceded that such anticipations have been correctly formed. The development of Canadian territory, or of British territory immediately adjacent to it, could never be a matter of indifference to the Government or people. Though young in years, still Canada cannot forego those aspirations regarding the future which are naturally suggested by the magnificent domain which, stretches along the northern portion of the Continent. It is for Canadians to occupy and eventually to govern it, and any means which point to the furtherance of an object which may be called spontaneous in the Canadian mind must engender solicitude and evoke encouragement.

"'When Messrs. Howland and Sicotte were in England, they expressed their opinion that Canada would be willing to aid the "Atlantic and Pacific Transit Company" in their enterprise of opening up communication across the Continent through British territory. Upon their return to this country, the matter was fully discussed, and it was understood, subsequently, that the Government of that day was prepared to recommend an appropriation of $50,000 per annum, provided that the Company gave the necessary assurances of their ability to commence and carry out the work. Since that time, however, those who formed that Association appear to have enlarged the field of their operations, and have included the whole of the Hudson's Bay Company, with their territory, *prestige*, and appliances, within the scope of their operations. But the same general policy which suggested the recommendation of the $50,000 referred to, would also prompt similar assistance to the New Hudson's Bay Company. It can be of little moment to Canada by whose agency the western territory is developed—that which is wanted is development.

"'Judging, then, by what has gone before, and from the exigencies which the spirit of progress imposes upon all Governments, it is not improbable when the new Company has itself determined what they will do, in what shape their enterprise will be promoted, that reasonable assistance will be given them. At present, it seems hardly likely that any exact conclusion has been made by themselves in this matter. Mr. Watkin, in whom a wide and just confidence is placed, not only by the shareholders in the new enterprise, but by the British Government itself, is here, engaged, no doubt, in collecting from the various sources within his reach such information as will enable him to report fully upon the matter. That done, the Company will be able to make propositions and to solicit the kindly aid of Canada. Looking at the wide field for enterprise that will be opened up; at the speedy colonization that is likely to take place, consequent upon the recent discoveries of gold; at the prospect that Canada may be made the high road for commerce between the great East and West; that the trade of the St. Lawrence, and all the various and manifold interests connected with it, will be inspired with new and energetic vitality,—from these and many other considerations it must be evident that the policy for Canada, let her political position as to parties be what it may, is to extend a friendly and greeting hand to those who come with capital and confidence to become the pioneers of a new order of things, which cannot fail to pour riches into the lap of Canada, and to lay the foundation of a prosperity which can be at present but dimly imagined.'

"The importance of assisting the work of opening up the North-west for telegraphic and postal purposes would, I believe, be alluded to in the Governor-General's speech on the 15th. [Footnote: This was done, and the following is an extract from the speech of the Governor-General of Canada, on opening Parliament:—

"I have received a despatch from the Secretary of State for the Colonies, enclosing copies of a correspondence between Her Majesty's Government and the agent of the 'Atlantic and Pacific Transit and Telegraph Company,' in reference to a proposal made by that Company for the establishment of a telegraphic and postal communication between Lake Superior and New Westminster, in British Columbia. The importance of such an undertaking to the British North American Provinces, both in a commercial and in a military point of view, induces me to commend the subject to your consideration. Copies of the correspondence shall be laid before you, and I feel assured that should any proposal calculated to effect the establishment of such communication on terms advantageous to the province be submitted to you, it will receive encouragement at your hands."] But whatever may be the extent or the value—as to which latter point I fear my opinion does not, as I regretted to find, quite coincide with yours—of the sympathy and support of Canada, any new bias in favour of your projects, as promised in your prospectus, has been mainly aided by the belief which, entertaining it, I inculcated, that without loss of time, and with the promptness and energy of English merchants, the new Government of the Hudson's Bay Company would establish, with the aid of the provinces east and west of the Hudson's Bay territory, but without shirking its own share of duty, telegraphic and postal communication in British interests, available for commercial, and requisite for other and even more serious, purposes. That the works would be begun at once, and that the Hudson's Bay Company, so long obstructive, would now set an example of despatch, and that that which had long been hoped for and promised by others, would now be accomplished by them as the pioneer works of an early settlement of the cultivable portions of the country.

"It is obvious that, unless materials are supplied and plans arranged before the end of September, the overland operations must wait a year's time. Therefore, apparently under a misapprehension of your wishes or policy, as our interview of yesterday showed, I looked out for the best practical man I could find fit to undertake the construction of a telegraph and system of posts, enabling postal and telegraphic service to be worked together. I found that man in Mr. O. S. Wood, an American settled in Canada, the engineer and manager of the 4,000 miles of telegraph owned by the Montreal Telegraph Company, which pays 23 per cent, upon its capital of 100,000_l._; and believing him to be exactly the man for the occasion, I agreed with him, subject to your sanction, to superintend and be responsible for the erection and operation of a telegraph and system of posts between Fort Garry and Jasper House. I do not trouble you with the document, as it is to be cancelled, so far as your Company is concerned; but I may shortly state that it proposed the completion of the works by October, 1864, and in addition to a liberal, but not excessive, payment for Mr. O. S. Wood's work, responsibility, and experience, it awarded a percentage upon all savings on the total sum of L30,000_l._, the outside estimate taken for the whole job, and a small premium for all time saved in the completion of the work. These payments were to be so made that the integrity, completeness, and success of the work would be their main condition.

"I also made a very important conditional agreement with this Montreal Telegraph Company, under which they were to extend a new and independent, or precautionary, line of telegraph from Halifax (Nova Scotia) to Mirimichi and on to Father Point, connecting with the other existing telegraphs up to Arnprior (Ottawa), and another telegraph from Arnprior to the Sault St. Marie, where you have a trading port. On the other hand, subject to the aid of Canada and British Columbia, your Company were to extend, or obtain the extension of, a telegraph from the Sault by Lake Superior to Fort Garry, and another by Jasper House to Fort Langley. All these telegraphs were to be completed by October, 1865. The Montreal Company were also to obtain the extension of the Minnesota telegraph to your boundary near Pembina, you extending your telegraph to that point. Thus, assuming the Fort Carry and Jasper House telegraph to be completed by October, 1864, and knowing that this, and the telegraph from Fort Langley to Jasper House, could be finished as easily, a complete and independent Atlantic and Pacific telegraph, stretching for more than 1,000 miles through your territory, might have been secured,—always assuming that this season of 1863 were saved, which was the great practical object before me. I obtained, as a condition, that in dividing the rates paid for messages, your telegraphs should have a bonus of 33 per cent. so long as your capital did not pay a clear 10 per cent. dividend.

"To this end, I advised you to confirm the order of 175 tons of charcoal wire and of the insulators, post pins, batteries, and instruments needed for the length between Fort Garry and Jasper House (the wire from England, and the other material from Canada and the United States), at a total cost, already given you in complete detail, estimated, when delivered at Fort Garry, as not to exceed 10,000_l._. This statement of cost, and a reference to my past statements, will answer the question in Mr. Fraser's letter of the 13th, as to whether I had calculated the heavy expense of carriage— 20_l._ per ton to Fort Garry. The question shows that it had not been calculated in Fenchurch Street that the poles and timber would be got in the country, and that the whole weight of material to be sent to Fort Garry was about 200 tons at the most.

"I may pause, however, in answer to another similar question, about the relative prices of American and English wire, &c., to say, that the best market for wire is England; and the best market for the less important articles is the United States, while the proper prices chargeable for the best article by the best houses are known to all practical men. I may add, as I am asked what is the weight per mile of telegraphic wire, that 'best charcoal No. 9 electric wire' is 320 lbs. to the mile of 1,760 yards.

"On leaving this subject, I may add, that if on further consideration you determine to store the material above named (cost and carriage 10,000_l._) at Fort Garry, there is yet time to get it out to St. Paul, and some, if not all, may go through to Fort Gany. There is a post three days per week to Fort Garry, and posts go through all parts of your own territory regularly, the 'Winter Express' leaving Fort Garry on Christmas Day. Though, in my humble opinion, not the best thing, still the transmission and storage of that material would be looked upon as an evidence of your intentions, and would help to keep you right in Canada and in your own territory, as also in British Columbia, and would expedite a final and favourable decision as to the proposed subsidy. So strong is my opinion, that I am ready to join any four or five gentlemen of your Committee feeling an interest in the work, in providing and paying for the material itself, if you will send it through at once.

"It will, I assume, be apparent to you how necessary it is to keep the section of telegraph in your own special district in your own hands. Your organization, also, will enable you to convey and erect material very cheaply. As to all details, I refer to the papers already sent over containing full particulars, and showing quantities, kind, cost, means of conveyance, and, more important than all, character of country and proposed route; the latter from the personal experience and knowledge of the country of Governor Dallas and Mr. Hopkins, whose reliability and capacity as advisers no one will question.

"While in Upper Canada, I received proposals for the establishment of steamers on your rivers and lakes: and no doubt these could be arranged for; but as the telegraph is to stand over for the present, I do not add to the length of this paper by any statement on this head.

"I would call attention, however, to the exploration of Dr. Hector, on behalf of the Canadian Government, of the lands adjoining Lakes Huron and Superior. Dr. Hector has surveyed a line of road all the way up to Dog Lake; and Mr. McDougal, the present Commissioner of Crown Lands, appears ready to recommend the gradual, but rapid, construction of roads throughout this territory, and onwards to that of the Hudson's Bay Company. Possibly you may consider the suggestion which I made in reference to obtaining an independent outlet to Lake Superior, in the direction of Superior City, as well worthy of consideration.

"As respects the alleged discoveries of gold, upon which some doubt is thrown in Mr. Fraser's letter of the 13th, I have merely to add that the testimony of Governor Dallas is important, and that the report of Professor Hind appeared to me to contain valuable evidence and reasoning, which can be tested by the further explorations of a geographical commission, for which purpose either Professor Hind, or Sir William Logan, or Mr. Sterry Hunt, or all these well known Canadians, are at once available. Professor Hind's suggestion as to the supply of quicksilver by the Company to miners, may or may not be valuable to a Company desiring to retain the lead of trade in portions of its own territory; but a reference to his report will show that it was not proposed to you as an immediate measure, as surmised. In any case, it is undoubted that gold exists in districts east of the primary rocks of the east flanks of the Rocky Mountains, and that persons are seeking for it in greater or less numbers. We have yet to learn how far the information has spread, and what influence it may have upon the movement of the American population. But, great or small, it is a fact affecting the settlement of the community, which enlarges the general pressure for a decision as to how large tracts of your territory, suitable beyond doubt for human habitation, are hereafter to be governed for the good of the people who may come, and so as to preserve British ascendency in your part of the Continent. Both Governor Dallas and myself have had many discussions as to this, and you have before you already both his views and mine. But the paper gives a *resume* of the general case as presenting itself to many thoughtful persons, known to you in Canada, and belonging to the various political parties. It was desirable to record their ideas, and I present them for what they may be worth, wishing you to understand that the proposal for federation and a joint Custom-house is the view of Mr. George Brown. On the other hand, Mr. Cartier, and even Mr. Sandfield Macdonald, desire to see a separate Crown Colony established.

"I now come to the all-important matter of the wise, economical, and efficient working of the business of the Company in America. The paper drawn up under the instructions of Governor Dallas by Mr. Hopkins, and discussed at length between us, is offered to you as an attempt to solve a difficulty which must be got rid of if more business is to be done at less cost, and if the competition around you is to be met, as it easily may be, with thorough success. The deed poll is an arrangement standing in the way of change and extension of your operations: it covers legal questions which some day may give you trouble; and it may be modified in some such manner as that suggested by your assent in the first place, and by the judicious action of Governor Dallas, who should receive your instructions soon, consequent thereon.

"The proposal to substitute a contingent and temporary interest in so much stock of the Company for the 40 per cent. of profits now given to the chief factors and traders, may assist you in placing your unissued shares, in a mode leading to a very large annual saving, to be accompanied by an evident increase of efficiency. For, able as your staff is in general, there are many useless, and even mischievous, persons under pay or profits; and the unfortunate propensities of Sir George Simpson did not lead in his latter years, I fear, to the improvement of the moral tone of your servants. There are cases of favouritism and abuse not at all creditable, such as that of the employment of Sir George's illegitimate son, and the retention of a chief trader notoriously useless and drunken, for many years after the chief factor of his district had reported his demerits to the local governor. But the service is popular, and there can be no difficulty in keeping up a staff fully able to cope with the sharp and energetic men employed by the American traders,—your permanent rivals in business.

"It is perhaps unnecessary further to explain the reasons of my not proceeding to Red River. As before stated, I had expected to do so in company with Captains Glyn and Synge, without whom I should have hesitated to undertake the more extended and responsible task at first proposed. I did not in any event expect that Governor Dallas would come to Canada prior to the receipt of your official letter of the 6th July, and for which I had been waiting from the 30th June until the 20th July; and when he arrived, and especially when I found that the purposes of my proposed journey had been in great measure previously fulfilled by him, it became a question of whether it ought not to be postponed. He had already folly advised the Governor and Committee of the 'state of the Red River Settlement,' of its 'suitability for settlement,' and of the general and highly favourable features of the tracts, over which he had travelled for 1,800 miles in various directions. The best route for a telegraph could be, and was, suggested, to you from his own observations, corroborated and added to by the personal experience of Mr. Hopkins and others, who had often traversed the districts, and had resided for years therein. The entire feasibility of constructing a telegraph across the Continent was not only confirmed by these experiences, but by the practical views of persons consulted, who had set up lines through even more difficult and wilder tracts of country.

"Therefore the objects you appeared to have before you were realized, if not directly through me, yet through the colleague you had selected for me, your own local governor, of whom I cannot express too high an opinion, having been his almost constant companion for above a month, during which every detail, so far as we could grasp it, was thoroughly discussed.

"Having given my best attention and labours to the whole subject for some years, and believing that I might be of more service to you here, since Governor Dallas could not be spared to come home, and could not prudently have left Canada until he had put all your business there in order, I exercised no unwise discretion in returning to England.

"I have now to ask your forgiveness for the length of this paper, and to express my readiness to give any further explanations in my power, while wishing you and your colleagues quite to understand that I have no desire whatever—but far the contrary—to obtrude myself upon you in the control of an enterprise which I honestly believe can be made completely successful by the exercise of even ordinary energy and skill, and which ought to be safe and certain in such experienced and able hands as yours.

> "I have the honour to be, dear Sir,
> "Yours faithfully,
> "EDWD. W. WATKIN.

"Sir E. W. HEAD, Bart.,

"*Governor of the Hudson's Bay Company.*"

One other object I desired to accomplish, was an exchange of boundary between the Hudson's Bay and the United States, with the view to Superior City being brought into British territory by a fair payment and exchange of land. The negociation looked very hopeful at one time, but it was not followed up in London, and it fell to the ground. There are few people who understand that it is not only desirable to do the right thing, but to do it at the right time—that is, when circumstances favour the doing.

I am entitled to say that, owing to the non-acceptance, at the time, of our proposals, much delay in realizing the great object of settling the government and colonizing the territory arose: inadequate terms for the sale and purchase of the vast landed estate of the Company had to be accepted from Canada; and the "wintering partners," not made real partners, as recommended by Governor Dallas and myself, but held at arm's length, had, at last, to be compensated for giving up the old "deed poll" with a sum of 107,055_l._, paid in 1871—ten years after the date of our report to Sir Edmund Head.

But, "all's well that ends well," and the great work is, at last, accomplished.

Chapter XII
The Hudson's Bay Company and the Select Committee of 1748-9

The history of the old co-partnery, the "Governor and Company of Adventurers of England trading into Hudson's Bay," ought to be written by some able hand. Samuel Smiles or Goldwin Smith, with the aid of the archives held by the Governor and Committee, would make a book which would go round the world. To publish such a record is a duty incumbent upon Mr. Eden Colville and his colleagues. From no merit or prevision of theirs, a happy and profitable transformation has been made of their undertaking. The individuals, as well as Canada as a State, and the Empire, also, have gained largely. The monopoly has been broken up, under liberal and generous treatment of the monopolists—monopolists who had deserved their monopoly by their able administration; and those who ran the risk, paid the cost, and incurred the anxiety, neither complain nor ask for the credit of their work. The merchant adventurer trading to the Eastern Indies, and the merchant adventurer trading into Hudson's Bay, each on his side of the world, has preserved vast territories to the Crown and people of England. Their conquests have cost the taxpayers of England nothing; while the trade and enterprise they promoted have enriched millions, and have opened careers, often brilliant, for men of courage and self denial, many of whose names will go down to posterity in fame and honour.

The Hudson's Bay Company was constituted under a charter of Charles the Second. That charter began thus: "Charles the Second, by the grace of God King of England, Scotland, France, and Ireland, Defender of the Faith, to all to whom these presents shall come greeting:

"Whereas our dear intirely beloved cousin, Prince Rupert, Count Palatine of the Rhine, Duke of Bavaria and Cumberland; George Duke of Albemarle, William Earl of Craven, Henry Lord Arlington, Anthony Lord Ashley, Sir John Robinson, and Sir Robert Vyner, Knights and Baronets; Sir Peter Colleton, Baronet, Sir Edward Hungerford, Knight of the Bath, Sir Paul Neele, Sir John Griffith, Sir Philip Carteret, and Sir James Hayes, Knights; John Kirke, Francis Millington, William Prettyman, John Fenn,

Esquires, and John Portman, citizen and goldsmith of London, have at their own great costs and charges undertaken an expedition for Hudson's Bay, in the Northwest parts of America, for the discovery of a new passage into the South Sea, and for the finding of some trade for furs, minerals, and other considerable commodities; and by such their undertaking have already made such discoveries as do encourage them to proceed farther in pursuance of their said design, by means whereof there may probably arise great advantage to us and our kingdom:

"And whereas the said undertakers, for their further encouragement in the said design, have humbly besought us to incorporate them, and grant unto them, and their successors, the whole trade and commerce of all those seas, streights, and bays, rivers, lakes, creeks, and sounds, in whatsoever latitude they shall be, that lie within the entrance of the streights commonly called Hudson's Streights; together with all the lands, countries, and territories upon the coasts and confines of the seas, streights, bays, lakes, rivers, creeks, and sounds aforesaid, which are not now actually possessed by any of our subjects, or by the subjects of any other Christian Prince or State."

And the adventurers were made "one body corporate and politic, in deed and in name," by the name of "The Governor and Company of Adventurers of England trading into Hudson's Bay."

They were granted "the sole trade and commerce" of "all those seas," &c., &c., "in whatever latitude they shall be;" "together with all the lands and territories upon the countries, coasts, and confines of the seas, bays, lakes, rivers, creeks and sounds aforesaid;" "with the fishing of all sorts of fish, whales, sturgeons, and all other royal fishes;" "together with the royalty of the sea upon the coasts within the limits aforesaid, and all mines royal, as well discovered as not discovered, of gold, silver, gems, and precious stones, to be found and discovered within the territories, limits, and places aforesaid; and that the land be from henceforth reckoned and reputed as one of our plantations or Colonies in America, called Rupert's Land."

All this was to be "holden" "of us, our heirs and successors, as of our manor of East Greenwich, in the County of Kent, in free and common soccage, and not in capite or by knight's service; yielding and paying yearly to us, our heirs and successors, for the same, two elks and two black beavers, whensoever and as often as we, our heirs and successors, shall happen to enter into the said countries, territories, and regions hereby granted."

The adventurers were further granted "not only the whole, intire, and only liberty of trade and traffick, and the whole, intire, and only liberty, use and privilege of trading and traffick to and from the territories, limits, and places aforesaid, but also the whole and intire trade and traffick to and from all havens, bays, creeks, rivers, lakes, and seas into which they shall find entrance, or passage by water, or land, out of the territories, &c. aforesaid; and to and with all the natives and people, inhabitants, or which shall inhabit within the territories, &c."

The charter proceeds to grant the fullest powers for the government of the countries by the adventurers; every power, in fact, provided the laws in force in England were administered. And then it authorizes "free liberty and license, in case they conceive it necessary, to send either ships of war, men, or ammunition, into any of their plantations, forts, factories, or places of trade," "for the security and defence of the same." "And to choose commanders and officers over them, and to give them power and authority, by commissions under their common seal, or otherwise, to continue, or make peace or war with any prince or people whatsoever, that are not Christians, in any places where the said Company have plantations, forts, or factories, or adjacent thereunto, as shall be most for the advantage and benefit of said Governor and Company, and of their trade;" "and also to right and recompense themselves upon the goods, estate, or people of those parts."

Thus, the adventurers had exclusive rights of trade, exclusive possession of territories, exclusive powers of government, and the right to make war, or conclude peace.

By an Order of Council of 4th February, 1748, a petition from one Arthur Dobbs, Esq., and from members of a committee appointed by the "subscribers for finding out a passage to the Western and Southern Ocean of America," was referred to the consideration of "A. Ryder" and "W. Murray," who heard counsel for and against the Hudson's Bay Company, and finally decided that, "Considering how long the Company have enjoyed and acted under this charter without interruption or encroachment, we cannot think it advisable for his Majesty to make any express or implied declaration against the validity of it till there has been some judgment of a court of justice to warrant it."

On the 24th April, 1749, a Select Committee of Parliament reported, through Lord Strange, upon "the state and condition of the countries adjoining to Hudson's Bay, and the trade carried on there." The report begins by stating —

"The Committee appointed to inquire into the state and condition of the countries adjoining to Hudson's Bay, and the trade carried on there; and to consider how those countries may be settled and improved, and the trade and fisheries there extended and increased; and also to inquire into the right the Company of Adventurers trading to Hudson's Bay pretend to have, by charter, to the property of lands, and exclusive trade to those countries;— have, pursuant to the order of the House, examined into the several matters to them referred, and find the particular state thereof to be as follows:—

"Your Committee thought proper, in the first place, to inquire into the nature and extent of the charter granted by King Charles the Second to the Company of Adventurers trading to Hudson's Bay; under which charter the present Company claim a right to lands, and an exclusive trade to those countries; which charter being laid before your Committee, they thought it necessary, for the information of the House, to annex a copy thereof to this Report, in the Appendix No. 1. Your Committee then proceeded to examine the following witnesses:—

"The witnesses were Joseph Robson, who had been employed in Hudson's Bay for six years as a stonemason; Richard White, who had been a clerk at Albany Fort and elsewhere; Matthew Sergeant, who had been employed in the Company's service, and 'understood the Indian language'; John Hayter, who 'had been house-carpenter to the Company for six years, at Moose River'; Mathew Gwynne, who 'had been twice at Hudson's Bay'; Edward Thompson, who had been three years at Moose River, as surgeon; Enoch Alsop, who had been armourer to the Company at Moose River; Christopher Bannister, who had been armourer and gunsmith, and had resided in the Bay for 22 years; Robert Griffin, silversmith, who had been five years in the Company's service; Thomas Barnett, smith, who went over to Albany in 1741; Alexander Brown, who had been six years at Hudson's Bay as surgeon; Captain Thomas Mitchell, who had commanded a sloop of the Company's; Arthur Dobbs, 'Esquire,' 'examined as to the information he had received from "a French Canadese Indian" (since deceased), and who was maintained at the expense of the Admiralty, on a prospect of his being of service on the discovery of a North-west Passage,' 'and who informed your Committee that the whole of that discourse is contained in part of a book printed for the witness in 1744, to which he desired leave to refer'; Captain William Moore, who 'had been employed in Hudson's Bay from a boy'; Mr. Henry Spurling, merchant, who 'had traded chiefly in furs for 28 years past, during which time he had dealt with the Hudson's Bay Company'; Captain Carruthers, who had been in the Hudson's Bay service 35 years ago; Arthur Slater, who had been employed by the Company on the East Main."

It will be seen that one object aimed at in granting a charter to the Hudson's Bay Company was to further the discovery of the "North-west Passage." Beginning in 1719, and ending, probably in despair, in 1737, the Hudson's Bay Company fitted and sent out in the whole six separate expeditions, which the Committee record in their Appendix, as follows (The instructions to the commanders usually ended, "So God send the good ship a successful discovery, and to return in safety. Amen"):—

A List of Vessels fitted out by the Hudson's Bay Company for Discovery of a North-West Passage.

1719. *Albany*, frigate, Captain George Berley, sailed from England on or about 5th June. *Never returned.*

1719. *Prosperous*, Captain Henry Kelsey, sailed from York Fort, June 19th. Returned 10th August following.

Success, John Hancock, master, sailed from Prince of Wales' Fort, July 2nd. Returned 10th August.

1721. *Prosperous*, Captain Henry Kelsey, sailed from York Fort, June 6th. Returned 2nd September.

Success, James Napper, master, sailed from York Fort, June 26th. Lost 30th of same month.

1721. *Whalebone*, John Scroggs, master, sailed from Gravesend 31st May, wintered at Prince of Wales' Fort.

1723. Sailed from thence 21st June. Returned July 25th following.

1737. The *Churchill*, James Napper, master, sailed from Prince of Wales' Fort, July 7th. Died 8th August, and the vessel returned the 18th.

The *Mus-quash*, Robert Crow, master, sailed from Prince of Wales' Fort, July 7th. Returned 22nd August.

It must be observed that, in 1745, Parliament had offered a reward of 20,000_l_. for the discovery of the North-west Passage. The Act was entitled "An Act for giving a publick reward to such person, or persons, His Majesty's subjects, as shall discover a North-west Passage through Hudson's Streights to the Western and Southern Ocean of America." In the evidence before the Committee, varied opinions were given as to this Northwest Passage. Mr. Edward Thompson, who had been a ship-surgeon, being examined as to the probability of a North-west Passage, said, "He had the greatest reason to believe there is one, from the winds, tides, and black whales; and he thinks the place to be at Chesterfield's inlet; that the reason of their coming back was they met the other boat which had been five leagues further, and the crew told them the water was much fresher and shallower there; but where he was the water was fifty fathoms deep, and the tide very strong; the ebb six hours and the flood two, to the best of his remembrance; that it is not common for the tide to flow only two hours; but he imagines it to be obstructed by another tide from the westward; that the rapidity of the tide upwards was so great, that the spray of the water flew over the bow of the schooner, and was so salt that it candied on men's shoes, but that the tide did not run in so rapid a manner the other way." Captain William Moore, being asked whether he believed there was a North-west Passage to the South Seas, said, "He believes there is a communication, but whether navigable or not he cannot say; that if there is any such communication 'tis further northward than he expected; that if it is but short, as 'tis probable to conclude from the height of the tides, 'tis possible it might be navigable; and it was the opinion of all the persons sent on that discovery that a north-west wind made the highest tides." Captain Carruthers said, "That he don't apprehend there is any such passage; but if there is, he thinks it impracticable to navigate it on account of the ice; that he would rather choose to go round by Cape Horn; and that it will be impossible to go and return through such passage in one year; and he thinks 'tis the general opinion of seamen that there is no such passage." Mr. John Tomlinson, merchant, of London, said, "He was a subscriber to the undertaking for finding a North-west Passage; which undertaking was dropped for want of money: that he should not choose to subscribe again upon the same terms; that he cannot pretend to say whether there is such a passage or not, or whether, if found, it could be ever rendered useful to navigation."

The merchant witnesses were in favour of throwing open the trade of Hudson's Bay; and this Mr. Tomlinson said more ships would be sent, and more people brought down to trade. "This is confirmed," he said, "by the experience of the Guinea trade, which, when confined to a company, employed not above ten ships, and now employs 150;" and "that the case of the Guinea trade was exactly similar (to the Hudson's Bay), where the ships near one another, and each endeavours to get the trade; and the more ships lie there, the higher the price of negroes."

The capital of the Hudson's Bay Company, increased by doublings and treblings of its nominal amount, was, in 1748, 103,950_l_., held by eighty-six proprietors.

The trade between London and Hudson's Bay was carried on in 1748, and for some previous years, by four ships. The cost of the exports was in 1748 5,102_l_. 12_s_. 3_d_., and the value of the sales of furs and other imports in that year amounted to 30,160_l_. 5_s_. 11_d_d. The "charge attending the carrying on the Hudson's Bay trade, and maintaining their factories," in 1748, is stated at 17,352_l_. 4_s_. 10_d_. The original cash capital was 10,500_l_. That capital was "trebled" in 1690, making the nominal capital 31,500_l_.; in August, 1720, it was proposed to augment the cash capital, and to make the nominal total 378,000_l_. But at a "General Court," held on the 23rd December, 1720, it was resolved to "vacate" the subscription "by reason of the present scarcity of moneys, and the deadness of credit." And it was further "Resolved, that in the opinion of this Committee, that each subscriber shall have 30_l_. stock for each 10_l_. by him paid in," "which resolutions were agreed to by this Court." Anyhow, the capital in 1748 is stated at 103,950_l_. A trade which, by sending out about 5,000_l_. a year, brought back a return of 30,000_l_., was no doubt worth preserving; and even taking the outlay for working and maintenance of forts and establishments, there was over 8 per cent, on the nominal capital left, or probably 40 per cent on all the cash actually paid in; not too great a reward for the benefits gained by the country from this trade.

Some particulars of the regulation of exchange of commodities may here be interesting.

The system of trade was simple barter. The equivalent of value was beaver skins; while skins of less value were again calculated as so much of each for one beaver. A kettle was exchanged for one beaver. A pound and a half of gunpowder, one beaver. One blanket, six beavers. Two bayonets, one beaver. Four fire-steels, one beaver. One pistol, four beavers. Twelve needles, one beaver. One four-foot gun, twelve beavers. Three knives, one beaver, and so on over a long list of various articles. Some of the things exchanged nearly 130 years ago, show that the Indians had a good knowledge of trade, and of objects used by civilised people. For example; brandy (English), one gallon, four beavers. Vermilion, one and a half ounces, one beaver; and combs, egg-boxes, files, glasses, goggles, handkerchiefs, hats (laced), hawk-bells, rings, scissors, spoons, shirts, shoes, stockings, and thimbles.

The factors were accused of imposing upon the Indians by using defective weights and measures; and it was said that the doubtful profit thus made, in opposition to the standards sent out from England, was called the "overplus-trade."

In the year 1748, the forts and settlements of the Hudson's Bay Company "in the Bay" were:—

Latitude

Moose Fort 51 28
Henley House, or Fort 52
The East Main House 52 10
Albany Fort 52 18
York Fort 57 10
Prince of Wales' Fort 59

This limited occupation contrasts in a marked manner with the area of posts, all over the continent, at this later date; see a list at pp. 222-226, and a map in front of this volume.

The skins and other articles imported, and sold at the Company's warehouse, in the City of London, by the "inch of candle"—a mode of auction common in those days (under which the bidding went on till the inch of lighted wax, candle went out)—fluctuated in the ten years between the years 1739 and 1748 very much. In that period the highest and lowest prices were for:—

```
                      L s d L s d_
Beaver (per lb ) 0 7 101/4 0 5 3
Martin (per skin) 0 6 8 0 5 11/4
Otter " 0 13 6 0 5 5
Cat " 0 18 0 0 10 101/4
Fox " 0 11 71/4 0 6 71/4
Wolverines " 0 7 0 0 5 5
Bear (per skin) 1 6 71/2 0 12 101/4
Mink " 0 4 8 0 2 0
Wolves " 0 18 11 0 9 01/4
Woodshock " 0 12 0 0 8 0
Elk " 0 11 7 0 6 1
Deer " 0 0 9 0 2 01/4
Bed feathers (per lb ) 0 1 41/4 0 1 0
Castorum " 0 13 21/4 0 6 1
Ivory " — — — — 0 0 61/4
Whale Fins " 0 2 9 0 1 101/4
Wesakapupa " 0 2 4 0 0 61/4
Whale Oil (per tun) 18 13 0 10 1 0
Goose quills (per 1,000) 0 18 0 0 11 7
```

"Ivory" only appears once, viz. in the sale of 1738-9. This article may have been, simply, bones of the whale; and "whale oil" only appears four times in the ten years quoted.

The report of Lord Strange's Committee quotes many quaint and solid instructions, as well in times of war as of peace, to the governors and agents on the Bay. A letter from London, dated 10th May, 1744, says, "The English and French having declared war against each other, and the war with Spain still continuing, we do hereby strictly direct you to be always on your guard and to keep a good watch; and that you keep all your men as near home as possible. We do hereby further direct that you cut away all trees, hedges, bushes, &c., or any other cover for an enemy; and lay all level and open round the factory, further than cannon shot, which we compute to be a mile; in order to hinder the enemy from attacking you unawares, and from being sheltered from the factory's guns. But you are to keep up, and repair, your palisadoes, for your defence." ... "You are to fire point blank upon any ship, sloop, or vessel that shall come near the factory, unless they make the true signal, and answer yours. The letter proceeds to offer 30_l_. to the widow or children of any man killed in defence of the factory; to every one who should lose a leg, or an arm, 30_l_. Compensation to men receiving smaller wounds; and especial reward to such of the "chiefs, officers, and common men" as might specially distinguish themselves.

The 18th paragraph of this remarkable letter says: "In case you are attacked at Henley House, and, notwithstanding a vigorous resistance, you should have the misfortune to be overpowered, then you are to nail up the cannon, blow up the house, and destroy everything that can be of service to the enemy, and make the best retreat you can to the factory."

Grand old London merchants, these!

Chapter XIII
The Hudson's Bay Posts—to-day

In their Report of 28th June, 1872, the Governor and Committee report the details of the varied posts from Ocean to Ocean of the Hudson's Bay Company, as follows:—

Statement of Land belonging to the HUDSON'S BAY COMPANY, exclusive of their claim to one-twentieth of the Land set out for settlement in the "Fertile Belt," or the district coloured green in the accompanying Map [in front of this volume].

— — — — — — — — — — — — — — | | Acres District | Post | of | | Land — — — — — — — — — — — — LAKE HURON | 1 | La Cloche | 6,400 TEMISCAMINQUE | 2 | Kakababeagino | 10 SUPERIOR | 3 | Long Lake | 10 UNITED STATES | 4 | Georgetown | 1,133 MANITOBA, or }| 5 | Fort Garry | 500 RED RIVER SETTLEMENT }| 6 | Lower Fort | 500 }| 7 | White Horse Plains | 500 MANITOBA LAKE | 8 | Oak Point | 50 PORTAGE LA PRAIRIE | 9 | | 1,000 LAC LA PLUIE | 10 | Fort Alexander | 500 | 11 | Fort Frances | 500 | 12 | Eagles Nest | 20 | 13 | Big Island | 20 | 14 | Lac du Bennet | 20 | 15 | Rat Portage | 50 | 16 | Shoal Lake | 20 | 17 | Lake of the Woods | 50 | 18 | White Fish Lake | 20 | 19 | English River | 20 | 20 | Hungry Hall | 20 | 21 | Trout Lake | 20 | 22 | Clear Water Lake | 20 | 23 | Sandy Point | 20 SWAN RIVER | 24 | Fort Pelly | 3,000 | 25 | Fort Ellice | 3,000 | 26 | Qu'Appelle Lakes | 2,500 | 27 | Touchwood Hills | 500 | 28 | Shoal River | 50 | 29 | Manitobah | 50 | 30 | Fairford | 100 | | | CUMBERLAND | 31 | Cumberland House | 100 | 32 | Fort la Corne | 3,000 | 33 | Pelican Lake | 50 | 34 | Moose Woods | 1,000 | 35 | The Pas | 25 | 36 | Moose Lake | 50 | 37 | Grand Rapid Portage | 100 | | |50 Acres | | |at each | | |end of | | |Portage SASKATCHEWAN | 38 | Edmonton House | 3,000 | 39 | Rocky Mountain House | 500 | 40 | Fort Victoria | 3,000 | 41 | St Paul | 3,000 | 42 | Fort Pitt | 3,000 | 43 | Battle River | 3,000 | 44 | Carlton House | 3,000 | 45 | Fort Albert | 3,000 | 46 | Whitefish Lake | 500 | 47 | Lac la Biche | 1,000 | 48 | Fort Assiniboine | 50 | 49 | Lesser Slave Lake | 500 | 50 | Lac St Anne | 500 | 51 | Lac la Nun | 500 | 52 | St Albert | 1,000 | 53 | Pigeon Lake | 100 | 54 | Old White Mud Fort | 50 | | | ENGLISH RIVER | 55 | Isle a la Crosse | 50 | 56 | Rapid River | 5 | 57 | Portage da Loche |

20 I 58 I Green Lake I 100 I 59 I Cold Lake I 10 I 60 I Deers Lake I 5 I I I
YORK I 61 I York Factory I 100 I 62 I Churchill I 10 I 63 I Severn I 10 I 64
I Trout Lake I 10 I 65 I Oxford I 100 I 66 I Jackson's Bay I 10 I 67 I God's
Lake I 10 I 68 I Island Lake I 10 I I I NORWAY HOUSE I 69 I Norway
House I 100 I 70 I Berens River I 25 I 71 I Grand Rapid I 10 I 72 I Nelson's
River I 10 I I I ALBANY 73 I Albany Factory I 100 I 74 I Martin's Falls I
10 I 75 I Osnaburg I 25 I 76 I Lac Seul I 500 I I I EASE MAIN I 77 I Little
Whale River I 50 I 78 I Great Whale River I 50 I 79 I Fort George I 25 I I I
MOOSE I 80 I Moose Factory I 100 I 81 I Hannah Bay I 10 I 82 I Abitibi I
10 I 83 I New Brunswick I 25 I I I RUPERT'S RIVER I 84 I Rupert's House
I 50 I 85 I Mistassing I 10 I 86 I Temiskamay I 10 I 87 I Woswonaby I 10
I 88 I Meehiskun I 10 I 89 I Pike Lake I 10 I 90 I Nitchequon I 10 I 91 I
Kamapiscan I 10 I I I KINOGUMISSEE I 92 I Matawagauinque I 50 I 93 I
Kuckatoosh I 10 I I I LABRADOR I 94 I Fort Nascopie I 75 I 95 I Outposts
do. I 25 I 96 I Fort Chimo (Ungava) I 100 I 97 I South River, Outposts I 30
I 98 I George's River I 50 I 99 I Whale River I 50 I100 I North's River I 25
I101 I False River I 25 I I I ATHABASCA I102 I Fort Chippewyan I 10 I103
I Fort Vermilion I 500 I104 I For t Dunvegan I 50 I105 I Fort St John's I 20
I106 I Forks of Athabasca River I 10 I107 I Battle River I 5 I108 I Fond du
Lac I 5 I109 I Salt River I 5 I I I MCKENZIE RIVER I110 I Fort Simpson I
100 I111 I Fort Liard I 300 I112 I Fort Nelson I 200 I113 I The Rapids I 100
I114 I Hay River I 20 I115 I Fort Resolution I 20 I116 I Fort Rae I 10 I117 I
Fond du Lac I 10 I118 I Fort Norman I 10 I119 I Fort Good Hope I 10 I120
I Peel's River I 10 I121 I Lapierre's House I 10 I122 I Fort Halkett I 100

WESTERN DEPARTMENT

VANCOUVER'S ISLAND I123 I Victoria, including I
   I I Town Lots, about I 70
   I124 I Esquimault (Puget's Sound I
   I I Company Land I 2,300
   I125 I Uplands Farm I 1,125
   I126 I North Dairy Farm I 460
   I I I
BRITISH COLUMBIA I127 I Fort Alexander I 100
   I128 I Fort George I 100
   I129 I Fraser's Lake I 100
   I130 I Stuart's Lake I 100
   I131 I McLeod's Lake I 100
   I132 I Connolly's Lake I 100
   I133 I Babine I 100

| 134 | Chilcotin | 100
| | Five other places | 100
| 135 | Fort Dallas | 50
| 136 | Fort Berens | 50
| 137 | Fort Shepherd | 100
| 138 | Fort Simpson | 100
| 139 | Salmon River | 50
| 140 | Langley and Langley Farm | 2,220
| 141 | Yale, sundry small blocks |
| 142 | Hope | 5
| 143 | Kamloops | 1,976
| 144 | Similkameen | 1,140
| | Barkerville) | Town
| | Quesnel) | Lots

Chapter XIV
"Uncertain Sounds"

I may illustrate the consequences of vacillation and delay in the vigorous government of the Hudson's Bay territory, and in all distant parts of the Empire, by giving a verbatim copy of a Bill ordered to be "printed and introduced" in July, 1866, into the "House of Representatives" of the United States, at Washington, providing for relieving the Queen of her sovereign rights in the British territories between the Atlantic and Pacific Oceans. The only excuse—an excuse far from valid for so monstrous a proposal—was that no one knew what the British Government were inclined to do; and at Washington no one believed that John Bull would "make a fight of it;" while everyone knew that if a similar Bill, with the object of enabling the Southern States to come under the dominion of the Queen, had been introduced into the British House of Commons, the United States Ambassador "to the Court of St. James'" would have been recalled—to begin with. The British Ambassador took no notice, made no remonstrance; but the advent of Mr. Disraeli to power discouraged such outrages, and led in the following year to the passing of the Act for Confederation. In printing this Bill, my object is to show the mischief, mischief which half-a-dozen times in my lifetime has placed before my countrymen the alternative of ignominious concessions or war between English-speaking people, of "uncertain sounds." It is essential to continued peace, trade and prosperity, that it should be known to all the world that the broad lands between the two great oceans are an integral part of the Empire; that they will never be parted with without a struggle, in which all our forces will be amply used; and that either invasion, or the insidious agitations which from time to time are hatched in the United States with an eye to rebellion, will be put down by force.

Here is this insulting document printed verbatim. I challenge the quotation of any similar outrage on the part of any civilized nation at peace with the Empire attacked:—

"[Printer's No., 266.

"39TH CONGRESS, 1ST SESSION.

"H. R. 754.

"IN THE HOUSE OF REPRESENTATIVES.

"JULY 2, 1866.

"Read twice, referred to the Committee on Foreign Affairs, and ordered to be printed.

"Mr. BANKS, on leave, introduced the following Bill:

"A BILL

"For the admission of the States of Nova Scotia, New Brunswick, Canada East, and Canada West, and for the organization of the Territories of Selkirk, Saskatchewan, and Columbia.

"*Be it enacted by the Senate and House of Representatives of the United States of America in Congress assembled*, That the President of the United States is hereby authorized and directed, whenever notice shall be deposited in the Department of State that the Governments of Great Britain and the Provinces of New Brunswick, Nova Scotia, Prince Edward Island, Newfoundland, Canada, British Columbia, and Vancouver's Island have accepted the proposition hereinafter made by the United States, to publish by proclamation that, from the date thereof, the States of Nova Scotia, New Brunswick, Canada East, and Canada West, and the Territories of Selkirk, Saskatchewan, and Columbia, with limits and rights as by this Act defined, are constituted and admitted as States and Territories of the United States of America.

"SEC. 2. *And be it further enacted*, That the following articles are hereby proposed, and from the date of the proclamation of the President of the United States shall take effect, as irrevocable conditions of the admission of the States of Nova Scotia, New Brunswick, Canada East, and Canada West, and the future States of Selkirk, Saskatchewan, and Columbia, to wit:

ARTICLE I

"All public lands not sold or granted; canals, public harbors, lighthouses, and piers; river and lake improvements, railway stocks, mortgages, and other debts due by railway companies to the provinces; custom-houses and post-offices, shall vest in the United States; but all other public works and property shall belong to the State governments respectively, hereby constituted, together with all sums due from purchasers or lessees of lands, mines, or minerals at the time of the union.

"ARTICLE II

"In consideration of the public lands, works, and property vested as aforesaid in the United States, the United States will assume and discharge the funded debt and contingent liabilities of the late provinces, at rates of interest not exceeding five per centum, to the amount of eighty-five million seven hundred thousand dollars, apportioned as follows: to Canada West, thirty-six million five hundred thousand dollars; to Canada East, twenty-nine million dollars; to Nova Scotia, eight million dollars; to New Brunswick, seven million dollars; to Newfoundland, three million two hundred thousand dollars; and to Prince Edward Island, two million dollars; and in further consideration of the transfer by said provinces to the United States of the power to levy import and export duties, the United States will make an annual grant of one million six hundred and forty-six thousand dollars in aid of local expenditures, to be apportioned as follows: To Canada West, seven hundred thousand dollars; to Canada East, five hundred and fifty thousand dollars; to Nova Scotia, one hundred and sixty-five thousand dollars; to New Brunswick, one hundred and twenty-six thousand dollars; to Newfoundland, sixty-five thousand dollars; to Prince Edward Island, forty thousand dollars.

ARTICLE III

"For all purposes of State organization and representation in the Congress of the United States, Newfoundland shall be part of Canada East, and Prince Edward Island shall be part of Nova Scotia, except that each shall always be a separate representative district, and entitled to elect at least one member of the House of Representatives, and except, also, that the municipal authorities of Newfoundland and Prince Edward Island shall receive the indemnities agreed to be paid by the United States in Article II.

ARTICLE IV

"Territorial divisions are established as follows:—(1) New Brunswick, with its present limits; (2) Nova Scotia, with the addition of Prince Edward Island; (3) Canada East, with the addition of Newfoundland and all territory east of longitude eighty degrees and south of Hudson's Strait; (4) Canada West, with the addition of territory south of Hudson's Bay and between longitude eighty degrees and ninety degrees; (5) Selkirk Territory, bounded east by longitude ninety degrees, south by the late boundary of the United States, west by longitude one hundred and five degrees, and north by the Arctic circle; (6) Saskatchewan Territory, bounded east by longitude one hundred and five degrees, south by latitude forty-nine degrees, west by the Rocky Mountains, and north by latitude seventy degrees; (7) Columbia Territory, including Vancouver's Island, and Queen Charlotte's Island, and bounded east and north by the Rocky Mountains, south by latitude forty-nine degrees, and west by the Pacific Ocean and Russian America. But Congress reserves the right of changing the limits and subdividing the areas of the western territories at discretion.

ARTICLE V

"Until the next decennial revision, representation in the House of Representatives shall be as follows:—Canada West, twelve members; Canada East, including Newfoundland, eleven members; New Brunswick, two members; Nova Scotia, including Prince Edward Island, four members.

ARTICLE VI

"The Congress of the United States shall enact, in favour of the proposed Territories of Selkirk, Saskatchewan, and Columbia, all the provisions of the Act organizing the Territory of Montana, so far as they can be made applicable.

ARTICLE VII

"The United States, by the construction of new canals, or the enlargement of existing canals, and by the improvement of shoals, will so aid the navigation of the Saint Lawrence river and the great lakes that vessels of fifteen hundred tons burden shall pass from the Gulf of Saint Lawrence to Lakes Superior and Michigan: *Provided*, That the expenditure under this article shall not exceed fifty millions of dollars.

ARTICLE VIII

"The United States will appropriate and pay to 'The European and North American Railway Company of Maine' the sum of two millions of dollars upon the construction of a continuous line of railroad from Bangor, in Maine, to Saint John's, in New Brunswick: *Provided*, That said 'The European and North American Railway Company of Maine' shall release the Government of the United States from all claims held by it as assignee of the States of Maine and Massachusetts.

ARTICLE IX

"To aid the construction of a railway from Truro, in Nova Scotia, to Riviere du Loup, in Canada East, and a railway from the city of Ottawa, by way of Sault Ste. Marie, Bayfield, and Superior, in Wisconsin, Pembina, and Fort Garry, on the Red River of the North, and the valley of the North Saskatchewan river, to some point on the Pacific Ocean north of latitude forty-nine degrees, the United States will grant lands along the lines of said roads to the amount of twenty sections, or twelve thousand eight hundred acres, per mile, to be selected and sold in the manner prescribed in the Act to aid the construction of the Northern Pacific Railroad, approved July two, eighteen hundred and sixty-two, and Acts amendatory thereof; and in addition to said grants of lands, the United States will further guarantee dividends of five per centum upon the stock of the Company or Companies which may be authorized by Congress to undertake the construction of said railways: *Provided*, That such guarantee of stock shall not exceed the sum of thirty thousand dollars per mile, and Congress shall regulate the securities for advances on account thereof.

ARTICLE X

"The public lands in the late provinces, as far as practicable, shall be surveyed according to the rectangular system of the General Land Office of the United States; and in the Territories west of longitude ninety degrees or the western boundary of Canada West, sections sixteen and thirty-six shall be granted for the encouragement of schools; and after the organization of the Territories into States, five per centum of the net proceeds of sales of public lands shall be paid into their treasuries as a fund for the improvement of roads and rivers.

ARTICLE XI

"The United States will pay ten millions of dollars to the Hudson Bay Company in full discharge of all claims to territory or jurisdiction in North America, whether founded on the charter of the Company or any treaty, law, or usage.

ARTICLE XII

"It shall be devolved upon the Legislatures of New Brunswick, Nova Scotia, Canada East, and Canada West, to conform the tenure of office and the local institutions of said States to the Constitution and laws of the United States, subject to revision by Congress.

"SEC. 3. *And be it further enacted*, That if Prince Edward Island and Newfoundland, or either of those provinces, shall decline union with the United States, and the remaining provinces, with the consent of Great Britain, shall accept the proposition of the United States, the foregoing stipulations in favour of Prince Edward Island and Newfoundland, or either of them, will be omitted; but in all other respects the United States will give full effect to the plan of union. If Prince Edward Island, Newfoundland, Nova Scotia, and New Brunswick shall decline the proposition, but Canada, British Columbia, and Vancouver Island shall, with the consent of Great Britain, accept the same, the construction of a railway from Truro to Riviere du Loup, with all stipulations relating to the maritime provinces, will form no part of the proposed plan of union, but the same will be consummated in all other respects. If Canada shall decline the proposition, then the stipulations in regard to the Saint Lawrence canals and a railway from Ottawa to Sault Ste. Marie, with the Canadian clause of debt and revenue indemnity, will be relinquished. If the plan of union shall only be accepted in regard to the north western territory and the Pacific Provinces, the United States will aid the construction, on the terms named, of a railway from the western extremity of Lake Superior, in the State of Minnesota, by way of Pembina, Fort Garry, and the valley of the Saskatchewan, to the Pacific coast, north of latitude forty-nine degrees, besides securing all the rights and privileges of an American territory to the proposed territories of Selkirk, Saskatchewan, and Columbia."

So much for an outrage of a character unheard of and unparalleled. It was the result of "uncertain sounds;" of "duffer" government.

Let me give some illustrations. Before we began the, finally successful, movement for the Intercolonial Railway, the confederation of the Provinces of North America, and the final completion of a railway binding the coasts of the Atlantic and Pacific together, the Right Hon. C. B. Adderley, M.P., wrote a "letter to the Right Hon. B. Disraeli, M.P., on the present relations of England with the Colonies." It was a skinflint document, and here are a couple of quotations:—

"I would have the Canadian Government, in the right time and manner, informed that after a. certain date, unless war were going on, they would have to provide for their own garrisons, as well as all their requisite peace establishments, as they might deem fit; and that they should be prepared to hold their own in case of foreign attack, at least till the forces of the Empire could come to their aid."

"Let Canada, however, by all means look to England in the hour of peril also; but if the sight of English red-coats, at all times, has become a needful support of Canadian confidence, and English pay has ceased to be resented as a symptom of dependence, we must bow humbly under the conviction that Canada is no longer inhabited by men like those who conquered her."

Then I must quote my revered friend, Mr. Cobden, who, addressing his relative, Colonel Cole (at one time administrator of New Brunswick), on the 20th March, 1865, only thirteen days before his ever-to-be-lamented death, wrote about Canada: "We are two peoples to all intents and purposes, and it is a perilous delusion to both parties to attempt to keep up a sham connection and dependence, which will snap asunder if it should ever be put to the strain of stem reality. It is all very well for our cockney newspapers to talk of defending Canada at all hazards. It would be just as possible for the United States to sustain Yorkshire in a war with England as for us to enable

Canada to contend against the United States. It is simply an impossibility. We must not forget that the only serious danger of a quarrel between these two neighbours arises from the connection of Canada with this country. In my opinion it is for the interest of both that we should, as speedily as possible, sever the political thread by which we are, as communities, connected, and leave the individuals on both sides to cultivate the relations of commerce and friendly intercourse as with other nations." ... "There is, I think, an inherent weakness in the parody of our old English constitution, which is performed on the miniature scenes of the Colonial capitals, with their speeches from the throne, votes of confidence, appeals to the country, changes of ministry, &c., and all about such trumpery issues that the game at last becomes ridiculous in the eyes of both spectators and actors."

Speaking in the House of Commons on the second reading of the British North America Bill, in 1867, Mr. Bright said: "Is this new State—or this new nation, as I think Lord Monck described it—to be raised up under the authority of an Act of Parliament—is everything to be done for it? Is it intended to garrison its fortresses by English troops? At present there are, I believe, in the Province 12,000 or 15,000 men. There are persons in this country, and there are some also in the North American Provinces, who are ill-natured enough to say that not a little of the loyalty that is said to prevail in Canada has its price. I think it is natural and reasonable to hope that there is in that country a very strong attachment to this country. But if they are constantly to be applying to us for guarantees for railways, and for fortresses, and for works of defence; if everything is to be given to a nation independent in everything except Lord Monck and his successors, and except in the contributions we make for these public objects, then I think it would be far better for them, and for us—cheaper for us, and less demoralising for them—that they should become an independent State, and maintain their own fortresses, fight their own cause, and build up their own future, without relying upon us. And when we know, as everybody knows, that the population of Canada, family for family, is in a much better position as regards the comforts of home than family for family are in the great bulk of the population of this country—I say the time has come when it ought to be clearly understood that the taxes of England are no longer to go across the ocean to defray expenses of any kind within the confederation which is about to be formed. The Right Honorable gentleman the Under-Secretary of the Colonies (Mr. Adderley) has never been an advocate for great expenditure in the Colonies by the Mother Country. On the contrary, he has been one of the members of this House who have distinguished themselves by what I will call an honest system to the Mother Country, and what I believe is a wise system to the Colonies. But I think that when a measure of this kind is being passed, having such stupendous results upon the population of these great Colonies, we have a right to ask that there should be some consideration for the Revenue and for the taxpayers of this country."

In speaking on the Canada Railway Loan Bill in the House on the 28th March, 1867, Mr. Gladstone, alluding to Canada, said: "We have carried it to this point, that as far as regards the Administration, I believe it may be said that the only officer appointed by the Colonial Secretary is the Governor; and I believe there cannot be a doubt that if it were the well-ascertained desire of the Colonies to have the appointment of their own Governor, the Imperial Parliament would at once make over to them that power."

I may, perhaps without presumption, here add two short speeches of mine in the House of Commons: one, in reply to Mr. Bright in the discussion on the Confederation, or British North America Bill, on the 28th February, 1867; the other, in reply to Mr. Lowe, on the Canada Loan Bill, on the 28th March, 1867.

Language affecting the relations between the Mother Country and the Colonies, such as I have quoted, does infinite mischief—more mischief than those who do not mix with the people can understand. It is as bad in its consequences as the unfortunate policy of Mr. Gladstone: the "Majuba Hill" policy.

[*Hansard, vol. 185, page 1187, Feb. 28, 1867.*]

"Mr. Watkin said he fully concurred in the statement of the right hon. gentleman (Sir John Pakington), that the House of Representatives and the Senate of Nova Scotia had approved the scheme of Confederation. The representative body approved it in 1861—not 1862, as the right hon. gentleman the First Lord of the Admiralty had stated.

"There was a general election in 1863, and the Prime Minister (Mr. Tupper) went through the country preaching this Confederation of the Provinces. It was brought under the notice of the electors at every polling-booth, and at every hustings the issue was distinctly raised. Well, after that general election, the plan of the Government was sustained by an enormous majority in the House of Representatives, and delegates were sent to the Conference to carry out the plan. If there was any question on which the British North American Provinces not only had enjoyed an opportunity of expressing, but had actually expressed, opinion, it was on this very question of Confederation.

"Mention having been made of the name of Mr. Howe, whose acquaintance he had the honour of possessing, he might state his own conviction that a man of purer patriotism, or one who had rendered more able and distinguished service to the Crown of this country, did not exist. He remembered the speech delivered by Mr. Howe some years ago at Detroit on the question of whether the Reciprocity Treaty should be continued or not; and he believed it was in no small degree owing to that remarkable speech—one of the most eloquent ever heard—that the unanimous verdict in favour of continuing the treaty had been arrived at. It was matter of surprise and regret to him that the valuable and life-long services of Mr. Howe had not received recognition at the hands of either the late or the present Government.

"The hon. member for Birmingham seemed dissatisfied with the phrase used by Lord Monck respecting the establishment of a new nation. Now he (Mr. Watkin) supported the Confederation, not as the establishment of a new nation, but as the confirmation of an existing nation. It meant this, that the people of the confederated colonies were to remain under the British Crown—or it meant nothing. He joined issue with those who said, 'Let the Colonies stand by themselves.' He dissented from the view that they were to separate from the control of the British Crown the territory of this enormous Confederation. But there was a vast tract beyond Canada, extending to the Pacific; and the House should bear in mind that more than half of North America was under British dominion.

"Did the hon. member (Mr. Bright) think that it was best for civilization and for public liberty that this half of the Continent should be annexed to the United States? If that were the opinion of the hon. gentleman, he did not think it was the opinion of that House. Every man of common sense knew that these territories could not stand by themselves; they must either be British or American—under the Crown or under the Stars and Stripes. The hon. member for Birmingham (Mr. Bright) might think that we should be the better for losing all territorial connection with Canada; but he could not agree with that doctrine. Extent and variety were amongst the elements of Imperial greatness.

"Descending to the lowest and most material view of the subject, he did not believe that, as a mere money question, the separation would be for our interest.

"Take, again, the question of defence. Our North American possessions had a coast line of 1,000 miles on the east, and 800 on the west, and possessed some of the finest harbours on that Continent, and a mercantile marine entitling it to the third rank among maritime nations. The moment these advantages passed into the hands of the United States, that country would become the greatest naval power in the world. In preserving commercial relations with the United States, the Canadian frontier line of 3,000 miles was likewise extremely useful.

"As long as British power and enterprise extended along one side of this boundary line, and as long as the tariff of extremely light duties was kept up by us, and that imposed only for the purposes of revenue, it would be impossible for the United States to pursue what might be called a Japanese policy.

"If England, therefore, desired to maintain her trade, even apart from other considerations, it was desirable for her to maintain her North American possessions.

They had lately had to pass through a cotton famine, and they had been taught the inconvenience of the prohibition of the export of cotton by the American Government.

"A large proportion of the corn imported into this country was brought from America, and in what state would England find herself if all the food exports of North America were placed under the control of the Government of Washington? If the frontier line became the sea coast, what might be looked for then? Scarcely three years had elapsed since Mr. Cobden declared that if there had not been a plentiful harvest in America he did not know where food could have been procured for the people of this country.

"Now, the corn-growing fields of Upper Canada alone ranked fifth in point of productiveness. Did England not wish to preserve this vast storehouse? Suppose that Canada belonged to America: in the event of a quarrel with England there was nothing to prevent the United States from declaring that not an ounce of food should leave its territories, which would then extend from the Arctic regions to the Gulf of Mexico. He had hoped that upon this Bill, not only both sides of the House, but every section of the House, might have been found in unison.

"It was no use blinking the question. This would not be a decision affecting Canada merely. We had sympathies alike with Australia and the other Colonies. If it were seriously proposed that England should denude herself of her possessions—give up India, Australia, North America, and retire strictly within the confines of her own Islands, to make herself happy there,—the same result might be brought about much more easily by those who wished it. They might become citizens of some small country like Holland, and realize their ideas of happiness in a moment. But he hesitated to believe that the people of England did really favour any such policy.

"If any one were to hoist the motto, 'Severance of the Colonies from the Crown,' he did not believe that one per cent. of the people would adopt it. He believed that the people of England felt a deep attachment to their Empire, and that not a barren rock over which the flag of England had ever waved would be abandoned by them without a cogent and sufficient reason. Every argument used in support of the necessity of giving up the Provinces, which lay within eight days of our own shores, would apply with equal force in the case of Ireland, if the people of the United States chose to demand possession.

"Was this country prepared to give up Gibraltar, Malta, Heligoland, all its outlying stations, merely because some strong power took a fancy to them? He did not believe that the people of England would ever act in such a spirit.

"As to the argument of expense, if Canada chose to pick a quarrel on her own account, clearly she ought to pay the bill; but if she were involved in war on Imperial considerations, then he maintained that the Imperial revenues might properly be resorted to.

"The British Empire was one and indivisible, or it was nothing. And what was the principle upon which the United States acted? If any portion of the territory of the Union was touched, were there one of its citizens who would not be ready and forward to defend it? Should we then be less determined to maintain intact the greatness and the glory of the British Empire?

"He, for one, would not give up the opinion that Englishmen were prepared to maintain, in its integrity, the greatness and glory of the Empire; and that such a feeling would find a hearty response in that House."

"CANADA RAILWAY LOAN.

"[*March* 28, 1867.]   ¬

"In reply to Mr. Lowe and others, "Mr. Watkin said that, in following the right hon. gentleman (Mr. Lowe), he felt very much as a quiet Roman citizen must have done on passing the chief gladiator in the street— inclined to pass over to the other side, and to have nothing to say to him, for fear of the consequences.

"But some years ago he was requested by the late Duke of Newcastle to make inquiries, which convinced him that the hobgoblin fears expressed that night in regard to the construction of this 375 miles of railway were unfounded.

"Let hon. members remember that Her Majesty's American dominions extended over an area equal to one-eighth of the habitable globe. This

Railway gave us communication, not only with Canada and with 10,000 miles of American railways, but with the vast tract of British territory extending across to the Pacific. The consequence of making this Railway would be, that two days would be saved in going from England to the northern continent of America, including the great corn- growing district of the West.

"If the House had seen, as he had seen, the Canadian volunteers turn out in bitter winter to repel a threatened invasion, without a red-coat near them, they would think that the right hon. gentleman's taunts might have been spared.

"The British Provinces had taxed themselves 360,000_l_. a-year for the execution of these works, which Lord Durham had proposed in 1838, with the object of binding together, by the means of physical communication, the varied sections of the Queen's American dominions.

"The evidence of every military man, including Sir John Michell, the present Commander-in-Chief in Canada, was that this Railway was absolutely necessary for the military defence of the Colonies. It was, however, to be defended not only on that ground, but upon the ground of its great commercial advantages.

"There were now in the Government offices memorials from many of the large towns in the three kingdoms, concurring in the commercial necessity and advantages of the measure which the House was now asked to agree to. Therefore, originating as it did with Lord Durham,— sanctioned as it was by Lord Grey's proposals of 1851—adopted by the late and present Governments,—demanded for purposes of defence, as also for the more genial and generous objects of commerce and peace,— he hoped the House would support the construction of the Railway by a guarantee, which would not cost this country a shilling."

The motion for giving the guarantee was carried by 247 votes to 67—or by a majority of 180.

Chapter XV
"Governor Dallas"

I should do injustice to my own loving memory of the man, if I did not publish some letters from the late Governor Dallas, which are, to my mind, especially interesting. Though some of his views, in 1863, as to the value of the Hudson's Bay lands, and their settlement, did not accord with my own, yet his experience should plead against mine. No one was more pleased than he to find that the country was in process— after many delays, over which he and I used to groan in concert—of successful colonization.

"MONTREAL, "*17th August*, 1863.

DEAR SIR,

"With reference to our late conversations upon various matters connected with the past and future of the Hudson's Bay Company, I take the liberty of calling your attention to several points of the business requiring immediate attention, in a more explicit manner than I may have done in desultory conversation.

"The government of the territory is come almost to a dead-lock in the Red River Settlement, and nothing short of direct administration under the authority of the Crown will, in my opinion, remedy the evil. Two prisoners have been, in separate instances, forcibly rescued from jail, and they, with about thirty to fifty others implicated in the riots, are still at large, fostering discontent, and creating great disquiet. Their secret instigator controls the only paper published in the settlement, and its continued attacks upon the Company find a greedy ear with the public at large, both in the settlement and in Canada. The position of those in authority is so disagreeable that I have had great difficulty in persuading the magistrates to continue to act. Mr. William Mactavish, Governor of Assiniboin, has resigned his post, and I have only been restrained from following his example, for a short time, in the hope that a remedy would speedily be applied, and that I should be relieved from the unfair position in which I find myself placed, with all the responsibility, and the semblance of authority over a vast territory, but unsupported, if not ignored, by the Crown. In the absence of a just grievance, the cry of 'the Company' is quite a sufficient watchword amongst the ignorant and discontented.

"The open malcontents are few in number, and I had ample volunteer force at my back to protect the jail and support my authority, but, as I have already explained to you, I could exercise but little control over my friends, who were keen for what would have ended in a free fight, with the certain death of the sheriff and ringleaders on both sides, and led to endless animosities. It required more resolution on my part to follow the course I did, than to have resisted the rioters. For details of the transactions I refer you to my official letters to the Board, which you will find in the Hudson's Bay House.

"Of the settlers, the greater number, including the French Canadians, are our staunch personal friends, while the openly disaffected are but few. There is still, however, a considerable portion of the people who, though taking no open part, are yet dissatisfied. Some of these last named have real or imaginary grievances, of long standing to complain of, and nothing but the extinction of the governing powers of the Company will satisfy them. I came amongst them as free from prejudice as you can be, and determined to redress every grievance and meet their wishes in every reasonable way, but to no avail. I have already transmitted to the Board evidence in the 'Nor' Wester,' that our unpopularity arises entirely from the *system* of government, and not from any faults in its administrators.

"A continuance of this state of matters may lead to the formation of a provisional government by the people themselves, and to annexation to the United States, as have been threatened. With the opening up of the St. Paul's route, there has been a large increase of the 'American' element in the settlement; and in the enclosed copy of the 'Nor' Wester' of the 22nd July, you will observe that the United States Government is quietly recruiting for its army in British territory. This matter, I trust, may be in the meantime brought to the notice of the proper authorities pending further information upon my return to Red River.

"The trust which the Board has placed in my hands, and the confidence reposed in my ability to guide you in forming your plans for the future, impose on me no little responsibility and anxiety. I must relieve my shoulders of this weight by stating plainly my belief that the opening up of the country by waggon road and telegraph, and by the encouragement of settlement, must prove so far detrimental to the current commercial business of the Company as to render it difficult, if not impossible, to provide a fair dividend upon the portion of its capital embarked in the trade. I do not, however, the less recognize the necessity of opening up the country and its communications. It is not at all clear to my mind how you are to secure a remunerative dividend upon the extra sum to be embarked in the erection of the telegraph, formation of roads, &c., &c. In a commercial point of view,

I do not consider it safe to enter upon these extended operations till secure of a sufficient subsidy from the different Governments interested.

"Upon a mature consideration of the whole subject, I entirely concur in the views expressed by Mr. Johnstone in his letter, of which I have already sent only an *extract* to Sir Edmund Head, viz., that with the government of the country the territorial right should also revert to the Crown, upon whatever terms might be arranged. Anything short of a full measure of this sort would fail to satisfy the settlers and the public at large, who seem inclined to view with distrust the present position of Her Majesty's Government in its supposed alliance with the new Board of Direction.

"It is a question for consideration whether the northern region of the country beyond the limits of probable settlement should not still remain under the control of the Company, with such a monopoly of trade as would induce them to undertake the responsibility of managing the Indian tribes, and excluding the introduction of ardent spirits. I make this suggestion solely on behalf of the Indians, upon whom free intercourse with white men will, in my opinion, be ultimately destructive.

"Having already impressed upon you the necessity of procuring from Her Majesty's Secretary of State for the Colonies such instructions to the Governors of Vancouver's Island and British Columbia as may put an end to all proceedings against us in the local courts, and place us in possession of proper titles to our lands, I have now, in reminding you of the importance of the matter, to hand you the enclosed extract of a private letter which I received yesterday from Mr. D. Mactavish, senior member of our Board of Management in Victoria, which speaks for itself.

"Though I have marked this communication 'private,' I shall be obliged by your laying it before Sir Edmund Head, as I am so very hurried that I have not time at present to write officially to the Board.

"I remain, dear Sir, yours faithfully,
"A. G. DALLAS.

"E. WATKIN, Esq., London.

"P.S.—The undoubted discoveries of gold diggings in the Saskatchewan and other portions of the territory is another strong reason why the land should revert to and be administered by the Crown. Large grants to the Company would be looked upon with great disfavour by the public.

A. G. D."

Extract private letter from D. Mactavish, Esq., to A. G. Dallas, dated Victoria, Vancouver's Island, 13th July, 1863:—

"We hear nothing of our land question from the Governor, and there is no getting him to give titles for the Company's lands at Hope, Yale, and Langley. Orders have come out for the Royal Engineers to go to England immediately after the new year, so that Colonel Moodie and his staff of surveyors will do no more work, their time being so nearly up—this is worrying, but cannot be helped. The Governor has so much to do, making roads and so forth in British Columbia, that there is no drawing his attention to our matters, and when we do call on him to act, his invariable answer is, that he cannot get Moodie to do anything, and I daresay there is some truth in it, as it is shrewdly surmised that His Excellency has had more to do with the recall of the Engineers home than anyone else, and they all feel that they are leaving under a cloud."

"MONTREAL, "17_th Augt._ 1863.

MY DEAR MR. WATKIN,

"Along with this I send you a letter which, though marked private, treats only of our affairs, in such a manner that it may be laid before the Duke of Newcastle. It ought, I think, also to be laid before Sir Edmund Head, and I shall refer him to it for my views. It is very important that *the whole* of Johnstone's letter, and of my account of affairs at Red River, in regard to the Corbett riots, addressed to the Board, should be read along with the above letter. I do not think that we can ever make anything out of our lands, [Footnote: Experience has shown that this was an error.] and I am therefore strongly of opinion that they should be transferred to the Government upon certain terms, excepting only such lands around our forts as may be necessary for our business, and our farms, &c. in actual occupation.

"Although a great outcry has been raised against us on account of our being a 'stop in the way,' and enjoying a monopoly of trade, the cry is groundless. It may, therefore, be well for you to know that for a number of years past we have enjoyed *no monopoly* of trade whatever, and that there is no impediment to the settlement of the country by any one who pleases. A settler may squat wherever he thinks fit, without question, or being called upon to pay for lands yet unsurveyed, and of which the Indian titles are not yet extinguished. The small portion of surveyed land in the district of Assiniboin has been all long since occupied, though not paid for. With a recognized Government, there would be no difficulty in obtaining payment for these lands from the occupiers.

"In erecting the telegraph, the Indian titles to the land ought to be extinguished by annual payments; but the absence of a recognized and respected Government will be of itself a great bar to the successful erection of the apparatus, and the preserving it and the various stations in good order. Though, by increased energy and supervision, the fur trade *may* for a time be maintained, yet you must not *count upon* increased profits, as with the opening up of the country the furs are costing us more, and many of our posts are so distant that they cannot, from that and a variety of causes, be placed all at once upon a proper footing, and it is very difficult to exercise a proper supervision over them. It behoves the Company, therefore, to look out for other sources of profit. One of these is that of banking operations, both here and at Red River, and probably also at Victoria and at St. Paul, or other suitable locality in the U. S. On this head I may again address you from Red River, and Mr. Hopkins will afford you every information in regard to the prospects at this place, which are represented to be *very great*, when you come out in September.

"I am just about starting for Lake St. John's on the Saguenay River, and shall be absent about ten days. Upon my return I shall be ready to return to Red River—say, about the 1st September.

"Hoping you have had a pleasant passage, believe me,

"Yours very truly,
"E. WATKIN, Esq., London.

A. G. DALLAS.

"P.S.—I do not see how the Company can make anything out of placer gold diggings in such a country. The miners must be encouraged, and mining licences cannot be expected to do more than pay the cost of collection, magistracy, police, &c. The surrender of all this territory to the Crown, however, is a question to be dealt with by the Board. My aim is to disabuse you of the idea that the Company can of itself turn the territory to profit by sale of lands, mining rights, making roads, telegraph, &c.

A. G. D."

"MONTREAL, "18_th August,_ 1863.

MY DEAR MR. WATKIN,

"I left New York the evening of the day I parted from you, and reached this place on the Saturday night, *via* Boston and Portland, quite done up, having travelled two nights without undressing. The crowds were such as they were on the Hudson, and my mind often reverted to the good things I left at the door of the steward's pantry in the 'Scotia,'

"Brydges is not yet back from Quebec, and Hopkins and I start to-morrow for the Saguenay and St. John's Lake, where affairs require to be looked after.

"I have a letter to-day from St. Paul, in which Kittson says that the railroad gentry were anxiously expecting you, and making much capital out of the expected visit. He adds, 'The people of the State will not be so blind to their own interest as to decline to undertake to complete the portion of telegraph required. I have no doubt that a company could immediately be formed to accomplish the object.'

"Reverting to *my grievance* against the old Board, I wish to state what I complain of, viz., that I am charged with my passage across the Atlantic, and with a sum of L50, drawn to cover travelling expenses to Montreal. These were charged against me in February, 1862, and *have borne interest against me* since then.

"2ndly. I complain that I am charged interest on all sums drawn by me in each year—though *within* the amount of that year's salary. I surely am entitled to draw my pay from time to time to cover my expenditure? Officers in this country manage under the existing system of accounts to get the benefit of funds, even in excess of their pay, for two years without interest.

"3rdly. I had charge of the Puget Sound Company's affairs, which, with great labour, I placed upon a satisfactory footing—including the recovery of large sums from Government, and the terminating complicated and ruinous engagements with bailiffs or tenants and partners. I paid my expenses to Vancouver's Island, and devoted my whole time to the above matters, from 1st January, 1857, to the period of my leaving the Island in 1861, without having received one shilling of recompense. For the latter portion of the time I was paid by the H. B. Co., when I had the sole charge of its affairs during a most anxious and harassing period—constantly involved with all around me defending the rights of both companies.

"I say nothing as to my scale of pay under the old Board, but in making the changes which they did I think they ought not to have assumed that I should continue to act for the same remuneration.

"The pay was not my inducement to come to the country, but when overtures were first made to me, nothing being said to the contrary, I expected that I should at least receive the same pay and be placed on an equally good footing with the late Sir George Simpson, who for a number of years past lived at his ease at Lachine, and attended more, apparently, to his own affairs than to those of the Company. The latter bear evidence in every district of having been left entirely to themselves, while extreme discontent prevails in consequence of favouritism having regulated the promotions.

"Though not a ground of complaint, or a matter requiring redress— yet I may call attention to the inadequacy of my pay hitherto, when it is taken into account, that, from the unsettled life I have led in the Company's service, I have been obliged to neglect my private affairs. I have never received anything for outfit, and I was unlucky enough on my way out to have the most of our traps burnt the night before we embarked at Liverpool, in the Adelphi Hotel. The clothes ordered to replace these have all gone to the bottom in the 'Anglo Saxon.'

"I do not allude to these matters now with the view of obtaining higher pay for the future, as you know my intention is to return to England in the spring, and with the business in fair working order I can be of more avail there.

"It so happens that the fruits of my labours in America, both as regards the Hudson's Bay and Puget Sound Companies, will be reaped mainly by the present proprietors. At the same time, all such claims as the above ought to have been settled up to 31st May last by the old Board.

"A grumbling fellow is, I know, looked upon with great disfavour, especially when there is nothing more to be got out of him. This, therefore, is intended for your own eye alone. The substance of my complaint you may make use of as you see fit.

"Excuse this scrawl, and believe me in haste,
                    "Very truly yours,
                    "A. G. DALLAS.
"E. WATKIN, Esq., London."

"FORT GARRY, RED RIVER, "16th October, 1863.

MY DEAR MR. WATKIN,

"I arrived here on the 9th instant, after a wet, cold, and very miserable ride on horseback, of 520 miles, from St. Cloud, and was not sorry to get *home* again.

"After parting from you I went to the Saguenay River and Lake St. John's, where I need say no more than that my presence was very much wanted. No practical supervision had ever been exercised over the posts in that district, so far as I could learn.

"Brydges accompanied me to St. Paul; but I could not induce him to come any further, as he said he had a wife, eleven hundred children, and six miles of railway (more or less of either) to look after.

"You will doubtless have seen what I have written to the Board in regard to the telegraph across the Continent. The more I consider the subject the more satisfied I am that next year's operations ought to be confined to a survey of the line, and to bring the material to Fort Garry. In addition to sending a practical man, I would recommend that Mr. Wood himself come to Fort Carry. By following the 'Crow Wing' route he will get a perfect idea of the difficulties to be encountered along the whole line, as perfectly as a pinch of flour would represent the contents of the whole sack.

"I wish to call your particular attention to a letter which I have this day addressed to the Board, upon the subject of Indian claims to lands, and the officious part taken by the editor of the 'Nor' Wester,' in the hope that you may be able to exercise some influence over the Duke of Newcastle in prevailing upon him to discourage such men in some marked manner. As my residence in that country will now be a very short one, and as I have no pecuniary interest in the Company or the country, I write disinterestedly, and this knowledge may induce his Grace to pay some attention to my warnings. There will be serious trouble hereafter with the Indians and half-breeds, unless the local government is better supported, and such men as Ross and others are discountenanced.

"My interest in the old Company was a nominal one, merely sufficient to qualify myself for a seat on the Direction. That interest I sold out on accepting my present appointment. During my residence at Vancouver Island and on this side, I have been working for *honorary occupation*—my pay having formed no inducement, and being quite inadequate in countries where, in matters of expenditure, a dollar passes for little more than a shilling in England, and liable, as I was, from my wandering life, and with a family—to the losses incurred by a frequent breaking up of establishment. I allude to these matters, not for the purpose of complaint, but in support of the position that, as a disinterested and impartial administrator of the affairs entrusted to my charge, I was actuated by no selfish or pecuniary motives.

"The formation of the colony of British Columbia could not have been carried on as it was but for the assistance rendered by the H. B. Co., and I considered I was acting as much for the Government as for the Company, in the services then rendered, which, being unofficial, have not been in any way recognized. The unscrupulous way in which Douglas wished to saddle all expenses on the Company, and his attempts to deprive us of the lands which he himself made over to me as Company's property, led to serious differences between him and me, and which may have caused me to be looked on with probably a hostile eye by the Government, when I was actuated by the most impartial motives, and did at the same time everything I could to help the local government in its elections and other views, where our influence was overwhelming.

"Since assuming office on this side, I have been thoroughly disheartened, in the midst of very trying and difficult circumstances, between the Americans, Sioux Indians, and local disturbances on one hand, and the want of any encouragement or support by Government on the other hand. We have been not only ignored, but the worst enemies of the country have direct access to the Colonial Office, and though, probably, not attended to, are yet encouraged, from the fact of their petitions being received. No temptation would induce me to continue longer in office, even were it considered desirable that I should continue to hold my appointment, which for the good of the country I ought not. At the same time. Her Majesty's Government cannot continue much longer to ignore this territory. By such a course they are only sowing the seeds of further trouble, which I shall not be sorry to escape.

"I am afraid I have let my pen run away with me; but in our isolation local matters absorb our whole energies, and we look upon the affairs of Europe, or even the fall of Charleston, as of minor importance.

"Believe me, yours very truly,
"A. G. DALLAS.
"EDWARD WATKIN, Esq., London."

The extract from the "Grit" paper, the "Nor 'Wester" was as follows:—

THE HUDSON'S BAY TERRITORY

[*"From the 'Nor' Wester.'*]

IMPORTANT STATEMENT OF PEGOWIS, THE INDIAN CHIEF

"A few weeks ago, the venerable Chief of the Red River Indians, William King, or 'Pegowis,' left his home at the Indian Settlement—a most unusual thing for him—and came up to Fort Carry to make a formal statement, once for all, of the arrangement made by the late Earl of Selkirk with the Indians of this region in regard to their land. This statement, which he made voluntarily and deliberately, for the benefit of all whom it may concern, and for future reference if necessary, he desired to be published in this journal, and a copy thereof to be forwarded to the Duke of Newcastle. His immediate reason for doing this at present, is, he says, because he is now the only surviving Chief of the five who treated with Lord Selkirk, and as there have been many misrepresentations, he desires to see the facts placed on record before he passes off the earthly stage.

"The following is his account, taken down at his own request, by one of the editors of this journal:—

"'This transaction happened a long long time ago. I am now a very old man—I was then in the prime and vigour of manhood. We were taken by surprise when, all of a sudden, those who came before, disembarked. We had not been apprised of the coming of the foreigners—when they landed, we were greatly surprised and wondered what they meant. We were in this neighbourhood at the time. They only spoke among themselves, while the agents of the North-west Company were here. We did not know what it meant, when they asked the North-westers into the plain. As soon as they were done speaking among themselves the cannons were fired. We said, "What can it mean? It must be some great affair." The apparent harmony of the two Companies did not last long. The same summer differences arose which led to fighting: they fought twice that summer. We wondered at their proceedings—meeting in friendly council together, and then, immediately after, taking each others' lives!

"'As soon as the fighting was over, the report came that Lord Selkirk had arrived at Fort William. The ensuing winter, I called together all the Indians round here—those at Red Lake, at the Manitobah, and at the mouth of the Red River; I also invited the Crees on the Upper Assiniboine. "Come," said I—"assemble here—come and listen—this great man cannot be coming for nothing." A large multitude had gathered here early in the spring, when the Earl arrived with 30 canoes.

"'The day after he arrived, about noon, he sent for us. There were many of us, and we all left our tents at his call, and marched to the place of conference. There lay before us six kegs. He said—"Friends, I salute you." Immediately after the salutations, a day was fixed for a Council. Two personages were appointed to meet us. On the day named, one gentleman arrived, the other did not. He said—"Let us do without him who did not come." But the other soon came.

"'As soon as we had taken our seats, he said—"Friends, I have come to ask you about the lands, if you will give them to me. I do not want much—give what you choose. Will you give me as far from the river as you can distinguish the belly of a horse? It is to put settlers here— people far off, who have misery in their own country. This is why I want it. They will not trespass upon or spoil your lands that you retain outside of the limits I have named. I wish to put inhabitants upon it to cultivate the soil. I will endeavour to make the country like my own country. If I succeed in accomplishing what I intend, there will be merchants and traders from one end of the Settlement to the other, who will furnish you with goods. They will be at a little distance from each other, and you will have a chance of seeking out the best places for trading. All this I will do, if we can arrange about the land."

"'We were five Chiefs. I represented this district, the other Chiefs, other districts. The Earl said to me—"Speak you first—how much land will you give me?" I said—"I will speak last: let the others speak before me." KITCHE OTTAWA (Grand Courte-Oreille) spoke first. He mentioned Riviere aux Rose Aux. The Earl made no reply to this; whereupon the Chief mentioned as far as Pembina. The Earl said—Yes. Then he appealed to Mahkatayihkoonaya, *Le Grand Noir*, and asked what *he* would give. He said, from Pembina to Red Lake. Then he turned to *La Robe Noir*, who said as far as Portage Laprairie. At this the gentlemen hummed among themselves for a little, and the end was a question from the Earl. Is there no stream about there which you could mention as a limit? Mahkatayihkoonayai replied— Yes, there is la Riviere Champignon, a little beyond. The Earl said—There, that will be the limit. Then he asked Senna the Cree Chief, who said—No, I do not want agriculturists, I only want traders! The Earl said—Do you think you will ever see your trader again? (referring to the North-West Company). Never: he (the N. W. Co.) has done a bad thing—he has killed people. The Earl added—Then you do not wish to get a load of powder, a knife or a steel from *settlers*? Well, work diligently at the furs, and you will find a trader (meaning the H. B. Co.). The nobleman then said to me—Your turn, speak. I said—This is my place. How much will you give me for the part between this and the Rapids? I will then go below that. He said—a little further down, if you will. I replied— Yes, I will give you to the bend of the river above Sugar Point. That point I like very much—I cannot part with it— it is for my children. This satisfied the Earl, and he said further—Fear not: the people I plant here will not trouble your wild animals—they will merely work the soil. If they pass beyond the two-miles limit, do not allow them: they have no right there. At present we cannot conclude the arrangement, for I have nothing to pay you with. Let us leave the matter as it stands. I will come back, and then we will close the negociations. I am in a hurry, and cannot remain longer, but I will be sure to return. I want to go to the States and get cattle, that we may eat. That is the meat *we* eat. Perhaps even *you* may desire to get some of our cattle when you see them with the inhabitants here. But before I leave, I would like to give you something in consideration of the arrangement, which is to be made when I come back. What would you like to have? I said—Powder is useful to Indians, and tobacco they like— rum, too, they would fain have. We got what we asked. When we were done speaking, the Earl said—I want you to put your names to a paper, to show in England what we propose to do. We all said, No—wait till you come back. He asked us again to sign, but we refused, saying it would be time enough when the arrangement was completed. The Earl said—If your names were down, it would be easier for me to conclude the affair when I get back; besides, your young men would see, in the event of your deaths, what you had proposed to do. So we consented. Our names and marks were put down. We did not see why he pressed us to sign; but I now think it was in order to have us in his power, should he not do what he promised. He did not tell us what was in the paper, and I regret to say we did not even ask him what was in it. That was our ignorance. It was a great mistake, as after events showed; Lord Selkirk never came back, and never completed the arrangements about the lands. Our lands have not been bought from us—we have not received payment for them. We got some things from time to time—small supplies—but less and less as time rolled along, until we got nothing. These little presents we looked upon as a consideration for the use of our land until a bargain should be properly made. Besides, we were friendly to the settlers, and often saved them from harm. We thought this also a reason why we got things. For my part, there was a great reason why I should receive something, irrespective of the land. I was the means one time of saving Lord Selkirk's life. When he was going off, some half- breeds wished to kill him—they asked us to take pemican to an ambush ahead. I refused, and prevented them doing it. The Earl thanked me for this. The things we got, I repeat, were not in payment for our lands. We never sold them. We only proposed to do so; but the proposal was never carried out, as Lord Selkirk never came back. At the time we held council with him, there was no mention of the Hudson's Bay Company. They were not spoken of, or taken into account at all. All of a sudden, some years afterwards, it turned out that they were claiming to be masters here.

"'And now I wish this statement to go across the waters to my great and good Mother, and I pray her to cause a proper settlement to be made with us for our lands, so that our children, and our children's children, whose lands are being taken possession of by foreigners, may receive what is just and fair for the loss of their lands. I am old and feeble. I am the only surviving Chief of those who spoke to Lord Selkirk. I pray the great Mother, whose medal I have, to feel for us and help us.

"'(Signed)
"WILLIAM KING.'"

I should like here to add a very interesting letter from the agent of the Hudson's Bay Company in the United States:—

"52, CEDAR STREET, NEW YORK, "24th August, 1863.

DEAR SIR,

"If in addressing you, and expressing a sincere hope that you had a pleasant voyage to Liverpool per the steamer 'Scotia,' I seem to take too much liberty, I beg your pardon, as it is not my nature to be intrusive'.

"A friend, knowing that I am interested in the fur and skin trade, handed me, to-day, a copy of the (London) 'Economist' of 4th ulto., calling my attention to the article headed 'The Hudson's Bay Company.' As you are interested in the 'International Financial Society,' I thought it proper, even at this late date, to call your attention to the ignorance, if not malice, displayed by the editor.

"He says: '*Civilization destroys wild animals, we all know. An eager trade destroys them, too. The moment they become either valuable to man, or disagreeable to man, they cease to live.*' This sounds very like Dr. Johnson, *without Dr. Johnson:* for any farmer, trapper, or trader knows, that as the United States territory becomes settled, *furred* animals increase, because the refuse of civilization — the hen-roosts, the corn-fields, &c. — feed, directly and indirectly, the smaller animals, such as musquash, minks, foxes, racoons, opossums, skunks, and others; but the larger animals, such as buffaloes, bears, wolves, deer, elk, and others, would suffer from civilization were it not that they retire to the deserts, of which there will be enough for hundreds of years. Germany (it is said) produces more red-foxes than all America; and wolves are plentiful in France. As to an '*eager trade,*' or excessive hunting, destroying wild animals, it is impossible. If the 'catch' is excessive this year, the supply will exceed the demand, and prices will fall; the hunt will be less *eager* next year, and the animals will increase. In the March sales in London this year, there were only 3,094 skunks, and the demand was greater than the supply, so that the price was as high as 7s. 2d., which stimulated the United States collectors so much that very likely C. M. Lampson & Co. will have about 100,000 in their September sale, and prices will very likely fall to 1s., or lower. The result will be, that the skunks will live in peace, and increase and multiply for some years to come. The skunk is the most 'disagreeable' of animals to man; but it is not, therefore, destroyed. I have a catalogue (Row, Row, Goad & Reece, brokers) of a fur sale (by the candle) at the London Commercial Sale Room, Mincing Lane, on the 21st and 22nd March, 1821, which I compare below with catalogues of fur sales in London on 27th and 28th January, and 2nd, 3rd, 4th, 5th, 6th, 9th, and 11th March, 1863. I include January, because musquash and beaver are sold in that month. This statement does not embrace many other, but lesser, sales, which take place about the same time. *A vast quantity goes direct from here to Germany, which, in past years, went to London.*

1821 1863 — — — —

300 Musquash 1,289,773
6,380 Bears 3,962
None Beaver 95,557
8,290 Otter 12,933

3,280 Fisher 5,485
108,850 Martens 66,827
10,340 Minks 25,989
8,190 Foxes 28,369
2,500 Wolves 3,322
370 Wolverines 918
57,100 Racoons 204,888
None Skunks 3,094
None Opossums 560
None Badgers 1,370
23,000 Rabbits 46,151
5,631 Lynx 4,276
2,285 Cats 100

"Do the above data of forty-two years prove his assertion, that '*the fur trade, by which old profits were made, is a peculiar trade, tending to disappear*' or do they prove the reverse? The value or price of furs has steadily advanced also.

"Again: '*The hunters in the Hudson's Bay Company are as perishable a race as the animals hunted.*' Any trader knows this is false, except in the sense that we are all perishable. Applied to the United States Indians, it is true, from the cause assigned—rum—and worse causes— the vices of civilization. The cost of transportation to any portion of the Hudson's Bay territory heretofore has been so great that the rum used there must, *to be profitable,* be the purest that can be found, as there is water enough in Prince Rupert's Land with which to dilute it: so that what the Indian gets will not hurt him. The rivers in the United States (the Mississippi, the Missouri, the Yellowstone, the Arkansas, the Platte, and others) easily and cheaply carry '*rot- gut*' and death to the United States Indian. It seems to be the aim, and will be the gain, of the United States to exterminate the Indian; it ought to be the aim, and would be the gain, of the 'International Financial Society' to preserve him.

"Again: '*The climate forbids effectual fertility, and the distance from more habitable regions forbids effectual transit. The regions to be colonized are mostly very cold and very barren.*' If such is the case, of what value, applied to the new Company, are his assertions: 'Civilization destroys wild animals,' &c., and 'The hunters are as perishable,' &c.? The shareholders of the International Financial Society need have no fears of a failure of the fur trade, whatever may become of the 'sale of lands to new settlements, and the communication with British Columbia.'

"Again: '*In fact, the whole of the Red River region, such as it is, is best accessible from the United States, and, in case of war, would be exposed to an inroad from Minnesota, which adjoins it, without the possibility of aid from England.*' If the editor would undertake to travel from St. Paul to Pembina (about 600 miles), and also read the accounts of expeditions in pursuit of hostile Indians in Minnesota, he would quickly get rid of his fear of the Americans ever invading the British North Western Territory. One of my correspondents, an old Indian trader, writes me on the 30th ult. that he had just reached Pembina, after a 'dirty and disagreeable trip' of 25 days from St. Paul. So long as the British Indians are treated as they have been, they could, and they would, sweep Minnesota clean of any army, even although as invincible as the 'army of the Potomac.' Even if the redskins did not want help, the United States Indians would unite with the British Indians, in order to be revenged on the pale faces.

"To my mind, the worst feature in the new Company is that of allowing a foreigner (American) to hold office. He owes allegiance to the United States, *and his position gives him, knowledge which no American should possess.* 'Blood is thicker than water,' says the proverb. Besides, he has his own fur trade to attend to, and it is as true now, as it was in old times, that 'no man can serve two masters.' Although he should withdraw from his own firm, still 'blood is thicker than water.' As to the idea that, being in the fur trade, his experience and influence will benefit the new Company, will any furrier believe that? If the new Company will sell *all the furs they may have in their warehouse at the time of their regular sales,* HOLDING BACK NONE TO RAISE PRICES, they will always have the confidence of the buyers, always get full value, and never require the influence or experience of any man. I am, unfortunately for myself, not a shareholder in either the old or the new Company, but if I were, I would never rest satisfied while an American was in the management.

"Should you ever visit this city, I will feel honoured if you call on me, and be glad to hear from you, or be of service to you, at any time.

"With great respect, yours truly,
"WM. MACNAUGHTAN.

"E. W. Watkin, Esquire,
"Care Hon. Hudson's Bay Co., London."

"Dunean, Inverness,
"*29th October, 1872. Midnight.*

"My dear Sir Edward,

"Your letter reached me to-night, just in the nick of tune, and I enclose a letter which I was just about to send to the Editor of the London 'Standard.' Please send it to that or any other paper you like, barring the 'Times,' 'Saturday Review,' or 'Pall Mall Gazette.' I wrote another letter to the 'Times,' by which they corrected the discrepancy between their statement of the 18th Oct. and that of the 26th, that the Emperor had three channels to consider, but they never published or acknowledged my letter. I suppose because it exposed their blunder, and attacked the Government. I had written both to the 'Pall Mall' and 'Saturday Review' in summer, pointing out that we had virtually surrendered our position by departing from the words of the Treaty of 1846, on the American demand; but for certain reasons they would not publish the letter, and you will observe that they now refrain from laying the blame on our Government. You must read carefully the articles in the 'Times' of 18, 25 and 26 October, and in the 'Standard' of Saturday last. The 'Standard' attacks our Government fairly and ably. You may give my name as the writer of the enclosed letter, but not for publication, as I do not wish to make an enemy of the 'Times.' Send me a copy of the paper in which it may appear, or make any use you may like of it.

"I send you Tuckerman's Report. It is very satisfactory and re- assuring.

"I and some others here were much pleased at your expose of Fowler. He tried to set up here as the cock of all our railways, but he got the worst of it, and now he has got his quietus (that is, if you intend to let him rest), and has lost what he was very ambitious of, viz., high social position in the North. The Duke of Sutherland and others with whom he had gained a footing, have given him the cold shoulder, and I hope you will, by some means or other, enlighten his friends at the Egyptian Embassy. I may write a few lines to you tomorrow—being now in great haste,

"Yours truly,
"A. G. DALLAS.

"P.S.—I have not kept a copy of my San Juan letter, which I have only just hurriedly written."

"Dunean, Inverness, N.B.
"30 October, 1872.

"My dear Sir Edward,

"I wrote you a few hurried lines last night, with an enclosure, for publication, on the subject of the San Juan Arbitration.

"In the 'Times' of yesterday there is a letter signed 'The Ghost,' which, like all that the 'Times' permits to appear in its columns, is intended to throw dust in the eyes of the public, and direct attention from the real authors of the calamity, viz., the present Government, to that of Lord Aberdeen, or the German Emperor. The letter says, 'It is difficult to understand how an arbitrator could have accepted the task imposed upon him,' &c., alluding to his being debarred from deciding on the middle channel. An arbitrator will, of course, decide upon any conditions laid down; but is it not much more difficult to understand *why* we should have imposed such conditions on the arbitrator, on the demand of America, when we had the simple words of the Treaty to go by?

"The same letter, in alluding to Harney's invasion, says, 'It is pleasant to remember how promptly the American Government disavowed the act of their officer.' They never did so practically. They never withdrew the offensive troops, and forced us to maintain an equal number of men there since that date, at who can tell what cost to this country, and for what good end?

"In considering the main question, I all along held that we erred in claiming the Rosario Channel; for the reason that although I have no doubt whatever it was the channel intended in the Treaty (as against the Haro Channel, and excluding consideration of the middle channel), we cannot prove to demonstration that it was so. In getting up a grievance it is now doubly dangerous to claim it, as we know that, comparing it with the Haro Channel, it is decided against us, on what we must suppose to be good reasons. On the above contention, too, we absolve our Government of their blunder, and make a scape-goat of the Emperor of Germany. The words of the Treaty define the boundary to be a line drawn southerly through the centre of the channel from the centre of the channel separating Vancouver's Island from the mainland. Had the existence of three channels been then known, one of them—the one meant—would certainly have been named. Only one channel, Rosario, was known at the time, and the presumption is that it was meant. Making too sure of this we claimed it. It is, however, clear to my mind that the whole space between the Continent and Vancouver Island was treated as one channel. The Douglas, or middle channel, would then fulfil to the letter the words of the Treaty, and give us all we wanted, and still leave a channel free to the Americans. It was, I contend, a fatal error to abandon this position. Having done so and departed from the words of the Treaty, it was really a toss up which of the two other channels was selected by the umpire. Though we argued that Rosario was the only channel known at the time of the Treaty, the Americans argue (as you know how) that it was not so, and moreover that there was no intention to give us more than Vancouver Island. Why such a red herring as this was allowed to decoy us from the straight path of the words of the Treaty is what, in the words of Dundreary, 'No fellah can understand.'

"I hope I have made myself clear to you, and that you will ventilate the subject in Canada (through the press), where and in British Columbia there must be a deep feeling of disappointment and disgust, without a just appreciation of how we came to be so befooled.

"Don't forget to send me any paper that may be published on the subject through you. I feel as if I had been personally swindled and insulted, and have lost all confidence in our present ministry. I am writing this again at midnight, having been from home all day.

"Yours truly,
"A. G. DALLAS.

"P.S.—Laing passed through Inverness to-day, on his way to canvass the Orkneys."

At Victoria, Vancouver's Island, in a fine position fronting the sea, there is a granite pedestal to record the services of Sir James Douglas, K.C.B., the father-in-law of Governor Dallas. The services of Sir James, were rendered to the great benefit, not only of the island, but of British Columbia generally. The colonist roads along the great mountain sides, across rivers, and, through the forests, are of his doing, with the practical co-operation of ex-Governor Trutch, a very able engineer; and to Douglas, Trutch, Sir Mathew Begbie, Mr. Dunsmuir, and a few others, the order, obedience to the law, and progress of the country must be mainly attributed. But no stone marks the services of Governor Dallas; no honour was offered him by our Government at home; and he received scant reward from the Governor and Committee of the Hudson's Bay Company sitting in London. Surely those who have profited by his self-denying labours might consider whether his great services should be allowed to fall into oblivion for want of some adequate monument to his memory.

Chapter XVI
The Honorable Thomas d'Arcy McGee

Amongst the men, able and earnest, who carried the union of the British, separated, Provinces, and made the "Dominion," no man gave more soul and substance to the cause, by his eloquence, than Mr. d'Arcy McGee. His had been a chequered career. Beginning, like Sir George Etienne Cartier, in revolt against what he believed to be British tyranny, he ended his life, one of the most loyal, as he was one of the most eloquent, of Her Majesty's subjects. In 1848 he was one of the "Young Ireland" party, and became an exile from his country; and, at length, a denizen of the United States. From thence he came to Canada. In Canada he found all the liberty, without very much of the license, of politicians in the United States. In Canada he could think for himself; in the United States he must think the thoughts of some secret organization—or perish. In Canada he was welcomed, and soon made a position. I first met him, in a casual way, in Ireland, in the time of O'Connell, I think in 1844; and in 1861 I made his acquaintance, and I knew him well until his untimely death, by Fenian assassination, at Ottawa. He had faults—what politician has not? But he was honorable and kindly; no man's enemy, unless it were his own. He was remarkable in appearance; of middle height, very dark complexion, and with hair so curious and curly that he always joked about his popularity with the negroes of Canada. He told a story of a meeting in Montreal at a little public-house called "Uncle Tom's Cabin." Here he was addressing an audience containing a considerable number of dark men. Mr. Holton, his colleague, had orated about differential duties, very dry and Yankee-like, as usual. McGee followed in one of his arousing speeches. When he sat down, the respected negro landlord of "Uncle Tom's Cabin" got up to move a vote of confidence. And, according to McGee's story, said: "Bredren, we all on us heah came to dis land on a venter. Mr. McGee he came heah on a venter. Dis child know nothing bout dem disgreable duties. All we wants, bredren, is to pick out de best man. How is we to do dat? Bredren, best way is to follow de hair. Mr. McGee has hair like good nigger. Bredren, let us follow our hair." The result was McGee was adopted unanimously.

In 1865 a volume of Mr. McGee's speeches was published by Chapman & Hall. He did me the favour to dedicate the book to me in these, too complimentary, terms: "To E. W. Watkin, Esq., M.P. for Stockport, whose intimate connection with many great enterprises in which the material future of British America is interwoven, and, still more, whose high-spirited advocacy of a sound Colonial policy, both in and out of Parliament, has conferred lasting obligations, upon these Provinces, this volume is very sincerely and cordially dedicated."

The last speech in this volume was delivered in the Legislative Assembly of Canada, at Quebec, on the 9th February, 1865. I venture to record some portion of it in this book:—

"With your approbation, Sir, and the forbearance of the House, I will endeavour to treat this subject in this way:—First, to give some slight sketch of the history of the question; then to examine the existing motives which ought to prompt us to secure a speedy union of these Provinces; then to speak of the difficulties which this question has encountered before reaching its present fortunate stage; then to say something of the mutual advantages, in a social rather than political point of view, which these Provinces will have in their union; and, lastly, to add a few words on the Federal principle in general: when I shall have done. In other words, I propose to consider the question of Union mainly from within, and, as far as possible, to avoid going over the ground already so fully and so much better occupied by hon. friends who have already spoken upon the subject.

"So far back as the year 1800, the Hon. Mr. Uniacke, a leading politician in Nova Scotia at that date, submitted a scheme of Colonial Union to the Imperial authorities. In 1815, Chief Justice Sewell, whose name will be well remembered as a leading lawyer of this city, and a far-sighted politician, submitted a similar scheme. In 1822, Sir John Beverley Robinson, at the request of the Colonial Office, submitted a project of the same kind; and I need not refer to the report of Lord Durham, on Colonial Union, in 1839. These are all memorable, and some of them are great, names. If we have dreamed a dream of Union (as some of you gentlemen say), it is at least worth while remarking that a dream which has been dreamed by such wise and good men, may, for aught we know, or you know, have been a sort of vision—a vision foreshadowing forthcoming natural events in a clear intelligence: a vision—I say it without irreverence, for the event concerns the lives of millions living, and yet to come—resembling those seen by the Daniels and Josephs of old, foreshadowing the trials of the future, the fate of tribes and peoples, the rise and fall of dynasties. But the immediate history of the measure is sufficiently wonderful, without dwelling on the remoter predictions of so many wise men. Whoever, in 1862, or even in

1863, would have told us that we should see even what we see in these seats by which I stand—such a representation of interests acting together, would be accounted, as our Scotch friends say, 'half daft'; and whoever, in the Lower Provinces, about the same time, would have ventured to foretell the composition of their delegations which sat with us under this roof last October, would probably have been considered equally demented. But the thing came about; and if those gentlemen who have had no immediate hand in bringing it about, and, therefore, naturally feel less interest in the project than we who had, will only give us the benefit of the doubt— will only assume that we are not all altogether wrong-headed—we hope to show them still farther, though we think we have already shown them satisfactorily, that we are by no means without reason in entering on this enterprise. I submit, however, we may very well dismiss the antecedent history of the question for the present: it grew from an unnoticed feeble plant, to be a stately and flourishing tree; and, for my part, any one that pleases may say he made the tree grow, if I can only have hereafter my fair share of the shelter and the shade. But in the present stage of the question, the first real stage of its success —the thing that gave importance to theory in men's minds, was the now celebrated despatch, signed by two members of this Government and an honourable gentleman formerly their colleague (Hon. Mr. Ross), a member of the other House. I refer to the despatch of 1858. The recommendations in that despatch lay dormant until revived by the Constitutional Committee of last Session, which led to the Coalition, which led to the Quebec Conference, which led to the draft of the Constitution now on our table, which will lead, I am fain to believe, to the union of all these Provinces. At the same time that we mention these distinguished politicians, I think we ought not to forget those zealous and laborious contributors to the public press, who, although not associated with governments, and not themselves at the time in politics, yet greatly contributed to give life and interest to this question, and, indirectly, to bring it to the happy position in which it now stands. Of those gentlemen I will mention two. I do not know whether honorable gentlemen of this House have seen some letters on Colonial Union, written in 1855—the last addressed to the late Duke of Newcastle—by Mr. P. S. Hamilton, an able public writer of Nova Scotia, and the present Gold Commissioner of that province; but I take this opportunity of bearing my testimony to his well-balanced judgment, political sagacity, and the skilful handling the subject received from him at a very early period. There is another little book, written in English, six or seven years ago, to which I must refer. It is a pamphlet, which met with an extraordinary degree of success, entitled Nova Britannia, by my honorable friend, the member for South Lanark (Mr. Morris); and as he has been one of the principal agents in bringing into existence the present Government, which is now carrying out the idea embodied in his book, I trust he will forgive me if I take the opportunity, although he is present, of reading a single sentence, to show how far he was in advance, and how true he was to the coming event which we are now considering. At page 57 of his pamphlet—which I hope will be reprinted among the political miscellanies of the Provinces when we are one country and one people—I find this paragraph:—

"'The dealing with the destinies of a future Britannic empire, the shaping its course, the laying its foundations broad and deep, and the erecting thereon a noble and enduring superstructure, are indeed duties that may well evoke the energies of our people, and nerve the arms and give power and enthusiasm to the aspirations of all true patriots. The very magnitude of the interests involved, will, I doubt not, elevate many amongst us above the demands of mere sectionalism, and enable them to evince sufficient comprehensiveness of mind to deal in the spirit of real statesmen with issues so momentous, and to originate and develop a national line of commercial and general policy, such as will prove adapted to the wants and exigencies of our position.'

"We, on this side, Mr. Speaker, propose for that better future our plan of Union; and, if you will allow me, I shall go over what appear to me the principal motives which exist at present for that Union. My hon. friend the Finance Minister mentioned the other evening several strong motives for Union—free access to the sea, an extended market, breaking down of hostile tariffs, a more diversified field for labour and capital, our enhanced credit with England, and our greater effectiveness when united for assistance in time of danger. The Hon. President of the Council, last night also enumerated several motives for Union in relation to the commercial advantages which will flow from it, and other powerful reasons which may be advanced in favour of it. But the motives to such a comprehensive change as we propose, must be mixed motives—partly commercial, partly military, and partly political; and I shall go over a few—not strained or simulated— motives which must move many people of all these Provinces, and which are rather of a social, or, strictly speaking, political than of a financial kind. In the first place, I echo what was stated in the speech last night of my hon. friend, the President of the Council—that we cannot stand still; we cannot stave off some great change; we cannot stand alone—Province apart from Province— if we would; and that we are in a state of political transition. All, even honorable gentlemen who are opposed to this description of Union, admit that we must do something, and that that something must not be a mere temporary expedient. We are compelled, by warning voices from within and without, to make a change, and a great change. We all, with one voice who are Unionists, declare our conviction that we cannot go on as we have gone; but you, who are all anti-Unionists, say—'Oh! that is begging the question; you have not yet proved that.' Well, Mr. Speaker, what proofs do the gentlemen want? I presume there are the influences which determine any great change in the course of any individual or State. First—His patron, owner, employer, protector, ally, or friend; or, in our politics, 'Imperial connection.' Secondly—His partner, comrade, or fellow-labourer, or near neighbour; in our case, the United States. And, thirdly,—The man himself, or the Province itself. Now, all three have concurred to warn and force us into a new course of conduct. What are these warnings? We have had at least three. The first is from England, and is a friendly warning. England has warned us by several matters of fact, according to her custom, rather than verbiage, that the Colonies had entered upon a new era of existence, a new phase in their career. She has given us this warning in several different shapes—when she gave us 'Responsible Government'—when she adopted Free Trade—when she repealed the Navigation Laws—and when, three or four years ago, she commenced that series of official despatches in relation to militia and defence which she has ever since poured in on us, in a steady stream, always bearing the same solemn burthen- 'Prepare! prepare! prepare!' These warnings gave us notice that the old order of things between the Colonies and the Mother Country had ceased, and that a new order must take its place. About four years ago, the first despatches began to be addressed to this country, from the Colonial Office, upon the subject. From that day to this there has been a steady stream of despatches in this direction, either upon particular or general points connected with our defence; and I venture to say, that if bound up together, the despatches of the lamented Duke of Newcastle alone would make a respectable volume—all notifying this Government, by the advices they conveyed, that the relations—the military apart from the political and commercial relations—of this Province to the Mother Country had changed; and we were told in the most explicit language that could be employed, that we were no longer to consider ourselves, in relation to defence, in the same position we formerly occupied towards the Mother Country. Then, Sir, in the second place, there came what I may call the other warning from without—the American warning. Republican America gave us her notices in times past, through her press, and her demagogues, and her statesmen, but of late days she has given us much more intelligible notices—such as the notice to abrogate the Reciprocity Treaty, and to arm the lakes, contrary to the provisions of the Convention of 1818. She has given us another notice in imposing a vexatious passport system; another in her avowed purpose to construct a ship canal round the falls of Niagara, so as 'to pass war vessels from Lake Ontario to Lake Erie;' and yet another, the most striking one of all, has been given to us, if we will only understand it, by the enormous expansion of the American army and navy. I will take leave to read to the House a few figures which show the amazing, the unprecedented, growth (which has not, perhaps, a parallel in the annals of the past) of the military power of our neighbours, within the past three or four years. I have the details here by me, but shall only read the results, to show the House the emphatic terms of this most serious warning. In January, 1861, the regular army of the United States, including of course the whole of the States, did not exceed 15,000 men. This number was reduced, from desertion and other causes, by 5,000 men, leaving 10,000 men as the regular army of the United States. In December, 1862, that is, from January, 1861, to January, 1863, this army of 10,000 was increased to 800,000 soldiers actually in the service. No doubt there are exaggerations in some of these figures — the rosters were, doubtless, in some cases filled with fictitious names, in order to procure the bounties that were offered; but if we allow two-thirds as correct, we find that a people who had an army of 10,000 men in 1861, had in two years increased it to an army of 600,000 men. As to their munitions and stock of war material at the opening of the war — that is to say, at the date of the attack upon Fort Sumter — we find that they had of siege and heavy guns 1,952; of field artillery, 231; of infantry firearms, 473,000; of cavalry firearms, 31,000; and of ball and shell, 363,000. At the end of 1863, the latest period to which I have statistics upon the subject, the 1,052 heavy guns had become 2,116; the 231 field pieces had become 2,965; the 473,000 infantry arms had become 2,423,000; the 31,000 cavalry arms had become 369,000; and the 363,000 ball and shell had become 2,925,000. Now as to the navy of the United States, I wish also to show that this wonderful development of war power in the United States is the second warning we have had, that we cannot go on as we have gone. In January, 1861, the ships of war belonging to the United States were 83; in December, 1864, they numbered 671, of which 54 were monitors and iron-clads, carrying 4,610 guns, with a tonnage of 510,000 tons, and manned by a force of 51,000 men. These are frightful figures; frightful for the capacity of destruction they represent, for the heaps of carnage they represent, for the quantity of human blood spilt they represent, for the lust of conquest they represent, for the evil passions they represent, and for the arrest of the onward progress of civilization they represent. But it is not the figures which give the worst view of the fact — for England still carries more guns afloat even than our well-armed neighbours. It is the change which has taken place in the spirit of the people of the Northern States themselves which is the worst view of the fact. How far have they travelled since the humane Channing preached the unlawfulness of war — since the living Sumner delivered his addresses to the Peace Society on the same theme! I remember an accomplished poet, one of the most accomplished the New England States have ever produced, taking very strong grounds against the prosecution of the Mexican war, and published the Bigelow Papers, so well known in American literature, to show the ferocity and criminality of war. That poet made Mr. Bird-o'-Freedom Sawin sing:

> "'Ef you take a soaord an droar it,
> An go stick a feller thru,
> Guv'ment won't answer for it,
> God'll send the bill to you!'

This was slightly audacious and irreverent in expression, but it was remarkably popular in New England at that time. The writer is now one of the editors of a popular Boston periodical, and would be one of the last, I have no doubt, to induce a Northern soldier to withdraw his sword from the body of any unhappy Southerner whom he had, contrary to the poet's former political ethics, 'stuck thru.' But it is not the revolution wrought in the minds of men of great intelligence that is most to be deplored—for the powerful will of such men may compel their thoughts back again to a philosophy of peace; no, it is the mercenary and military interests created under Mr. Lincoln which are represented, the former by an estimated governmental outlay of above $100,000,000 this year, and the other by the 800,000 men, whose blood is thus to be bought and paid for; by the armies out of uniform who prey upon the army in uniform; by the army of contractors who are to feed and clothe and arm the fighting million; by that other army, the army of tax- collectors, who cover the land, seeing that no industry escapes unburthened, no possession unentered, no affection even, untaxed. Tax! tax! tax! is the cry from the rear! Blood! blood! blood! is the cry from the front! Gold! gold! gold! is the chuckling undertone which comes up from the mushroom *millionaires*, well named a shoddy aristocracy. Nor do I think the army interest, the contracting interest, and the tax-gathering interest, the worst results that have grown out of this war. There is another and equally serious interest— the revolution in the spirit, mind, and principles of the people, that terrible change which has made war familiar and even attractive to them. When the first battle was fought—when, in the language of the Duke of Wellington, the first 'butcher's bill was sent in' —a shudder of horror ran through the length and breadth of the country; but by- and-by, as the carnage increased, no newspaper was considered worth laying on the breakfast table unless it contained the story of the butchery of thousands of men.

'Only a thousand killed! Pooh, pooh, that's nothing!' exclaimed Mr. Shoddy, as he sipped his coffee—in his luxurious apartment; and nothing short of the news of ten or fifteen thousand maimed or slain in a day could satisfy the jaded palate of men craving for excitement, and such horrible excitement as attends the wholesale murder of their fellow-creatures. Have these sights and sounds no warning addressed to us? Are we as those who have eyes and see not; ears and hear not; reason, neither do they understand? If we are true to Canada—if we do not desire to become part and parcel of this people—we cannot overlook this, the greatest revolution of our own times. Let us remember this, that when the three cries among our next neighbours are shoddy, taxation, blood, it is tune for us to provide for our own security. I said, in this House, during the session of the year 1861, that the first gun fired at Fort Sumter had a 'message for us;' I was unheeded then; I repeat now that every one of the 2,700 great guns in the field, and every one of the 4,600 guns afloat, whenever it opens its mouth, repeats the solemn warning of England—-Prepare! prepare! prepare! I think, Sir, I am justified in regarding the American conflict, as one of the warnings we have received; and the third warning, that things cannot go on in this country as they are, is a warning voice from within—a warning voice from our own experience in the government of these Provinces. On these internal constitutional difficulties existing among ourselves, which were so fully exposed last evening by my hon. friend, the President of the Council, I need say little; they are admitted to have been real, not imaginary, on all hands. An illustration was used in another place in explaining this part of the subject by the venerable and gallant knight, our Premier, than which nothing could be more clear. He observed that when we had had five administrations within four years, it was full time to look out for some permanent remedy for such a state of things. True—most true— Constitutional Government among us had touched its lowest point when it existed only by the successful search of a messenger or a page after a member willingly or unwillingly absent from his seat. Any one might in those days have been the saviour of his country. All he had to do was, when one of the five successive Governments which arose in four years was in danger, to rise in his place, say 'Yea!' and *presto* the country was saved. This House was fast losing, under such a state of things, its hold on the country; the administrative departments were becoming disorganized under such frequent changes of chiefs and policies; we were nearly as bad as the army of the Potomac before its 'permanent remedy' was found in General Grant. Well, we have had our three warnings: one warning from within and two from without. Some honorable gentlemen, while admitting that we have entered, within the present decade, on a period of political transition, have contended that we might have bridged the abyss with that Prussian pontoon called a Zollverein. But if any one for a moment will remember that the trade of the whole front of New Brunswick and Nova Scotia gravitates at present along-shore to Portland and Boston, while the trade of Upper Canada, west of Kingston, has long gravitated across the lakes to New York, he will see, I think, that a mere Zollverein treaty without a strong political end to serve, and some political power at its back, would be, in our new circumstances, merely waste paper. The charge that we have not gone far enough—that we have not struck out boldly for a Consolidated Union, instead of a union with reserved local jurisdictions—is another charge which deserves some notice. To this I answer that if we had had, as was proposed, an Intercolonial Railway twenty years ago, we might by this time have been perhaps, and only perhaps, in a condition to unite into one consolidated government; but certain politicians and capitalists having defeated that project twenty years ago, special interests took the place great general interest might by this time have occupied; vested rights and local ambitions arose and were recognized; and all these had to be admitted as existing in a pretty advanced stage of development when the late conferences were called together. The lesson to be learned from this squandering of quarter centuries by British Americans is this, that if we lose the present propitious opportunity, we may find it as hard a few years hence to get an audience, even for any kind of union (except democratic union), as we should have found it to get a hearing last year for a legislative union, from the long period of estrangement and non- intercourse which had existed between these Provinces, and the special interests which had grown up in the meantime in each of them. Another motive to union, or rather a phase of the last motive spoken of, is this, that the policy of our neighbours to the south of us has always been aggressive. There has always been a desire amongst them for the acquisition of new territory, and the inexorable law of democratic existence seems to be its absorption. They coveted Florida, and seized it; they coveted Louisiana, and purchased it; they coveted Texas, and stole it; and then they picked a quarrel with Mexico, which ended by their getting California. They sometimes pretend to despise these our colonies as prizes beneath their ambition; but had we not had the strong arm of England over us we should not now have had a separate existence. The acquisition of Canada was the first ambition of the American Confederacy, and never ceased to be so, when her troops were a handful and her navy scarce a squadron. Is it likely to be stopped now, when she counts her guns afloat by thousands and her troops by hundreds of thousands? On this motive a very powerful expression of opinion has lately appeared in a published letter of the Archbishop of Halifax, Dr. Connolly. Who is the Archbishop of Halifax? In either of the coast colonies, where he has laboured in his high vocation for nearly a third of a century, it would be absurd to ask the question; but in Canada he may not be equally well known. Some of my honorable friends in this and the other House, who were his guests last year, must have felt the impress of his character as well as the warmth of his hospitality.

Well, he is known as one of the first men in sagacity, as he is in position, in any of these colonies; that he was for many years the intimate associate of his late distinguished *confrere*, Archbishop Hughes of New York; that he knows the United States as thoroughly as he does the Provinces,—and these are his views on this particular point; the extract is somewhat long, but so excellently put that I am sure the House will be obliged to me for the whole of it:—

"Instead of cursing, like the boy in the upturned boat, and holding on until we are fairly on the brink of the cataract, we must at once begin to pray and strike out for the shore by all means, before we get too far down on the current. We must at this most critical moment invoke the Arbiter of nations for wisdom, and abandoning in time our perilous position, we must strike out boldly, and at some risks, for some rock on the nearest shore—some resting-place of greater security. A cavalry raid, or a visit from our Fenian friends on horseback, through the plains of Canada and the fertile valleys of New Brunswick and Nova Scotia, may cost more in a single week than Confederation for the next fifty years; and if we are to believe you, where is the security even at the present moment against such a disaster? Without the whole power of the Mother Country by land and sea, and the concentration in a single hand of all the strength of British America, our condition is seen at a glance. Whenever the present difficulties will terminate—and who can tell the moment?—we will be at the mercy of our neighbours; and, victorious or otherwise, they will be eminently a military people, and with all their apparent indifference about annexing this country, and all the friendly feelings that may be talked, they will have the power to strike when they please; and this is precisely the kernel and the only touch-point of the whole question. No nation ever had the power of conquest that did not use it, or abuse it, at the very first favourable opportunity. All that is said of the magnanimity and forbearance of mighty nations can be explained on the principle of sheer inexpediency, as the world knows. The whole face of Europe has been changed, and the dynasties of many hundred years have been swept away within our own time, on the principle of might alone—the oldest, the strongest, and, as some would have it, the most sacred of all titles. The thirteen original States of America, with all their professions of self-denial, have been all the time, by money, power, and by war, and by negociation, extending their frontier until they more than quadrupled their territory within sixty years; and believe it who may, are they now of their own accord to come to a full stop? No; as long as they have the power, they must go on onward: for it is the very nature of power to grip whatever is within its reach. It is not their hostile feelings, therefore, but it is their power, and only their power, I dread; and I now state it as my solemn conviction, that it becomes the duty of every British subject in these Provinces to control that power, not by the insane policy of attacking or weakening them, but by strengthening ourselves—rising, with the whole power of Britain at our back, to their level, and so be prepared for any emergency. There is no sensible or unprejudiced man in the community who does not see that vigorous and timely preparation is the only possible means of saving us from the horrors of a war such as the world has never seen. To be fully prepared is the only practical argument that can have weight with a powerful enemy, and make him pause beforehand and count the cost. And as the sort of preparation I speak of is utterly hopeless without the union of the Provinces, so at a moment when public opinion is being formed on this vital point, as one deeply concerned, I feel it a duty to declare myself unequivocally in favour of Confederation as cheaply and as honourably as possible—but Confederation at all hazards and at all reasonable sacrifices.

"'After the most mature consideration, and all the arguments I have heard on both sides for the last month, these are my inmost convictions on the necessity and merits of a measure which alone, under Providence, can secure to us social order and peace, and rational liberty, and all the blessings we now enjoy, under the mildest Government and the hallowed institutions of the freest and happiest country in the world.'

"These are the words of a statesman—of a mitred statesman—one of that order of mighty men, powerful in their generation, whose statesmanly gifts have been cast in the strong mould of theological discipline— such men as were Ximenes and Wolsey, Laud and Knox. The next motive for Union to which I shall refer is, that it will strengthen rather than weaken the connection with the Empire, so essential to these rising Provinces. Those who may be called, if there are any such, the anti- Unionists, allege, that this scheme now submitted will bring separation in its train. How, pray? By making these countries more important, will you make them less desirable as connections to England? By making their trade more valuable, will you make her more anxious to get rid of it? By reducing their Federal tariff, will you lessen their interest for England? By making them stronger for each other's aid, will you make her less willing to discharge a lighter than a greater responsibility? But if the thing did not answer itself, England has answered that she 'cordially approves' of our plan of Union,—and she has always been accounted a pretty good judge of her own Imperial interests. She does not consider our union inimical to those interests. Instead of looking upon it with a dark and discouraging frown, she cheers us on by her most cordial approval, and bids us a hearty 'God speed' in the new path we have chosen to enter. But I put it on provincial grounds as well. When Canada proposed to move, in 1859, Newfoundland alone responded; when

Nova Scotia moved, in 1860, New Brunswick alone agreed to go with her; at all events, Canada did not then concur. Of late years the language of the Colonial Office, of Mr. Labouchere, of Sir Bulwer Lytton, and of the lamented Duke of Newcastle, was substantially: 'Agree among yourselves, gentlemen, and we will not stand in the way.' Ah! there was the rub—'Agree among yourselves!' Easier said than done, with five Colonies so long estranged, and whose former negotiations had generally ended in bitter controversies. Up to the last year there was no conjunction of circumstances favourable to bringing about this union, and probably if we suffer this opportunity to be wasted we shall never see again such another conjunction as will enable us to agree, even so far, among ourselves. By a most fortunate concurrence of circumstances—by what I presume to call, speaking of events of this magnitude, a providential concurrence of circumstances—the Government of Canada was so modified last spring as to enable it to deal fearlessly with this subject, at the very moment when the coast Colonies, despairing of a Canadian union, were arranging a conference of their own for a union of their own. Our Government embraced among its members from the western section the leaders of the former Ministry and former Opposition from that section. At the time it was formed it announced to this House that it was its intention, as part of its policy, to seek a conference with the Lower Colonies, and endeavour to bring about a general union. This House formally gave the Government its confidence after the announcement of that policy, and although I have no desire to strain terms, it does appear to me that this House did thereby fully commit itself to the principle of a union of the Colonies, if practicable. Everything we did was done in form and with propriety, and the result of our proceedings is the document that has been submitted to the Imperial Government as well as to this House, and which we speak of here as a treaty. And that there may be no doubt about our position in regard to that document, we say, Question it you may, reject it you may, or accept it you may, but alter it you may not. It is beyond your power, or our power, to alter it. There is not a sentence—not even a word—you can alter without desiring to throw out the document. Alter it, and we know at once what you mean—you thereby declare yourselves against the only possible union. On this point, I repeat, after all my hon. friends who have already spoken, for one party to alter a treaty, is, of course, to destroy it. Let us be frank with each other; you do not like our work, nor do you like us who stand by it, clause by clause, line by line, and letter by letter. Well, we believe we have here given to our countrymen of all the Provinces the possible best—that we have given them an approximation to the right— their representatives and ours have laboured at it, letter and spirit, form and substance, until they found this basis of agreement, which we are all confident will not now, nor for many a day to come, be easily swept away. And first, I will make a remark to some of the French Canadian gentlemen who are said to be opposed to our project, on French Canadian grounds only. I will remind them, I hope not improperly, that every one of the Colonies we now propose to re-unite under one rule—in which they shall have a potential voice—were once before united as New France. Newfoundland, the uttermost, was theirs, and one large section of its coast is still known as the 'French shore;' Cape Breton was theirs till the final fall of Louisburgh; Prince Edward Island was their Island of St. Jean; Charlottetown was their Port Joli; and Frederickton, the present capital of New Brunswick, their St. Anne's; in the heart of Nova Scotia was that fair Acadian land, where the roll of Longfellow's noble hexameters may be heard in every wave that breaks upon the base of Cape Blomedon. In the northern counties of New Brunswick, from the Mirimichi to the Metapediac, they had their forts and farms, their churches and their festivals, before the English speech had ever once been heard between those rivers. Nor is that tenacious Norman and Breton race extinct in their old haunts and homes. I have heard one of the members for Cape Breton speak in high terms of that portion of his constituency; and I believe I am correct in saying that Mr. Le Visconte, the late Finance Minister of Nova Scotia, was, in the literal sense of the term, an Acadian. Mr. Cozzans, of New York, who wrote a very readable little book the other day about Nova Scotia, describes the French residents near the basin of Minas, and he says, especially of the women, 'they might have stepped out of Normandy a hundred years ago!' In New Brunswick there is more than one county, especially in the North, where business, and law, and politics, require a knowledge of both French and English.

"I think it is to their honour, that the Highlanders in all the Lower Provinces preserve faithfully the religion, as well as the language and traditions of their fathers. The Catholic Bishop of Charlottetown is a McIntyre; his Right Rev. Brother of Arichat (Cape Breton) is a McKinnon; and in the list of the clergy, I find a. constant succession of such names as McDonald, McGillis, McGillvary, McLeod, McKenzie, and Cameron—all 'Anglo-Saxons' of course, and mixed up with them Fourniers, Gauvreaus, Paquets, and Martells, whose origin is easy to discover. Another of the original elements of that population remains to be noticed—the U. E. Loyalists, who founded New Brunswick (as they founded Upper Canada), for whom New Brunswick was made a separate Province in 1784, as Upper Canada was for their relatives in 1791. Their descendants still flourish in the land, holding many positions of honour; and as a representative of the class, I shall only mention Judge Wilmot, who the other day declared, in charging one of his grand juries, that if it were necessary to carry Confederation in New Brunswick, so impressed was he with the necessity of the measure, to the very existence of British laws and British institutions on this continent, he was prepared to quit the Bench and return to politics. There are other elements also not to be overlooked. The thrifty Germans of Lunenberg, whose homes are the neatest upon the land, as their fleet is the tightest on the sea; and other small sub-divisions; but I shall not prolong this analysis. I may observe, however, that this population is almost universally a native population of three or four or more generations. In New Brunswick, at the most there is about twelve per cent. of an immigrant people; in Nova Scotia, about eight; in the two Islands, even less. In the eye of the law, we admit no disparity between natives and immigrants in this country; but it is to be considered that where men are born in the presence of the graves of their fathers, for even a few generations, the influence of the fact is great in enhancing their attachment to that soil. I admit, for my part, as an immigrant, of no divided allegiance to Canada and her interest; but it would be untrue and paltry to deny a divided affection between the old country and the new. Kept within just bounds, such an affection is reasonable, is right and creditable to those who cherish it. Why I refer to this broad fact, which distinguishes the populations of all the four seaward Provinces, as much as it does Lower Canada herself, is, to show the fixity and stability of that population; to show that they are by birth British-Americans; that they can nearly all, of every origin, use that proud phrase when they look daily from their doors, 'This is my own, my native land.' Let but that population and ours come together for a generation or two—such are the elements that compose, such the conditions that surround it—and their mutual descendants will hear with wonder, when the history of these present transactions is written, that this plan of union could ever have been seriously opposed by statesmen in Canada or elsewhere. I am told, however, by one or two members of this House, and by exclusive-minded Canadians out of it, that they cannot get up any patriotic feeling about this union with New Brunswick or Nova Scotia, and that they cannot look with any interest at those Colonies, with which we have had hitherto so little association. 'What's Hecuba to me, or I to Hecuba!' Well, I answer to that, Know them, and my word for it, you will like them. I have made several journeys there, and I have seen much of the people, and the more I have seen of them, the more I respected and esteemed them. I say, then, to these gentlemen, that if you desire any patriotism on the subject; if you want to stir up a common sentiment of affection between these people and ourselves, bring us all into closer relation together, and, having the elements of a vigorous nationality within us, each will find something to like and respect in the other; mutual confidence and respect will follow, and the feeling of being engaged in a common cause for the good of a common nationality will grow up of itself without being forced by any man's advocacy. The thing who shuts up his heart against his kindred, his neighbours, and his fellow-subjects, may be a very pretty fellow at a parish vestry, but do you call such a forked- radish as that, a man? Don't so abuse the noblest word in the language.

"But there is one special source of wealth to be found in the Maritime Provinces, which was not in any detail exhibited by my hon. friends—I allude to the important article of coal. I think there can be no doubt that, in some parts of Canada, we are fast passing out of the era of wood as fuel, and entering on that of coal. In my own city every year, there is great suffering among the poor from the enormous price of fuel, and large sums are paid away by national societies and benevolent individuals, to prevent whole families perishing for want of fuel. I believe we must all concur with Sir William Logan, that we have no coal in Canada, and I may venture to state, on my own authority, another fact, that we have—a five months' winter, generally very cold.

"Sir W. E. Logan demonstrated by a laborious survey the thickness or depth of the whole group in Northern Nova Scotia to be over 2 3/4 miles, an amount which far exceeds anything seen in the coal formation in other parts of North America; in this group there are seventy-six coal beds one above the other.

"These exhaustless coal fields will, under our plan—which is in fact our Reciprocity Treaty with the Lower Provinces—become, hereafter, the great resource of our towns for fuel. I see the cry is raised below by the anti-Unionists, that to proceed with Confederation would be to entail the loss of the New England market for their coals. I do not quite see how they make this out, but even an anti-Unionist might see that the population of Canada is within a fraction of that of all New England put together, that we consume in this country as much fuel per annum as they do in New England; and, therefore, that we offer them a market under the Union equal to that which these theorizers want to persuade their followers they would lose. Sir, another cry raised by the anti-Unionists below is, that they would have to fight for the defence of Canada—a very specious argument. What, Sir, three millions and one million unite, and the one million do the fighting for all! In proportion to their numbers no doubt these valiant gentlemen will have to fight, if fighting is to be done, but not one man or one shilling more than Canada, *pro rata*, will they have to risk or spend. On the contrary, the greater community, if she should not happen to be first attacked, would be obliged to fight for them, and in doing so, I do not hesitate to say, on far better authority than my own, that the man who fights for the valley and harbour of St. John, or even for Halifax, fights for Canada. I will suppose another not impossible case. I will suppose a hostile American army, on a fishery or any other war, finding it easier and cheaper to seize the Lower Colonies by land than by sea, by a march from a convenient rendezvous on Lake Champlain, through Lower Canada, into the upper part of New Brunswick, and so downward to the sea—a march like Sherman's march from Knoxville to Savannah. While we obstructed such a march by every means in our power, from the Richelieu to Riviere du Loup, whose battles would we be fighting then? Why, the seaports aimed at, for our common subjugation. But the truth is, all these selfish views and arguments are remarkably short-sighted, unworthy of the subject, and unworthy even of those who use them. In a commercial, in a military, in every point of view, we are all, rightly considered, dependent on each other. Newfoundland dominates the Gulf, and none of us can afford to be separated from her. Lord Chatham said he would as soon abandon Plymouth as Newfoundland to a foreign power, and he is thought to have understood how to govern men. Nova Scotia and New Brunswick are Siamese twins, held together by that ligature of land between Baie Verte and Cumberland Basin, and the fate of the one must follow the fate of the other. Prince Edward Island is only a little bit broken off by the Northumberland Strait from those two bigger brethren, and Upper and Lower Canada are essential to each other's prosperity.

"If the honest and misguided would but reflect for a moment the risks they run by defeating, or even delaying this measure, I am sure they would, even yet, retract. If we reject it now, is there any human probability that we shall ever see again so propitious a set of circumstances to bring about the same results? How they came about we all know. The strange and fortunate events that have occurred in Canada; the extraordinary concessions made by the leaders of the Governments below—Dr. Tupper, the Nova Scotian Premier, for instance, admitting to his confidence, and bringing with him here as his co- representatives, the Hon. Messrs. Archibald and McCully, two of his most determined political opponent—can we ever expect, if we reject this scheme, that the same or similar things will occur again to favour it? Can we expect to see the leader of the Upper Canadian Conservative party and the leader of the Upper Canadian Liberals sitting side by side again, if this project fails to work out, in a spirit of mutual compromise and concession, the problem of our constitutional difficulties? No, Sir, it is too much to expect. Miracles would cease to be miracles if they were events of every-day occurrence; the very nature of wonders requires that they should be rare; and this is a miraculous and wonderful circumstance, that men at the head of the Governments in five separate Provinces, and men at the head of the parties opposing them, all agreed at the same time to sink party differences for the good of all, and did not shrink, at the risk of having their motives misunderstood, from associating together for the purpose of bringing about this result. I have asked, Sir, what risks do we run if we reject this measure? We run the risk of being swallowed up by the spirit of universal democracy that prevails in the United States. Their usual and favourite motto is—

"'No pent-up Utica contracts our powers,
But the whole boundless continent is ours.

That is the popular paraphrase of the Monroe doctrine. And the popular voice has favoured—aye, and the greatest statesmen among them have looked upon it as inevitable—an extension of the principles of democracy over this continent. Now, I suppose a universal democracy is no more acceptable to us than a universal monarchy in Europe would have been to our ancestors; yet for three centuries—from Charles V. to Napoleon—our fathers combated to the death against the subjugation of all Europe to a single system or a single master, and heaped up a debt which has since burdened the producing classes of the Empire with an enormous load of taxation, which, perhaps, none other except the hardy and ever-growing industry of those little islands could have borne up under. The idea of a universal democracy in America is no more welcome to the minds of thoughtful men among us than was that of a universal monarchy to the minds of the thoughtful men who followed the standard of the third William, or who afterwards, under the great Marlborough, opposed the armies of the particular dynasty that sought to place Europe under a single dominion.

"But if we are to have a universal democracy on this continent, the Lower Provinces—the smaller fragments—will be 'gobbled up' first, and we will come in afterwards by way of dessert. The proposed Confederation will enable us to bear up shoulder to shoulder; to resist the spread of this universal democracy doctrine; it will make it more desirable to maintain on both sides the connection that binds us to the parent State; it will raise us from the position of mere dependent colonies to a new and more important position; it will give us a new lease of existence under other and more favourable conditions; and resistance to this project, which is pregnant with so many advantages to us and to our children, means simply this, ultimate union with the United States. But these are small matters, wholly unworthy of the attention of the Smiths, and Annands, and Palmers, who have come forward to forbid the banns of British-American Union. Mr. Speaker, before I draw to a close the little remainder of what I have to say— and I am sorry to have detained the House so long—

I beg to offer a few observations *apropos* of my own position as an English-speaking member for Lower Canada. I venture, in the first place, to observe that there seems to be a good deal of exaggeration on the subject of race, occasionally introduced, both on the one side and the other, in this section of the country. I congratulate my honorable friend, the Attorney-General for this section, on his freedom from such prejudices in general, though I still think in matters of patronage and the like he always looks first to his own compatriots for which neither do I blame him. But this theory of race is sometimes carried to an anti-christian and unphilosophical excess. Whose words are these—'God hath made of one blood all nations that dwell on the face of the earth'? Is not that the true theory of race? For my part, I am not afraid of the French Canadian majority in the future local government doing injustice, except accidentally; not because I am of the same religion as themselves; for origin and language are barriers stronger to divide men in this world than is religion to unite them. Neither do I believe that my Protestant compatriots need have any such fear. The French Canadians have never been an intolerant people; it is not in their temper, unless they had been persecuted, perhaps, and then it might have been as it has been with other races of all religions.

"All who have spoken on this subject have said a good deal, as was natural, of the interests at stake in the success or failure of this plan of Confederation. I trust the House will permit me to add a few words as to the principle of Confederation considered in itself. In the application of this principle to former constitutions there certainly always was one fatal defect, the weakness of the central authority. Of all the Federal constitutions I have ever heard or read of, this was the fatal malady: they were short-lived, they died of consumption. But I am not prepared to say that because the Tuscan League elected its chief magistrates but for two months and lasted a century, that therefore the Federal principle failed. On the contrary, there is something in the frequent, fond recurrence of mankind to this principle, among the freest people, in their best times and in their worst dangers, which leads me to believe, that it has a very deep hold in human nature itself—an excellent basis for a government to have. But, indeed, Sir, the main question is the due distribution of powers in a Federal Union—a question I dare not touch to-night, but which I may be prepared to say something on before the vote is taken. The principle itself seems to me to be capable of being so adapted as to promote internal peace and external security, and to call into action a genuine, enduring, and heroic patriotism. It is a fruit of this principle that makes the modern Italian look back with sorrow and pride over a dreary waste of seven centuries to the famous field of Legnano; it was this principle kindled the beacons which yet burn on the rocks of Uri; it was this principle that broke the dykes of Holland and overwhelmed the Spanish with the fate of the Egyptian oppressor. It is a principle capable of inspiring a noble ambition and a most salutary emulation. You have sent your young men to guard your frontier. You want a principle to guard your young men, and thus truly defend your frontier. For what do good men who make the best soldiers fight? For a line of scripture or chalk line—for a text or for a pretext? What is a better boundary between nations than a parallel of latitude, or even a natural obstacle?—what really keeps nations intact and apart?—a principle. When I can hear our young men say as proudly, 'our Federation,' or 'our Country,' or 'our Kingdom,' as the young men of other countries do, speaking of their own, then I shall have less apprehension for the result of whatever trials the future may have in store for us. It has been said that the Federal Constitution of the United States has failed. I, Sir, have never said it. The Attorney- General West told you the other night that he did not consider it a failure; and I remember that in 1861, when in this House I remarked the same thing, the only man who then applauded the statement was the Attorney-General West,—so that it is plain he did not simply adopt the argument for use the other night when advocating a Federal Union among ourselves. It may be a failure for us, paradoxical as this may seem, and yet not a failure for them. They have had eighty years' use of it, and having discovered its defects, may apply a remedy and go on with it eighty years longer. But we also were lookers on, who saw its defects as the machine worked, and who have prepared contrivances by which it can be improved and kept in more perfect order when applied to ourselves. And one of the foremost statesmen in England, distinguished alike in politics and literature, has declared, as the President of the Council informed us, that we have combined the best parts of the British and the American systems of government; an opinion deliberately formed at a distance, without prejudice, and expressed without interested motives of any description. We have, in relation to the head of the Government, in relation to the judiciary, in relation to the second chamber of the Legislature, in relation to the financial responsibility of the General Government, and in relation to the public officials whose tenure of office is during good behaviour instead of at the caprice of a party—in all these respects we have adopted the British system; in other respects we have learned something from the American system, and I trust and believe we have made a very tolerable combination of both.

"The principle of Federation is a generous principle. It is a principle that gives men local duties to discharge, and invests them at the same time with general supervision, and excites a healthy sense of responsibility and comprehension. It is a principle that has produced a wise and true spirit of statesmanship in all countries in which it has ever been applied. It is a principle eminently favourable to liberty, because local affairs are left to be dealt with by local bodies, and cannot be interfered with by those who have no local interest in them, while matters of a general character are left exclusively to a General Government. It is a principle inseparable from every government that ever gave extended and important services to a country, because all governments have been more or less confederations in their character. Spain was a Federation, for although it had a king reigning over the whole country, it had its local governments for the administration of local affairs. The British Isles are a *quasi*-Confederation, and the old French dukedoms were confederated in the States-General. It is a principle that runs through all the history of civilization in one form or another, and exists alike in monarchies and democracies; and having adopted it as the principle of our future government, there were only the details to arrange and agree upon. Those details are before you. It is not in our power to alter any of them even if the House desires it. If the House desires, it can *reject* the treaty, but we cannot, nor can the other Provinces, which took part in its negociation, consent that it shall be *altered* in the slightest particular.

"Mr. Speaker, I am sorry to have detained the House so long, and was not aware till I had been some time on my legs, that my physical strength was so inadequate to the exposition of those few points which, not specially noticed by my predecessors in this debate, I undertook to speak upon. We stand at present in this position: we are bound in honour, we are bound in good faith, to four Provinces occupied by our fellow colonists, to carry out the measure of Union agreed upon here in the last week of October. We are bound to carry it to the foot of the Throne, and ask there from Her Majesty, according to the first resolution of the Address, that she will be graciously pleased to direct legislation to be had on this subject. We go to the Imperial Government, the common arbiter of us all, in our true Federal metropolis— we go there to ask for our fundamental Charter. We hope, by having that Charter, which can only be amended by the authority that made it, that we will lay the basis of permanency for our future government. The two great things that all men aim at in free government, are liberty and permanency. We have had liberty enough—too much, perhaps, in some respects—but, at all events, liberty to our hearts' content. There is not on the face of the earth a freer people than the inhabitants of these Colonies. But it is necessary there should be respect for the law, a high central authority, the virtue of civil obedience, obeying the law for the law's sake; for even when a man's private conscience may convince him sufficiently that the law in some cases may be wrong, he is not to set up his individual will against the will of the country, expressed through its recognized constitutional organs. We need in these Provinces, and we can bear, a large infusion of authority. I am not at all afraid this Constitution errs on the side of too great conservatism. If it be found too conservative now, the downward tendency in political ideas which characterises this democratic age is a sufficient guarantee for amendment. Its conservatism is the principle on which this instrument is strong, and worthy of the support of every colonist, and through which it will secure the warm approbation of the Imperial authorities. We have here no traditions and ancient venerable institutions; here, there are no aristocratic elements hallowed by time or bright deeds; here, every man is the first settler of the land, or removed from the first settler one or two generations at the farthest; here, we have no architectural monuments calling up old associations; here, we have none of those old popular legends and stories which in other countries have exercised a powerful share in the government; here, every man is the son of his own works. We have none of those influences about us which, elsewhere, have their effect upon government just as much as the invisible atmosphere itself tends to influence life, and animal and vegetable existence. This is a new land—a land of young pretensions because it is new; because classes and systems have not had that time to grow here naturally. We have no aristocracy but of virtue and talent, which is the best aristocracy, and is the old and true meaning of the term. There is a class of men rising in these Colonies, superior in many respects to others with whom they might be compared. What I should like to see, is—that fair representatives of the Canadian and Acadian aristocracy should be sent to the foot of the Throne with that scheme, to obtain for it the royal sanction—a scheme not suggested by others, or imposed upon us, but one the work of ourselves, the creation of our own intellect and of our own free, unbiassed, and untrammelled will. I should like to see our best men go there, and endeavour to have this measure carried through the Imperial Parliament—going into Her Majesty's presence, and by their manner, if not actually by their speech, saying—'During Your Majesty's reign we have had responsible Government conceded to us: we have administered it for nearly a quarter of a century, during which we have under it doubled our population, and more than quadrupled our trade. The small Colonies which your ancestors could hardly see on the map, have grown into great communities. A great danger has arisen in our near neighbourhood. Over our homes a cloud hangs, dark and heavy. We do not know when it may burst. With our own strength we are not able to combat against the storm; but what we can do, we will do cheerfully and loyally. We want time to grow; we want more people to fill our country, more industrious families of men to develop our resources; we want to increase our prosperity; we want more extended trade and commerce; we want more land tilled—more men established through our wastes and wildernesses. We of the British North-American Provinces want to be joined together, that, if danger comes, we can support each other in the day of trial. We come to Your Majesty, who have given us liberty, to give us unity, that we may preserve and perpetuate our freedom; and whatsoever charter, in the wisdom of Your Majesty and of Your Parliament, you give us, we shall loyally obey and observe as long as it is the pleasure of Your Majesty and Your Successors to maintain the connection between Great Britain and these Colonies.'"

Chapter XVII
1851.—First Visit to America: a Reason for it

My first visit to America was mainly induced by a misfortune which happened to me in the spring of 1846. The year 1845 had been one of excitement, and my hands had been very full at that time. I was to a great extent a water drinker. I had the habit of sticking to my work, various and complicated as much of it was, day by day, until that day's work was done. It often happened that I forgot to eat the modest lunch carefully put in my pocket by my wife on my leaving home, in early morning. And often and often I did not get home till nine o'clock at night, so tired that occasionally I fell asleep over my dinner; and my wife, seeing my condition of fatigue, got into the habit of carving our frugal joints, a habit which has become permanent. Thus, when I say, as a bit of pleasantry, that where the lady carves, you learn who is the master of the house, Lady Watkin will retort by mentioning this old story of past and anxious times.

Well, the Trent Valley Railway, of which I was Secretary and Manager, was sold, at a large profit—I think 438,000_l._—to the London and Birmingham and Grand Junction Companies, then about to amalgamate under the name of the "London and North Western." In the spring of 1846 it became necessary to close our accounts, and balance our books, with a view to give each shareholder his share of principal and profit. It was arranged that the shareholders should call at the office in Norfolk Street, in Manchester, for their cheques on and after a day in April, 1846. Two days before this date, my Scotch book-keeper came to me to report that in balancing the books he was out the small sum of 1_s_. 10_d_. (I think it was), and he proposed to carry that to profit and loss ("Profeet and Loasse," he said). To which I, of course, replied, "My good friend, a failure to balance of even a penny may conceal errors on the two sides of the account by the hundred. Set all hands to work to call over every item." We set to work, and I was up the best part of one, and the whole of another, night. I was so anxious that I did not feel to want food; and drink I was unused to. A beefsteak and a pint of stout would have saved me from ten years, more or less, of suffering, weakness, and all kinds of misery. In the early morning of the day on which we were to begin paying off our shareholders, the books balanced. We had discovered errors, both to debit and credit, probably a hundred at least in number.

It was a clear, cold morning. I went out to a little barber's shop and got shaved. I did not feel in want of food—and took none. At ten o'clock shareholders began to arrive: got their cheques, and went away satisfied. One of them, who would gain about 30,000_l._, actually gave me a 5_l._ note for the clerks, which was the only expression of gratitude of a practical character, so far as I remember, now. About noon Mr. Henry Houldsworth, the father of the present member for Manchester, called for his cheque; and, chatting with him at the time, as I was making the upstroke of the letter H in "Houldsworth," I felt as if my whole body was forced up into my head, and that was ready to burst. I raised my head, and this strange feeling went away. I thought, how strange! I tried again, the same feeling came again and again, till, with a face white as paper, that alarmed those about me, I fell forward on the desk. Water was given me; but I could not swallow it. I never lost entire consciousness; but I thought I was going to die. I never can forget all that in those moments passed through my brain. They put me into a carriage, and took me to the consulting room, in Mosley Street, of my old friend William Smith, the celebrated Manchester surgeon, nephew of the great Mr. Turner, the surgeon. He placed me on a sofa, and asked me what it was,—feeling, or trying to find, my pulse the while. I whispered, "Up all night—over-anxious—no food." He gave me brandy and soda water, and a biscuit, and told me to lie still. I had never tasted this popular drink before. In about a quarter of an hour I felt better, got up, and said, "Oh! I am all right now." But Mr. Smith, nevertheless, ordered me to go home at once, go to bed, take a pill—I assume, a narcotic—which he gave me, and not to get up till he had seen me in the morning. I insisted on calling at the office. I felt able to go on with my work. But at the office, something in my looks induced them to send a faithful clerk with me in the cab to our house, Woodland Cottage, Higher Broughton. So he and I went away. I found afterwards, that some of the clerks said, "We shall never see him again." But they did—shaky and seedy, as he was, for many a long day.

Well, just as our cab mounted the small hill on which our house stood, the faithful clerk, with more zeal than discretion, said, "You look awful ill, sir; why your face is as white as my shirt." I looked at his shirt, seemingly guiltless, for days past, of the washerwoman.

But I was within three minutes of home: and I was distressed at the thought of alarming my wife, who was not in a condition to be alarmed. So, with what little strength I had left, I rubbed my forehead, face, nose, lips, chin, with my clenched fist, to restore some slight colour. Entering our door, I said, "I am rather worn out, and will go to bed. Up all night. Work done. Now, please, I will go to bed."

So, after every affectionate care that a good wife could pay, I swallowed my narcotic pill—and slept, slept, slept—till, at eight in the morning, the sun was coming in, charmingly, through the windows. Nothing seemed to ail me. What weakness, what nonsense, said I. But I had promised to remain in bed till Mr. Smith came. But I sent down for my clerks, and at 11 a.m. I was in full activity, dictating to one man, listening to another, and giving orders to a third, in, as I thought, the fullest voice—when in came Mr. Smith. He looked round in doubt, and then went down stairs. I have only just forgiven him for that. For in a moment up came my wife. "Edward," she said, "Mr. Smith declares that if you do not give over at once, you will have brain fever." Oh! unwise Smith. The words were hardly out of my wife's mouth, when I felt I could do no more. Had the world been offered to me, I could have done no more.

Alas! my *nerve* was gone.

At that tune I was working for a livelihood. Fortunate that it was so, otherwise a lunatic asylum, or a permanent state of what the doctors call hypochondriasis, might have followed.

After some years of struggle with this nerve-demon, the child of overwork, I wrote, in 1850:—

"I am not fond of writing, and I know I must do it badly. Still I feel that the little narrative I am about to put together may do some good to some few people who may be suffering. I know that the roughest and dullest book ever written, had it contained a similar relation to this of mine, would have brought balm to my mind and hope to my heart not many years ago. And who knows but that other men (for the scenes of this world, and its good and evil, are very much alike), may be suffering as I did, and may therefore be influenced by my rude scribbling, as I might have been by some of theirs?

"There was a time, and not a very distant one either, when I was utterly ignorant of two things—first, the existence, in my particular case, of the thing called the human stomach; and secondly, the reality of those mysterious telegraphic wires—yclept NERVES. Often nave I sneered at 'bilious subjects,' 'dyspepsia,' and that long string of woes which one hears of, in such luxuriance of description, usually over breakfast, at Clifton, Tonbridge, or Harrogate. Like the old Duchess of Marlborough, too, I used 'to thank God I was born before nerves came into fashion.'

"But 'live and learn.' I have lived; and I have learnt the utter misery which a deranged digestion and jarring nerves, acting and reacting upon each other, can inflict upon their victims. To be laid up in bed for a month with a violent disease is nothing. You are killed or cured; made better, and your illness forgotten even by yourself; or quietly laid under the dust of your mother earth, to lie there in oblivion, the busy world moving on, unheeding, over your cold remains, till the great day of judgment. But to have, as it were, your whole 'mind, body, soul, and strength' turned, with a resistless fascination, into the frightened study of your own dreadful anatomy. To find your courage quail, not before real danger, but at phantoms and shadows—nay, actually at your own horrid self—to feel every act of life and every moment of business a task, an effort, a trial, and a pain. Sometimes to be unable to sleep for a week—sometimes to sleep, but, at the dead of night, to wake, your bed shaking under you from the violent palpitation of your heart, and your pillow drenched with cold sweat pouring from you in streams. But, worst of all, if you are of a stubborn, dogged, temper, and are blessed with a strong desire to 'get on'—to feel yourself unable to make some efforts at all, to find yourself breaking down before all the world in others, and to learn, at last, in consequence, almost to hate the half-dead and failing carcase tied to your still living will. This, not for months only, but for YEARS. Years, too, in what ought to be your prime of manhood. Ah! old age and incapacity at thirty is a bitter, bitter punishment. Better be dead than suffer it; for you must suffer it alone and in silence—you may not hope for sympathy—you dare not desire it—you see no prospect of relief—you wage a double warfare, with the world and with yourself. I do not, I dare not, exaggerate. Indeed, a lady of a certain age could hardly feel more abashed at the sudden production of her baptismal certificate than I—a man, a matter-of-fact man, a plain, hard-headed, unimaginative man of business—do, at this confession. Suffice it to say, that in the last four years I have lived the life of a soul in purgatory or an inhabitant of the 'Inferno,' and though I have worked like a horse, determined, if possible, to rout out my evil genii—the wave of health has gradually receded, till, at last, an internal voice has seemed solemnly to say, 'Thus far shalt thou go and no farther.'

"If any one, who has not suffered similarly, has patience to read thus far (which is doubtful), before now he has said, with Mr. Burchell in the 'Vicar of Wakefield'—'FUDGE.' No matter—I should have so exclaimed once; and I now envy him his healthy ignorance. The history of my derangements is told above in one word: that word is—OVERWORK.

"If any one who may not just like an actual dissection, will look at one of Quain's 'Plates of the Bones, Muscles, and Nerves of the Human Body,' he will see that, growing as it were out of the walls of the stomach, there are, in our wonderful human machine, great bunches of nerves, called, by the medicals, the 'great ganglionic system,' and he will observe that these nerves are in intimate and inseparable connection with the spinal cord, and the brain. Then, if he recollects that a perpetual series of conversations and signals goes on by those agents between the stomach and the brain—that, in fact, the two are talking together every moment (without even the delay of that inappreciable interval for which the electric current lingers on the wires in its wondrous progress of intelligence)—he will see that he cannot abuse either great organ without a 'combination of parties' against his administration.

"My unfortunate mistake, therefore, was this: I *overworked my brain*. It rebelled. Stomach joined the outbreak. Heart beat to the rescue; and all the other corporal powers sympathised in the attempt to put me down. They would not stand ten days' work a week, and no Sunday,—relieved though the labour might be by the amusement of speeches and leading articles.

"The first explosion of the conspiracy laid me fainting at the desk. A sort of truce followed this. I consented for a few days to the terms of the belligerents.

I rested. But resting, I was restless. Unfit to work, I was tormented by an unnatural desire for action. Thus I roused myself early—rode to the office (for I was too weak to walk), buried myself amidst my letters, reports and accounts—and rushed on with the day's duties as if all the work of the world had to be done in that one day, and that one day was the last. But an hour or two usually settled the contest. Head swam, heart beat, fluttered, stopped, struggled,—knees knocked together,—and out oozed that cold clammy sweat which reminds one of weakness and the grave. So with a pale face, anxious eye, and hollow cheek, I had to quit the desk again and ride mournfully home, the remainder of the day being consumed in a rest, which only increased my melancholy feelings, because it made me more than ever conscious of my feebleness and excitability.

"But by great care and management of myself, by desperate strivings to get a little health, I *did* improve. Two hours a day at work, two or three times a week, became two or three hours every working day of the week. Then, as a wonderful achievement, at last I managed to endure half a day's business at a time. And at the end of some months (one beautiful day in August, bless the sunlight) I actually did a *whole* day's work! And so, at last, I got before the wind sufficiently to engage again in the competition of business life, with some credit and success. None of those, however, with whom I had to compete, and to whom work (as it should be to every man in health) was easy and pleasant, knew the cost of many of my weary days and nights of labour, or the nervous suffering and physical weakness; in spite of which I endeavoured always to meet my compeers in the working world with pleasantry, or at least with a smile.

"I had many relapses—but I hardly ever laid up for more than an hour or two. In these cases a loll, or rather a recumbent pant, upon the sofa, and a dose of some bitter tonic, or a strong glass of brandy, usually brought down the palpitation, and enabled me to set to work again as if nothing had happened. Indeed, as the eels get accustomed to skinning, so I got used to all this; and it became at last an old habit, and bearable.

"Thus I went on from 1846 until 1850. Four years of incessant and various labour, relieved only by the confidence and appreciation of those who directed, and the good feeling of those who were engaged, like me, in the executive management of the great corporation with which, during this (to me) memorable period of my life, I was connected. I need not repeat how thoroughly I was sustained and comforted by the assiduity of one of the best of women. I tried to thank her by making light of my many miseries.

"This sort of life was, however, too great and continued a strain for a rickety machine to last. And at times, when I gave way to those strange thoughts about the use and end of human existence, which crowd upon the mind in nervous disease—it seemed to me as if I could weigh and measure the particles of vitality from my daily diminishing store— expended in each unnatural effort of labour—as if every stroke of my business craft represented so much of that daily shortening distance which lay between me and the end. I felt the price I was paying for the privilege of labour, and for its remuneration. But I thought, ever, of my wife and little babies, and the thought roused me to a kind of desperation, and made me feel for the time as if I could trample weakness under foot, and tear out, break in pieces, and cast away those miserable, oversensitive organs, which chained, cramped, and hindered me. I like work, too. And I had a sort of shame of confessing myself incapable. I morbidly derided the sympathising regret likely to be shown by my friends, and I pictured the moribund predictions likely to follow a temporary desertion of my post.

"But the estates of my mortal realm stepped in again.

"At the end of a time of hard, anxious, and difficult labours, I went down into the country on business, and was seized, in the streets of a little town, with violent palpitation, and with faintness. I had to take refuge in a shop; to resort to brandy, physic, and a doctor; and, at the close of a day's confinement to my room, to sneak back to London, as miserable as any poor dog, who, having run about all day with a tin kettle at his tail, is, at last, released, to go limping and exhausted home.

"I struggled with this, too, and for some time would not 'give in.' But my face, now, would not answer to my will. It would look pale and miserable. My friends began to commiserate me. This was dreadful. So I at last yielded to the combined movement, of my own convictions of necessity, the wishes of my friends, the orders of my physician, and, most effective of all, the kind commands of one whom I deem it an honour, as it is a necessity, to obey in most things—I went away from business. I went away without hope. I did not expect cure. I believed functional derangement had become, at last, organic disease—and that my days were numbered. I tried the water cure, homoeopathy, allopathy— everything. Some day, I must recount my consultations, on the same Sunday, with Sir James Clarke, Her Majesty's physician, and Dr. Quin, homoeopathist, jester, and, as some said, quack."

At the end of five years of my suffering, I went to America. The trip did me good. It did not cure me. I wrote a book—a very little one. Half-a-crown was its price. The present First Lord of the Treasury, Mr. W. H. Smith, published it. All the edition was sold. I did not venture another. I will quote some portions of it, as a preface to what is to follow.

When this book was just out of the press, I received the following letters from Mr. Cobden:—

"DUNFORD, NEAR MIDHURST, SUSSEX,

"*6th January*, 1852.

MY DEAR WATKIN,

"When lately in Manchester I heard from S. P. Robinson that you had been to the United States; that you had been much struck with what you saw there; that we were being fast distanced by our young rival, &c. Since then I have seen an extract in a paper from a work published by you; but being in an outlying place here, have no means of informing myself further about it. Now, if the book be not large, and can be sent through the post, I wish you would let me have a copy. I know how unreasonable it is to ask an author to give away his works; for, as Dr. Johnson said to Thrale, the brewer, in vindication of his own rule never to make a present of his writings, 'You do not give away your porter, Sir;' but I feel very anxious to know what you think of the United States.

"I have long had my notions about what was coming from the West, and recorded my prophecy on my return from America in 1835. People in England are determined to shut their eyes as long as they can; but they will be startled out of their wilful blindness some day by some gigantic facts proving the indisputable superiority of that country in all that constitutes the power, wealth, and real greatness of a people.

"Hoping that you are quite well after your holiday, which you would not allow to be a holiday.

"I remain, very truly yours,

"R. COBDEN.

"EDWD. WATKIN, Esq."

In reference to a paragraph in the following, I should mention that in my letter transmitting the book, I had written about my meetings with Kossuth, the Hungarian patriot, and had referred to his visit to the United States.

"DUNFORD, NEAR MIDHURST,

"*8th January*, 1852.

MY DEAR WATKIN,

"Many thanks for your kindness in sending me a copy of your work, which, so far as I have gone, pleases me much. You could not have done a wiser and more patriotic service than to make the people of this country better acquainted with what is going on in the United States. It is from that quarter, and not from barbarous Russia, or fickle France, that we have to expect a formidable rivalry—and yet that country is less studied or understood in England than is the history of ancient Egypt or Greece. I should like to go once more to America, if only to see Niagara again. But I am a bad sailor, and should dread the turmoil of public meetings when I arrived there.

"My impression of Kossuth's *phrenology* was that there was not power or animal energy sufficient to account for the ascendancy he acquired over a turbulent aristocracy and a rude uncivilized democracy. The secret lies evidently in his eloquence, in which he certainly surpasses any modern orator; and, taking all things into account, he is in that respect probably a phenomenon without equal in past or present times. I fear when the French news reaches America, it will damp the ardour of his friends there, and make them more than ever resolved to 'stand upon their own ground' rather than venture into the quagmire of European politics. It has confirmed me in my non-intervention policy. It is evident that we know nothing about the political state of even our next neighbours, and how are we likely to be better informed about Germany or Italy? *Their ways are not our ways.* Let us not attempt to judge them by our standard. Let us endeavour to set them a good example. If 36 millions of Frenchmen, or 46 millions of Germans, submit to a despotic Government, it is because they do not really desire anything better.

"If they wished for a different form of Government they could have it. What presumption in *us* to think that our interference in the matter can be necessary!

"Believe me, faithfully yours,

"RICHARD COBDEN.

"EDWD. WATKIN, Esq."

I venture here a few extracts from my little book of 1851, as detailing my views, new and fresh as they were, on American questions.

"I have presumed to think that these hasty Letters, destitute as they are of all literary merit, written during a visit to the 'New World,' may be, just now, worth presenting to 'every-day sort of people,' like myself, who have little time to travel; and, unable to do both, would rather watch the free growth of a new country, than observe the decadence and decrepitude of old ones. For just now, when a large part of our labouring population is strangely awakening to the impression, that a dollar a-day and a vote at elections in the United States are better than eightpence a-day in Ireland; the New Home to which our fellow-countrymen are thus flocking—and in which, somehow or other, they prosper and are independent—is especially interesting.

"Steam navigation and railways have so far reduced the difficulties and uncertainties of Western travel, that it is now as easy and as cheap to spend one's autumn holidays, as I have done, in a trip to America of some eleven thousand miles out-and-home, as fifteen years ago it was to get to John o' Groats and back by land conveyance, or to go a-shooting in Sutherlandshire—which, by-the-bye, is an out of the way and dismal sort of county even yet.

"Every one ought to know how easy it is, and how pleasant and instructive, to travel in the States. But, though many people do know this, the plague of English travellers which annually overspreads Europe, from July to December, and disturbs even the quiet of the Nile, has hardly touched America. And while one cannot enter the drawing-room of any decent house without hearing descriptions of scenery and manners in Germany, Italy, or Russia,—to have visited America almost involves the suspicion of some commercial connection with that country. Yet no other land in the world has so close an alliance with our own; and, while we are culpably ignorant of almost everything but its peculiarities and its vices, no other country studies our history, and watches our progress, with greater interest or more solicitude. Any English youngster will tell you that Americans speak through their noses, spit, and hold slaves; but how few, even of the most intelligent, know that better English is spoken by the mass of Americans, than by the majority of English citizens, and that education is practically an institution of the United States, and universal; though at home it hardly exists as a system, and can never be extended in any truly national direction without exciting a war of parties! Be the reason what it may, we have been in the habit of looking down on America. We shall soon perhaps have to look up to it.

"It is but sixty-two years since the foundation of the Republic. It then consisted of thirteen small States. It now comprises twenty-nine States; without reckoning the new dominions of Oregon, California, New, Mexico, and Texas. Ten years ago its area was 2,000,000 square miles, or more than 1,300,000,000 acres. That area has become, in 1850, 3,252,689 square miles, or 2,081,717,760 acres. It is thus nearly thirty times the size of Great Britain and Ireland.

"The Republic now possesses an ocean coast of 5,140 miles, viz.,—1,920 on the Atlantic, 1,620 on the Pacific, and 1,600 on the Gulf of Mexico.

"Its population in 1790 was less than 4,000,000; in 1840 it stood at 17,000,000; it is now 25,000,000. And if its vast territory, with a more productive soil, and greater resources of all kinds, should some day become as thickly peopled as our own island, it will then contain a population of 800,000,000 of souls speaking the English tongue. If the Federation hold together in peace, why should this result, though distant, be doubtful? For it now comprises almost every variety of soil, climate, vegetable productions, and mineral wealth.

Its 20,000 miles of river and lake navigation—its 10,000 miles of railway—its 4,000 miles of canal—and its 11,000 miles of telegraphic wire— connect every part of its vast territory together, and give to an interminable continent the compactness of a small island. The facilities of communication, too, place at the command of the people of one part of the country the climate of every other. When the thermometer is below zero at New York, a journey of three days will bring the traveller to Savannah, where a genial temperature of 60 degrees, clear skies, and verdant nature, await him. And when a scorching sun is filling New Orleans with fever, the cool weather of the North, and upon the great lakes, is healthy and delightful. The apple bloomed at Natchez, in 1850, as early as the 24th March; while at Montpelier, in Vermont, it bloomed on the 10th June. The distance between the two places is but three or four days' travel.

"One can hardly name a staple article of production which some part or other of the States will not grow—not as a mere garden curiosity, but as an article of profitable cultivation. The champagne of Cincinnati is beginning to be noted, and tea is under experimental cultivation in South Carolina.

"The mineral resources of the country are enormous; and their development is only limited by the present want of capital to work them more efficiently. The coal of Pennsylvania—the iron in various parts of the Union—the copper of Lake Superior—the lead about Galena on the Mississippi; and lastly, the gold of California, which has already put in circulation a coinage of 15,000,000_l_. sterling—all these are but the first tapping of almost boundless resources.

"In 1791, the public debt of the United States was $75,000,000. It is now, with six times the population, only $64,000,000; and in the same period, the imports of the country have increased from a value of $52,000,000 to $147,000,000; the exports from $19,000,000 to $145,000,000; and the tonnage of shipping from 500,000 tons to 3,300,000 tons.

"The post-office statistics show how the transmission of intelligence has outstripped even the march of population. In 1790, the number of post-offices in the entire States was 75; in 1850, the number was 16,789. In 1790, there were 4,875 miles of post routes; in 1850, there were 167,703. In 1790, the whole post-office revenue was 37,905 dollars; in 1850, it was 4,905,176 dollars; which sum consisted of 4,082,762 dollars for letters, and 819,016 dollars for newspapers and pamphlets. The mileage run in transportation of letters in 1850, was 42,544,069 miles, at a cost, for transportation only, of a little more than twopence-halfpenny per mile. And the total number of letters conveyed was 67,500,000; 62,000,000 of which were paid, and 5,500,000 free and franked.

"To come from letters to arms; it is a curious fact, as exhibiting the real military strength of this great country, that the militia force of the States amounts to 1,960,265 men, or as many as the whole population of Canada, or two-thirds of that of Scotland, who could be called out and in the field in less than a month.

"The school funds belonging to the respective States, swelled by the constant addition of every sixteenth section of government land sold, are very large. Those belonging to seventeen free States amounted, in 1850, in fixed value, to 21,400,000 dollars. Popular education is the condition on which all new States are admitted into the Union.

"There are 121 colleges in the States; with a total of 950 instructors; 50,115 alumni; 9,028 ministers; and 11,565 students; and having 769,079 volumes in their libraries.

"And without a farthing from the State, or from any source beyond the free-will offerings of the people, to support them, there are in this country of yesterday, 30,217 churches (exclusive of those belonging to the

Wesleyans) connected with the various sects of Christians: 26,588 ministers; and 4,558,168 communicants, or 1 in 5 1/2 of the population.

"This country, then, possesses all the elements which are usually considered as contributing to civilization and to power. It has far outstripped us in the rate of its progress; and it becomes every day, more and more, the refuge for the industrious poverty, not only of Great Britain, but of Europe.

"Those who wish to gaze at ruins need not go to it. Those who only yearn for the sight of crown jewels, or ancient armour, had better stay away. But to all who would see the realm which Nature has spread out, in her largest features, for the development of the Anglo-Saxon race, under institutions once deemed Utopian, and even yet wondered at as experimental—to all who would see how a people can GROW—North America is the country of irresistible attraction."

As to slavery, I wrote:—

"Maryland is a slave State, and Baltimore exhibits traces of the existence of the 'Institution.' At the railway stations—the one belonging to the line which connects Baltimore with Philadelphia, for instance—are notices, stating 'that coloured persons desiring to go by the cars, must be at the depot two hours before the starting of the train, to have their names registered and their papers examined, or they will not be allowed to travel.'

"The following announcements in the 'Baltimore Clipper,' were amongst similar advertisements:—

"'SLAVES WANTED.—We are at all times purchasing Slaves, paying the highest *cash* prices. Persons wishing to sell, will please call at 242, Pratt-street. (Slatter's Old Stand.) Communications attended to.'

"'NEGROES WANTED.—I will pay the highest prices, in cash, for any number of Negroes with good titles, slaves for life, or for a term of years, in large or small families, or single Negroes. I will also purchase Negroes restricted to remain in the State, that sustain good characters. Families never separated. Persons having Slaves for sale, will please call and see me, as I am always in the market with the cash. Communications promptly attended to, and liberal commissions paid, by John D. Denning, No. 18, South Frederick-street, between Market and Second-streets, with trees in front of the house.'

"Maryland has 89,000 slaves, and the number is decreasing. Virginia, its neighbour State, has 448,000—the total number in the Union being 2,487,000.

"I have found throughout my tour, what all English travellers must find—that slavery is a question which it is better not to go out of one's way to discuss. For, although I have had many friendly conversations with its most ardent supporters and most violent opponents, I soon discovered, on the one hand, that the question is practically compromised by the great political parties in the Free States, from time to time, in order to conciliate Southern votes; and, on the other, that the slave-owners consider the word 'abolition' as synonymous with confiscation and civil war. The latter meet you at the outset of the argument by stating that their whole property consists of land and slaves. That their lands of course derive their value from cultivation; and that, apart from the mere question of cost, that cultivation is impossible in the hands of the white man. They tell you, that while the negro endures the labour of the rice field mid-leg deep in water, and with a scorching sun above his head, without danger, and can withstand the miasma-hanging in the night air on the plantations— the white man is attacked with hopeless fever if he exposes himself to these influences. They declare that the unconditional abolition of slavery, in a country abounding in unappropriated lands, where men may squat without being disturbed, means simply the confiscation of three hundred millions sterling, the value of the slaves, in the first place, and the abandonment and destruction of the entire planting interest, in the second. To urge the morality of the question with these men, would be as successful as a similar appeal to our opium traders; to the maker of fire-arms certain to burst; or, to use an American free State illustration—to the successful manufacturer of wooden nutmegs.

"After hearing these statements, doubtless exaggerated, but which were made with earnestness, and are at least partially true, I was not surprised to learn, that since the forcible seizure of a slave at Boston, some months ago, by the abolitionists of that city, many of the Southern merchants have transferred their purchases of manufactured goods to New York, to an extent which, were it not stated on authority, would be beyond belief. Indeed I learn, that so strong is this anti- abolition feeling, that where any option exists, the avowed abolitionists are systematically avoided in business dealings. A first- class firm in New York, having a magnificent shop in the Broadway, see their old Southern customers pass by to a rival establishment in the same street, the only reason being that they are known to be earnest abolitionists, while their rival has never publicly expressed any opinion on the question.

"This feeling, showing itself in an endless variety of shapes, is just now most-fierce, owing to an outrage which has occurred in Pennsylvania, in which a Mr. Gorsuch has been shot down, and his son seriously wounded, in an attempt to seize a fugitive slave (under the provisions of the 'fugitive slave law'), which was resisted by a rising of the free black population, and of some white abettors.

"The 'fugitive slave law' is, indeed, simply a declaratory act. For it is unfortunately the fact, that the Southern States gave in their adhesion to the Federal Republic solely on condition that, while the slave trade should cease, the institution of slavery should be respected, and they should have the right to follow and seize fugitive slaves in any part of the Union. The 'fugitive slave law' was the work of the 'Union' party—a party composed of men of all shades of opinion, who wished, by conciliation, to prevent the threatened withdrawal of South Carolina and other slave States from the Union.

"Greatly as all just and dispassionate men must abhor slavery, every one must admit the difficulties with which its immediate abolition is here surrounded. The negro does not possess the cordial sympathy of the white man. For while a small, and, politically speaking, uninfluential, party are prepared to make every sacrifice and run all risks in order to blot out slavery on the instant, the influential and acting leaders of the majority, whatever their occasional language of denunciation, and affectation of horror, are not disposed to brave the rebellion of the South, and the possible disruption of the Republic, for the sake of shortening the thraldom of the negro some fifty years. They profess to rely upon the natural progress of events, which, by quiet change, has already banished slavery from the majority of the States originally parties to the Union; and has, within the last few years, forbidden the future existence of slave States north of latitude 36 degrees 3o'—for the gradual extinction of the system; and in the meantime they are prepared to alleviate the lot of the slave; to refuse any extension of slavery; and, as far as concession can obtain it, to narrow the area which it now occupies.

"Perhaps, should these cold political views still hold possession of the moving spirits of the country, the next practical step in advance may be to secure to the slave a personal right to some small portion of the day, and to the produce of his labour in that portion;—to say, in fact, that after a stipulated number of hours' labour for his master, the remainder of his time shall be his own. The effect of this would be to enable him legally to accumulate property. And if, in addition, a minimum price be fixed at which his master should be bound to allow him to redeem himself, and savings' banks were opened to receive the produce of his free earnings—some glimmering of daylight would dawn upon his lot, and his condition, as a 'chattel' to be bought and sold, would not be hopeless."

Referring to what I hereafter relate of the incident at Saratoga, I may, at this point, remind the reader that, as late as 1862, President Lincoln, a sincere abolitionist, could not see his way to declare the freedom of the slave. He told a deputation from Chicago that "a Pope once issued a Bull against an eclipse, but the eclipse came along nevertheless." The moment

I saw black soldiers in Northern uniform, carrying Northern muskets, at the end of 1863, I made up my mind that the North had won. In 1865 Dr. Mackay, registrar, showed me the registry of the passage of John Brown's, corpse through New York. I quote from memory; but if I recollect rightly, it was this:—

— —
— — —- | Date. Name. Age. Occupation. Cause of Death. | | — —- — —- — —
— — — — —- — — — — — — —- | | Nov., 1859. John Brown 59 Farmer Hanging
| | | | Remarks. | | | | Tried and found guilty of treason and of inciting slaves to | | rebel against their masters. | — — — — — — — — — — — —
— — — — — — — — — — — — — — — -

"CHAMPION STEAMER, UP THE ST. LAWRENCE,
"Thursday, September 4, 1851.

"Owing to the locomotive habits of the people, the hotels of America are more extensive and more systematized than ours. One of their features is the system of charging a fixed sum per day, which covers all the annoying extras of English hotel bills. On entering an hotel, you write your name and address in a book, have the number of your bedroom placed opposite your name, and receive a key, which, when you go out you leave in the office. The breakfast, lunch, dinner, and tea, take place at stated hours, and are managed with great precision and discipline.

"At the 'United States Hotel,' Saratoga, the waiters are blacks, and are commanded by a black maitre d'hotel. On dinner being served, the gong is sounded, and each guest takes his appointed place. All being seated, the maitre d'hotel claps his hands, and in an instant, at one *coup*, the covers are nipped away, as if with the same hand, by waiters stationed at regular distances around the tables. Then the serious work of eating commences. If any embarrassment arises, a clap of the hand calls attention to it, and a sign directs its immediate remedy. Then, as each course is finished, another clap stations the waiters again at their old places, and at a wave of the hand all the dishes skip off the table. Then, the table being cleared of dinner dishes, the whole posse of waiters march two and two round the tables, and leave the room by a side door. In a few seconds they return again in the same order, each man bearing three dishes, and fall again into their places. Then, all eyes being fixed upon the maitre d'hotel, *clap one*, and down goes one dish from the hands of each waiter all along the tables. *Clap two* brings down dish the second; and *clap three* drops the third. And at a table of nearly 400 persons all are thus served with dessert, as before they had been with each course, in about half a moment, and each at the same time. Even in changing knives, forks, and plates, a system is adopted. A portion of the waiters, obeying a sign, fall out of line, and divide into threes; one of each three bears the plates, one the knives, and one the forks; and each party goes round its allotted length of table. Black No. 1 dots down a plate opposite each person; No. 2 plants a knife on one side of it; No. 3 puts down a fork on the other side. The men do this with an even regularity of movement, and a gravity which is quite amusing. All this rapid and regular action drives dinner on amazingly; indeed, it almost hurries you. In fifty minutes all is over, and the table cleared. The Americans, who seem to know the value of time, generally get up and decamp immediately after the last mouthful, which is perhaps a sensible plan.

"At Saratoga we found a party of Indians. Eighteen of these children of the forest, who had been down to New York to sell toys and ornaments, which they manufacture in the winter, were on their return home, and were encamped outside the village during Sunday. They showed little of the costume of their tribe, or rather, I suppose I should say, want of costume; one man wearing a pair of red plush breeches, and some of the women having bonnets. Still there were the features, the attitudes, and the language of the aborigines. We visited their camp at night, a collection of gipsy-like tents, and conversed with one or two of them, which led others to steal out and listen. I say steal out, for it was only upon turning round, that I became aware that we were suddenly almost surrounded. One man spoke very good English. He said they were Oneidas, or as he pronounced it 'Onidehs,' and were going back to their country, where they would remain with their tribe, about two hundred and eighty of whom were left, till next year, and then come down again.

"On Sunday evening I witnessed another and a very different spectacle. A Methodist preacher came into the village in a little four-wheeled car, with a square black hood over it, and preached from his car, on what is termed by the common voice 'Nigger abolition.' He was accompanied by a young woman and a very pretty little child, who both sat behind him. He soon got an audience, amongst whom were several men from the Southern States. He denounced slavery in no very measured terms, and soon provoked the Southern men to interject—'Why don't you go into the South?' 'Why, Sir,' was the reply, 'you know, it would be as much as my life is worth.' 'Nonsense! we will give you five hundred dollars to go, and you shall be safe.' 'To what State, Sir?' 'Georgia,' replied one voice; 'Alabama,' another; 'North Carolina,' another. 'Why,' was the rejoinder, 'three of our preachers were expelled from those very States not a month ago.' 'Your niggers here are free, and they are worse off than ours; why don't you mend their condition first?' And so the attack and reply went on (this was Sunday evening) for half an hour, amidst laughter, jeers, and the occasional propulsion, by fellows behind, of some unlucky lad or other against the poor preacher's horse; a movement which endangered the woman and child especially, but which appeared to give great satisfaction to many, and which no one interfered in any manner to prevent. I left the spot in disgust. I have seen, however, as much petty intolerance at home. I returned from my walk in time to hear the preacher pronounce his benediction, in the midst of which there arose a hideous yell: three or four boys were shot against the horse, and the car was nearly overthrown; after which a shouting multitude followed the retreating abolitionist for some distance, to harass and annoy him, as he drove with difficulty away.

"On Monday morning, recruited by the previous day's rest, I left Saratoga, and travelled forty-one miles by railway through a partially cleared, and, in many parts, very beautiful country, to Whitehall, which is at the southern end of Lake Champlain, where we took a steamer, a nice, orderly, and comfortable boat, and steamed to Rouse's Point, 132 miles further. The scenery of the lake is very beautiful. The ruins of the old fortress of Ticonderoga rise upon it, standing upon a steep rocky headland, and commanding the lake, which narrows at this point; a wide expanse of water swelling out both above and below. Ticonderoga was taken from the French by the English, by the use of artillery fired down from the mountain above it. In the American war of independence it was taken from us by surprise by one Colonel Ethen Allen. It is reported that Allen awakened the commandant, who was in bed, and told him to surrender. 'By what authority?' said the half- awakened officer. 'By the authority of the Lord Jehovah and the Continental Congress,' replied Allen.

"About the middle of the lake is the thriving town of Burlington, the chief town of Vermont. Here we stopped to take in passengers, and were pleased with the bustle and activity of the place. The wharf was crowded; and, as the day was hot, straw hats and shirt-sleeves, also the mitigated form of comfort — viz., coat and trousers without waistcoat — were abundant.

"It was dusk when we arrived at Rouse's Point, and we had not so good a view as I could have wished of the extensive wharves and landings; the boat, 300 feet long, built to carry over whole trains; and the extensive station works of the Northern or Ogdensburgh Railroad, which is just opened. 'I had been introduced, at Saratoga, to the superintendent of this line, Colonel Schlatter, by Mr. Van Ransellaer, of the Saratoga and Washington line. Both these gentlemen were very polite, and gave me orders to pass over their railways when I pleased. The Ogdensburgh line extends from Rouse's Point to Ogdensburgh, near the head of Lake Ontario. It forms, with other lines, a complete system from Boston and New York to Lake Ontario, and has many difficult and extensive works in its course.

"From Rouse's Point we took the Champlain and St. Lawrence line, opened two days ago, and at Isle aux Noix passed into British-American territory, and heard the old French patois of the 'habitans' of that locality, from the mouths of a crowd of curious people awaiting the arrival of the train. At La Prairie we joined the ferry boat, an immense vessel as usual, and dropped down the St. Lawrence for nine miles, to Montreal, where I got to bed at Donnegana's hotel, at one o'clock on Tuesday morning, desperately tired.

"Montreal is a flourishing town of 50,000 inhabitants. It is built upon an island formed by the confluence of the St. Lawrence and the Ottawa. The 'island' belonged to the Catholic priesthood of the place, who still exercise rights over it similar to those of the 'lords' in cases of English copyholds, and who obtain an annual revenue of some 30,000_l_. or 40,000_l_. from it. The city was founded about 250 years ago, and has still many of the features of a French town, though the improvements of the last twenty years, by obliterating single story and wooden houses from the best quarters, have altered its character. In old times it was the depot for the great fur trades. Now, however, it receives its furs almost entirely back from England, to which country the Hudson's Bay Company send their whole supply, to be dressed and prepared for re-exportation. It is the commercial emporium of this district; and, though it has suffered from the equalization of duties, it is now recovering. The facilities for communication with the United States, by the systems of railroad made and making, which may bring it within twelve hours of Boston and New York, will doubtless urge forward its prosperity.

"Montreal has considerable general commerce, commanding, as it does, the St. Lawrence, now connected by railway directly with the United States, and being at the outlet of the Ottawa river district. The island upon which it stands is some thirty miles long, and contains much fine and valuable land, mostly under cultivation, and abounding in good farms and gardens, and fine orchards. From the 'Mountain' above Montreal, a splendid view is obtained of the St. Lawrence and its wooded shores; the dark forests of the Ottawa valley; the fine bright lands of the islands; the city, and its villaed suburbs. In the distances, north and south, the 'green mountains' of Vermont, and the distant summits which separate the cultivated parts of Lower Canada from those far-off and savage regions, in which the trappers of the Hudson's Bay Company and some scattered Indians are the sole monarchs of the woods—are visible. There can be no view more beautiful, few more extensive. It gives all the peculiarities of this North American scenery in its largest and finest features. And seen again from the high towers of the Catholic Cathedral (the cathedral will hold several thousand people, and is the largest church in Canada), to which I mounted, up 268 steps, it again delights the eye with its extent and beauty. From this latter point, too, the St. Lawrence is seen just below, and you may watch the rushing of the nearest rapids, and the struggles and windings of the boats and steamers, in passing on their upward voyages.

"Montreal and Quebec (more especially) have the distinctive features of French towns with many of the peculiarities of English ones. Here is the well-known countenance of the northern parts of France. Carts such as might have been seen, no doubt, hundreds of years ago in France. The Norman breed of horses: small, round, strong, and enduring. Every other signboard presents a French name; the blacksmith styling himself 'forgeron;' the baker, 'boulanger;' the ladies' attendant, 'sage- femme;'—and so on. The professional man generally has two plates upon his door:—one telling you that he is 'M. Charles Robert,' 'avocat;' and the other, that he is 'Mr. C. Robert,' 'attorney at law.' In the 'Cote des Neiges,' behind the mountain, at Montreal, and in the suburb or quarter 'St. Henry,' this French appearance is universal. 'Notre Dame des Neiges,' in the former, with its gaudily painted inside and unpretending outside, its wooden roof and tin-covered steeple, would recall to you the wooded districts of France; and the houses in both quarters, the people with their 'bonnets rouges' (as distinguished from the 'bonnets bleus' and 'bonnets gris' of the Quebec district), and innocence of English and English ways of living, working, farming, and thinking, are even more French than the French themselves. Indeed, so little have they changed since the settlement of the country two hundred years ago, that they speak the French of that time without the alloy since introduced into the language. Their old modes of farming are still in vogue; and they despise all change, satisfied to live in quiet and simple comfort, without the worry of improvements. In the Quebec district the farmers singe their pigs when they have killed them, and despise the use of hot water. Just as farmers do in Normandy, and in some parts of the south of England. This pig-singeing is a great event; and on one occasion during the Rebellion, the singeing of two or three pigs on a hill-side at night, caused the Quebec garrison and the country volunteers to turn out, under the belief that the light seen was that of a beacon fire, and that the enemy were at hand.

"Montreal, and Quebec also, abound in fine Catholic churches, and the streets swarm with comfortable-looking priests, dressed in black cassocks and bands, and wearing big-buckled shoes and broad-brimmed hats.

"The difference in language, customs, and religion, divides the population into two distinct sections, and is a bar to united effort and to the improvement of the country; which nevertheless does improve in spite of this difficulty, though not as rapidly as it might and ought. I did not fully appreciate this until I visited the Superior Law Court, then sitting in Montreal. This court is held, during the erection of the new court-house, in the old, low-walled, high-roofed, building in which the French Government conducted their public affairs a hundred and fifty years ago. In this building, in 1839, the Privy Council decided to place the country under martial law, and the proclamation was issued from it.

"The judges sitting when I visited the court were Smith, Van Feloon, and Mondelet, the latter a French Canadian. The first case argued was a long-pending one between Sir John Stewart and an architect, who had superintended the erection of some buildings on one of Sir John's farms. The counsel were not over clever, but sufficiently verbose, and full enough of 'instances,' both ancient and modern. The counsel for Sir John laid great stress upon the erroneous manner in which the action had been laid, and contended that as the English form of' assumpsit' had been taken, in order to get both debt and damages, instead of a single action of damages being brought, all the consequences of the form adopted must be taken by the plaintiff, who, not having proved *damages*, or even stated them, must be held by the court to have made out no case, and be cast accordingly. The counsel quoted the old French law, and a French law-writer of 1700, Chardon, and also English and Canadian authorities. The French Canadian judge having, during the oration, thrown in an observation or two in English, which he did not speak over fluently, at length uttered in French a long comment upon the fallacy of the argument—which sounded strangely. The counsel for the architect went at the argument of his opponent with great vigour, stimulated by the expressed opinion of Judge Mondelet, and went back to the days of ancient Rome to show that forms of action had been difficult even in those days, having once caused a revolt. He declared that even in England they were as unsettled as ever; and wound up by propounding as a dogma, that the Canadian law was neither English, French, Roman, nor of any other precedent, but was founded upon common sense, which was the only guide and authority in the administration of it. In corroboration of this, the little black eye of Judge Mondelet brightly twinkled, and he nodded his head in dignified approbation. Judge Van Feloon, who seemed more phlegmatic, quietly settled the matter by saying, that he supposed if a man *did* work for another, and the other had agreed to pay him, he was entitled to the money, and that therefore the court would have to see that a bargain had been made, and the work duly performed, and then decide. The next case argued arose out of a fraudulent assignment; and in this, too, French authorities, in the old language of a hundred and fifty years since, were often appealed to—Chardon being apparently the standard book of reference. The mixture of custom evidently caused embarrassment, and it was clear that no fixed decisions could regulate disputes concerning property, while the precedents relied upon were based upon the differing laws of two separate countries—laws, perhaps, not now operating in those very countries themselves.

"The tenure of property in Lower Canada is still in part based upon the old French feudal system. There are still 'seigneurs' who hold lands, and have 'censitaires' or tenants, paying fee-rent in produce, services, and money. It is true that a law has been passed enabling a fixed commutation, in money, of these seigneurial rights; but I am told that the parties adhere in most cases to the old usage, and despise innovation.

"A singular custom, too, prevails. Parents, when old and tired of labour, assign their property to their children, or to one of them, in consideration of a string of conditions for their own maintenance and comfort, each one of which is recited in the deed with minute exactness. They stipulate usually for a house, so much meat, bread, sugar, tea, &c.; a caleche and horse to take them to church on Sundays and holidays; so much tobacco or snuff; so many gowns and bonnets, or suits of clothes and hats; and so on. These gifts lead to frequent law- suits; and one can quite understand how, in a country with large tracts of its land held upon tenures of the most complex character, under a system which has passed away even in the country from whence it came, and where to this mass of difficulty is added the cause of dispute just alluded to, the legal profession should flourish,—which I understand it does.

"Many of the public buildings of Montreal are excellent. The Bon Secours Market is a very fine building, and puts many of ours at home to shame. The Jesuits' College is large and sombre; and some of the convents and institutions are well worth a visit, both as buildings and as institutions of the place.

"In the country little progress appears; but you see no misery, and much comfort and joyfulness. Indeed, these French settlers seem happy upon their small properties, surrounded by their old customs, and in the enjoyment of the fetes and holidays which their religion allows. They look upon the rush of improvement with calmness, though often with a sort of incredulity as to the agency by which it is brought about, and the righteousness of its existence. 'Mais, croyez-vous que le bon Dieu permettra tout cela?' said one of them on seeing a train move along, dragged by no visible horseflesh, and propelled without birds' wings. They are quite a contrast to their American neighbours, who have often suggested that Lower Canada might go ahead if the French population were 'improved off the face of the earth.'

"The priests set a good example of taking matters enjoyably and peacefully: their country farm outside Montreal, at the foot of the mountain, for example. The house is situated so as to command a beautiful view of the basin of the St. Lawrence, which, on a fine day, shows its river gliding on with broad tranquil surface, peacefully towards the sea, and exhibits the gardens, woods, and orchards, which cover the country with a fertile and smiling landscape. The grounds are large and well planted; and the rude gaze of the multitude is shut out by a high wall, which extends half round the farm itself. Here the good fathers come for a few days at a time, and in turns, to recruit exhausted nature, and spend their hours in exercise and reading. Fine old fellows! we need not envy them; but rather hope that all men may some day have as many of the means of quiet and simple happiness to resort to.

"The short summer of Lower Canada causes great activity in business during the 'seasons.' The summer and autumn are therefore the times of business; the short interval between them the time for visits to the seaside, or to Saratoga, or the Caledonia Springs; while the winter, with its snow and ice and long endurance, brings round a continuous carnival of pleasant racket, and is really the season of society amongst all ranks of the people. I heard magnificent accounts of the balls, parties, sleighings, and country frolics, which take place; also of the walking expeditions far out into the wilds, with snow shoes, tents to sleep in, and Indian attendants; and of the wild sport in hunting the moose-deer, and other tenants of the wood — during this winter season. Some of the English agents spend five business months in Canada, and all the rest of the year in England, going home in November and returning in April.

"The residences in the suburbs of Montreal are usually well built, large, and beautifully situated. We drove through the suburbs to Monklands, which is on the western side of the mountain, and commands a fine view of the country. This house, which is capacious and handsome, is now used as an hotel. It was the seat of the Governor-General, Lord Elgin; and the landlord showed us a point at the end of the now dilapidated, but some time beautiful, garden, from whence, he said, his lordship viewed afar off the burning of the Parliament Houses at Montreal a year or two back. Lord Elgin shut himself up in Monklands for about three months after this outrage, and the Parliament and court were removed to Toronto, which, until the turn comes round to some other place, has the exclusive honour of hearing the rather strong oratory of the Upper Province. The country about Monklands is very beautiful, and there are still abundant openings on the mountain sides for villas, similar to the very handsome and tasteful erections with which they are at present pretty thickly studded.

"Leaving Montreal one evening by steamer, I dropped down to Quebec. The St. Lawrence below Montreal is broad, deep, and, in some places, winding. The principal population of Lower Canada is on its immediate shores; and the numerous cottages and houses, with cultivated fields around them, would lead to a belief that the whole population of the country, so thickly appearing on the margin of the river, was greater than it is. The sail by daylight must be beautiful, and as the hours of day, which going and returning allowed, enabled me to see a great part of the distance, I only regretted that I could not see more of so noble a river, and of the industry and the people settled on its banks.

"When within five miles of Quebec, coming down the river, there commences a succession of wharfs, to which the timber, which forms so great a trade here, is floated down stream, and from which it is loaded into vessels for Europe and other parts of the world. The stock of timber balks floating in the basins about these wharfs and landings is now so great, that for three miles the margin of the river looks like one great raft. We passed two immense rafts of timber, floating down the stream, to be stowed here, one of which was some 400 yards long, had eighteen sails set, and four wooden houses complete, erected upon it.

"Quebec is admirably placed as a fortified city, and also as a point for commerce. It stands on a high point of land opposite the Isle of Orleans, which here divides the St. Lawrence into two large streams. The citadel overlooks the Bay of Quebec, the Isle of Orleans, and the high banks of the St. Lawrence. The view from it is most extensive, in whichever direction the eye wanders. Forty miles of the St. Lawrence are seen from it. The white wooden houses on the hill-sides, and the broad fields of yellow grain, set off the dark wood; and the river—its bay, fronting the point of land on which the city is placed, covered with sails and glistening in the sun—mellows the landscape most exquisitely. Quebec, as seen from the river, too, has a fine commanding aspect. The Citadel crowning the height does not give so great an appearance of extent or strength as it possesses. In reality, Gibraltar preeminent over all, it is one of the most impregnable strongholds in the world; and its underground works, I am told, are so extensive that 5,000 men may be garrisoned and hidden within the bowels of the earth beneath it. Visitors are not allowed to walk on the west ramparts; and on complaining of this to a distinguished military officer, I was assured that the workmen, who are still employed in the excavations below, are taken in blindfold—that the engineer officer alone knows the form and shape of the works in progress, and that the plan of the remainder is kept sealed up in the hands of the commandant, to be opened only in case of actual need.

This is mystery with a vengeance, and but for the authority from whence I received the statement, I should doubt the fact—most decidedly.

"The lower town of Quebec stands upon the river bank, beneath the almost perpendicular face of rock, surmounted by the Citadel. It is old, and the houses are principally of wood, and ultra-French in appearance. The streets are narrow and not over clean. To reach the upper town you drive up a very precipitous road, or walk up a long flight of timber steps, which shorten the steepest portion of the way. The upper town is built on the acclivity and on the slopes of the hill- side, which slide down to the river St. Charles, to the north. The fire of 1845 improved the town, by clearing out miserable old wooden dwellings; and the buildings erected on the site are of good brick or stone. Since these fires, too, it has been forbidden to build houses of wood, within the walls; and the use of shingles for roofing has been prohibited. The roofs are mostly covered with tin, which shines and glares in the sun at mid-day, but reflects the morning light very pleasantly.

"The Protestant and Catholic Cathedrals are fine buildings, as are the new Catholic church outside the suburbs, the Catholic seminary, and many other edifices. But the narrow streets, steep ascents, and ancient buildings, take away all beauty from the town itself, delightful as is its situation, and beautiful as are the vistas and views from various parts of it.

"A pilgrimage to the Plains of Abraham, about a mile from the Citadel, which consist of the high tableland between the St. Lawrence and the St. Foix road and St. Charles river, was to me a traveller's duty.

"It was on the night of the 12th of September, 1759, that Wolfe, checked by the French, at Montmorenci, two months before, dropped down the St. Lawrence with his army in boats, and succeeded in landing at a little bend of the river, still half hidden by trees, where the high and precipitous shores are most accessible, though yet most difficult of ascent. The troops scaled the heights, meeting little opposition, formed into line across the plains, and waited the attack of the French, who had marched that morning from Beauport, near to which the battle of Montmorenci had been fought. The French came on gallantly, and the English stood their fire until they approached within forty yards, and then delivered theirs. The French wavered, and Wolfe charged at the head of his men, Montcalm heading his. A desperate fight took place, and Wolfe fell, struck by the third ball, just as the French line broke in confusion, and the English cheer of victory burst from his conquering army. Montcalm was mortally wounded immediately afterwards.

"On the spot where Wolfe fell, on the extreme right of his line, a plain unpretending pillar is placed, bearing the simple inscription,—

'HERE DIED WOLFE, VICTORIOUS, SEPT. 13, 1759.'

Near the Citadel, and in the town, another monument has been erected, which bears the name of Wolfe on one side and that of Montcalm on the other.

"To see the country, I had a drive of twenty-five miles along the St. Charles river, through the Indian village of Lorette, and back through the fine open district to the westward of the town. Our road was good for a few miles, but then became such a collection of deep pits and heaps of mud, that, but for a rude fence and wheel-marks, it would hardly have been distinguished from the fields. The course of the St. Charles, however, at this point, is between precipitous and sometimes rocky banks, covered with trees and jungle: and in enjoyment of the scenery, the fresh pure air, cooled by the previous night's rain, and the sweet scents thrown out by the trees and wild-flowers, the slow progress of the vehicle and the bumping of one's sides, were forgotten.

"Lorette was originally a colony of Christianized Huron Indians, to whom lands were granted by the French. The village is now principally inhabited by whites and half-breeds, though there are some of the pure race left—the men wearing European dresses, the women adhering to the ancient costume. Their cottages are generally neat and clean. Andre Romain, the chief, resides in the centre of the village, a high pole denoting his residence and rank. I found him bending over his simple dinner of milk and coarse bread. He was dressed in old, and somewhat ragged, garments. He seemed so extremely old, that I did not trouble him with more than a very short conversation, in French. He showed me a portrait of George IV., given to him, he said, from the hands of that monarch, and a coloured engraving of the installation of one of the royal princes as chief of the Hurons. The poor old man, broken down with extreme age, had still the remains of a commanding presence, which even his miserable dress, unshaven beard, and bleared and misty eye, could not altogether extinguish.

"This village gives an example of the fate of all the Indian tribes. Here, once brought together to live after the manner of the whites, this tribe has been reduced in number, and finally all but absorbed; and in a few years not one of the unmixed race will remain, and the language of the tribe will be obliterated.

"At Lorette are the falls of the St. Charles, which are very interesting. After seeing them, I had some milk at the 'Billy Button,' a public-house kept by a Yankee, who deals in the Indian ornaments made in the village, and shows the falls, and then drove round to Quebec, through a fine and richly-tilled district; and, in passing, saw a hotly-contested heat run upon the course on the plains of Abraham—for it was Quebec races."

"TORONTO, "Saturday, September 6th, 1851.

"Returning to Montreal, I spent Thursday in visiting various institutions of that city, and drove out with Mr.—— to see the country residence of a friend of his, which is hidden in a sweet little glen, from whence, however, glimpses of the St. Lawrence river are obtained. This gentleman lives here in summer, and employs his leisure in the cultivation of the fruits and flowers, which a fine soil and a forcing climate produce in perfection. He complains of the destruction of the large trees in his vicinage, regretting that those who own the neighbouring woods should be impelled to bring down, first, the oldest and finest timber, and should be unable to preserve even so much of it as might illustrate hereafter the magnificent proportions of the native forest wood. This is truly one of the sad features of advancing civilization. The fine old forests, like the native Indians, lose their noblest chieftains, and, degenerating to a few dwarfed and scattered specimens, at last disappear and are forgotten.

"Mr.—— told us much of the happy and comfortable lives of the farmers and settlers hereabouts. All have land; food in abundance, including sugar from their own maple-bush; cattle; horses; light spring waggons, which serve as family coaches when not required for the week-day's work; good homely furniture and clothing: in short, an abundance of all the essentials of existence, and even wealth—but they possess little money. In many cases, and now that agricultural improvement has become a necessity, this want of money is found to be a great evil. The ordinary sized farms, of 100 acres of good land, all in cultivation, are worth from 500_l_., to 1,000_l_.; and very often an expenditure of 200_l_. or 300_l_. in improvements would double their value. The legal rate of interest here is 6 per cent.; and as high a rate as 7 or 8 per cent could be got for small loans on mortgages for these purposes were the money to be had. The banks, however, do not, as a rule, lend money on mortgage, and the monied men of the country have usually lands of their own requiring the same sort of development. Foreign capital is therefore looked to; and doubtless it will ultimately be procured in abundance, the security being undeniable, and the rate of interest so high.

"Mr.—— does not consider the long winter any impediment to farming, but rather the contrary, as the sudden burst of spring, and the rapid growths of summer, make up for it; while in a country like this, where roads are so scanty, many of the farmers' operations are performed more easily during the snow and hard frosts which prevail.

"Leaving Montreal, by a short railroad of nine miles in length, constructed to avoid the rapids of a bend of the St. Lawrence, I came to Lachine. Here are the head-quarters of the Hudson's Bay Company, and the house of Sir George Simpson, the Governor; and hence, annually, towards the end of April, proceed the 'maitre-canots,' or large canoes, of the company, manned by its officers and hardy 'voyageurs,' up the waters of the Ottawa to Lake Nipissing, and down the Riviere des Francais into Lake Huron.

"At Lachine I took the 'Champion,' a fine new steamer, built and equipped at Montreal, and worked up the St. Lawrence, along Lake Ontario, to Toronto, a journey of 450 miles, and occupying about forty hours in the performance.

"The navigation of the St. Lawrence is impeded by several large 'rapids,' formed by the action of the suddenly descending current upon sunken rocks deep below the surface of the water. On the upward voyage these are impassable for merchandize vessels; and, though the large steamers struggle through many of them, there are others which no force can cope with. To remedy these impediments, several fine canals, equal to any similar works in the world, have been constructed. The first of these, the Beauharnois Canal, connects, by a cut eleven miles long, the broad embayment called 'Lake St. Louis,' above Montreal, with the similar reach called 'Lake St. Francis;' and in the narrow passage between these unruffled waters are the principal rapids—the 'Coteau du Lac,' the 'Cedars,' and the 'Cascades.' The passage through this 'sixteen miles' declivity of boiling waters' is exciting. The large steamers rush down with the rapidity of the wind, through waves lashed into foam—sweeping close past the rocks and islets in the stream, and only kept in safety in their course by the united exertions of six or seven 'voyageurs,' and a pilot, at the wheel.

"The upper shores of the St. Lawrence are populous and well cultivated. In stopping to take in our supply of wood, which we had to do several times during the day and night, usually at quiet secluded nooks along shore, or on some little island, I had many opportunities of seeing the comfort of the people, and the progress of the country. The houses, usually of wood, painted white, or of some showy colour, and having verandas covered with climbers, looked both commodious and gay. It might be mistake, but I fancied that improvement was more perceptible when, passing the point where line 45 degrees 'strikes' the river, we came into the American territory. I was particularly struck with one farm near Warrington, over which I had half-an-hour's walk, upon the best fields of which were still protruding the heavy stumps of the forest trees, cut down ten or twenty years ago. The owner told us he had 160 acres, which he bought, partly cleared, seventeen years ago, for ten dollars an acre. He had, a year ago, refused twenty dollars an acre for it, intending to make it worth fifty; and during his occupation he had brought up a large family in comfort and independence upon it, and saved money. The crop of oats he was now clearing was a poor one, he said,—only forty-five bushels per acre.

"Arrived at Ogdensburgh, on the American side of the river, I spent some time, while waiting the arrival of the train bearing Boston and other eastern passengers, in going through the extensive and commodious depot of the Northern Railway. The works are not quite completed. They will cover an area of some forty acres, and comprise warehouses for the stowage of corn and other produce, a fine passenger shed, and large engine-houses and sheds for cars. The quantity of corn and flour stored here in the fall is very large. Last year it was 80,000 barrels. Unfortunately, however, for the railways, the rate for conveyance of these staples is brought down by the competition of the steamers to a very low point; the charge from Toronto to Montreal being but one shilling per barrel of 218 lbs., or a farthing per ton per mile.

"Opposite Ogdensburgh is the village of Prescott, remarkable as the scene of a deadly conflict during the rebellion, the traces of which it still exhibits, in dismantled houses, and a windmill in ruins.

"On the evening of this day we entered a part of the river, called, from the unceasing abundance of islets which gem its surface, the 'Lake of the Thousand Isles.' These islets, above fifteen hundred in number, vary in size from tiny things, little bigger than an upturned boat, to areas of many hundred acres. They are a succession of rocky excrescences, mostly covered with wood, which grows, or overhangs, down to the water's edge. Some of them are cultivated, but the mass are just as nature left them, when—their broken and jutting strata having settled into bearings far down below the stream, on the morrow of some vast convulsion and upheaving of nature— the forest era was at last established. How long a time elapsed before the action of the weather had produced, from the hard face of the stone itself, soil enough for the lichen and the moss, or for these, in their turns, to become the receptacle of the seeds of forest trees, blown from some distant region—is a problem. In threading these islands, sometimes our vessel passed through tortuous passages apparently blocked up at the end, and within a few yards of land, but by a sudden turn emerged into fine large basins, and so wound and twined its way along. As the sun declined, every island made a full, clear reflection in the glassy surface of the water; and the boughs and branches, the flowers by the water's edge, the very marks upon the rocks, were repeated upside down, as if in a perfect mirror. The whole scene bore an air of such complete seclusion, that our noisy passage through it appeared like a rude intrusion into some fairy realm, before time uninvaded by mortal visits. The birds were disturbed from amongst the trees, and the wild ducks and other water-fowl skimmed away, scared at the splashing of our paddles and the panting of our engine.

"At sunset we stopped to take in wood at Gannanoque, a village sweetly placed on a swelling hillock above the river. Here I entered some of the houses, and found considerable comfort, plenty of dirt, and a good many pigs, who seemed on the best possible terms with the children. An Irishwoman, standing at her door, her eldest son in her arms, a fine bright-eyed urchin, told me, in return for my compliments on the healthy appearance of the child, that she 'had been afther bathing him; for sure he had made himself dirty with playing with the pig.'

"The full moon had risen high when we left the last of the isles behind us; and late at night we emerged from the St. Lawrence, and arrived at Kingston, the tin roofs of which shone brightly in the moonlight.

"Kingston is an important town, and is the port of the Rideau Canal, which connects Bytown and the Ottawa with Lake Ontario. A walk through the streets by moonlight enabled us to see the market-house, a stone building, considered to be the finest in Upper Canada.

"Keeping along the north shore of Lake Ontario, we stopped at several thriving little ports, and arrived in Toronto early on the afternoon of Saturday.

"Toronto is the chief city of Upper Canada, and is evidently a highly prosperous place. It has a thoroughly Anglo-Saxon cast about it, and looks new and bright. The streets are long and wide, the houses generally of brick, high and regular; and everywhere is the appearance of vigorous trade and rapid extension. The houses of the richer classes are fully equal to those in the suburbs of Montreal; while no old dilapidated dwellings, like those which appear in that city, are here visible. There are many fine public buildings—St. Lawrence Hall, the Banks, the Parliament House, and many others. The grounds of King's College are well worth a visit. Toronto is at present the seat of Government, and the Governor-General resides here.

"This city, and its people, present many points of favourable contrast with the older cities and population of Lower Canada. The soil and climate may perhaps be more favourable, and the vicinity of American energy may have some effect; but the secret of the greater growth of this province may be traced to its settlement by American Loyalists in 1783. These men, driven away from their country by their adherence to the British Crown, here found a refuge and new home. The whole land along the St. Lawrence, above the French settlements, was formed into townships, and farms were allotted to these, the 'United Empire Loyalists,' who thus became the fathers of Upper

Canada. The population of Upper Canada was not more than 210,000 in 1830, now it is nearly 1,000,000. Much of the land in the Province is equal to any in the world; and nature seems to have given every aid to the formation of a great country. All that is wanting would seem to be that independence, which, with all its reputed vices, would appear to be the condition of Anglo-Saxon progress. Canada has been hitherto the resort of British settlers only, while the United States have become a home for all the world."

What precedes was written nearly thirty-six years ago. I need not apologise for its crudeness, for I only represent, in plain words, the impressions of the time. And I think I have troubled the reader quite enough about my "first visit to America, and the reason for it." I may say, however, that my trip induced many other visits to the growing countries of North America. I was, to some extent, a pioneer traveller to the other side of the Atlantic.

Chapter XVIII
The Reciprocity Treaty with the United States

After asking various questions in the House of Commons, to which I received unsatisfactory replies, I brought the subject of the Reciprocity Treaty with the United States before the House of Commons late one night in February, 1865. My observations, as reported in "Hansard," were:—

"That the hour was too late to permit more than a speech in outline as to the Reciprocity Treaty and the Bonding Acts. Under the latter, articles chargeable with duty could be sent through United States territory and Canada in bond, and as Canada was for the present, and would be until the completion of railway communication to Halifax on the Atlantic, cut off from access to the ocean for five winter months of the year, the Bonding Acts enabled her commerce with the outside world to pass unimpeded. The Northwestern States received in return corresponding facilities of access through Canada. The Reciprocity Treaty included three essential provisions—the rights of fishery on a shore line of 1,500 miles, the free navigation of the St. Lawrence, and the free interchange of productions between the British Provinces and the United States. (The beneficent theory of the treaty was to make two countries, politically distinct, commercially one, and to induce the two peoples, otherwise opposed, to live in co-operation and in peace.) The provision as to the fisheries had settled for the time difficult questions leading, in past days, and over and over again, to dispute, collision, and sometimes the imminence of war. The free navigation of the St. Lawrence and of Lake Michigan had removed jealousies and fostered the idea of common interests in the great waterways to the ocean, while the results of trade had been so happy that a total annual interchange of commodities of a value of nearly 10,000,000_l. a year in amount between the British Provinces and the United States now existed. They were now threatened with the termination of this treaty at the end of twelve months, and no hope appeared to be held out, so far, of an amicable revision and extension of its benefits. The consequences to commerce were evident, and at first would be most serious. Trade at last, no doubt, would take other channels, and the British Provinces, trading between each other and with the Mother Country, and reducing their duties to a low rate, might at the end be largely benefited at the price of a present loss; but that was merely the money view, and such a gain would be dearly purchased at the cost of humanity and civilization if it broke up the commercial and social union heretofore existing. He held that peace and progress and the future good relations between Great Britain and the United States, on which peace and progress were largely based, would suffer by such an isolation, and he would look with distrust upon a prosperity which was not still shared between the people on each side of the border. He had travelled much on both sides of the British lines, and it was cheering to see there how thoroughly one the two peoples had become, socially and commercially. They traded together, went into partnership together, visited together. A Canadian or New Brunswicker would often have a farm on each side of the, practically imaginary, boundary line; and a citizen of the United States often lived on his own and traded or manufactured on the other side of the border. In fact, the border jealousies which had caused such bitterness and danger even in our own country had in this generation all but disappeared in this case, under the operation of high-minded and far-sighted legislation. Considering, therefore, the magnitude of the commercial interests, the grave questions of navigation, ocean rights, and free communication, he must express the most anxious, surprise to learn that Her Majesty's Government had allowed the matter to drift into its present position. He was told that no effort whatever had been made to preserve the treaty as it was, or as it might be amended, by negociations at Washington. His honorable friend, the Under-Secretary for Foreign Affairs, had said, in answer to a question he had put in that House last May, that no negociations were pending as to the Reciprocity Treaty, and that Government had no official information upon the subject of the Bonding Acts. He was bound to take that answer as a correct statement; and he then asked, Was it possible that her Majesty's Government could remain inactive when a trade of 10,000,000_l_ a year and the issues of future peace or disturbance were in the balance? Were the proposed notice to terminate the treaty any matter of suddenness or by way of surprise, he might comprehend it; but for above three years the subject had been agitated and discussed in Congress, in Canada, and in all the Chambers of Commerce in the North-west. It had been notorious to everybody that one party desired isolation from the British Provinces and another desired the operations of the treaty to be extended. It was, therefore, a question to be discussed in advance of the present entanglement; and, as Canada had no treaty-making power, the responsibility rested with the Government at home. This was a question so serious from every point of view that the House would have to take it up as soon as the noble lord at the head of the Government laid upon the table the notice which he had told them would be given on the 15th March next. Then would be the time to discuss it fully and in all its bearings.

His object now was to prepare for that discussion by obtaining all the facts. The papers laid before the House last week did not go back far enough. It appeared that in the autumn of 1861 the New York Chamber of Commerce memorialized Congress for a revision of the treaty, and a committee reported upon it in February, 1862. That report he had here. It did not advocate notice; no, it advocated adherence to the principles of free exchange, and it proposed that commissioners should negociate an extension of the treaty. In March, 1864, Mr. Ward reported resolutions appointing commissioners for that purpose, and ultimately the discussion was postponed to December, 1864. During all this time surely communications of some kind passed to or from this country; and it was self-apparent that the treaty might have been revised and extended before recent causes of irritation had appeared. Those causes had led to much bitter feeling, and it might now be too late to restore the principle of the treaty and of the Bonding Acts in all their integrity. He now moved for all papers subsequent to December, 1861, with a view to further discussion hereafter. He would call attention to a very singular letter, given at pages 70 and 77 in the papers printed last week. That letter had been intercepted by General Augur, and was stated by Mr. Seward to be undoubtedly genuine. He would ask whether any explanation of that letter had been offered by his Excellency the American Minister, Mr. Adams? And, if so, why that explanation had not been printed? The letter was from a Confederate agent residing in Canada, apparently to Mr. Seddon, the Confederate Secretary for War. It must have been written at the end of October last year. It stated that the writer had made an arrangement with parties 'powerful and influential with the Government of the United States' to deliver supplies of meat in exchange for cotton, 'at any port Mr. Secretary Seddon may designate on the east side of the Mississippi,' or on 'the west side,' and after this delivery it was said that 'the way was perfectly clear to deliver anywhere within General Butler's department.' He adds, that he has made another contract with another Federal American citizen, 'by which supplies of meat will be furnished at Mobile by written permission of the President of the United States to the free passage of the blockading fleet at that port.' His contract, he says, is for 5,000,000 lbs. of meat in exchange for 5,000,000 lbs. of cotton. Now, if this were true, it opened up a very large question. Merchants in England who had run the blockade had been most properly censured for the practice. Their having done so was naturally matter of diplomatic complaint; but here were the seal and the signature of the President of the United States himself made use of to send supplies to the enemy on the one hand, and to give cotton to the manufacturers of the Northern States on the other. He thought that letter ought not to have been printed without some comment. If explanations had been given by Mr. Adams and were not printed, the omission was a slight; and he thought a good understanding with the United States, desired so sincerely by, he hoped, the House at large, would not be promoted by its publication."

The "Observer," referring to this speech, made the following remarks:—

"There is a great disadvantage in bringing any important question before the House of Commons at a late hour of the night, because in such a case it is impossible, arising from the exigencies of the morning papers, that full justice can be done by the parliamentary reporters to the speech of the speaker. An illustration, of this occurred on Friday evening. Mr. Watkin, in moving for papers respecting the Reciprocity Treaty between the United States and the British North American Provinces, entered at considerable length and with great ability into that important subject. His speech will be found in another part of our impression. It would not be easy to overrate the importance of the interests to this country involved in the question which Mr. Watkin so lucidly brought before the House. He showed that under the operation of the existing treaty British trading interests to the extent of 10,000,000_l_. per annum were involved. This is no inconsiderable sum. Assuredly it is much too large to be heedlessly sacrificed if means can be found consistent with the honour of the country to prevent it. And yet, notwithstanding the great and manifest importance of the subject, and though the United States have given notice of their intention to terminate the treaty in twelve months from the present time, it would appear that no steps have yet been taken on the part of the Imperial Government to avert the evils of which the termination of that treaty would be productive to the British North American Provinces, and through them to the Mother Country; for, apart from the stoppage that would ensue to the international trade now existing between the States and Canada and her sister provinces, the old vexed question as to the right of Americans to participate in the fisheries in the Gulf of the St. Lawrence, along a shore upwards of 1,500 miles in length, is again raised. To call attention to these facts was the main object of Mr. Watkin's speech. He had no wish to embarass the Government in any way, but was simply desirous of impressing on it the importance of early action in the matter, with the view to the preservation or modification of the Reciprocity Treaty. It is to be hoped, now the matter has been so fully and ably brought before the British Government, that steps will be immediately taken to enter into such negotiations with the United States as will secure this desirable result. If this were done, we cannot doubt that the Government of the United States will respond in a friendly spirit to the wishes of our own Government, and that not only the best results will follow as regards the treaty in question, but also as regards the general commercial relations between the United States, the British North American Provinces, and this country."

I felt so strongly that great opportunities had been lost owing to the negligence and incapacity of our rulers, that I drew up and widely circulated, various memoranda, intended to inform public opinion in England. I felt convinced that, if once this wise and fraternal treaty were allowed to expire, the future relations of the British Provinces and Canada must gravitate towards antagonism, or towards annexation. My forebodings are, at this moment, justified by the action of the United States Congress in the matter of the fisheries. Because Canada has enforced the provisions of the, still existing, and recognized, Treaty of 1818, the Congress of the United States has, in 1887, by statute, instructed the President to put in operation odious "reprisals"— reprisals which throw the "Milan Decrees" of the first Napoleon into the shade of barbarism. The President, believed to be an enlightened man, threatens to put his powers into strict operation. If he goes to the full length of this unique enactment, he may practically close all industrial, and even social, intercourse between the British territory —a territory larger in area than that over which he rules—and the United States. Such legislation, so eagerly acted on, is simply sickening. Talk of fraternity and liberty for all mankind. Delusion —mockery.

A concise *resume* of this question, written by me in 1865, here follows:—

"A treaty of amity and commerce between Great Britain and the United States of America, known as the 'Reciprocity Treaty,' [Endnote 1] has been allowed to expire with the expiry of the twelve months' notice, given on the 17th March, 1865, by the Government at Washington, under the authority of the Senate.

"No explanation has been given to Parliament; nor has a single paper of any kind been laid upon the table of the House by Her Majesty's Government. It is, therefore, thought to be time to ask for explanations, and thereby, so far as may now be possible, to prevent that gradual 'drifting' into serious complication which disfigured the transactions of the Whig Government in 1854 (Russian war), in 1861-2 (Poland), and in 1863-4 (Denmark). The Reciprocity Treaty provided not merely for free interchange of commodities between Her Majesty's North American Colonies and the United States, but it settled the fishery complications, on a coast line of 4,000 miles, and provided for the international navigation of the St. Lawrence (1,200 miles), and of the canals and locks of that mighty river, and of Lake Michigan and its tributaries. It thus dealt with questions which, unsettled and in doubt, had led to antagonism and the recurring danger of war; and, in the twelve years of its existence, its operation has alike enlarged the commerce and the friendship of the neighbouring subjects of the two powers parties to the treaty. Perhaps no convention of modern times has more tended to produce material prosperity and peace and goodwill amongst those concerned. But it has been, it is repeated, allowed to expire, and, as will be shown, owing mainly to the culpable negligence and maladroit management of those who have had charge of British interests.

"On the 27th June, 1854, Lord Clarendon said in the House of Lords, in answer to a question put by Lord Fitzwilliam (see 'Hansard's Debates,' 27th June, 1854):—

"'It appeared to Her Majesty's Government that the return of Lord Elgin to Canada afforded an opportunity which ought not to be neglected, of endeavouring to settle those numerous questions which for years past have been embarrassing the two Governments. One of those questions especially, that relating to the fisheries, has given rise to annually increasing causes of contention, and has sometimes threatened collisions, which, I believe, have only been averted for the last two years by the firmness and moderation of Sir George Seymour and of the British and American naval commanders, and by that spirit of friendship and forbearance which has always characterized the officers of both navies. But, my Lords, your Lordships are aware that there are other questions which have given rise to embarrassing discussion between the Governments of the two countries — questions which involve the commercial relations of our North American possessions with the United States, and that those questions, which involve very divergent interests, have become so complicated as to render their solution a matter of extreme difficulty.' And he added, 'I trust, therefore, that nothing will occur to mar the completion of this great work, which, I firmly believe, more than any other event of recent times, will contribute to remove all differences between two countries, whose similarity of language and affinity of race, whose enterprise and industry, ought to unite them in the bonds of cordial friendship, and to perpetuate feelings of mutual confidence and goodwill.'

"In the conversation which ensued all parties coincided as to the vast importance of the treaty, and Lord Derby, while doing so, took the opportunity of insisting that Her Majesty's Government should keep such treaty negociations affecting the whole Empire in their own hands, and not permit them to be dependent upon the will or consent of the local authorities. He said (see 'Hansard,' 1854):—

"'He was afraid that if we had to consult the Colonies, with respect to a treaty with a foreign country, the effect would be that in such questions the Colonies would be independent.'

"It is well specially here to note, that the Government of that day, speaking by Lord Clarendon, considered it as a condition, that the person highest in dignity, authority, and ability should be selected as the fittest negociator; and that Lord Derby gave a caution which all who regard the British Empire as 'one and indivisible,' must coincide in. It will be seen hereafter how, in the present case, the actual Government has departed from both the condition and the caution.

"An extract from a letter from Mr. John Bright, M.P., to Mr. Joseph Aspinall, of Detroit, Michigan, in response to an invitation to attend the Reciprocity Convention, held last year, will illustrate the benevolent idea of the treaty, and exhibit the opinion of a distinguished admirer of the United States upon the renewal of the instrument. The letter, itself, is dated London, 10th June, 1865. 'The project of your convention gives me great pleasure. I hope it will lead to a renewal of commercial intercourse with the British North American Provinces, *for it will be a miserable thing* if, because they are in connection with the British Crown, and you acknowledge as your Chief Magistrate your President at Washington, there should not be *a commercial intercourse between them and you, as free as if you were one people, living under one Government.'*

"To make 'one people,' though living under two separate Governments, was the great, and has been the successful, object of Lord Elgin and Mr. Marcy. But the 'miserable thing' has happened, and the treaty is at an end.

"On the 23rd May, 1864, I put a question on the subject of the renewal of this treaty. The question and the answer of the Under-Secretary for Foreign Affairs were as follows:—

[*From* "HANSARD," *Monday, May 2nd, 1864.*]

"'Mr. Watkin said he wished to ask the Undersecretary of State for Foreign Affairs to state the present position of negociations with the Government of the United States in reference to the proposed termination or repeal by the United States of the "Reciprocity Treaty," and of the "Bonding Act," under which instruments facilities for mutual commercial interchange have been afforded, and a large and increasing trade has grown up with the colonies of British North America?

"'Mr. Layard, in reply, said there were no negociations pending with regard to the suspension or repeal of the Reciprocity Treaty, and the Government had received no official information upon the subject of the "Bonding Acts."'

"On the 17th February, 1865, I again called attention to the question becoming more and more urgent, by moving for 'Copies of all papers in the possession of Her Majesty's Government respecting the Reciprocity Treaty and the Bonding Acts, of dates subsequent to December, 1861.'

"In reply, the Under-Secretary for Foreign Affairs said (see 'Hansard,' 17th Feb. 1865):—

"'He had only to report what was stated by the noble lord the other night, that there were no papers on the subject of the Reciprocity Treaty; as the hon. gentleman was aware, no notice with respect to the treaty had been given to Her Majesty's Government. Resolutions on the subject had been submitted to Congress, but there had been no intimation given to Her Majesty's Government, consequently, there were really no papers to lay on the table.'

"Thus we have it on the direct declaration of the organ of the Government, that no negociations were undertaken having any reference to the retention or renewal of the treaty up to the 23rd May, 1864; and that there were no 'papers' even in the possession of the Government up to the 17th February, 1865, bearing upon so momentous an international question.

"The Bonding Act, or Acts, are above alluded to; and it will be well here to state, that under these Acts of the Congress of the United States, goods liable to United States duties may be sent in bond through United States territory into and through Canada or New Brunswick. In fact, but for this privilege, Canada would be, under present circumstances, shut out for the five months of her winter from access to Europe. That access could, of course, be given by the construction of the remaining links of the 'Inter-colonial' Railway (about 360 miles), connecting Halifax, Nova Scotia, with Quebec and the Canadian railway system; but pending such construction, it is in the power of the United States thus to isolate Canada. Being in their power, we may ask, What is their intention? and we may ask, What have the Government done to ascertain the one and prevent the other? Have they ever thought of danger? Certainly, in May, 1864, both Mr. Cardwell, the Colonial Secretary, and Mr. Layard, the Undersecretary for Foreign Affairs, were puzzled to know what was meant by the 'Bonding Acts.'

"Particulars of these Acts are given in a note below. [Endnote 2]

"We must now briefly sketch the history of the discussions and events which more immediately preceded the notice of the 17th March, 1865, given by the United States Government and Senate, to put an end to the treaty. Subsequent to the treaty (1854) Great Britain (1859) founded the Colonies of British Columbia and Vancouver's Island on the North Pacific. For this we are indebted to the then colonial minister, Sir E. Bulwer Lytton. The first gave a new gold field; the second contains all the bituminous coal to be found on the west side of the great North American Continent. These new countries were not embraced in the operation of the treaty; nor does it seem that after Sir E. Bulwer Lytton left office, any effort was made to enlarge the operations of the treaty. But of course American commerce was anxious to extend itself, and Californian and American cruisers in the Pacific wanted the coal of Vancouver. Hence a party in the States was formed for an extension of the area of the treaty. Then Canada, having established her railway system by the aid of British capital, and having expended large sums to promote public works generally, got into debt and had to raise her taxation; and as import duties are, and must always be, most easy of collection in a new country, and the most popular, or rather the least unpopular, mode of taxation, she raised her import duties generally to a scale as high on many articles, if not higher, than the import duties of the United States. This led to complaint; and hence a party was formed in the United States for an extension of the 'free list,' or list of articles to be admitted duty free into Canada. It is but fair to bear in mind that the Canadian import duties on United States goods were the same as those on *British* goods; so that whatever ground of complaint might be set up, Great Britain had the right to the largest share of it, because she had the ocean freights to add to the duty, and *pro tanto* was at a disadvantage in competing for Canadian custom with the manufacturers of the States.

"In 1861 the Chamber of Commerce of New York moved Congress on the whole subject. Their object was the extension of the area and purposes of the treaty: in no sense its termination. Congress, hereupon, referred the matter to the 'Committee on Commerce,' Mr. Ward being chairman. That committee reported in February, 1862, in a most able document, usually known as Mr. Ward's report. This report also recommended a more extended area, and *more* extended purposes; but in no sense the abrogation of the treaty.

In March, 1864, Mr. Ward proposed a resolution in Congress for the appointment of commissioners to negociate an extended and improved treaty with Great Britain. That resolution was laid over by Congress till December, 1864. In the summer and autumn of 1864 a correspondence sprang up between Earl Russell, Mr. Seward, Mr. Adams and others in reference to the dangers of the invasion of the territory of the United States by Confederate agents asylumed in Canada. Mr. Seward and Mr. Adams strongly urged that preventive measures should be taken by Great Britain, but Earl Russell could not see it—did nothing, and the burning of United States steamers engaged in peaceful commerce, and the robbery and murders at St. Albans and Vermont followed. Correspondence in reference to the 'St. Albans' raids' was laid before Parliament last year. The following is an extract, bearing, too, indirectly upon the Reciprocity Treaty, from one of the letters of Mr. Adams, United States Ambassador in London, to Earl Russell, echoing a despatch of Mr. Seward's and dated November 23rd, 1864:—

'In the use of the word exigency, the full sense of its effect is perfectly understood. The welfare and prosperity of the neighbouring British Provinces are as sincerely desired on our part as they can be by Great Britain. In a practical sense they are sources of wealth and influence for the one country only in a less degree than for the other, though the jurisdiction appertain only to the latter. That this is the sincere conviction of my Government has been proved by its consent to enter into relations of reciprocal free commerce with them almost as intimate as those which prevail between the several States of the Union themselves. Thus far the disposition has been to remain content with those relations under any and all circumstances, and that disposition will doubtless continue, provided always that the amity be reciprocated, and that the peace and harmony on the border, indispensable to its existence, be firmly secured. The fulfilment of that obligation must be, however, as your Lordship cannot fail to perceive at a glance, the essential and paramount condition of the preservation of the compact. Even were my Government to profess its satisfaction with less, it must be apparent that by the very force of circumstances peace could scarcely be expected to continue long in a region where no adequate security should be afforded to the inhabitants against mutual aggression and reprisal.

'Political agitation, terminating at times in civil strife, is shown by experience to be incident to the lot of mankind, however combined in society. Neither is an evil confined to any particular region or race. It has happened heretofore in Canada, and what is now a scourge afflicting the United States may be likely at some time or other to re- visit her. In view of these very obvious possibilities, I am instructed to submit to Her Majesty's Government the question whether it would not be the part of wisdom to establish such a system of repression now as might prove a rock of safety for the rapidly multiplying population of both countries for all future time.

"'I pray, &c.,
"'(Signed) CHARLES FRANCIS ADAMS.'

"But the 'Alabama' correspondence was also going on, and a new Congress had to sit in 1865. Was it then surprising that on the 17th March, 1865, notice to put an end to the treaty was given?

"But in July, 1865, a convention, already alluded to (see Mr. Bright's letter), composed of delegates from New York, Philadelphia, Baltimore, Cincinnati, St. Louis, Boston, Portland, and in fact from almost every important town and district of the States north of Washington, assembled at Detroit to consider the expiry of the treaty and the question of its renewal.

After long and earnest deliberations they unanimously approved the notice given, and as unanimously passed the following resolution for transmission to the Government of the United States:—

"'That the convention do respectfully request the President of the United States to enter into negociations with the Government of Great Britain, having in view the execution of a treaty between the two countries, for reciprocity and commercial intercourse between the United States and the several Provinces of British North America, including British Columbia, the Selkirk Settlement, and Vancouver's Island, upon principles which should be just and equitable to all parties, and which also shall include the free navigation of the St. Lawrence and other rivers of British North America, with such improvements of the rivers, and enlargement of the canals, as shall render them adequate for the requirements of the west communicating with the ocean.'

"At the time of passing this resolution a 'Revenue Commission' was sitting, and its members recommended the Secretary of the Treasury, Mr. McCulloch, to have a special report upon the treaty and its renewal. The task was, thereupon, committed to Mr. E. H. Derby, of Boston. The Commission also includes this subject in their report. Their report (dated January, 1866,) says:—

"'In accordance with the resolutions of Congress and the notification of the Executive, the commercial arrangement known as the "Reciprocity Treaty," under which the trade and commerce between the United States and the British Provinces of North America have been carried on since 1854, expires on the 17th day of March, 1866. The consideration of the effect which the termination of this important commercial arrangement is likely to have upon the revenue, as well as upon the trade and commerce of the United States, has legitimately formed a part of the duties devolving upon the Commission; and has also been especially commended to their attention by the Secretary of the Treasury. The Commission do not, however, propose to present in this connection any review of the history of the treaty, or of the circumstances which, in the opinion of Congress, have rendered its termination expedient. This work has already been performed, under the auspices of the Treasury Department, by E. H. Derby, Esq., of Boston, to whose able and exhaustive report the Commission would refer, without, however, endorsing its conclusions. There are, however, certain points connected with this subject to which the Commission would ask special attention.

"'The first of these is, that during the continuance of the Reciprocity Treaty the trade and commerce between the United States and the British North American Provinces *has increased* in ten years *more than threefold*, or from seventeen millions in 1862 to sixty-eight millions in 1864: so that at present, with the exception of Great Britain, the commercial relations between the United States and the British North American Provinces outrank in importance and aggregate annual value those existing between this country and any other foreign state. [Footnote: The value of the import and export trade of the United States with the following countries for the year ending June 30th, 1864, was, according to the Treasury Report, as follows (in round numbers):

Great Britain $317,000,000
British North America 68,000,000
Spanish West Indies 57,000,000
France 29,000,000
Hamburg and Bremen 29,000,000
Mexico 20,000,000
Brazil 19,000,000
China 19,000,000
British West Indies .... 12,000,000]

"'It may also, they think, be fairly assumed that taking into consideration the growth of the two countries in population and wealth, (that of Canada for the last ten years having preserved a nearly equal ratio in this respect with that of the United States,) the trade as at present existing is really but in its infancy, and that the future may be expected to develop an increase equally as great as that of the past.

"'A change in the conditions under which a reciprocal commerce of such magnitude is carried on, and is now developing, ought not, therefore, to be made without the most serious consideration.

"'As regards the present treaty, the Commission, as the result of their investigations, have been led to the conclusion that its continuance, under existing circumstances, unless accompanied with certain important modifications, is not desirable on the part of the United States.

"'They, however, are also unanimous in the opinion, that, in view of the close geographical connection of the United States with the British Provinces—rendering them in many respects but one country—and of the magnitude of the commercial relations existing between them, it would be impolitic and to the detriment of the interests of the United States to decline the consideration of all propositions looking to the re- establishment of some future and satisfactory international commercial arrangement. Such a course would be in entire opposition to the spirit of the age, the liberality of our people, and the policy of rapidly developing our resources as a means of diminishing the burden of our public debt.

"'In view of such an arrangement, the question of whether either of the parties to the treaty has, or has not, conformed to the spirit of its stipulations, is of little importance. It is the future, not the past, that we are to consider; and if advantageous terms for the future are offered—terms which are calculated to promote the development of the trade and commerce of the United States, encourage good feeling and prevent difficulties with our neighbours, and at the same time protect the revenues of the country from serious and increasing frauds—it would be, in the opinion of the Commission, most impolitic to disregard them.

"'The offer on the part of the provincial authorities to re-negociate in respect to the commercial relations of the two countries, is in itself an expression of desire to make an arrangement that must be, in every respect, reciprocal; inasmuch as it is evident that no treaty can, for any length of time, continue that does not conduce to the benefit of both parties.

"'It is evident that the necessities of the United States will for many years require the imposition of high rates of taxation on many articles, and that with the production of such articles free, or assessed at low rates of duty, in the British Provinces, the enforcement of the excise laws on the borders will be a matter of no little difficulty, annoyance and expense; and under all ordinary conditions a large annual loss of the revenue must inevitably occur. The experience of all the nations of Europe has shown that to attempt to wholly prevent smuggling, under the encouragement of high rates of duty, is an utter impossibility. If, however, such an arrangement can be made with the British Provinces as will ensure a nearly or quite complete equalization of duties—excise and customs—it must be apparent that all evasions of the revenue laws by smugglers would instantly come to an end; and that the attainment of the above result would be of immense advantage to the United States in a revenue point of view.

"'Again: it is also urged that under the existing system the products of American industry subject to high rates of excise, are injuriously brought into competition with similar products of provincial industry which are subjected to little or no excise, and then admitted into the United States free of duty. That such is the fact cannot be denied; and is itself a reason why the abrogation or modification of the present Reciprocity Treaty has become imperative. But if it were possible to effect such an arrangement with the British Provinces as would allow the imposition of duties equivalent to the American excise on all articles of provincial production passing into the United States, it seems clear that the afore-mentioned objection would be entirely removed.

"'As the whole subject, however, is now before Congress for consideration, the Commission do not consider it as within their province to submit any specific recommendations; but would content themselves with merely pointing out that, under certain circumstances, conditions of great advantage to the United States, in a revenue point of view, might be secured.'

"Mr. Derby's report contains much that is sensational, and many curious admissions, but its general tenor is strongly in favour of a new treaty, regard being had to the revenue necessities of the United States; *i.e.*, that articles admitted into the United States from Canada should pay a duty equivalent to the internal revenue tax on the same articles charged in the States. This is just as if Great Britain said that brandy from France coming into England should pay a duty equivalent to the English excise duty upon spirits, which would be quite fair.

"The next fact in the history is that delegates from Canada, New Brunswick, and Nova Scotia, are found at Washington on the 24th January, 1866, and that they remain there till the 24th February, on which day they report that after many days' discussion they have failed to do anything, and that the Reciprocity Treaty is finally at an end.

"Our Government having done nothing, the Provinces, it would appear, had, at the last moment, to send 'delegates' themselves to negociate; a mode of procedure altogether very unlike the action of 1854.

"The following papers give a *resume* of the discussion : —

"WASHINGTON,
"*February 7th*, 1866.

"'SIR,

"'We have the honour to inform Your Excellency that our negociations for the renewal of Reciprocal Trade with the United States have terminated unsuccessfully. You have been informed from time to time of our proceedings, but we propose briefly to recapitulate them.

"'On our arrival here, after consultation with Your Excellency, we addressed ourselves with your sanction to the Secretary of the Treasury, and we were by him put in communication with the Committee of Ways and Means of the House of Representatives. After repeated interviews with them, and on ascertaining that no renewal or extension of the existing treaty would be made by the American authorities, but that whatever was done must be by legislation, we submitted as the basis upon which we desired arrangements to be made the enclosed paper (marked A).

"'In reply we received the Memorandum from the Committee, of which a copy is enclosed (B). And finding after discussion that no important modifications in their views could be obtained, and that we were required to consider their proposition as a whole, we felt ourselves under the necessity of declining it, which was done by the Memorandum also enclosed (C).

"'It is proper to explain the grounds of our final action.

"'It will be observed that the most important provisions of the expiring treaty, relating to the free interchange of the products of the two countries, were entirely set aside, and that the duties proposed to be levied were almost prohibitory in their character. The principal object for our entering into negociations was therefore unattainable, and we had only to consider whether the minor points were such as to make it desirable for us to enter into specific engagements.

"'These points are three in number.

"'With regard to the first—the proposed mutual use of the waters of Lake Michigan and the St. Lawrence—we considered that the present arrangements were sufficient, and that the common interests of both countries would prevent their disturbance. We were not prepared to yield the right of interference in the imposition of tolls upon our canals. We believed, moreover, that the privilege allowed the United States of navigating the waters of the St. Lawrence was very much more than an equivalent for our use of Lake Michigan.

"'Upon the second point—providing for the free transit of goods under bond between the two countries—we believed that in this respect, as in the former case, the interests of both countries would secure the maintenance of existing regulations. Connected with this point was the demand made for the abolition of the free ports existing in Canada, which we were not disposed to concede, especially in view of the extremely unsatisfactory position in which it was proposed to place the trade between the two countries.

"'On both the above points, we do not desire to be understood as stating that the existing arrangements should not be extended and placed on a more permanent basis, but only that, taken apart from the more important interests involved, it did not appear to us this time necessary to deal with them exceptionally.

"'With reference to the third and last point—the concessions of the right of fishing in provincial waters—we considered the equivalent proposed for so very valuable a right to be utterly inadequate. The admission of a few unimportant articles free, with the establishment of a scale of high duties as proposed, would not, in our opinion, have justified us in yielding this point.

"'While we regret this unfavourable termination of the negociations, we are not without hope that, at no distant day, they may be resumed with a better prospect of a satisfactory result.

"'We have the honour to be,
"'Your Excellency's most obedient Servants,

"'A. T. GALT, Minister of Finance, Canada.
"'W. P. HOWLAND, Postmaster General, Canada.
"'W. A. HENRY, Attorney General, Nova Scotia,
"'A. J. SMITH, Attorney General, New Brunswick.

"'To His Excellency, SIR FREDERICK BRUCE, K.C.B., &c., &c., &c.'"

"'MEMORANDUM A.

"'The trade between the United States and the British Provinces should, it is believed, under ordinary circumstances, be free in reference to their natural productions; but as internal taxes exceptionally exist in the United States, it is now proposed that the articles embraced in the free list of the Reciprocity Treaty should continue to be exchanged, subject only to such duties as may be equivalent to that internal taxation. It is suggested that both parties may add certain articles to those now in the said list. With reference to the fisheries and the navigation of the internal waters of the continent, the British Provinces are willing that the existing regulations should continue in effect; but Canada is ready to enter into engagements with the view of improving the means of access to the ocean, provided the assurance be given that the trade of the Western States will not be diverted from its natural channel by legislation; and if the United States are not prepared at present to consider the general opening of their coasting trade, it would appear desirable that, as regards the internal waters of the Continent, no distinction should be made between the vessels of the two countries.

"'If the foregoing points be satisfactorily arranged, Canada is willing to adjust her excise duties upon spirits, beer and tobacco upon the best revenue standard which may be mutually adopted after full consideration of the subject; and if it be desired to treat any other articles in the same way the disposition of the Canadian Government is to give every facility in their power to prevent illicit trade.

"'With regard to the transit trade, it is suggested that the same regulations should exist on both sides and be defined by law. Canada is also prepared to make her patent laws similar to those of the United States.

"'WASHINGTON, D.C., "'Feb. 2, 1866.'"

"'MEMORANDUM B.

"'In response to the Memorandum of the Hon. Mr. Galt and his associates, Hon. Mr. Smith, Hon. Mr. Henry, and the Hon. Mr. Howland, the Committee of Ways and Means, with the approval of the Secretary of the Treasury, are prepared to recommend to the House of Representatives for their adoption a law providing for the continuance of some of the measures embraced in the Reciprocity Treaty, soon to expire, viz.—For the use and privileges as enjoyed now under said treaty in the waters of Lake Michigan, provided the same rights and privileges are conceded to the citizens of the United States by Canada in the waters of the St. Lawrence and its canals as are enjoyed by British subjects, without discrimination as to tolls and charging rates proportioned to canal distance; also for the free transit of goods, wares, and merchandize in bond, under proper regulations, by railroad across the territory of the United States to and from Portland and the Canada line; provided equal privileges shall be conceded to the United States from Windsor or Port Sarnia, or other western points of departure to Buffalo or Ogdensburg, or any other points eastward, and that the free ports established in the Provinces shall be abolished; also the bounties now given to American fishermen shall be repealed, and duties not higher imposed upon fish than those mentioned in Schedule A., provided that all the rights of fishing near the shores existing under the treaty heretofore mentioned shall be granted and conceded by the United States to the Provinces, and by the Provinces to the United States.

"'It is also further proposed that the following list of articles shall be mutually free:—

> Burr Millstones, unwrought.
> Cotton and Linen Rags.
> Firewood.
> Grindstones, rough or unfinished.
> Gypsum or plaster, unground.

'SCHEDULE A

FISH—Mackerel $1 50 per bbl
" Herrings, pickled or salted 1 00 "
" Salmon 2 50 "
" Shad 2 00 "
" All other, pickled 1 50 "

"'Provided that any fish in packages other than barrels shall pay in proportion to the rates charged upon similar fish in barrels.

All other Fish 1/3 cent per lb

"'As to the duties which will be proposed upon the other articles included in the treaty, the following are submitted, viz.-

Animals, living, all sorts 20 per cent ad val
Apples and Garden Fruit and Vegetables 10 " "
Barley 15 cts per bushel
Beans (except Vanilla or Castor Oil) 30 " "
Beef 1 ct per lb
Buckwheat 10 cts per bushel
Butter 4 " lb
Cheese 4 " "
Corn (Indian) and Oats 10 cts per bushel
Corn-meal (Indian) and Oatmeal 15 " "
Coal, bituminous 50 " ton
  " all other 25 " "
Flour 25 per cent, ad val
Hams 2 cts per lb
Hay $1 00 per ton
Hides 10 per cent ad val
Lard 3 cts per lb
Lumber—
Pine, round or in the log $1 50 per M
" sawed or hewn 2 50 "
" planed, tongued and grooved or finish'd 25 per cent ad val
Spruce and Hemlock, sawed or hewn $1 00 per M
Planed, finished or partly finished 25 per cent ad val
Shingle bolts 10 " "
Shingles 20 " "
All other, of Black Walnut, Chesnut, Bass,
White Wood, Ash, Oak, round, hewed or sawed 20 " "
Planed, tongued and grooved or finished 25 " "
Ores 10 " "
Peas 25 cts per bushel
Pork 1 ct per lb
Potatoes 10 cts per bushel
Seed, Timothy, and Clover 20 per cent ad val
Trees, Plants and Shrubs, Ornamental and Fruit 15 " "
Tallow 2 cts per lb
Wheat 20 cts per bushel

'MEMORANDUM C

"'In reference to the Memorandum received from the Committee of Ways and Means, the Provincial Delegates regret to be obliged to state that the proposition therein contained in regard to the commercial relations between the two countries is not such as they can recommend for the adoption of their respective Legislatures. The imposts which it is proposed to lay upon the productions of the British Provinces on their entry into the markets of the United States are such as in their opinion will be in some cases prohibitory, and will certainly seriously interfere with the natural course of trade. These imposts are so much beyond what the delegates conceive to be an equivalent for the internal taxation of the United States, that they are reluctantly brought to the conclusion that the Committee no longer desire the trade between the two countries to be carried on upon the principle of reciprocity. With the concurrence of the British Minister at Washington, they are therefore obliged respectfully to decline to enter into the engagement suggested in the memorandum, but they trust that the present views of the United States may soon be so far modified as to permit of the interchange of the productions of the two countries upon a more liberal basis.

"'WASHINGTON,
"'*February 6th*, 1866.'

"This abortive negociation was followed (March, 1866) by a United States Bill for enabling a new treaty upon impossible terms; that Bill was at last hung up in Congress, and so the matter ended, so far as the States were concerned.

"The operation of the treaty from 1854 to 1866 may now be considered.

"The Report of the Revenue Commissioners shows that the trade under it increased from 20,000,000 dollars, to 68,000,000 dollars in 1864, and that this trade was larger than the trade of the United States with any country in the world except Great Britain. It was 31/2 times more than with China; 31/2 times more than with Brazil; above 3 times more than with even Mexico; 21/4 times more than with Hamburg and Bremen, notwithstanding the direct line of steamers to and from New York; 21/4 times more than with France, with all its wines, silks, and fashions; and one-third more than with Cuba and the Spanish West Indies.

"Then, on the whole, 'the balance of trade,' as it is called, was in favour of the States during the whole period of the treaty by a sum of 56,000,000 dollars.

"As regards coal, the quantity taken in 1865-6 from Pennsylvania and other States to Upper Canada was about 180,000 tons; while the quantity of Nova Scotian coal taken to Boston and the Eastern States was about 200,000 tons. Thus the supply of districts 1,000 miles apart had nearly balanced itself under the treaty. As regards fishing rights, the United States appeared largely to have the advantage, for they had, by the treaty, access to excellent fishing grounds and passage through the Gut of Canso, while the provincial fishermen rarely troubled the coasts of Maine or Massachusetts—'bare pastures' for fish. As an example, the boats employed by the United States in the mackerel fishery in 1852 were 250, the tonnage 18,150 tons, and the value 750,000 dollars, while the catch of fish was 850,000 dollars; while in 1864 it showed 600 vessels, 54,000 tons, 9,000 men, and a catch worth 4,567,500 dollars.

"Upon the general question, Mr. Derby says in his report:—

"'If the Maritime Provinces would join us spontaneously to-day— sterile as they may be in the soil under a sky of steel—still with their hardy population, their harbours, fisheries, and seamen, they would greatly strengthen and improve our position, and aid us in our struggle for equality upon the ocean. If we would succeed upon the deep, we must either maintain our fisheries, *or absorb the Provinces.*'

"'No negociations' and 'no papers'—say our Government. This may be true. Or it may be true that the Foreign Office have had papers, and the Colonial not. Or that the Board of Trade have had papers, and the Foreign and Colonial people have not; but, however that may be, Canada has made, in good time, very serious representations. It is believed that her Government had long before made personal appeals to both the Colonial and the Foreign Offices, but the following document (19th February, 1865), will speak for itself; and the Government at home cannot deny that they had it, but which of the three departments will admit its receipt is yet to be seen; always let it be remembered that in *May,* 1865, there were 'no papers:'—

"'*Copy of a Report of a Committee of the Honorable the Executive Council,* approved by his Excellency the Governor-General on the 19th February, 1865.

"'The Committee of the Executive Council deem it to be their duty to represent to Your Excellency that the recent proceedings in the Congress of the United States, respecting the Reciprocity Treaty, have excited the deepest concern in the minds of the people of this Province.

"'Those proceedings have had for their avowed object the abrogation of the treaty at the earliest moment consistent with the stipulations of the instrument itself.

"'Although no formal action indicative of the strength of the party hostile to the continuance of the treaty has yet taken place, information, of an authentic character, as to the opinions and purposes of influential public men in the United States has forced upon the Committee the conviction that there is imminent danger of its abrogation, unless prompt and vigorous steps be taken by Her Majesty's Imperial advisers to avert what would be generally regarded by the people of Canada as a great calamity.

"'The Committee would specially bring under Your Excellency's notice the importance of instituting negotiations for the renewal of the treaty, with such modifications as may be mutually assented to, before the year's notice required to terminate it shall be given by the American Government; for they fear that the notice, if once given, would not be revoked; and they clearly foresee that, owing to the variety and possibly the conflicting nature of the interests involved on our own side, a new treaty could not be concluded, and the requisite legislation to give effect to it obtained before the year would have expired, and with it the treaty. Under such circumstances—even with the certain prospect of an early renewal of the treaty—considerable loss and much inconvenience would inevitably ensue.

"'It would be impossible to express in figures, with any approach to accuracy, the extent to which the facilities of commercial intercourse created by the Reciprocity Treaty have contributed to the wealth and prosperity of this Province; and it would be difficult to exaggerate the importance which the people of Canada attach to the continued enjoyment of these facilities.

"'Nor is the subject entirely devoid of political significance.

"'Under the beneficent operation of the system of self-government, which the later policy of the Mother Country has accorded to Canada, in common with the other Colonies possessing representative institutions, combined with the advantages secured by the Reciprocity Treaty of an unrestricted commerce with our nearest neighbours in the natural productions of the two countries, all agitation for organic changes has ceased—all dissatisfaction with the existing political relations of the Province has wholly disappeared.

"'Although the Committee would grossly misrepresent their countrymen if they were to affirm that their loyalty to their Sovereign would be diminished in the slightest degree by the withdrawal, through the unfriendly action of a foreign Government, of mere commercial privileges, however valuable these might be deemed, they think they cannot err in directing the attention of the enlightened statesmen who wield the destinies of the great Empire, of which it is the proudest boast of Canadians that their country forms a part, to the connection which is usually found to exist between the material prosperity and the political contentment of a people, for in doing so they feel that they are appealing to the highest motives that can actuate patriotic statesmen—the desire to perpetuate a dominion founded on the affectionate allegiance of a prosperous and contented people.

"'The Committee venture to express the hope that Your Excellency will be pleased to bring this subject and the considerations now submitted under the notice of Her Majesty's Imperial advisers.

'W. H. LEE, C. E. C.'

"Does it not seem as if the whole business was let alone, neglected, despised?

"What were our Government doing from 1861 to 1865?

"POLAND exercised the minds of the Foreign Office from an early date, and they have given us papers from July 31st, 1862, December 31st of that year, and on to April 23rd, 1863, when that affair ended.

"DENMARK revived their old discussions in 1863, and they began to write despatches about them. They have given Parliament papers about the 'Conference,' which only began January 23rd, 1864, and ended March 26th, 1864.

"The whole number of papers printed for Parliament, and laid on the table in 1864, was 369. Yet there was not, out of these, one single paper about the Reciprocity Treaty.

"The whole number of papers printed for Parliament, and laid likewise upon the table in 1865, was 170, but not a line appears about the Reciprocity Treaty. So much for the attention of the people we pay to watch over our affairs.

"The question, as regards our relations with the States, Was a great opportunity lost? arises. Let us see. 1st, the Chamber of Commerce of New York, and its 1,300,000 people, ask for a treaty in 1861; 2nd, Congress asks for it by appointing a committee in 1861; 3rd, the committee ask for it by their report of 1862 and by their resolutions of 1864; 4th, Mr. Seward endorses it even so late as November, 1864; and 5th, the Convention at Detroit ask for it so late as the 14th July, 1865. In further testimony, a member of Congress said, on the 14th March, 1866, on the debate on the *abortive Bill* for regulating trade with British North American Provinces:—

"Mr. Brooks, 'Dem. N. Y.,' said, 'that he would not have risen to obtrude any remarks on the committee on a subject that had been discussed with an ability and ingenuity reminding him, of ancient times in the House, and demonstrating that upon subjects which interest our own race there is as much ability here as of old, if he had not voted last year, with others, for an abrogation of the Reciprocity Treaty, and if he did not see now, from the tendencies and sympathies of the House, that the moment the Bill passed from the hands of the committee of the whole it would receive its final death blow. He did not believe there would have been thirty votes obtained in this House last year for the abrogation of the Reciprocity Treaty with Canada, but for the explicit understanding that some sort of reciprocity in trade would be forthwith re-established, either through the treaty-making power, or through the legislative power of the Government. The people of the United States were ground down by the internal revenue taxation, and he had not felt at liberty to let the Reciprocity Treaty stand, without being at liberty to make some sort of bargain with the people of Canada, that whatever our internal revenues might be, the same would be levied, either by them or by us, on our imports from them. It was exclusively on that understanding that he had voted for the abrogation of the treaty. And he now saw in the additional claims of those who represented the lumber interests, and the coal and other interests of the country, that advantage was to be taken of the present opportunity, and that never again were we to have reciprocity with the neighbouring Provinces. On the contrary, we were to impose as high duties as could be imposed upon their products, higher if possible than those now levied under the general tariff bill. If that were to be so, he never should regret any vote that he gave in his life as he would regret his vote of last winter to abrogate the treaty. He had given it with the understanding that it should be substantially renewed. He spoke of the people of the Provinces as being connected with us by kindred and by blood, and as rightfully belonging to us; and he hoped to live to see the day when the seats on this floor and in the Senate would be occupied by representatives and senators from Canada, New Brunswick, Nova Scotia, Prince Edward's Island, and all the other American dependencies of Great Britain.'

"Then it will not be forgotten that the Government and Congress of the States ratified a treaty with Great Britain, which never could before be acted on, viz., that affecting the African slave trade, on the 7th April, 1862, and they agreed to the important additional article on the 17th February, 1863. At these dates the Government and people of the United States were most anxious, therefore, for friendly relations with us. But Earl Russell lost the golden opportunity. British interests were entirely neglected.

"We must now look at the new features of difficulty which have sprung up; and first, there is now a Congress with a Republican majority, and the majority of that majority are Protectionists: while a considerable number are Annexationists.

"The Convention at Detroit was appealed to by the latter. Mr. Consul Potter, United States Consul at Montreal, Canada, and Mr. O. S. Wood, Manager of the Montreal Telegraph Company, appear in the following report of a speech of the Consul at a meeting specially convened by him at Detroit:—

"Mr. Consul Potter, at Detroit, July 12th, 1865, said, "'I would meet the people of Canada on the most friendly footing, but I would say to them, in making an arrangement, we must look to our own interest as well as yours, and in looking to our interest we cannot forget that the policy we may adopt in relation to reciprocity will have a very great influence on the future relations of the two countries. Now, we are ready to give you in Canada the most perfect reciprocity. We will give you complete free trade, but we ask you to come and share with us the responsibilities of our own government. We make this proposition, but not in a spirit of conquest, for, as I remarked before, if it were positively certain that by one day of war we could obtain possession of the whole Provinces for ever I would say—No!—for this reason, that after the conquest you would find a feeling of opposition to the United States and our government on the part of the people of Canada which would prevent any harmonious working. When they come, let them come by their own consent, let them come as brothers, and let us be all brothers with one flag, under one destiny. The question then is, Shall we simply be content to give the Canadians all the privileges of our markets? For the true policy is, that in getting those privileges they should be placed on equal footing with our own citizens in relation to our responsibilities and in relation to taxation. I believe I express the general feeling of those who are the most friendly to the United States in Canada when I say it is not the policy of our Government, or our policy, to continue this treaty, and I believe that in two years from the abrogation of the Reciprocity Treaty, the people of Canada themselves will apply for admission to the United States. I repeat that I believe in two years they would ask for admission. I have a letter which I received on the evening of my departure for Detroit, and I may say I came here, with the consent of my own Government, to express my views on reciprocity. This letter is from a gentleman in Montreal, than whom none stands higher—a gentleman of intelligence and wealth, and whose judgment is as good as that of any person in Canada on these matters:—

"'MONTREAL,   "'July
10th.

'MY DEAR. MR. POTTER,

"'I am much delighted to hear that you have decided to attend the Detroit Convention, as it is in my opinion of the greatest importance that the real friends of the United States who reside here shall be represented at Detroit, or that our friends, before committing themselves to a renewal of the Reciprocity Treaty, may know our views on the subject; and I can assure you, from the knowledge I have of the sentiments of those who have been and still are the friends of the United States in this country, that not one in fifty of them wants a renewal or extension of the treaty. On the other hand, every man who has been openly hostile to us is for the renewal. The reasons are obvious, as it is clear to all intelligent men that a failure to renew the treaty will result in thorough reciprocity. All the friends of the Western States here, and they are rapidly increasing in numbers and influence, would rejoice to submit to temporary inconvenience and loss, for the purpose of accomplishing this result, while those who are against us wish for a renewal of the treaty which, during the last four years, has given so much trouble to both sides. They know that a renewal of the treaty would be the only effectual check on the annexation movement. I believe the renewal of it would be one of the greatest political blunders on the part of the United States. This is the feeling of our friends on this side, and I am sure our friends on the other side of the frontier who have already suffered so much, will join us heartily in this additional sacrifice, if such it should prove.'

"As Mr. Potter closed reading the letter there were loud cries from the Canadian delegates of 'Name, name.'

"Mr. Potter gave the name, 'O. S. Wood, Superintendent of the Montreal Telegraph Company'—a gentleman, he said, of wealth and the highest respectability in Montreal.

"Some one asked whether Wood was a born Canadian.

"Mr. Potter replied he was not, but came originally from New York.

"The Republican journals in the West have since taken up this tone, and Mr. Morrill, the Protectionist chairman of the 'Committee of Ways and Means,' echoed it even in conference with the provincial delegates at Washington last February:—Witness the following:—

"'Chicago Tribune' (Republican), Jan. 6th, 1866.

"The 'Tribune' concludes:—'The Canadians will soon discover that free trade and smuggling will not compensate them for the loss of the Reciprocity Treaty. They will stay out in the cold for a few years and try all sorts of expedients, but in the end will be constrained to knock for admission into the Great Republic. Potter was right when he predicted that the abrogation of the treaty would cause annexation.'

"(Mr. MORRILL, Chairman of Ways and Means, "Washington, Feb. 6th, 1866.)

"'Mr. GALT: We would not build those canals for our own trade alone. I think, indeed, it might well be considered whether it would not suit both parties to put this trade on a better footing. I am not authorized to make any proposition looking to this end, but my idea is that these waters might be neutralized with advantage to both.

"'Mr. MORRILL: That will have to be postponed until *you, gentlemen, assume your seats here.'*

"Mr. Derby coolly discusses the question as to whether concession or coercion will best succeed in inducing the British Provinces to 'come over,' and his recipe for all outstanding grievances is the following. He says, in his report of January 1st, 1866:—

"'And if as an inducement for this treaty and in settlement of Alabama claims we can obtain a cession of Vancouver's Island, or other territory, it will be a consummation most devoutly to be wished for.'

"Would our Government 'devoutly wish' such a consummation?

"Mr. O. S. Wood had to resign his position as manager of the Montreal Telegraph Company: that was done by public opinion in Canada. But Mr. Potter, who attends a meeting to enforce the annexation of a part of the Queen's dominions, by the consent of the Washington Government, is still Consul at Montreal.

"But what are these dominions which Mr. Potter would annex? Read what Mr. Ward's Report of 1862 says:—

"'The great and practical value of the British North American Provinces and possessions is seldom appreciated. Stretching from the Atlantic to the Pacific Oceans, they contain an area of at least 3,478,380 square miles—more than is owned by the United States, and not much less than the whole of Europe, with its family of nations!

"'The climate and soil of these Provinces and possessions, seemingly less indulgent than those of tropical regions, are precisely those by which the skill, energy, and virtues of the human race are best developed. Nature there demands thought and labour from man as conditions of his existence, and yields abundant rewards to a wise industry.'

"Specially, as regards Canada; let us recapitulate her progress, as compared with that of her giant neighbour, the United States.

"During the interval between the last census and the preceding one (1850-1860), the decennial rate of increase of population in Canada exceeded that in the United States by nearly 51/2 per cent.—Canada adding 40.87 per cent. to her population in ten years, while the United States added only 35.58 per cent. to theirs. She brought her wild land into cultivation at a rate, in nine years, exceeding the rate of increase of cultivated lands in the United States in ten years by nearly 6 per cent.,—Canada in 1860 having added 50 acres of cultivated land to every 100 acres under cultivation in 1851, while the United States in 1860 had only added 14 acres to every 100 acres under cultivation in 1850. The value per cultivated acre of the farming lands in Canada in 1860 exceeded the value per cultivated acre of the farming lands of the United States—the average value per cultivated acre in Canada being $20.87 and in the United States $16.32. In Canada a larger capital was invested in agricultural implements, in proportion to the amount of land cultivated, than in the United States—the average value of agricultural implements used on a farm having 100 cultivated acres being in Canada $182 and in the United States $150. In proportion to population, Canada in 1860 raised twice as much wheat as the United States—Canada in that year raising 11.2 bushels for each inhabitant, while the United States raised only 5.50 bushels for each inhabitant. Bulking together eight leading staples of agriculture—wheat, corn, rye, barley, oats, buckwheat, peas and bean, and potatoes,—Canada, between 1851 and 1860, increased her production of these articles from 57 millions to 123 millions of bushels—an increase; of 113 per cent.; while the United States in ten years, from 1850 to 1860, increased their productions of the same articles only 45 per cent. In 1860 Canada raised, of those articles, 49.12 bushels for each inhabitant, against a production in the United States of 43.42 bushels for each inhabitant. Excluding Indian corn from the list—Canada raised of the remaining articles 48.07 bushels for each inhabitant, almost three times the rate of production in the United States, which was 16.74 bushels for each inhabitant. And as regards live stock and their products, Canada in 1850, in proportion to her population, owned more horses and more cows, made more butter, kept more sheep, and had a greater yield of wool, than the United States.

"Our British Government having thus allowed the treaty to expire, and having thereby damped the energies of the colonies, and excited the hopes of the Protectionist and Annexationist parties in the States, what are we to do?

"In the first place, Parliament should express its condemnation of the failure of the executive; in the second, its desire for peace and fraternity with the United States; and in the third, its determination to stand by the Queen's dominions on the other side of the Atlantic. Language so just and so clear would lead to the inevitable result of renewed negociation. But who should negociate? The incapable, nonchalant people who have so signally perilled the interests of Great Britain,—or new and capable men? Or should the whole state of our relations with the United States be remitted to a plenipotentiary?

"What ought we to seek now to secure, in the interests of peace and civilization?

"1. A neutralization of the 3,000 miles of frontier, rendering fortifications needless.

"2. A continuance of the neutrality of the lakes and rivers bordering upon the two territories.

"3. Common navigation of the lakes and the outlets of the sea.

"4. An enlargement of canals and locks, to enable the food of the west to flow unimpeded and at the smallest cost direct in the same bottom to Europe, or any other part of the world.

"5. Neutrality of telegraphs and post routes between the Atlantic and Pacific, no matter on which territory they may traverse.

"6. A free interchange of untaxed, and an exchange, at internal revenue duty rate only, of taxed, commodities.

"7. The passage of goods in bond through the respective territories as heretofore.

"8. A common use of ports on both sides of the Continent."

It seems to me, now, in 1887, that this paper sums up a question of the past, now re-appearing in full prominence. It also sums up what ought to be done if civilization and friendship between English-speaking nations still exist.

[Endnote 1]

The Government of the United States being equally desirous with Her Majesty the Queen of Great Britain to avoid further misunderstanding between their respective citizens and subjects in regard to the extent of the right of fishing on the coasts of British North America secured to each by Article I of a Convention between the United States and Great Britain, signed at London on the 20th day of October, 1818; and being also desirous to regulate the commerce and navigation between their respective territories and people, and more especially between Her Majesty's possessions in North America and the United States, in such manner as to render the same reciprocally beneficial and satisfactory, have respectively named Plenipotentiaries to confer and agree thereupon—that is to say, the President of the United States of America, William L. Marcy, Secretary of State of the United States; and Her Majesty, the Queen of the United Kingdom of Great Britain and Ireland, James, Earl of Elgin and Kincardine, Lord Bruce and Elgin, a peer of the United Kingdom, knight of the most ancient and most noble Order of the Thistle, and Governor General in and over all Her Britannic Majesty's provinces on the continent of North America and in and over the island of Prince Edward—who, after having communicated to each other their respective full powers, found in good and due form, have agreed upon the following articles:—

ART. I. It is agreed by the high contracting parties that, in addition to the liberty secured to the United States fishermen by the above- mentioned convention of October 20, 1818, of taking, curing, and drying fish on certain coasts of the British North American Colonies therein defined, the inhabitants of the United States shall have, in common with the subjects of Her Britannic Majesty, the liberty to take fish of every kind, except shell-fish, on the sea-coasts and shores, and in the bays, harbours, and creeks of Canada, New Brunswick, Nova Scotia, Prince Edward's Island, and of the several islands thereunto adjacent, without being restricted to any distance from the shore; with permission to land upon the coasts and shores of those colonies and the islands thereof, and also upon the Magdalen Islands, for the purpose of drying their nets and curing their fish: provided that, in so doing, they do not interfere with the rights of private property or with British fishermen in the peaceable use of any part of the said coast in their occupancy for the same purpose.

It is understood that the above-mentioned liberty applies solely to the sea fishery, and that the salmon and shad fisheries, and all fisheries in rivers and the mouths of rivers, are hereby reserved exclusively for British fishermen.

And it is further agreed that, in order to prevent or settle any disputes as to the places to which the reservation of exclusive right to British fishermen contained in this article, and that of fishermen of the United States contained in the next succeeding article, apply, each of the high contracting parties, on the application of either to the other, shall, within six months thereafter, appoint a commissioner. The said commissioners, before proceeding to any business, shall make and subscribe a solemn declaration that they will impartially and carefully examine and decide, to the best of their judgment and according to justice and equity, without fear, favour, or affection to their own country, upon all such places as are intended to be reserved and excluded from the common liberty of fishing under this and the next succeeding article, and such declaration shall be entered on the record of their proceedings.

The commissioners shall name some third person to act as an arbitrator or umpire in any case or cases on which they may themselves differ in opinion. If they should not be able to agree upon the name of such third person, they shall each name a person, and it shall be determined by lot which of the two persons so named shall be the arbitrator or umpire in cases of difference or disagreement between the commissioners. The person so to be chosen to be arbitrator or umpire shall, before proceeding to act as such in any case, make and subscribe to a solemn declaration in a form similar to that which shall already have been made and subscribed by the commissioners, which shall be entered on the record of their proceedings. In the event of the death, absence, or incapacity of either of the commissioners, or of the arbitrator or umpire, or of their or his omitting, declining, or ceasing to act as such commissioner, arbitrator, or umpire, another and different person shall be appointed or named as aforesaid to act as such commissioner, arbitrator, or umpire in the place and stead of the person so originally appointed or named as aforesaid, and shall make and subscribe such declaration as aforesaid.

Such commissioners shall proceed to examine the coasts of the North American Provinces and of the United States embraced within the provisions of the first and second articles of this treaty, and shall designate the places reserved by the said articles from the common right of fishing therein.

The decision of the commissioners and of the arbitrator or umpire shall be given in writing in each case, and shall be signed by them respectively.

The high contracting parties hereby solemnly engage to consider the decision of the commissioners conjointly, or of the arbitrator or umpire, as the case may be, as absolutely final and conclusive in each case decided upon by them or him respectively.

ART. 2. It is agreed by the high contracting parties that British subjects shall have, in common with the citizens of the United States, the liberty to take fish of every kind, except shell-fish, on the eastern sea-coasts and shores of the United States north of the 36th parallel of north latitude, and on the shores of the several islands thereunto adjacent, and in the bays, harbours, and creeks, of the said sea-coasts and shores of the United States and of the said islands, without being restricted to any distance from the shore, with permission to land upon the said coasts of the United States and of the islands aforesaid for the purpose of drying their nets and curing their fish; provided that, in so doing, they do not interfere with the rights of private property, or with the fishermen of the United States in the peaceable use of any part of the said coasts in their occupancy for the same purpose.

It is understood that the above-mentioned liberty applies solely to the sea fishery, and that salmon and shad fisheries, and all fisheries in rivers and months of rivers, are hereby reserved exclusively for fishermen of the United States.

ART. 3. It is agreed that the articles enumerated in the schedule hereunto annexed, being the growth and produce of the aforesaid British Colonies or of the United States, shall be admitted into each, country respectively free of duty:—

SCHEDULE.

Grain, flour and breadstuffs of all kinds.
Animals of all kinds.
Fresh, smoked, and salted meats.
Cotton-wool, seeds, and vegetables.
Undried fruits, dried fruits.
Fish of all kinds.
Products of fish, and all other creatures living in the water.
Poultry, eggs.
Hides, furs, skins, or tails, undressed.
Stone or marble, in its crude or unwrought state.
Slate.
Butter, cheese, tallow.
Lard, horns, manures.
Ores of metals of all kinds.
Coal.
Pitch, tar, turpentine, ashes.
Timber and lumber of all kinds, round, hewed and sawed,
unmanufactured,
in whole or in part.
Firewood.
Plants, shrubs, and trees.
Pelts, wool.
Fish oil.
Rice, broom-corn, and bark.
Gypsum, ground or unground.
Hewn or wrought or unwrought burr or grindstones.
Dye-stuffs.
Flax, hemp, and tow, unmanufactured.
Unmanufactured tobacco.
Rags.

ART. 4. It is agreed that the citizens and inhabitants of the United States shall have the right to navigate the river St. Lawrence, and the canals in Canada, used as the means of communicating between the great lakes and the Atlantic Ocean, with their vessels, boats, and crafts, as fully and freely as the subjects of Her Britannic Majesty, subject only to the same tolls and other assessments as now are or may hereafter be exacted of Her Majesty's said subjects; it being understood, however, that the British Government retains the right of suspending this privilege on giving due notice thereof to the Government of the United States.

It is further agreed that, if at any time the British Government should exercise the said reserved right, the Government of the United States shall have the right of suspending, if it think fit, the operation of article three of the present treaty, in so far as the Province of Canada is affected thereby, for so long as the suspension of the free navigation of the river St. Lawrence or the canals may continue.

It is further agreed that British subjects shall have the right freely to navigate Lake Michigan with their vessels, boats, and crafts, so long as the privilege of navigating the river St. Lawrence, secured to American citizens by the above clause of the present article, shall continue; and the Government of the United States further engages to urge upon the State Governments to secure to the subjects of Her Britannic Majesty the use of the several State canals on terms of equality with the inhabitants of the United States.

And it is further agreed that no export duty or other duty shall be levied on lumber or timber of any kind cut on that portion of the American territory in the State of Maine watered by the river St. John and its tributaries, and floated down that river to the sea, when the same is shipped to the United States from the Province of New Brunswick.

ART. 5. The present treaty shall take effect as soon as the laws required to carry it into operation shall have been passed by the Imperial Parliament of Great Britain and by the Provincial Parliaments of those of the British North American Colonies which are affected by this treaty on the one hand, and by the Congress of the United States on the other. Such assent having been given, the treaty shall remain in force for ten years from the date at which it may come into operation, and further, until the expiration of twelve months after either of the high contracting parties shall give notice to the other of its wish to terminate the same; each of the high contracting parties being at liberty to give such notice to the other at the end of the said term of ten years, or at any time afterwards:

It is clearly understood, however, that this stipulation is not intended to affect the reservation made by article four of the present treaty, with regard to the right of temporarily suspending the operation of articles three and four thereof.

ART. 6. And it is further hereby agreed that the provisions and stipulations of the foregoing articles shall extend to the Island of Newfoundland, so far as they are applicable to that colony. But if the Imperial Parliament, the Provincial Parliament of Newfoundland, or the Congress of the United States shall not embrace in their laws, enacted for carrying this treaty into effect, the Colony of Newfoundland, then this article shall be of no effect; but the omission to make provision by law to give it effect, by either of the legislative bodies aforesaid, shall not in any way impair the remaining articles of this treaty.

ART. 7. The present treaty shall be duly ratified and the mutual exchange of ratifications shall take place in Washington within six months from the date hereof, or earlier if possible.

In faith whereof we, the respective Plenipotentiaries, have signed this treaty, and have hereunto affixed our seals.

Done in triplicate at Washington, the fifth day of June, anno Domini one thousand eight hundred and fifty-four.

W. L. MARCY. [L.S.] ELGIN AND KINCARDINE. [L.S.]]

[Endnote 2:]

Act cap. 71 [Dunlop's Laws of the United States, Federal], passed March 3rd, 1845, page 1075

"SEC. 7. That any imported merchandize which has been entered, and the duties paid or secured according to law, for drawback, may be exported to the British North American Provinces, adjoining the United States; and the ports of Plattsburg, in the District of Champlain; Burlington, in the District of Vermont; Sackett's Harbour, Oswego, and Ogdensburg, in the District of Oswegatchie; Rochester, in the District of Genesee; Buffalo and Erie, in the District of Prequ'isle; Cleveland, in the District of Cuyahoga; Sandusky and Detroit, together with such ports on the seaboard from which merchandize may now be exported for the benefit of drawback, are hereby declared ports from whence foreign goods, wares and merchandize on which the import has been paid or secured to be paid, may be exported to ports in the adjoining British Provinces, and to which ports foreign goods, wares, and merchandize may be transported inland, or by water from the port of original importation, under existing provisions of law, to be thence exported for benefit of drawback. Provided, that such other ports situated on the frontiers of the United Sates, adjoining the British North American Provinces, as may hereafter be found expedient, may have extended to them the like privileges on the recommendation of the Secretary of the Treasury, and proclamation duly made by the President of the United States, specially designating the ports to which the aforesaid privileges are to be extended."

NOTE—Several other ports have since been proclaimed, viz., Whitehall, Lewiston, and others.

"SEC. 11. That the Secretary of the Treasury is hereby further authorized to prescribe such rules and regulations, not inconsistent with the laws of the United States, as he may deem necessary to carry into effect the provisions of this Act, and to prevent the illegal re- importation of any goods, wares, or merchandize which shall have been exported as herein provided; and that all Acts or parts of Acts inconsistent with the provisions of this Act, be, and the same are hereby repealed."

See, also, Warehousing Act of United States Congress, chapter 48, Dunlop's United States Statutes, page 1106, passed 6th August, 1846, in which it is enacted as follows:—

"And in case the owner, importer, consignee or agent of any goods on which the duties have not been paid shall give to the collector satisfactory security that the said goods shall be landed out of the jurisdiction of the United States in the manner now required by existing laws relating to exportations, for the benefit of drawback, the collector, &c., on an entry to re-export the same shall, upon payment of the appropriate expenses, permit the said goods, under the inspection of the proper officers, to be shipped without the payment of any duties thereon," &c.

Chapter XIX
The Defences of Canada

In February and March, 1865, I spoke in the House of Commons on the general question of the defences of Canada; and, also, on the special vote (carried by a majority of 235) of 50,000_l_. for the fortifications of Quebec. The first of these speeches was delivered on the 13th March, 1865; the second on the 23rd March. On the second occasion I was followed by Lord Palmerston; and I commend his speech, pithy and decisive as it was, to the statesmen who have to deal with our Imperial relations with Canada, and with her Canadian Pacific Railway.

"Hansard" reports that,—

"Mr. WATKIN said that having, like the right hon. gentleman the member for Calne, visited Canada not once but frequently, he felt unable to corroborate the description given of Quebec; nor could he agree as to what had been said of other places. The fortifications of Quebec were not those of the days of Wolfe; they had been systematically enlarged and strengthened. Quebec, naturally a position of enormous strength, was now most efficiently fortified, and so far from the nature of the surrounding country exposing it to attack, that country presented features enabling the speedy and easy construction of additional works rendering the fortress impregnable. In fact, it might easily be made the strongest work upon the continent. Nor was it fair to say, as the gallant member opposite had declared, that the guns were all antiquated and the gun-carriages rotten. It was true that many of the guns were old, but newer ordnance had been supplied; there were abundant stores of shot, shell, and rockets, and a considerable number of Armstrong guns had been received at the citadel very recently. Canada could be made capable of defence, without difficulty, though, of course, not without cost. No one would contend that the defence of Canada, if an Imperial duty, was simply an Imperial liability. Every one would admit that the colony should contribute, both in times of peace and of war, its fair share of the burden. Independence and defence were co-existent ideas, and Canada, desiring to be free of foreign control, should, and he hoped would, be ready to defray her just and honest share of the burden. He took this as admitted on all hands and on both sides of the Atlantic. His objection, then, to the proposal of the Government was that it was not worthy of that emergency which alone could justify the policy of the fortification of a frontier. But the question really before the House was not one of the extent of territory to defend, but plainly this—Was this House, was the country, ready to abandon—to alienate for ever from the British Crown—the vast expanse of territory lying between the Atlantic and Pacific Oceans? There was no half-way house between 'cutting the painter,' as one or two hon. gentlemen near him now and then suggested, in conversation only, as regarded Canada, and severing all connection, now and for ever, with Prince Edward's Island, Newfoundland, Nova Scotia, New Brunswick, and Canada, on the east; British Columbia, one of the most thriving and hopeful of the British possessions, on the west; and that vast intermediate country known as the 'Hudson's Bay Territory,' which they were told contained within itself fertile land enough to sustain 50,000,000 of people—and holding on to the Queen's possessions. Hon. gentlemen near him should remember their geography a little, and they would cease to speak of Canada as more than a section of that northern continent over which the Queen of Great Britain ruled, and which comprised an area larger than that of the Federal and Confederate States put together. Now what was that great property? He could not describe it better than in the language of the United States. If the House would refer to the report on the Reciprocity Treaty laid before the House of Representatives at Washington in 1862 by Mr. Ward, they would find a glowing description of the vast extent, the wonderful means of internal navigation, the richness of mineral resources, the bracing healthiness of climate, and the immense extent of fertile soil which British North America contained. The report said:—'The great and practical value of the British North American Provinces and possessions is seldom appreciated. Stretching from the Atlantic to the Pacific Oceans, they contain an area of at least 3,478,380 square miles—more than is owned by the United States, and not much less than the whole of Europe, with its family of nations.' And, again, it said—'The climate and soil of these Provinces and possessions, seemingly less indulgent than those of tropical regions, are precisely those by which the skill, energy, and virtues of the human race are best developed. Nature there demands thought and labour from man as conditions of his existence, and yields abundant rewards to a wise industry.' Indeed, the warmth of language used irresistibly suggested the idea that the people of the United States, with whom the love of territory was a passion, were disposed to cast a covetous eye upon these possessions of old England. Now, knowing something of America, he must express his belief that there was no very imminent danger of war with the United States. The issues of peace and war, however, depended upon the attitude of that House and of the country. Weakness never promoted peace, and an uncertain and half-hearted attitude was provocative of war. This country had, he believed, the desire to preserve its power and influence on the American continent. It was for the good of mankind that the rule of the British Crown and the influence of the wisely-regulated liberty of Britain and of the British Constitution should continue. The way to prevent war was not to talk of severing the connection with Canada or of withdrawing our troops from Canada for fear they should be caught in a net, but to announce boldly but calmly, in language worthy of the traditions of that House, that these vast American possessions are integral parts of the great British Empire, and come weal, come woe, would be defended to the last. If that language were held there would be no war in America. The only danger arose from impressions produced by speeches in that House and elsewhere, leading to the belief that we were indifferent to our duties or our interests on the American Continent; for we had duties as well as interests. Those who thus spoke—humanitarians by profession—could support the continuance of a war which, in his humble opinion, disgraced the civilization of our time; and, while professing to be Liberals, they were ready to thrust out from our Imperial home of liberty the populations of some of our most important possessions to satisfy some imaginary economical theory of saving. They spoke of the Empire as if it were this mere island, and they seemed enchanted with the idea of narrowing our boundaries everywhere. That was not a question of simple arithmetic, it was a question of empire; not a question of a single budget, but a question of the future destiny of our race. These gentlemen seemed to prefer to live in a small country. For his part, he hoped he should all his life live in a great one. No country could be stationary without becoming stagnant, or restrict its natural progress without inviting its decay. It was so in all human affairs; it was so even in ordinary business. Every man of business knew that if his enterprise ceased to grow bigger, it soon began to dwindle down; and so a country must grow greater or else must slide away to weakness, until at last it would be despised. Now the Government proposed to spend 50,000_l_. at Quebec; 50,000_l_., he repeated, was really nothing if it were necessary to carry out the fortification policy at all. He had two objections to make. One was, that Quebec was not the vulnerable point; that point was Montreal. Montreal was the key to Canada. Once holding that key, the enemy would cut Canada in two—would separate Upper and Lower Canada from each other. Yet the Government proposed to leave all that to the unaided resources of Canada—to do nothing, in fact, where, if action were necessary at all, that action was pressing and imperative. He should deplore to see this country commencing and carrying on a competition of expenditure on fortifications with the United States. The results must be, as he warned the House, excessive votes of money, of which this one was only the small beginning, and an entire change in the nature of those relations which had so happily subsisted between the United States and the British North American possessions. Let the House remember the case of France. England and France had for years been running a race of competition of this kind. If France raised a new regiment, or added a new ship of war, or built an ironclad, or erected a fortress, we must do the same. And thus it had been that the forces still remained on a measure of some sort of equality, notwithstanding a vast outlay, which had crippled the resources of both countries, and here at home had delayed fiscal reform and retarded, nay even prevented, the most obvious measures for the elevation and education of our people. Were we to play the same game over again with the States? Now, as regards the great lakes and water ways of America, possessing a coast line of above 3,000 miles, we had since 1817 neutralized these waters as regards armaments. Under that truly blessed arrangement, the sound of a hostile shot, or even of a shot fired for practice, had never been heard now for nearly half a century. Here was a precedent of happy history and worthy of all gratitude and of all imitation. Now, if they were to fortify, let it be done adequately, whatever the cost. That cost would, he repeated, be great and also uncertain. Now he would venture to make a suggestion to the Government. It was to try negociation. Place before the minds of American statesmen the neutralization of the lakes and ask if the frontiers could not be neutralized also. Was it not possible that if Her Majesty's Government took Brother Jonathan in a quiet mood, he might be disposed to save his own pocket and thereby to save ours, and unite with us to set a bright example to surrounding nations? The people of the United States had their faults and we had ours; but they were distinguished by their common sense. No people had more of it. This suggestion would, he thought, come home to it; for they would argue, if we lay out millions so will the British, and, after all, it is merely adding burdens to both and not really strength or dignity to either. Let the Government try. If they failed the trial would have shown them to be just and in the right. If they succeeded how happy would it be for us. Reference had been made by the right hon. gentleman to the fortifications at New York, Boston, and Portland; but no one had mentioned a very strong work within forty miles of Montreal itself. He had seen that work. It was called 'Fort Montgomery,' and there was a railway all the way from it to Montreal. It was now very strong. He believed it had embrasures for some 200 guns. All the time this war had been going on, this work had been going on also. Now this looked like menace. Our Government had been informed about it, but he failed to find that they had made any representation to Washington. Surely they might have said, and would have been justified in saying to a friendly nation—'If you must have 200 guns 40 miles from Montreal, we must have 250 at Montreal; and whatever you do, we must imitate—therefore, why should either of us lay out our money?' But Government had done nothing; and now, before attempting any negociation, they asked the House to agree to make fortifications. He had humbly offered a suggestion to the Government. Let them take one of two decided courses. Let them deal firmly and wisely with the question. Let them state, in no spirit of offence, to the United States that, as Canada was part of the British Empire, we would defend it at all cost; or let them endeavour to induce the Government of Washington to distinguish itself for ever by adopting the alternative—the neutralization of the lakes and the avoidance of hostile fortifications on both sides of the frontier."

The second speech is reported as follows:

"Mr. WATKIN, member for Stockport, said, that he felt concerned to hear the United States so often spoken of in the debate as 'the enemy;' and if he thought that the vote before the committee would in any manner increase international irritation, he should regret his vote in favour of the proposition of the Government. As it was, he felt that he could not quite agree with the policy the vote indicated. That policy was one of armament against an enemy. The proposition, in his opinion, went either too far or not far enough. It did not go far enough to inspire undoubted confidence and to deter attack by providing for absolute defence; and still it went far enough to raise suspicion and to excite or to aggravate a frontier feeling. But he thought that our actual relations with the United States were guiding considerations in reference to the policy of this vote. Government ought, therefore, to tell the House how far they could repeat the peaceful assurances of a former debate. Did the despatches by the mail just arrived tend towards peace or misunderstanding? Was it true, on one side, that formal notice had a few days ago been given to our Government by the United States to terminate the Reciprocity Treaty? and was it true that that notice had been entirely unaccompanied by any overture or suggestion for a re- discussion of the question? On the other and more friendly side, was it true that the vexatious passport system had been abrogated? and, above all, was it also true that the Government of Washington had expressed to Her Majesty's Government their intention to revoke the notice to terminate the arrangement of 1817, and to place gunboats on the great American lakes? If this was true, and if it should also appear that the notice to put an end to the Reciprocity Treaty had either not yet been given or had been accompanied by some friendly declaration of a desire to negociate anew, the House must receive the intelligence with satisfaction; but should it, unfortunately, be the fact that non- intercourse regulations were maintained, that the lakes were to be covered by armaments, and that international trade was to be interfered with, then he thought the House would consider the question as one affecting a hostile neighbour, whose unfriendly designs had to be met by preparation. He hoped, therefore, that the right hon. gentleman would give the House all the information at his command. Had he been in possession of all the facts, he should have been disposed to move as an amendment that it was inexpedient to consider a vote of money for the construction of fortifications adjoining the United States frontier until negociations had been undertaken and had failed, with a view to the suspension of such works under treaty obligation. He was strongly in favour of negociation. There was an example and precedent in the arrangement of 1817 for the neutralization of the lakes. That peaceful compact had endured for fifty years, and had alike saved the expense and obviated the dangers attending rival navies on the great internal waters of America. It was self-evident that we must either fortify efficiently or let it alone. The United States could not fail to see that if they laid out large sums on permanent works of defence, we must do the same; while if we voted money, they must follow us. And thus while both countries made themselves poorer in the process, neither became much stronger, because a sort of equilibrium of forces would after all be maintained. The Government at Washington surely had no present desire to enter upon a race of expenditure for military works on both sides of the frontier. If they had, the sooner we knew it the better, for then the House would only have one course, however they might deplore it, to pursue. But here was a case where the common sense of the American people could, he thought, be appealed to not in vain. Instead of fortifying, let us neutralize the frontier—let us agree to do away with the expenditure. [Mr. BRIGHT: On both sides the frontier?] Yes, on both sides. If the American people were appealed to as the hon. member for Rochdale appealed to the Emperor of the French in favour of the French treaty, he believed that similar earnestness and tact could bring about an arrangement. The Government at Washington would thereby set an example to all countries having long frontier lines, and a precedent would be established of inestimable value to the world. What could be more deplorable than to substitute for neutrality and the operation of the Reciprocity Treaty an armed frontier and practical non-intercourse? He had before stated, from much personal observation on the spot, that border feeling and jealousy had hardly an existence as between the people of our possessions, and of the United States; but so soon as rival fortresses, frowned at each other on both sides of the line, and an armed truce were, so to speak, established, all the feelings and prejudices of separate nationality would grow up in abundance. The free exchanges of industry would, perhaps, be at the same time arrested, and war itself might not be impossible. The Reciprocity Treaty practically made the people of the United States and of the British North American possessions, each living under a totally different form of government, one for all purposes of trade and intercourse. Why should they be separated? But unfortunately our Government did not appreciate the value of, or they did not appear disposed to undertake, negociations. Instead of endeavouring to come to some friendly understanding first, they came down to the House and asked for a vote of money, enough to change the aspect of discussion with the United States, but not enough to effectually protect from danger. They would spend money first, he supposed, and then negotiate; they would allow some great evil to happen, and remonstrate afterwards. The difficulties in Canada might have been avoided by previous precaution. The threatened notice to put an end to the treaty, which grew out of those difficulties, might have been avoided by a renewal of the engagement two years ago. But the Government had done nothing. They had been—how many months?— without a Minister at Washington at the most critical period of our relations with the United States. Now it was proposed to send out a gentleman of many attainments, but who certainly was not of the first order of diplomatists. Was he gone? [Mr. BRIGHT: They say he goes to-morrow.] His hon. friend the member for Birmingham said he was to leave to-morrow. Hitherto all the interests of this country had been left in the hands of Mr. Burnley, who, if only from his position, was not able to meet on equal terms the able men of whom Mr. Lincoln's Cabinet was composed. Ever since the 17th December a vexatious system of passports and consular regulations as to merchandize had been in force. These regulations were probably in force now. They had seriously impeded trade, produced uncertainty and alarm, and great losses to individuals. They had also created great exasperation; yet during all this time we had no ambassador at Washington. Since he entered the House, a letter, by the mail just in, had been placed in his hands, and he would, with the permission of the House, read an extract from it. The writer, under date Portland, March 11th, says:—'Some eighteen passengers, per "Belgian," arrived here without passports for Canada. The United States Government, by order of General Dix, has detained them, and sent a squad of soldiers to guard them on board the "Belgian." At this time of writing they are still in custody, one of them being a clergyman. Only fancy, United States soldiers taking charge of an English ship and English subjects! This is carrying the matter with a high hand.' Now, he did not believe that the Government of the United States had purposely and of malice aforethought committed this outrage, nor did he speak of it to increase irritation; but did it not show how wrong the Government had been in leaving the interests of this country so long without representation? What, in fact, was the use of an embassy at all if our ambassador was not at his post? The Embassy at Washington was now the most important of our diplomatic establishments abroad. We ought to place there the ablest man we could find, regardless of all party or personal considerations. The people of the United States knew our own estimate of our own officials well, and they took it as a slight if we did not send to Washington a man of the first rank as a diplomatist. He would appeal to the noble lord at the head of the Government to consider the suggestion he had ventured to make, and not to allow the country to embark, without any attempt at negociation, in an expenditure of which this was but the first beginning if the policy of it should be forced upon the House. Our fellow-subjects in Canada ought to be assured that, if an unjust war broke out, this country would stand by them at all hazards; but that assurance was quite consistent with the attempt which, he hoped, would be made after all, to neutralize the frontier and the lakes and to re-establish the Reciprocity Treaty. The House would, he felt assured, do nothing to raise up bitter feelings between the British Provinces and the United States, nor to alienate still further two peoples of common origin, who, for the sake of civilization itself, ought, as far as possible, to be one and united in the interests of commerce and of peace."

"Lord PALMERSTON: Sir, this is not a Canadian question, it is not a local question, it is an Imperial question. It is a question which affects the position and character, the honour, the interests, and the duties of this great country; and I hold it to be of the utmost importance to the character of the nation in a case like this, and when the great majority of the House seem to be of the same opinion, that it should not go forth to the world that there has been a difference of opinion on this motion; but that it should be seen to have been accepted by a unanimous House of Commons. Sir, there are one or two points with regard to which I think it right to express my dissent from some doctrines which have been laid down. Many gentlemen have argued this question as if there was a general impression and belief that war with the United States was imminent, and that this proposal of ours was for the purpose of meeting a sudden danger which we apprehended to be hanging over us. Now, I think there is no danger of war with America. Nothing that has recently passed indicates any hostile disposition on the part of the United States towards us; and, therefore, I do not base this motion on the ground that we expect war to take place between this country and America. But is it necessary that when you propose to put a country in a state of defence you should show that war with some powerful neighbour is imminent and likely soon to take place? Why, the whole practice of mankind is founded on an entirely different assumption. Every country which is able to do so fortifies its frontier if its neighbour is a powerful state, which might, if it thought fit, attack it. But it is said that you cannot defend Canada. Now, I utterly deny that proposition. I think that is assuming a conclusion which no man is entitled to assume. Does the example even of the war now going on tend to justify that conclusion? The territory of the Confederates is vast and extensive; have they attempted to defend every portion of that territory? They have fortified certain important points, and those important points, although the rest of the country may have been overrun, have resisted attack—some of them even to this day and others for three or four years of the contest. Look at Richmond; is Richmond taken? Has not Richmond been attacked for a great length of time? And what are its defences? Why, chiefly earthworks, with a force behind them; and, though that force is inferior in numbers to the force which threatens it, it has hitherto remained in Confederate hands. The mere occupation of territory by an army that traverses through it without reducing its fortresses is no conquest. The conquest is limited to the ground that the invading army occupies, and when that army passes to another part of the country its conquest passes away with it. But all countries fortify particular points, and when those points are secure they trust that the general bulk of the territory is safe from any permanent occupation or conquest by any enemy who may attack it. It is urged that Canada has an extended frontier; but are no other States similarly placed in that respect? What country has the largest frontier? What is the extent of our own frontier? Why, the whole coast of the United Kingdom; and we might as well say that it would be necessary for the security of this country that we should line our whole coast with defensive works because we may be attacked at any point of that great and extensive frontier. I maintain, therefore, that there is nothing that has passed—nothing that is now passing—between the Government of the United States and our Government which justifies any man in saying that the relations between the two countries are likely, as far as present circumstances go, to assume a character of hostility leading to war. But, then, the hon. member for Birmingham says that any danger which might threaten Canada and our North American Provinces must arise from political disputes between England and the United States. And, therefore, the hon. gentleman says the Canadians will find that their best security is, not in fortifications or in British support, but in separating themselves from Great Britain. Now, in the first place, that happens not to be the wish or inclination of the Canadians. The Canadians are most anxious to maintain the connection with this country. They are proud of that connection; they think it for their interest; they are willing to make every exertion that their population and resources enable them to achieve, and, in conjunction with the efforts of this country, to preserve that connection, and prevent themselves from being absorbed by a neighbouring power. Is it not, therefore, alike the duty and interest of this country, for the sake of that reputation which is the power and strength of a nation, when we find the Canadas and our other Provinces desirous of maintaining the connection, to do that which we may have the means of doing in assisting them to maintain that connection and remain united with

Great Britain? But, sir, is it true that the only danger which a smaller colonial state runs from a more powerful and larger neighbour arises from quarrels that may exist between the Mother Country and the foreign state? I say that is a total fallacy. Suppose these provinces separated from this country—suppose them erected into a monarchy, a republic, or any other form, of Government, are there not motives that might lead a stronger neighbour to pick a quarrel with that smaller state with a view to its annexation? Is there nothing like territorial ambition pervading the policy of great military states? The example of the world should teach us that as far as the danger of invasion and annexation is concerned, that danger would be increased to Canada by a separation from Great Britain, and when she is deprived of the protection that the military power and resources of this country may afford. If these American Provinces should desire to separate, we should not adopt the maxim that fell unconsciously from the hon. member for Birmingham, who maintained that the North was right in suppressing the rebellion of the South; we will not adopt his maxim, and think that we have a right to suppress the rebellion of the North American Provinces. We should take a different line, no doubt, and if these Provinces felt themselves strong enough to stand upon their own ground, and if they should desire no longer to maintain their connection with us, we should say, 'God speed you and give you the means to maintain yourselves as a nation!' That has not happened; but, on the contrary, they much dislike the notion of annexation to their neighbours and cling to their connection with this country. And I say that it will be disgraceful to this country—it would lower us in the eyes of the world—it would weaken our power and leave consequences injurious to our position in the world if, while they desire to maintain their connection with us, we did not do what we could to assist them in maintaining their position. I think that the Government are perfectly right in proposing this vote to the House. We are of opinion that all those examples which my right hon. friend behind me (Mr. Lowe) has adduced are not applicable. We all know that in winter the snow is so deep in Canada that if an army should march it could only be in one beaten track, and that it would be impossible to carry on siege operations in winter. We know that warlike operations must be limited to the summer months, and we think that we can, by the fortifications now proposed—some to be made by the Canadians and some by this country—put Canada into such a state of defence that, with the exertions of her own population, and assisted by the military force of this country, she will be able to defend herself from attack. My right hon. friend the member for Calne argued in a manner somewhat inconsistent with himself, for what did he say? He says that you cannot defend Canada because the United States can bring a military force into the field much superior to that which you can oppose to them. Yet the right hon. gentleman says we ought to defend Canada. You ought not to relinquish the connection, he says, but you should defend Canada elsewhere. Where? Why, as you are not able to cope with the United States in Canada, where you have a large army, and where you can join your forces to those of the Canadians, you should send an expedition and attack the people of the United States in their own homes and in the centre of their own resources, where they can bring a larger force to repel our invasion. If we are unable to defend Canada, we shall not have much better prospects of success if we land an army to attack New York or any other important city."

Chapter XX
Intended Route for a Pacific Railway in 1863

The result of mature consideration, reasoning carefully upon all the facts I had collected, was, that, at that time, 1863, the best route for a Railway to the Pacific was, to commence at Halifax, to strike across to the Grand Trunk Railway at Riviere du Loup, 106 miles east of Quebec, then to follow the Grand Trunk system to Sarnia; to extend that system to Chicago; to use, under a treaty of neutralization, the United States lines from Chicago to St. Paul; to build a line from St. Paul to Fort Garry (Winnipeg) by English and American capital, and then to extend the line to the Tete Jaune Pass, there to meet a Railway through British Columbia starting from the Pacific. A large part of this route has been completed. For instance, an "Intercolonial" Railway— constructed so as to serve many local, but no grand through, purposes; constructed to satisfy local interests, or, probably, local political needs—has been built. The Grand Trunk extension from Detroit to Chicago, an excellent Railway, has been completed, thanks to the indomitable efforts of Mr. Hickson, the Managing Director of the Grand Trunk. A line from St. Paul to Winnipeg has also been opened; but the route of the line from Winnipeg to the Pacific has been deviated from, and, to save distance, the Kicking Horse and Beaver River Passes have been chosen. I think needless cost has been incurred, and that future maintenance will be greater than it need have been.

The British Columbian Railway has been constructed from Fort Moody to Kamloops, and is now part of the Canadian Pacific.

It seemed to me, at that time, that the route of the Ottawa Valley, Lake Nipissing, and round by the head of Lake Superior, was a great project of the future; and that to accomplish so great a work, in such a country, the policy was to utilize existing outlays of capital, filling in vacant spaces rather than duplicating what we had got.

It seemed to me, also, that the use of existing railways in the United States was not only economical, but politic: and I knew that, at that time, the Government of the North would have made every reasonable advance to meet England in affairs of mutual interest. There was every desire, at that juncture, to work cordially with our Queen and her people. For example, the passing of the Slave Trade Bill, modelled on English legislation, in, I think, 1863, through both Houses of Congress at Washington, with hardly a hostile expression. *Apropos* of this Bill, Mr. Charles Sumner told me, in 1865, at his house at Boston, the following story. "The Bill for putting down the slave trade in association with England and the other anti-slave trade countries passed so quickly as to astonish its friends. Charles Sumner, on the final question being put, 'that the Bill do pass'—as we should put it at home—immediately ran across to Mr. Seward, opened the door of Mr. Seward's private office, without knocking, and found Mr. Seward asleep. He awoke him by calling out, 'Seward, Seward, the Bill is passed: the Bill is passed.' Seward gradually opened his eyes, stared under his bushy eyebrows, and said, 'Then what in — — has become of the "great democratic party?"'"

Again, it was the fault of our own Government at home that the Reciprocity Treaty, nearly expiring, was not renewed. Our Government did nothing. It was the "masterly inactivity" of Lord Granville, and other Whigs, which has done so much harm to the prestige and power of our Empire. Opportunities are everything—they are the statesman's chances. In this case the chance was lost. However, I had every reason to believe that Mr. Seward would have been willing to agree to the use of United States lines up to St. Paul (which he once predicted would become the centre, or "hub," of the United States) and through Minnesota to the boundary of the Hudson's Bay territory,—under a treaty of international neutralization. There were, it is true, difficulties at home. The authorities, at home, did not know what was to be the end of the Civil War. They did not know the country to be passed through. They doubted if there was any precedent. I quoted the treaty, of years before, between England, the United States, and other countries, for the neutralization of a railway, if made, across Honduras, and other analogous cases. But I failed to bring about any official action at that time. I think, in looking back for twenty-three years, I have nothing to modify as respects this. Had my proposals been carried out millions sterling would have been saved; throughout railway communication to the Pacific might have been secured fifteen years sooner; and a friendly agreement with the United States for a great common object would, no doubt, have led to many more equally friendly agreements.

As respects neutralization, I, unconsciously, put a spoke into my own wheel, and I was not aware of it until I had a conversation with Mr. Bright a good while afterwards. Had I known of the grievance at the time I would have gone right off to Washington and explained all about it. The facts were these:—

I was at Quebec in July, 1863. At that time, and previously, and after, there was a tall, long-legged, short-bodied, sallow-faced, sunken-eyed man, whose name, if he had reported it correctly, was Ogden. He was called "consul" for the United States at Quebec. He reported, I was told, direct to Mr. Seward at Washington. He was, in fact, the sort of diplomatist whose duties, as he apprehended them, were those of a spy. He was a person disagreeable to look at, as in his odd-coloured trousers, short waistcoat, and dark green dress-coat, with brass buttons, he went elbowing about amongst the ladies and gentlemen promenading the public walk, which commands so beautiful a view over the St. Lawrence, called the "Platform." Phrenology would have condemned him. Phrenology and Physiognomy combined, would have hung him, on the certain verdict of any intelligent jury.

One day, as I was preparing to go West, a deputation from the "Stadacona" Club of Quebec, of which I was a member, asked me to take the chair at a private dinner proposed to be given at the club to Mr. Vallandigham, the democratic leader of Ohio, who had come across country from Halifax, on his way homeward—through, free, Canada—after his seizure in bed, in Ohio, and deportation across the Northern frontier into the land of secession. It appeared that Mr. Vallandigham, not being a secessionist, merely desiring an honourable peace between North and South, which he had ably advocated, had gone on to Nassau, thence to Halifax, thence to Quebec: where he was.

I at first declined the honour. But I was much pressed. I was told that leading citizens of Quebec and members of the late Canadian Government would attend. That the dinner was merely hospitality to a refugee landed upon our shores in distress; and that my presidency would take away any suspicion that there was the slightest *arriere-pensee* in the matter. I concurred. The dinner took place. Not a word was said of the great pending contest, unless some words of Mr. Vallandigham, apologizing for the poverty of his dress, might be so construed. He said: "Mr. Chairman, I must apologize for my costume. I can only explain that I am standing in the clothes I was allowed to put on, after being taken out of my own bed, in my own house, without warning and without warrant, and I have not had the means to re-clothe myself."

The dinner was certainly about as non-political and as innocent as any such assembly could be. Mr. Vallandigham left for Niagara the same night. I saw him into the train. He declined a friendly loan; but he accepted a free passage to Niagara, where, later on, I spent two or three pleasant and interesting days in his society; our little party being Governor Dallas, of the Hudson's Bay Company, D'Arcy McGee, Dr. Mackay, who had acted as correspondent of the "Times," Professor Hind, my son, Mr. Watkin, and myself. The "consul" had, no doubt, misrepresented our proceedings.

Now this is the whole story. I never after this got any answers to letters to Mr. Seward; and, as stated above, I never knew of the grievance till spoken to by Mr. Bright, who had received a letter of complaint of me from somebody at Washington.

Chapter XXI
Letters from Sir George E.
Cartier—Question of Honors

The "Act for the Union of Canada, Nova Scotia, and New Brunswick, and the government thereof, and for purposes connected therewith," received the Royal Assent on the 29th of March, 1867.

The following letters may be of some interest to the friends of the late Sir George Etienne Cartier, and to mine:

"W. P. HOTEL, LONDON,
"30 April, 1867.

"My DEAR MR. WATKIN,

"I leave to-morrow for *Liverpool* on my way to *Canada*. Allow me, before my departure, to convey to you personally and for 'Canada' the most sincere and grateful thanks for all the kindnesses you have bestowed, on me since my *sojourn in* London, and for all the political services you have rendered to 'Canada' in having so *efficiently helped* the carrying of the *great confederation measure*. I hope that before long we will see you again in Canada, and rest assured that we will be delighted to demonstrate to you *our gratefulness*.

"Be kind enough to present my best respects to Mrs. Watkin, and to ask her to accept from me the within-enclosed photograph taken at 'Naples,' which I think is very good.

"Good bye, my dear Mr. Watkin, and believe me,
"Yours very truly,
"GEO. ET. CARTIER.

"E. W. WATKIN, Esq., M.P."

MISTAKE ABOUT HONORS.

When the Act for Confederation had been passed, and while some of the delegates were still in England, a notification was made of honors intended to be conferred by Her Majesty on some of those who had devoted anxious hours of labour to the great cause of Union. In my case, my name was mentioned for knighthood, while the names of Mr. Cartier and Mr. Galt were named for the honor of "C. B.," and Mr. Langevin's name appeared to be entirely omitted. When, how, or by whom, the leader of the great French-speaking section of the Canadian people was placed, thus, in a position inferior to that of the leader of Upper Canada, who was made "K. C. B.," I do not care, now, to inquire. But I felt at the time, and I feel now, that it would have been unjust— unselfish and earnest as my services had been— to give to a man like Mr. Cartier, an honor inferior to that which common report had attributed to me. I felt, also, that the proposal would be treated as a slight to the Catholic and French-speaking people. I did all in my, limited, power to represent the mistake and the danger to the leaders of the Government, at home; and, as will be shown in the next Chapter, I wrote to Mr. Disraeli on this serious question on the 3rd August, 1867.

"MONTREAL,   "23rd
August, 1867.

MY DEAR MR. WATKIN,

"I thank you very much for your kind letters. Really you are too good to *espouse, as it were,* my cause respecting the *honors conferred* in Canada. There is no doubt that——is the cause of all the *evil* in the matter of the *honors conferred.* Some *other parties* are also not exempt from blame. I have not as yet received a reply to my letter declining the C. B. *ship.* I presume I shall have it very soon. I have to tell you that I will make throughout *all* Lower Canada the *best electoral campaign* I have ever made. The *Rouges* will not elect 10 members out of the 65 *allotted* to *Lower* Canada. *Holton* and *Dorion,* the *leaders* of the Rouge Party, will very likely be defeated. I went to Chateaugay on Monday last to attend a meeting against Holton. I gave it to him as he deserved. I will tell you in *confidence* that *Gait and myself* through the large majority I will have in Lower Canada, will be stronger than ever. Mrs. Cartier and my girls are at Rimouska. I will deliver them your kind messages as soon as I see them. My kindest regards to Mrs. Watkin, and believe me,

"My dear Mr. Watkin,
"Yours very truly,
"GEO. ET. CARTIER.

"E. W. WATKIN, Esq, M.P.,
"London."

"MONTREAL,
"22_nd September_, 1867.

MY DEAR MR. WATKIN,

"Accept my most sincere thanks for your such unappreciable kindness in having made common cause with me in reference to the late distribution of honors in Canada. I do really think, and I am convinced, that you have allowed your good heart to go too far in having declined the honor and distinction offered to you, and which you so well deserved in every respect. I hope that *my matter* will not stand in the way of you having your public and political services in England, as well as in Canada, sooner or later fully recognized, and well rewarded by a proper and suitable distinction. I hope so, for your own sake as well as for that of Mrs. Watkin and your son and amiable daughter. The Chancellor of the Exchequer has written you a very nice letter, indeed. With regard to my *matter*, would you imagine that the Duke of Buckingham has written a *confidential note* to Lord Monck, telling to this latter that there *being no precedent* for a resignation of the C. B., the only way to have my wishes carried out would be by the *Queen* directing by *order* in the Gazette my name to be struck out from the Order, which proceeding, the Duke adds, would be *construed* by *outsiders* and *uninitiated* that it was for *misconduct*. Lord Monck having communicated to me the substance of the Duke's communication, I have asked Lord Monck to obtain from the Duke leave to communicate to me the substance of his note in *no confidential* manner, in order that I may reply to it. I do really think that the intention is to *frighten* me, in order to induce me to withdraw my letter asking leave to resign the C. B. That I *will not do*, and when the Duke's communication is under my *eyes* in *no confidential manner*, I will send such a reply that will make people understand the *injury done* to me, and the *slight* so absurdly *offered* to a *million* of *good and loyal* French Canadians. As a matter of course, all that I say to you in this letter is *strictly* in confidence to you.

"Mrs. Cartier and myself have had the pleasure, yesterday, to have the company at *dinner* of your friends Mr. and Mrs. Sidebottom. They are really a very nice couple, and we thank you for having given us the opportunity of making their acquaintance. Be kind enough to present on my behalf, and on that of Mrs. Cartier and my daughters, our best respects and regards to Mrs. Watkin, and to believe me, my dear Mr. Watkin,

> "Your devoted friend,
> "GEO. ET. CARTIER.

"E. W. WATKIN, Esq., M.P., London."

> "OTTAWA,   "24_th
> November_, 1867.

MY DEAR MR. WATKIN,

"I am so much thankful to you for your kind wish of the 10th of October last. I do appreciate with gratefulness your so kind expression of feelings towards me. I enclose you an extract of the 'Montreal Gazette,' giving the report of a debate which took place in our House some few days ago respecting the 'C.B.' matter, and also an 'extract' of the same paper, containing some editorial remarks on the same subject. I like to keep you *au courant* of that matter, since you are so good as to take interest in it. I took great care not to take any part in the debate. I have not as yet got a copy of the Duke of Buckingham's letter. I will follow your advice with regard to any answer to it on my part. I will never forget your disinterestedness in this question of *'honor'* and nothing will be more agreeable to me than to act in such a way, whenever the opportunity will offer itself, as to show by reciprocal action my thanks and my feelings.

"'The Grand Trunk Act' will be read a second time to-morrow (Monday). Mrs. Cartier and my girls are here for a few days. We were all sorry to hear that your son had an attack of fever. We all hope that he got over it, and that he is well again. Be kind enough to present to Mrs. Watkin and your dear son our best regards and kindest remembrance. I regret very much the retirement of 'Galt' from our government. You will have heard that I have replaced him by *Rose.* I could not do better under any circumstances.

"Believe me, my dear Mr. Watkin,

"Yours very truly,

"GEO. ET. CARTIER.

"E. W. WATKIN, Esq., M.P.,
"London, England."

"QUEBEC,

"15_th February_, 1868.

MY DEAR MR. WATKIN,

"I am very grateful to you for your three kind letters of the 2nd, 13th, and 15th January last. Be good enough to excuse me if I have not sooner acknowledged their receipt.

"I am in Quebec since a couple of weeks, attending the 'Local Parliament,' of which I am a member. Things are going on very well. I got elected to the 'Local Parliament' in order to help my *friends,* the '*Local Ministers*' to carry on the 'Local Government' and I must say they are doing it very well. The 'Quebec Legislature' carries this 'business' better than does the 'Ontario Legislature.' I will leave for Ottawa on the 17th instant, to be there on the 20th to attend the *Council Meeting* for deciding on the *route* of the *Intercolonial Railway.*

"I felt so sorry to hear that your dear son was so long unwell. I hope that by this time he is himself again.

"I gave to Mrs. Cartier and my daughters your kind message of good wishes for them and myself during this present year. We are all thankful to you. Have the goodness to accept in return from them and myself for you, Mrs. Watkin, and your dear son and daughter, our best wishes for the prosperity and happiness of you all.

"I must say, my dear Mr. Watkin, that with regard to the C. B. matter, you do really take too much trouble and interest for me. I am very thankful to you for it, and also to Mr. Baring and Lord Wharncliffe. If you have occasion to *intimate* to them my thankfulness, if any opportunity for so doing should offer itself to you, you would oblige me very much.

"Really it was too kind of Lord Wharncliffe to have brought that delicate matter before Lord Derby, and to have written you about it. I thank you for the enclosures you have made to me of what Lord Wharncliffe had written to you about the C. B.

"I have now to tell you something which happened about that subject since my last to you.

"You very likely must have seen or heard of the 'notification,' published in the 'London Gazette' at the end of the month of *December last*, about the *honors distributed* in Canada in connection with the 'Confederation.' In that 'notification' you must have seen that the names of 'myself and Galt' are omitted, and it was stated in that *notification* that it must be 'substituted' for the 'one' published on the 9th of July last, in which Galt's name and mine *were inserted* as C. B. Now, you must recollect that some months ago I wrote you about a 'confidential communication' of the Duke of Buckingham to Lord Monck, in order that it should be intimated to me and Gait, that there was no precedent of a resignation of the Order of the Bath, and that the only way left for the *carrying out* of Galt's wishes and mine would be by '*an order of Her Majesty ordering our names to be struck off the roll.*' The communication of the Duke having been made to me in a *confidential manner*, I had no opportunity to answer it. I had written to Lord Monck to ask the Duke's leave for communicating to me in no confidential manner the despatch of the Duke, in order to give me an opportunity to answer it. I never had any *answer* from Lord *Monck* to that request. To my great surprise, at the end of December last, I received from Lord Monck a note, accompanied by the copy of a despatch from the Duke, informing me that a *mode had been found* to meet my wishes and those of Galt, which consisted in the publication in the 'London Gazette' of a 'notification' omitting our names, and such notification to be substituted for the former one of July last.

"The reading of this last despatch more than astonished me, and my astonishment was greater when I saw by the 'London Gazette' that it was *carried into effect* by the *notification* above *alluded to*. I have had no more opportunity to answer the second despatch of the Duke than the *first one*, which was marked 'confidential.' Allow me to add, that the 'Duke' expressed in his 'first communication' that he did not like to suggest that my name should be struck off the roll, because an ungenerous construction now and hereafter might be made against me by those not acquainted *with the facts*. Now, by the course followed, as explained in his second despatch, I feel as badly treated as if the first course had been adopted. In one case my name would have been ordered to be struck off the roll, and by the second course followed up, my name was ordered to be omitted in the second notification. There is not much difference between these two courses. I have written a letter to Lord Monck to complain of the second course followed up, inasmuch as there being no reason assigned for the omission of my name in the second notification, a construction ungenerous to myself and my children after me could now and hereafter be made. Excuse me for troubling you so long about that C.B. matter. Now, with regard to the *Hudson Bay matter*, not the least doubt that the speech of 'John A.' was very uncalled for and injudicious. He had no business to make such a speech, and I told him so at the time— that he ought not to have made it. However, you must not attach too much importance to that speech. I myself and several of my colleagues, and John A. himself, have no intention to commit any spoliation; and, for myself in particular, I can say to you that I will never consent to be a party to a measure or anything intended to be an act of spoliation of the Hudson Bay's rights and privileges. I must bring this long epistle to a close.

"My kindest regards and respects to Mrs. Watkin.

"Remember me to your dear son, and believe me, my dear Mr. Watkin,

"Yours very truly,

"GEO. E. CARTIER.

"E. W. WATKIN, Esq."

UNFORTUNATE DISCUSSIONS.

These discussions were both unfortunate and embarrassing; in the course of them, I had suggested that the way out of the difficulty was generously to offer a baronetcy to Mr. Cartier. During the discussion Dr. Tupper arrived in England. He cordially agreed with me. He deplored the mistake made, and, acting from his official position, and with the great judgment which he has always shown, he was able to assist in the desired happy solution.

On the 22nd of April I received the following letter:—

"WESTMINSTER
PALACE HOTEL,   "*April*

22nd, 1868.

MY DEAR SIR,

"The Duke (of Buckingham) showed me (in *strict confidence* until after the official announcement here) the copy of his telegram to Lord Monck, announcing the fact that the Queen had conferred a baronetcy upon Mr. Cartier, and a C.B. upon Langevin, and was pleased to say that he was very much indebted to me for having suggested it. I told him that I was satisfied that his Grace had conferred a signal service to our country, which would be productive of much good. Knowing how much pleasure this will give you I cannot forbear mentioning it, of course in confidence.

"I enclose a letter received to-day from our late lamented friend. Be good enough to return it to me. Ought I to communicate his wishes to Messrs. Hurst &

Blackwell? I had a long interview with Mr. Cardwell to-day. He will do anything in his power to aid in putting matters right in Nova Scotia, and is anxious that I should see Mr. Bright. Mr. C. takes your view as to the Union question having been an issue before the people in 1863, in the strongest manner.

"Yours faithfully,
"C. TUPPER.

"E. W. WATKIN, Esq., M.P."

I feel assured that Mr. Cartier was moved, solely, by a regard for the honor of his compatriots.

"OTTAWA,
"*28th May*, 1868.

MY DEAR MR. WATKIN,

"On Friday last, the 21st instant, our Parliament was prorogued. We have had a very hard and laborious session. For my part, I had charge of the two most difficult measures, the Militia and the Fortifications measures, which I carried through successfully, and which were sanctioned on the 21st instant. Without being considered guilty of *boasting,* I can say, and every man in Parliament will say, that I was the only one who could carry through these measures. My Lower Canada Parliamentary strength supported me nobly. I consider that in carrying these two measures to successful issue, I have rendered a good service to Canada, to England, and to British transactions. I wanted to write you last week, before the closing of our session, but really I could not find a moment for so doing. During ten days we sat three times a day, and we had to attend our executive sittings during the very short intervals allowed us. I have not as yet answered your so kind letter of the 24th April last, nor your also kind former one of March last, and I hope you will have the goodness to excuse my delay. My dear Mr. Watkin, I do really not know how to thank you for all that you have done for me with regard to the injustice done me in the matter of the distribution of honors to the Confederation delegates, and with regard to the baronetcy which the Queen intends to confer on me. As you remark in your last note, I became aware of Her Majesty's intentions by a *cable* telegram to Lord Monck, and the last *mail* has brought a despatch to Lord Monck from the Duke of Buckingham to apprise me *officially* of Her Majesty's intentions, and to request me to send to the Colonial Office my pedigree and my coat of arms, for the preparation of the letters patent to be issued. I am now procuring all the information and things required by the Heralds' College. The first telegram to Lord Monck was to offer me the baronetcy, and to ascertain if I would accept of it. I took a few days to consider the matter, as I would not do anything which might not have been approved by Galt and Langevin. Both of them urged me to accept; and consequently I made Lord Monck aware of my acceptance. A few days afterwards came another *cable telegram*, informing Lord Monck that the Queen had conferred on me the baronetcy dignity, and the C.B. on Langevin. When the Queen's pleasure was announced in the House, there were cheers and approbation from both sides of the House. I have not the *least* doubt that I am under obligation to Lord Derby and to Lord Wharncliffe for their interference in my favour; and I must add, that I feel under stronger obligation to you for the honor conferred on me, first, for your having *moved* so kindly and so urgently Lord Wharncliffe, and, secondly, for your so chivalrous disinterestedness in having yourself declined the royal mark of favour offered to you by Mr. Disraeli, on the ground of the injustice at first done to me. My dear Mr. Watkin, I cannot forget such friendly and disinterested conduct on your part. I hope it will be in my power, in return, to be useful to you. Very likely I will have to go to England on the question of *defence* before the next Session of our Parliament, and I will not fail to say the *proper words* to the proper quarters; and if it were possible for me to do something by correspondence, I would gladly do it; but I don't know how to proceed, and *whom* to move. Besides, I would not like to do or write anything which might not meet your wishes. I would like very much to know your views on that delicate question. I thank you for your suggestion to write a few lines to Lord Wharncliffe. I enclose you a letter for him, which I leave open, in order that you should see it. If the letter meets your views, be kind enough to seal it and to mail it to Lord Wharncliffe. I was so pleased the other day to hear from our friend Brydges, that your dear son had arrived in Montreal, and that his health is improving. I have not failed to let Langevin know your kind congratulations to him. He feels very thankful for the interest you take in him. I showed him your last note to me. I have duly transmitted to Mrs. Cartier and my daughters your kind message,—and they all feel grateful to you. I enclose you the Militia and Fortification measures as they finally passed. I enclose you also the return to an *address* for the correspondence and despatches on the defence-fortification question. You may, perhaps, like to have all these papers. I enclose you also the *return* to an address for the correspondence on the C.B. matter, and the report of the *Select Committee* upon it; you will find the report of the *Committee* in the *Notes and Proceedings* of the 15th of May. It seemed to me, that you might like to have these documents, as you took such a degree of interest in Galt and myself. Do me the kindness to present my best regards to Mrs. Watkin, and to remember me kindly to your daughter when you write her.

"We are threatened with a *Fenian* invasion in the course of *June next*. We are preparing to meet it. It is too bad that the *Imperial Government* should allow such an hostile organization to be formed in the United States without a *word of remonstrance*. In the hope of hearing from you at your earliest convenience,

"Believe me, my dear Mr. Watkin,
"Your sincere and grateful friend,
"GEO. ET. CARTIER.

"E. W. WATKIN, Esq., M.P. London."

PERMITTED INVASION.

Sir George Cartier's allusion to the neglect by our Government in permitting, without remonstrance, the repeated invasion of Canada, makes one shiver with shame. As President Johnson said to me in 1865, "Why don't your people remonstrate?"

My countrymen may feel assured that if remonstrances, firm and dignified, had anticipated each known intended outrage—English and Irish-American conspiracies would have not been as now.

"ROSE   HILL,
NORTHENDEN,   near
MANCHESTER,   "12th
August, 1868.

MY DEAR SIR,

"I, gladly, enclose a copy of the Gazette notice of your Baronetcy.

"I have had the fees at the Heralds' College, and also the stamps and expenses, through the Home Office, duly paid, and I will send you the papers and receipts as soon as I receive them.

"The completion of this matter will close the somewhat intimate connection which now for some years has given me, if trouble and anxiety, still deep pleasure and satisfaction,—in reference to your now united Provinces.

"With best wishes allow me to remain,
"Yours very faithfully,
"EDW. W. WATKIN.

"To the Hon. Sir G. E. CARTIER, Bart.,
"Montreal, Canada."

"OTTAWA,
"*18th September, 1868.*

MY DEAR SIR EDWARD,

"The last English mail has brought us the happy news that the honor of knighthood has been conferred on you by the Queen.

"Allow me to offer you, Lady Watkin, and your dear son and daughter, my sincere and heartfelt congratulations on the bestowal on you of so well deserved a distinction. You must bear in mind that I do not forget that the honor so recently bestowed on you would have been conferred on you a long time ago, had not your generous feelings towards me prompted you at one time to decline the same distinction. Lady Cartier and my daughters gladly unite with me in this expression of congratulation, which I now offer you, Lady Watkin, and your son and daughter. I hope that your future election will not give you much trouble, and that Canada and the British people will have again the benefit of your presence in Parliament.

"I may see you before long in England. Be kind enough to accept for you and Lady Watkin the assurance of the kindest regards of myself, Lady Cartier, and my daughters, "And, believe me, my dear Sir Edward, "Yours very truly,

GEO. ET. CARTIER

"Sir EDWARD W. WATKIN, M.P., Kt., London."

"London,
"Westminster Palace Hotel,
"*20th November, 1868.*

"My dear Sir Edward,

"You cannot conceive how sorrowful I feel that the result of the election in Stockport was adverse to you. I was watching the incidents and proceedings connected with that election with such an interest and with such sure hope that you would be successful. You have no idea of my grief and disappointment when I became aware of your defeat. Our friend Brydges has mentioned to me some of the *causes* which have militated against you amongst your constituents, viz. your having attended at the laying of the corner stone of a Roman Catholic School, and your drinking the health of the 'Pope' at the *lunch* which *ensued*, and also the *displeasure* which you have *incurred from Mr. Bright* and some of his friends for not having supported *him* in *his motion* for Nova Scotia against the Confederation. I have already written to some of my colleagues in Canada to let them know there the *'liberality'* of these pretended 'Liberals' here. I hope you will not remain a long time *out of Parliament*, and that very soon some vacancy will occur which will give you an opportunity to be re-elected, and to serve and *advocate* again in the Imperial Parliament, not only the interests of the *three British Isles*, but also the Colonial interests, and particularly those of the Dominion of Canada, to which you have always attended with such ability, zeal, and ardour, that you have now the everlasting gratitude of every Canadian. I hope your electoral *contretems* will not deter you from your political pursuits. I would have had such a pleasure in congratulating Lady Watkin on your electoral success.

"I hope Lady Watkin, Miss Watkin, and your son are enjoying good health. Have the goodness to present my best regards to Lady Watkin, and to remember me kindly to your dear daughter and son; and, my dear Sir Edward, reiterating to you my sincere thanks for all you have done for me, and expecting the pleasure of seeing you very soon in London, believe me, as always,

"Your very sincere,
"And devoted friend,
"GEO. ET. CARTIER.

"Sir EDWARD W. WATKIN, 21, Old Broad Street, London.

"On my leaving Canada Lady Cartier and my daughters have asked me not to forget to present to you and Lady Watkin their best wishes and kindest regards, to remember them kindly to your son, and to offer their compliments to Miss Watkin, in the hope of making her acquaintance hereafter."

Chapter XXII
Disraeli—Beaconsfield

No one aided the cause of Canada more readily than Mr. Disraeli, and I ought to explain how I first gained his confidence and kindness. But Mr. Philip Rose, who was his solicitor, his friend, his executor; who had stuck by him "per angusta ad augusta," was of priceless service in placing before him, from time to time, the facts, affecting Confederation, as I collected them.

My first acquaintance with Mr. Disraeli was the consequence of my connection, as an honorary secretary, with the "Manchester Athenaeum," a literary institute, originated in 1835 by Richard Cobden, on his return from a visit to his brother in the United States, a country at that time on the rage for social clubs with classic names. The "Manchester Athenaeum," owing partly to defective management and architectural costliness, partly to some years of bad trade and deficient employment, and partly to an unfortunate sectarian conflict, had fallen into debt and difficulty; and a few of the younger members, who had profited by the existence of the institution, came to the rescue, and by various methods got rid of its debts, and set it fairly on the way again. One method was, the holding of a great literary soiree in the Manchester Free Trade Hall. The audience was more than 4,000. The President was Charles Dickens.

On the morning of the day before the soiree, which took place on Thursday, the 5th of October, 1843, I received a note, in these terms, from Mr. Cobden:—

"MOSLEY   St,
"Wednesday.

"Dear Sir,

"Mr. Benj'n Disraeli, the author of 'Vivian Grey,' is at the Mosely Arms Hotel, with Mrs. Disraeli.

"I wish you would call and invite them to the soiree.

"Yours truly,
"R. COBDEN.

"Mr. E. Watkin,
"High St."

I print the note exactly as it was written.

It has appeared to me, since, that Mr. Cobden at that time considered it necessary to identify Mr. Disraeli as Mr. "Benj'n" Disraeli, "the author of Vivian Grey."

I called accordingly, without delay. Mr. Disraeli was out, but I found Mrs. Disraeli at home. She was a little, plain, vivacious woman; one who, like an india-rubber toy, you have only to touch, and it issues sound. But she was obviously no common-place woman. Her comments upon what she had seen already in Manchester were acute, and, at times, decidedly humorous. They were those of a shrewd observer. We became good friends. She promised, both for herself and her husband, to attend the soiree; and, in answer to my further request that Mr. Disraeli would speak, she said, she "could almost promise that he would." The soiree of the next evening was brilliant. Dickens was at his very best; and it must have been difficult indeed to follow so admirable a speaker. But Mr. Disraeli certainly shared the honours and the applause of this great meeting. His speech, in fact, created so decided a sensation that I was asked to invite him to preside at the soiree of the coming year of 1844,—which he did. Few, who heard it, will forget the eloquent oration he delivered. I cannot forbear, out of place as it may seem to some, here to quote the concluding portions of this remarkable address; an address which I have never yet seen amongst the published speeches of Lord Beaconsfield:—

"If my description of what this institution offers to us, if my view of what it in some degree supplies, be just, what, I must inquire, is the reason that an institution, the prosperity of which now cannot be doubted, but so brief a time ago could have been apparently in the last stage of its fortunes? It is not an agreeable task—I fear it may be considered by some an invidious one—if I, who am a stranger among you, shall attempt to play the critic upon your conduct; but I feel confidence in your indulgence. I remember the kindness which has placed me in this honourable position, and therefore I shall venture to express to you the two reasons to which I think the dangerous state of our position must fairly be ascribed. I would say, in the first place, without imputing the slightest fault to the originators of this institution, wishing to be most distinctly understood as not only not imputing any fault to them, but most decidedly being of opinion that the fault does not lie at their door; still I cannot shut my eyes to the fact that, in the origin of this institution, by circumstances not foreseen, and which, certainly, were not intended, a party, a limited, and a sectarian feeling, in some degree pervaded its management. I confess, myself, that it appears to me that it would have been a marvel had it been otherwise. When we remember the great changes that had then but very recently occurred in this country—when we recall to our mind not only the great changes that had occurred, but the still greater that were menaced and discussed—when we remember what an influence is created when local jealousy blends with political passion—it is not difficult to imagine, because there are none of us present but in their sphere must have felt its influence—it is not wonderful that men of different political opinions should look with extreme jealousy upon each other. A combination of peculiar circumstances that created a balanced state of parties in those places where the struggle for dominion and power takes place, very much assisted this feeling; and that such a feeling existed throughout all England in a degree more intense and more virulent than has ever been equalled in the history of this country, I think no man will deny, and all must deplore. For my own part, I really believe that, had that party and sectarian feeling proceeded in the same ratio of virulence it has done for the last twelve or fourteen years, it must have exercised a barbarising influence upon public sentiments and public manners. There are some amongst us now, I know, who believe that the period has arrived when a great effort must be made to emancipate this country from the degrading thraldom of faction—to terminate, if possible, that extreme, that sectarian, and limited view, in which all human conduct is examined, observed, and criticized—to put an end to that exclusiveness, which, in its peculiar sphere, is equally deleterious as that aristocratical exclusiveness of manners which has produced so much evil; and, as far as I can form an opinion, these views have met with sympathy from every part of the country. I look upon it that to-night—I hope I am not mistaken—we are met to consummate and to celebrate the emancipation of this city, at least so far as the Athenaeum extends, from the influence of these feelings. I hope that our minds and our hearts are alike open to the true character of this institution, to the necessities which have created it, to the benefits to which it leads; and happy I shall be, and all, I am sure, who are assisting me this evening, if it prove that our efforts, however humble, may have assisted in so delightful and so desirable a consummation.

"Now that is one of the reasons, and one of the principal reasons, why I believe a blight seemed to have fallen over our fortunes. I think at the same time that there is another cause that has exercised an injurious effect upon the position, until recently, of this institution. I think that a limited view of its real character has been taken even by those who were inclined to view it in a spirit of extreme friendliness. It has been looked upon in the light of a luxury, and not of a necessity—as a means of enjoyment in the hour of prosperity, from which we ought to be debarred when the adverse moment has arrived; so that, when trade was prospering, when all was sunshiny, a man might condescend to occupy his spare hours in something else than in a melancholy brooding over the state of the country—that, when returns were rapid, and profits ready, one might deign to cultivate one's faculties, and become acquainted with what the mind of Europe was conceiving or executing; but these were delights to be reserved only for those chosen hours. Now that, I am bound frankly to say, is not the view which I take of this question—not the idea which I have formed of the real character of the Manchester Athenaeum. I look upon it as part of that great educational movement which is the noble and ennobling characteristic of the age in which we live. Viewing it in that light, I cannot consent myself that it should be supported by fits and starts. The impulse which has given us that movement in modern times, is one that may be traced to an age that may now be considered comparatively remote, though the swell of the waters has but recently approached our own shore. Heretofore society was established necessarily on a very different principle to that which is now its basis. As civilization has gradually progressed, it has equalized the physical qualities of man. Instead of the strong arm, it is the strong head that is now the moving principle of society. You have disenthroned Force, and placed on her high seat Intelligence; and the necessary consequence of this great revolution is, that it has become the duty and the delight equally of every citizen to cultivate his faculties. The prince of all philosophy has told you in an immortal apophthegm, so familiar to you all, that it is now written in your halls and chambers,—'Knowledge is power.' If that memorable passage had been pursued by the student who first announced this discovery of that great man to society, he would have found an oracle not less striking, and, in my mind, certainly not less true; for Lord Bacon has not only said that 'Knowledge is power,' but living one century after the discovery of the printing press, he has also announced to the world that 'Knowledge is pleasure.' Why, when the great body of mankind had become familiar with this great discovery— when they learned that a new source was opened to them of influence and enjoyment—is it wonderful that from that hour the heart of nations has palpitated with the desire of becoming acquainted with all that has happened, and with speculating on what may occur? It has indeed produced upon the popular intellect an influence almost as great as—I might say analogous to—the great change which was produced upon the old commercial world by the discovery of the Americas. A new standard of value was introduced, and, after this, to be distinguished—man must be intellectual. Nor, indeed, am I surprised that this feeling has so powerfully influenced our race; for the idea that human happiness is dependent on the cultivation of the mind, and on the discovery of truth, is, next to the conviction of our immortality, the idea the most full of consolation to man; for the cultivation of the mind has no limits, and truth is the only thing that is eternal. Indeed, when you consider what a man is who knows only what is passing under his own eyes, and what the condition of the same man must be who belongs to an institution like the one which has assembled us together to-night, is it—ought it to be—a matter of surprise that, from that moment to the present, you have had a general feeling throughout the civilized world in favour of the diffusion of knowledge? A man who knows nothing but the history of the passing hour—who knows nothing of the history of the past but that a certain person, whose brain was as vacant as his own, occupied the same house as himself, who in a moment of despondency or of gloom has no hope in the morrow because he has read nothing that has taught him that to-morrow has any changes—that man, compared with him who has read the most ordinary abridgment of history, or the most common philosophical speculation, is as distinct and different an animal as if he had fallen from some other planet, was influenced by a different organization, working for a different end, and hoping for a different result. It is knowledge that equalizes the social condition of man—that gives to all, however different their political position, passions which are in common and enjoyments which are universal. Knowledge is like the mystic ladder in the patriarch's dream. Its base rests on the primaeval earth—its crest is lost in the shadowy splendour of the empyrean; while the great authors, who for traditionary ages have held the chain of science and philosophy, of poesy and erudition, are the angels ascending and descending the sacred scale, and maintaining, as it were, the communication between man and heaven. This feeling is so universal that there is no combination of society in any age in which it has not developed itself. It may, indeed, be partly restrained under despotic governments, under peculiar systems of retarded civilization; but it is a consequence as incidental to the spirit and the genius of the Christian civilization of Europe as that the day should follow night, and the stars should shine according to their laws and order. Why, the very name of the institution that brings us together illustrates the fact—I can recall, and I think I see more than one gentleman around me who equally can recall, the hours in which we wandered amid

"Fields that cool Ilyssus laves.

At least, there is my honorable friend the member for Stockport (Mr. Cobden), who has a lively recollection of that classic stream, for I remember one of the most effective allusions he made to it in one of the most admirable speeches I ever listened to. But, notwithstanding that allusion, I would still appeal to the poetry of his constitution, and I know it abounds in that quality. I am sure that he could not have looked without emotion on that immortal scene. I still can remember that olive-covered plain, that sunset crag, that citadel fane of ineffable beauty! That was a brilliant civilization, developed by a gifted race more than two thousand years ago, at a time when the ancestors of the manufacturers of Manchester, who now clothe the world, were themselves covered with skins, and tattooed like the red men of the wilderness. But influences more powerful even than the awful lapse of time separate and distinguish you from that race. They were the children of the sun; you live in a distant, a rugged, and northern clime. They bowed before different altars; they followed different customs; they were modified by different manners. Votaries of the Beautiful, they sought in Art the means of embodying their passionate conceptions: you have devoted your energies to Utility; and by the means of a power almost unknown to antiquity, by its miraculous agencies, you have applied its creative force to every combination of human circumstances that could produce your objects. Yet, amid the toil and triumphs of your scientific industry, upon you there comes the undefinable, the irresistible yearning for intellectual refinement—you build an edifice consecrated to those beautiful emotions and to those civilizing studies in which they excelled, and you impress upon its front a name taken from—

"Where on AEgean shores a city rose,
Built nobly, dear the air, and light the soil,
Athens, the eye of Greece, mother of arts
And eloquence."

Beautiful triumph of immortal genius! Sublime incentive to eternal fame! Then, when the feeling is so universal, when it is one which modern civilization is nurturing and developing, who does not feel that it is not only the most benevolent, but the most politic thing you can do to avail yourselves of its influence, and to direct in every way the formation of that character upon which intellect must necessarily now exercise an irresistible influence? We cannot shut our eyes any longer to the immense revolution. Knowledge is no longer a lonely eremite, affording a chance and captivating hospitality to some wandering pilgrim; knowledge is now found in the market-place, a citizen, and a leader of citizens. The spirit has touched the multitude; it has impregnated the mass—

"——Totamque infusa per artus,
Mens agitat molem, et magno se corpore miscet.

"I would yet say one word to those for whom this institution is not entirely but principally formed. I would address myself to that youth on whom the hopes of all societies repose and depend. I doubt not that they feel conscious of the position which they occupy—a position which, under all circumstances, at all periods, in every clime and country, is one replete with duty. The youth of a nation are the trustees of posterity; but the youth I address have duties peculiar to the position which they occupy. They are the rising generation of a society unprecedented in the history of the world; that is at once powerful and new. In other parts of the kingdom the remains of an ancient civilization are prepared ever to guide, to cultivate, to influence, the rising mind; but they are born in a miraculous creation of novel powers, and it is rather a providential instinct that has developed the necessary means of maintaining the order of your new civilization than the matured foresight of man. This is their inheritance. They will be called on to perform duties— great duties. I, for one, wish, for their sakes and for the sake of my country, that they may be performed greatly. I give to them that counsel which I have ever given to youth, and which I believe to be the wisest and the best —I tell them to aspire. I believe that the man who does not look up will look down; and that the spirit that does not dare to soar is destined perhaps to grovel. Every individual is entitled to aspire to that position which he believes his faculties qualify him to occupy. I know there are some who look with what I believe is short-sighted timidity and false prudence upon such views. They are apt to tell us— 'Beware of filling the youthful mind with an impetuous tumult of turbulent fancies; teach youth, rather, to be content with his position—do not induce him to fancy that he is that which he is not, or to aspire to that which he cannot achieve.' In my mind these are superficial delusions. He who enters the world finds his level. It is the solitary being, the isolated individual, alone in his solitude, who may be apt to miscalculate his powers, and misunderstand his character. But action teaches him the truth, even if it be a stern one. Association affords him the best criticism in the world, and I will venture to say, that if he belong to the Athenaeum, though when he enters it he may think himself a genius, if nature has not given him a passionate and creative soul, before a week has elapsed he will become a very sober-minded individual. I wish to damp no youthful ardour. I can conceive what such an institution would have afforded to the suggestive mind of a youthful Arkwright. I can conceive what a nursing- mother such an institution must have been to the brooding genius of your illustrious and venerated Dalton. It is the asylum of the self- formed; it is the counsellor of those who want counsel; but it is not a guide that will mislead, and it is the last place that will fill the mind of man with false ideas and false conceptions. He reads a newspaper, and his conceit oozes out after reading a leading article. He refers to the library, and the calm wisdom of centuries and sages moderates the rash impulse of juvenescence. He finds new truths in the lecture-room, and he goes home with a conviction that he is not so learned as he imagined. In the discussion of a great question with his equals in station, perhaps he finds he has his superiors in intellect. These are the means by which the mind of man is brought to a healthy state, by which that self-knowledge that always has been lauded by sages may be most securely attained. It is a rule of universal virtue, and from the senate to the counting-house will be found of universal application. Then, to the youth of Manchester, representing now the civic youth of this great county and this great district, I now appeal. Let it never be said again that the fortunes of this institution were in danger. Let them take advantage of this hour of prosperity calmly to examine and deeply to comprehend the character of that institution in which their best interests are involved, and which for them may afford a relaxation which brings no pang, and yields information which may bear them to fortune. It is to them I appeal with confidence, because I feel I am pleading their cause — with confidence, because in them I repose my hopes. When nations fall, it is because a degenerate race intervenes between the class that created and the class that is doomed. Let them then remember what has been done for them. The leaders of their community have not been remiss in regard to their interests. Let them remember, that when the inheritance devolves upon them, they are not only to enjoy but to improve. They will one day succeed to the high places of this great community; let them recollect those who lighted the way for them; and when they have wealth, when they have authority, when they have power, let it not be said that they were deficient in public virtue and public spirit. When the torch is delivered to them, let them also light the path of human progress to educated man."

As time went on, I had many interviews and conversations with Mr. and Mrs. Disraeli. I learned to appreciate, more and more, that the oddities attributed to the latter were mainly of society manufacture; while her fine qualities had been kept in the background by the over- shadowing ability, and prominence, of her husband. She was a devoted wife, and the soul of kindness to every one she liked or respected. Peace and honor to her memory.

In the sad years which followed my misfortune of 1846, previously alluded to, it was enough for me, wearily, to get through the work of the day, and then to return to a home where there has always been sympathy, kindness, and cheerfulness in the darkest and most anxious hours of laborious and self-denying lives. In those years I rarely saw any of my old friends of prominence and station. My wife and I lived the lives of recluses until clouds ceased to lower. Health became restored, a moderate and augmenting fortune, laid in the foundations of carefulness, came to us; and we at last emerged into daylight, again.

When in Parliament, in 1857, I made a speech in the House of Commons, which some thought timely, upon the then pressing question of Indian railways. Mr. Disraeli did me the honor to listen to what I had to say. After his lamented death, one of his executors handed back to me, in an envelope, endorsed in his own hand, the letters which I had written to him in the years of the Manchester Athenaeum.

I may add, that Mr. Disraeli's ear was always open to me during the struggles for the Intercolonial Railway as a means, and the Confederation of the British Provinces in America as the great end, of our efforts. He was strongly in favour of Confederation; and, just as we owe the establishment of a Crown Colony in British Columbia to the sagacity of Bulwer Lytton, so we owe the final realization of Confederation, through the passing of an Act by the Queen, Lords, and Commons of Great Britain and Ireland, to the Government, no less sagacious on this question, of Lord Beaconsfield.

I think the following letters reflect no discredit upon my motives,— neither self-seeking nor selfish. At the same time they are further evidence of Mr. Disraeli's thorough kindness and feeling of justice towards all who had, in his judgment, "deserved well of their country."

"LONDON,   "3rd

August, 1867.

DEAR SIR,

"On my return from Scotland yesterday I learnt, confidentially, that you had been good enough to propose to present my name to the Queen for the honour of knighthood, in consideration of my services in connection with the union of the British North American Provinces under the Crown, and with their Intercolonial Railway. And I see that a semi-official statement to that effect is in some of the papers. Will you permit me to thank you very sincerely for such a recognition of the services of a political opponent whose known opinions will protect him from the suspicion of receiving, and you from that of giving, an unworthy reward.

"But the mail brings me tidings from Canada which convince me that the French Canadian population at large look upon the course pursued towards Messrs. Cartier and Langevin in the recent distribution of honors as an act of indifference towards themselves. It might be possible, therefore— but you will be the best judge—that the honor now proposed for me might lead to an aggravation of this feeling of dissatisfaction, which arises at the very inopportune moment of the birth of the 'new Dominion.'

"I think, therefore, that I should be as deficient in public duty as in generosity, if I did not evince my gratitude for your unsolicited remembrance by saying that, should the difficulty I allude to be found really to exist, I shall not feel myself slighted or aggrieved should your kindness proceed no further, pending such an unfortunate state of feeling.

"I ought to add, that my late most kind and indulgent friend, the Duke of Newcastle, suggested some little time before his death an even higher reward for the services, which he alone knew the real extent of; but at my request it was postponed until—all the manifold difficulties being one by one cleared away—the great question of policy which he had so much at heart should be finally realized in legislation.

"Having thus been led almost, to rely upon some adequate recognition of several years' gratuitous and arduous exertion on both sides of the Atlantic, I feel the sacrifice I propose to make. But a desire to avoid aggravating this unfortunate misunderstanding induces me to trouble you now.

"I have the honour to be, dear Sir,
"Yours very faithfully and obliged,
""E. W. WATKIN.

"THE RT. HON. THE CHANCELLOR OF THE EXCHEQUER."

"DOWNING STREET,
S.W. "*August 8, 1867.*

DEAR SIR,

"I have had the honor of receiving your letter of the 3rd instant, in which you refer to the rumoured intention of Her Majesty's Government to recommend your name to the Queen for the honor of knighthood, in consideration of services connected with the International Colonial Railway, and the influence of that undertaking on the union of the British North American Provinces; and in which you state your apprehension, that such an intention, in consequence of the recent intelligence from Canada with respect to the distribution of honors, might prove embarrassing to the Government.

"Under that impression you have, in a manner highly creditable to yourself, and most considerate to the Government, stated that you should not feel yourself slighted or aggrieved, if the views of Her Majesty's Government towards yourself were not proceeded with pending such an unfortunate feeling in Canada.

"It is quite true that it was the intention of Her Majesty's Government to recommend to Her Majesty to confer the honor of knighthood on you, in consideration of your services in question, thereby, as they believe, fulfilling the purpose of the late Duke of Newcastle, when his Grace was Secretary of State for the Colonies; but Her Majesty's Government, appreciating your motives in the suggestion which you have made, are of opinion that it may be expedient to suspend, for a time, conferring a distinction on you which, under the peculiar circumstances of the case, might occasion a painful, though an unfounded, feeling of jealousy.

> "I have the honor to remain,
> "Dear Sir, yours faithfully,
> "B. DISRAELI.

"E. W. WATKIN, Esq., M.P."

Time went on, and, one morning in the summer of 1868, I received this letter: —

> "10,   DOWNING
> STREET,   WHITEHALL,
> "*August 11, 1868.*

MY DEAR MR. ROSE,

"The Queen has been graciously pleased to order, that letters patent should be prepared, to confer the honor of knighthood on Mr. Watkin, the Member for Stockport.

"As I know you take a great interest in the welfare of that gentleman, I have sent you this line, that you may be the first to know the distinction that awaits him.

> "Sincerely yours,
> "B. DISRAELI.

"PHILIP ROSE, Esqre."

I may also add a curious bit of history of a personal character.

Mr. Disraeli was returned to Parliament, in 1837, for Maidstone, mainly, by the exertions and influence of his agent, Mr. Richard Hart, the eminent solicitor. Mr. Hart was my friend and agent on my return for the borough of Hythe, in 1874, and in 1880.

Mr. Hart had many interesting reminiscences of Mr. Disraeli to recount, and some day, in a more appropriate place, I hope to be able to recount them.

Chapter XXIII
Visits to Quebec and Portland, and Letters Home, 1861

Leaving Montreal by the night boat, I arrived at the wharf at Quebec; and, after a visit to the hotel and a walk round the city, called on Mr. Cartier, the Chief Minister of Canada, at the small house he then inhabited.

My first relation with Quebec was in acting as Honorary Secretary to a Committee in Manchester, which raised 7,500_l_. by subscription, and sent it out in money and goods to relieve the people, houseless and ruined by the great Quebec fires of May and July, 1845, when 3,015 houses were burnt down, and thousands of people were made homeless, and were starving. I also visited the city in 1851. Later on, in the year 1866, I was Chairman of the City of London Committee, which raised 23,800_l_. to alleviate the suffering caused by the great Quebec fire of that year.

In my walk round the city (in 1861) I was struck with the absence of precautions against fire, and the persistence in building wooden houses, when the cost of brick or stone could not be greatly more than of wood.

I may say, however, in my right as an old helper in these fire disasters, that on inspecting the city last September (1886), I was much impressed by the new building regulations in rigid force, and especially by the admirable system adopted for the effective repression of fires. There are central and subordinary fire stations, all connected together by telegraph and telephone. A constant watch is kept, engines are always ready to start off, and a sufficient number of men available for duty night and day.

But to come back to Mr. Cartier. After I had waited in his salon for a few minutes, he entered: A man under middle height, hair turning a little grey, eyes grey blue, sparkling and kindly; face almost Grecian; figure spare but muscular; well proportioned; manner full of almost southern fire, and restlessness. We discussed our Grand Trunk affairs. I explained the objects of our draft Bill, which were few and simple— (A) To raise 500,000_l_. as an "equipment" mortgage, to provide the railway with, much needed, plant and material; (B) to set aside all revenue derived from postal and military services; and upon the security of this revenue to issue "Postal and Military" Bonds, wherewith to pay the debts due by the Company in Canada and England. These debts were pressing, and were large. (C) To alter the administration of the Company in such wise that while the executive work would be done in Canada, with Montreal as headquarters, the seat of government would be in London, the stock and bonds being mainly held in England. I think, at that time, there were not more than 20,000_l_. of the original issue of Ordinary Stock of the Grand Trunk held in Canada.

Mr. Cartier knew, of course, all the ins and outs of the Grand Trunk. His Government had in previous years placed the loan of 3,100,000_l_. from Canada, expended in construction, behind other securities, to enable an issue of second bonds with which to complete the Trunk lines. But, unfortunately, as a condition of this concession, profitless branches were undertaken, branches, no doubt, locally useful, perhaps politically needful, but profitless nevertheless.

Mr. Cartier's sole query was, "Have you arranged with the Government at home as to the Military Revenue?"—to which I replied, that there was no occasion: the Government made no objection, and regularly paid the moderate charges made for the conveyance of men and material over the Railway: and we could, of course, if the Canadian Parliament passed our draft Bill into an Act, appropriate these receipts in any way the Act directed. With the Canadian Government it was different. The Canadian Government had, so far, delayed any settlement of our accounts for the costly conveyance of mail matter, by special trains, over long distances, so timed as to suit the Province but not to suit the Grand Trunk passengers; and one of my objects in coming out was to endeavour to induce Mr. Cartier and his colleagues to close up this pending matter for the past and to accord a just and adequate amount for the service of the future, such amount to be effective over a period of years. We then went into general conversation. I told Mr. Cartier I had been in Canada in 1851: and had at that time seen Papinean, Mackenzie, and others, whose resistance had led to peace and union, and greater liberty for all. This remark fired his eye; and he said, "Ah! it is eight years that I am Prime Minister of Canada; when I was a rebel the country was different, very different."

Mr. Cartier often preceded his observations, I believe, by the words "When I was a rebel;" and old George Crawford, of the Upper Province, a magnificent specimen of a Scotch Upper Canadian, once said, "Cartier, my frind, ye'll be awa to England and see the Queen, and when ye come bock aw that aboot ye're being a robbell, as no doobt ye were, will never be hard again. Ye'll begin, mon, 'When I was at Windsor Castle talking to the Queen.'" Years before, on Cartier being presented to the Queen by

Sir E. Bulwer Lytton, he told Her Majesty that a Lower Canadian was "an Englishman who speaks French."

But Mr. Cartier had been a rebel; and a gallant and brave one. One of the incidents was, that when Sir John Colborne's troops invested the Chateau of St. Eustache, Cartier, a young man of nineteen, was lowered from a window at night, crawled along to the Cache, then under range of fire, and brought back a bag of cartridges strapped round his waist, to replenish the exhausted ammunition of the defenders of the Chateau. And I believe that he was hauled up again amidst a rain of bullets, having been discovered,— which bullets, fortunately for Canada, missed the "rebel."

I may here mention that in the autumn of 1865 I had a long interview with President Andrew Johnson, at the White House at Washington, having been introduced by Mr. Rice, of St. Paul's, Minnesota, a man to whom the United States and Canada are each deeply indebted, for the completion of railways from St. Paul's to the Hudson's Bay post of Fort Garry, now the thriving town of Winnipeg. The President told me he had that morning received a letter from the wife of the ex-President of the just defeated Southern Confederacy, which he said was "the reverse of complimentary." He read a sentence or two; and smiled quietly at a reference to his, as assumed by the lady, early occupation of journeyman tailor. President Davis was at the moment in prison in the case-mates of Fort Hatteras. "It is, of course, difficult to know what to do with him." Well, I said, "Mr. President, I remember when you were a Senator you said to those who talked secession, that if they carried out their threats, and you had your way, you would 'hang them as high as Haman.'"

The President paused, and then lifted his head and replied, "So I did, Sir. But we must look at things all round; consider faults on both sides, and that we have to be fellow-citizens in future." I added, "Mr. President, I have just left Canada, and taken leave of Mr. Cartier, the Prime Minister of that country. The Queen has not a more loyal subject. Yet, in 1839, he was a rebel in arms against the Crown. He was a secessionist. For a while he was a refugee in the woods at Rouse's Point, on Lake Champlain. A reward of 500_l_. was offered for his apprehension. But our country removed grievances, recognized the equality of French and English Canadians, united the Provinces, and forgave the rebels. All that sad contest is now forgotten."

The President seemed much struck, and, after a pause, he said, "Sir, will you say that again?" I repeated the words, and he scribbled, as I spoke, some notes on the blotter of the portfolio before him. He then said, "A countryman of mine has been over to your side of the Atlantic to teach you to tame horses. This gentleman, Mr. Rarey, uses what he calls 'mild force.' Mild force will probably be useful with us." The Fenian demonstrations in the United States against England were named as a breach of comity. The President said, sharply, "Why don't your people remonstrate? We hear no complaint."

To return to my narrative, Mr. Cartier arranged an interview for me with the Governor-General, Sir Edmund Head, and I presented my letters from Mr. Baring, and was assured of all the help he could give me. "Your demands are very clear, and appear to me equally just. First you ask the Government of Canada to aid you in passing a Bill through Parliament, which clearly is for the benefit of Canada, because it proposes to increase the efficiency of the railway service by a further outlay of capital, and also to pay off debt, a considerable part of which is incurred in Canada; and secondly, you ask for an immediate and just settlement of the charge for the conveyance by you of the mails."

The Governor-General then sent for Mr. John A.

Macdonald, who came immediately, and the conversation which had taken place was repeated.

This was the first time I had seen either Cartier, Sir Edmund Head, or Macdonald.

Sir Edmund Head was a tall stately man, with thoughtful brow, and complexion a little purpled by cardiac derangement. As the don of a college he would have been great, and in his sphere: as the Governor of a Province with a self-asserting people, I doubt if he had found the true groove.

His despatches were scholastic essays. His simplest replies were grave and learned, sometimes too complex for ordinary comprehension. When he, subsequently, became Governor of the Hudson's Bay Company, he tried to manage a profit-and-loss undertaking as if he were governing a province: just as when he governed a province he administered all things as if he were dealing with Russia in Europe. He was, however, a man of the kindest heart, and the strictest honor. But, after all, he was one of the round men put into the square holes of Provincial Government by the "authorities" at home. Still, on the whole, a noble character, and in very truth a gentleman. His chronic ailment led to some irritability of temper; and when, during the visit of the Prince of Wales, one of the Governor's aides-de-camp was pushed over from the steamer at Detroit by the press of the crowd, and fell into the water, Colonel Irving said:—"Ah! there was no danger whatever to — —'s life. The Governor-General has blown him up so much that he could never sink." I was present at a farewell dinner to Sir Edmund Head at Mr. Cartier's, at Quebec, in the winter of 1861-2. In response to the toast of his health, he alluded to his infirmity of temper, admitted his suffering—before concealed from outside people—and expressed his apologies in a manner so feeling and so gentle that the tears came into everybody's eyes. I heard more than one sob from men whose rough exterior disguised the real tenderness of their hearts.

Mr. John A. Macdonald entered the Governor-General's presence with a manly deference. I was at once struck by an odd resemblance in some of his features and expressions to Disraeli—dark curly hair, piercing eyes, aquiline nose, mouth sometimes firm, almost stern in expression, sometimes so mild that he seemed especially fitted to play with little children. I soon learned that, in tact, fixed purpose, and resources, he was ahead of them all. And, after watching his career for a quarter of a century, I have seen no reason to alter that opinion. He is the statesman of Canada—one of the ablest men on the Continent. I wish he administered the Colonial relations of the whole Empire. Had he done so for the last ten years we should have escaped our mistakes in South Africa, and the everlasting disgrace of Majuba Hill. Why is it that such men are excluded from office at home? Sir John A. Macdonald (then Mr. Macdonald) was once taken by me under the gallery, by special order of Mr. Speaker, to hear a "great" speech of Mr. Gladstone, whom he had not before heard. When we went away, I said: "Well, what do you think of him?" He replied: "He is a great rhetorician, but—he is not an orator." Would that men would not be carried away in a torrent of happy words. One hour of the late Patrick Smyth was, to my mind, worth a week of all the great rhetoricians.

A day or two after these interviews, the Hon. John Ross took me down to Portland, to have an interview with the Hon. A. T. Galt, the Finance Minister of Canada. I at once recognized in Mr. Galt a reduced likeness of his father. Mr. Galt was about five feet eleven: his father, who I had seen when a boy, about six feet four, and "buirdly" and stout in proportion. The father wore spectacles—the son did not. The father was the author of the "Annals of the Parish," "Laurie Todd," and many works greatly read when I was young. He was, also, the founder of the town of "Guelph," and of other towns in Upper Canada. If anyone wants to see an admirable likeness of him, he had better consult "Fraser's Magazine," of one of the issues of 1830 to 1833, and he will there find a rough engraving of the hoisting of the Union Jack at Guelph. Mr. Galt, *pere*, was so very large a man that Mr. Archibald Prentice, of the "Manchester Times," used to tell a story about his pointing Mr. Galt out to a little humpbacked Scotchman in the High Street of Edinburgh: "Eh! Jamie, mon, there's the great Galt, author of the 'Annals of the Parish.'" "'Annals o' the Payrish,' Archie, hech, sirs, he's big eneuch to be the Payrish itself—let alone the annals o' it."

Mr. Galt, the Finance Minister, has done great services to Canada, and is doing them still, in developing the mineral resources of the West, and in other ways. Our conversation on Grand Trunk affairs was long and anxious. I could see that Mr. Galt would do everything in his power; but the public prejudice was strongly against the Grand Trunk. The Grand Trunk Arrangements Bill was passed, as herein stated, in May, 1862; but, alas, the question of postal payments by Canada stood over till the end of 1864.

In reference to my visit, of 1861, so far as my personal journeyings were concerned, I will merely transcribe a few letters sent home.

"STEAMSHIP 'PERSIA'
"(in the Gulf of St. Lawrence),
"*Sunday noon.*

"I have not had a pen in hand for a week—not since I wrote just as we were coming to Cork.

"Just now the weather is as like that of last Sunday as one pea is to another—rain and mist—mist and rain! Yet we have, on the whole, had wonderful weather—little sea—little wind—little of anything very unpleasant—nothing unbearable.

"Our church-service is just over: the Captain reads prayers and a sermon, and does it very well: the sailors are dressed in their best, and behave with great decorum, but show some sleepiness: the day is wet, and that, and the general devoutness, draws a large congregation, —indeed, the cabin is full.

"And now for a long letter:—

"When I left off, before, we were coming to Cork. It was blowing and raining, and the atmosphere was thick with mist. We went on till six. Captain looked anxious—the Cork pilot bothered, the passengers ill- tempered, and everything had a dismal dampness about it. At last we stopped, and the big boilers sent out their steam through the waste pipe with a loud roar. Around us was nothing but *mist*—the, to me, nastiest form of fog. We could not see more than three times the length of the ship. We tried the lead twice, and the second time got soundings. We then fired a gun—then another—then a third. Then we moved on—then stopped—then moved on. The Captain sent for his chart, and put on his eye-glasses. The pilot stared out into the fog, and pointed first in one direction, then in another. All no use. We knew we *ought* to be outside the Queenstown harbour—but we could see nothing. At last we heard a gun, and then in quick succession appeared a row boat and a steam tug with the passengers and mails; and, the mist breaking a little, we saw the land right a-head of us, about half-a- mile off. It was disagreeable, but it got over; and now came the transfer of bags, luggage, and passengers—only two or three of the latter. The tug came alongside and made fast, but there was a good deal of swell, and as she bobbed up and down it became highly amusing to see the crew and passengers scramble up the ladder, which sometimes was perpendicular, and at other times almost flat, as it followed the altering level of the tug. The ladder got broken—two or three ropes snapped—a deal of profane swearing took place—but it got over, too.

"The tug brought the news—the Confederates had defeated the Federal forces at Manasses Junction—three thousand killed and wounded—prisoners taken—artillery captured, &c., &c. I went up to one of the Misses Preston and hoped the news was happy—for she seemed delighted at what she had heard, and which then I had not. She said she 'did not quite know—it was for the South.' I replied that such news hardly could be happy for both sides, and, unless the news were *peace*, was unhappy for all the world. She did not quite agree—and then told me the tidings. But what a strange effect in such a little ship- confined community!

"The Southern people collected together in delight—the Northern in anger and disgust. The former predicted an early possession of Washington for the Palmetto flag; the latter talked of raising half-a- million of men, and 'crushing out' the South, right amain; while, as in any disaster, there is always someone to be blamed, many of the Northern men laid all the responsibility upon the 'lawyer-generals' and 'store-keeping-colonels,' who had assumed commands for which they were never fit. It is a sad, unhappy quarrel!

"But I must describe our circle to you. First, I should tell you that I have the honor to sit at the Captain's table, and on his left hand—a Miss Ewart sitting on his right. Our set consists of the Captain, Judkins—the right and left-hand passengers as aforesaid—Col. Preston, Mrs. Preston and the three Misses Preston.

Mr. Stone, Col. Stewart, Miss Warde, Mr. Still, and Mr. Hutton, of Sheffield, and his daughter. We have 134 passengers, *only*, on board—a slack muster, caused by the evil times in America—and all were at dinner on Saturday, the day we sailed, but the wind, rain, mist, and misery of the next three days sent many of them below, and for those days we had plenty of elbow-room. The weather, however, improved, the sun got now and then out, though it has, so far, been anything but warm, and out came the sick people again in renovated appetite—some epicurean and dainty, many others with a ravenous, all- devouring maw, reminding one of the 'worm that never dieth.'

"Now, Col. Preston is the late U.S. Ambassador to Madrid, where he has resided officially, and with his family, for the four years of the Buchanan Presidency. He is now replaced, I think, by a Mr. Falkner. He is a tall, stout, gentlemanly man, but, while a perfect gentleman in his conversation, and having less of the American accent than most Americans, his manner is somewhat ungainly—perhaps owing to his make, which is large and a little inclining to the unwieldy.

"Mrs. Preston has an Americo-Grecian face, and is a 'grand-dame.' She talks of the blessings of slavery, and of the vain and self-recoiling efforts of her mother, who liberated many slaves and educated more, to reduce the evil; and is full of the troubles and robberies of foreign house-keeping and of the gossip of the diplomatic circle.

"Her daughters are high-spirited, good-humoured, large-sized girls— fresh, natural and charming. One of them has a fine face with eyes of blue, just like those Bradley liked to paint—and the other two are good looking enough. They have, however, no conversation—lots of talk and gossip; much of it, too, amusing and quick witted, but it wants thought. They all come from Kentucky, where they are now going. Colonel Stewart is, I think, from Louisiana. He talks little, and does not interest me. Mr. Stone is a voluble high-spirited Northern man, with Southern tendencies. He says that the men who started this secession, and have made it what it is, ought (on both sides) to be hung, and he 'would go home on purpose.' It seems that a house in which he had a large sum has failed, and, to use a phrase I have heard both Mr. Preston and himself make use of, the civil war has 'shocked' his property above one half, *i.e.* has reduced its value above one half. They all agree, in fact, that the value of all property has gone down at least half, a loss, if the nation had to sell up—which it has not, but has only to 'liquidate'—of a sum greater than required to buy up all the slaves and set them free. Credit is gone—the faith of the people in their Government is weakened, and thousands are ruined in every city in the land. Sad civil war! Our passengers comprise all sorts of people—from all sorts of places, clothed in all sorts of dresses: anything will do at sea. We have, too, a good many old stagers of the Atlantic, who think nothing of 'going across.' This will console you—as you have to go 'across' next spring—to know that one man has been across 57 times, another 31, another 18, and another 13; and one lady has been 6—while the fat buxom stewardess has done a hundred, and is alive and well, and quite as ready to receive a half crown from a passenger, of any country, as ever!

"But I must give over writing for a little, till this breeze of wind is over.

"We have now only 1,000 miles to go, and shall be in New York on Wednesday.

"*Monday.*

"We had a bad night, and I could not sleep for the row and the motion. We have now got it over, and are going merrily along with a smart breeze, bright sun, and sparkling sea. It will be late on Wednesday, however, when we get in.

"A rough night at sea has its features. On board these ships there are strict rules and strict discipline. We breakfast, lunch, dine, and tea at hours which are kept to a moment. The bell rings, and down we sit. Then the bar closes at 11, and all lights are put out at 12. The lights in the cabins are placed inside a partition, glazed with ground glass, so that there is no glare, and you cannot get at them. No loose lights are allowed, and a passenger who struck a light would be severely handled. These are proper precautions against fire, and should be obeyed. But at 12 we are in total darkness—the ship rolls and pitches —every now and then a sea strikes her, and burr—hush—swish—goes the water over her sides or bows, and along her decks.

Then the men above run about, ropes are pulled, sails set or taken in, and a general hullabaloo goes on—no doubt in the interest of the passengers—but very disagreeable. Then the boatswain's whistle—Pee- ee-ee ah! Pee-ee-ee ah-h-h!—every now and then wakes you up. Light is a comfort, and darkness at sea seems to aggravate the strange feeling which now and then affects you, as you think you are following a great road without track or guide—save that which the stars, if visible, and the previous day's observations afford.

"On Saturday morning (10 August) I was called up to see the Great Eastern: and certainly an immense steamer was making its way eastward, about 15 miles due north of us. You will see by the date of her arrival if she was the object we saw or not. Saturday was very cold. We had heard at Queenstown, from a note from Capt. Stone to Judkins, that icebergs had been seen on the homeward passage, and at 3 o'clock we saw ahead of us something which looked like the wreck of a steamer—but which was pronounced to be ice. It was about 10 miles off. As we approached it we found it was a little mountain of ice, covering perhaps a couple of acres in area, and about 50 or 60 feet high. It assumed all sorts of shapes as we caught sight of it at different points—it looked, once, like a great lion crouching on the water—then it took an appearance like part of the causeway at Staffa. As soon as we got abreast of it we saw pack ice around it, and the light, then shining upon the whole mass, gave a fairy-like whiteness—transparent, snowy whiteness—which was very beautiful to see. While we were observing it, a great mass broke away, toppled over into the sea, sending up an immense snowy spray, and disappeared. The remainder stayed in sight, with the evening sun-light upon it, for a couple of hours.

"Yesterday, Sunday, morning, we sighted Cape Race, the eastern extremity of Newfoundland, and ran close in shore along a most desolate, dismal, coast, for a couple of hours. Abreast of the lighthouse and telegraph station a boat came off, and we pitched over a packet, with a little red flag attached, containing the latest news, to be telegraphed from thence to New York and other places, so that our passing would be known that afternoon everywhere—and if the steamer had not left Halifax it might bring the news thence to England; thus you may know of our safe arrival, so far, by about the 18th or 19th. I hope you may, as it will relieve your mind from various fears about me. It is very seldom indeed that the steamers actually sight Cape Race, as we did. However, we saw that desolate coast and the poor hermits of the place. Rounding the Cape, we enter the Gulf of St. Lawrence, which broke in rain and storm upon us. We saw several fishing sloops 'lying to,' to wait for better weather. These little craft are often run over by larger vessels, as they swarm in what is the great east and west track for steamers and other large ships; and when the wind is south, or south west, there is always fog and mist in the Gulf, and on the banks of Newfoundland outside.

"I find it a great comfort having a cabin to myself. I am now writing in my 'drawing-room'—*i.e.*, my upper berth, with my legs hanging down over my bed-room, or lower berth. All my property is stowed away and hung up, and the steward keeps all nice and clean—calls me in the morning, and at half-past seven brings me a foot-pan of fresh sea-water to bathe in. The *rum* is not very much diminished, as I have been very self-denying, being desirous of coming home in full vigour and hard health, if possible. It is very good, however, and when I finish this letter I shall reward good resolution by taking a little drop to drink your health—and God bless you!

"Taylor was excessively sick and ill, but is now all alive, and says he 'feels so light' he could run a race.

"I am pretty well. I have not been sick at all: I wish I had—but I ought to be thankful for a great deal of comfort in this long journey.

"I shall open this if anything worth recording takes place before we reach New York. If not, the receipt of this will tell you that we are 'safely landed.' I shall, however, write again from New York before I leave it for Boston—but I shall only remain a portion of a day and a night at New York."

"ST. LAWRENCE HALL,
MONTREAL.
"*Sunday, August 18.*

"From New York I went on, *via* Long Island Sound, to Boston, where I arrived at 7 a.m. on Friday. I stayed there all day, in conference with Mr. Baring's agent, Mr. Ward, and went on to Montreal, in the evening, *via* Lowel, Concord, and Rouse's Point. I engaged a double berth in a sleeping car, and slept pretty well and pretty comfortably from about 10 till 5—with sundry breaks, caused as hereafter stated. I got to Montreal at 10—washed, breakfasted, and then did a hard day's work, and dined at 7, with the internal satisfaction that I had done a good day's duty, and had a good appetite for both food and drink—the latter, however, moderate—only one pint and one cup of coffee and one cigar after—the first cigar which I have smoked since leaving England. The rum, thanks to similar moderation, holds out, and will last some time yet.

"New York is be-flagged and be-bannered to a wonderful extent. Every street is disfigured by huge streamers, some right across the street, others out of windows and from the tops of houses—while each occupant tries to vie with his neighbour in this sort of loyalty, till there seems almost to be hypocrisy in it. 'Stars and Stripes' everywhere, and on all occasions, opportune and inopportune. The main public place in New York is half filled by ugly wooden sheds, used as military store rooms and barracks, and, every now and then, with a frequency which is startling, are the head-quarters of all sorts of Volunteer regiments— American, Irish, German, Dutch, French, and Scotch. These rooms are adorned with flags, and transparencies showing the costume of the corps, or the portrait of the colonel, or general, shown generally on a big prancing horse, and sporting a savage-looking beard. All along the roads and routes—everywhere almost—are tents and wooden sheds, the encampments of companies and regiments; and every now and then bands and recruiting parties parade the street, and draw crowds of people after them. The mothers of America have taken up the question, too, and there are societies to make lint and bandages for the wounded, and to stitch together clothing for the new companies. Little Zouaves are plentiful—red vest, blue sash, and red fez and breeches.

"The day we arrived, the New York Firemen Zouaves (7th New York) returned from the defeat at Bull's Run—380 out of 1,000, who left two months ago under a young fellow named Ellsworth, as colonel. Ellsworth was shot by a public-house keeper, whose secession flag he hauled down —and the regiment was much cut up at Bull's Run. It has been very uproarious, and some of its men 'retreated' on the way from Bull's Run to New York, on the principle that, once ordered to retreat, they had better 'retreat right away home.' There can be no doubt, however, that the bulk of these men fought well—but were, like most of the regiments, badly officered—zealous men, but lawyers, store-keepers, and political partisans, who could do nothing in handling *bodies* of men.

"But to go back: about 60 miles from Boston, and just as I got into the bed-berth in the car, several companies of one of the Vermont regiments joined the train, having been discharged, on the expiration of their three months' term, the day before. These men had to be dropped in companies at various stations all along the road; and every hour or so I was wakened up by bell ringing, gun firing, and cheering, as each section got back home to their friends. In the morning I got amongst those who were left, and heard their adventures. They had been in nothing but skirmishing, however, and only had had three men wounded. They seemed a nice body of young fellows, many very young. All were voluble and in high spirits (*coming home*), and were very large about the hard biscuits they had eaten—some, as one 'boy' said—for they are all 'boys,' not 'men,' as with us—with the stamp of 1810 upon them,—of camping out—keeping sentry at night, &c., &c., &c. They had three young fellows, girlish-looking lads, with them, '*sick;*' two—one certainly—sick under death; just get home to die! I went into the baggage car and saw them lying on the floor, covered up in tarpaulins and blankets, poor fellows!

"I have been to the Catholic Cathedral at Montreal to-day, and heard high mass. I visited it in 1851. Fine church, fine music, and a good sermon, in French; but I thought I should have preferred Mr. Woolnough and the little church at home.

"The matter of business I have in hand is surrounded with difficulty, and there are here, I fear, two classes in connection with the concern. Mr. Baring and Mr. Glyn have been, I can see already, deceived by over sanguine estimates—and they do not know all yet, but they shall, if I can find it out.

"Letters leave here to-morrow, and I shall open this before I post it should there be any new feature. As at present advised, I shall go to Quebec on Wednesday night, and spend four or five days in that district. Then I shall come back here, and then go to Toronto and the western portion of the line. After that, all will depend upon whether the Government will call a special session, or not. We shall see. I shall know, perhaps, in time for the following post."

"HAMILTON,
"Sunday, I Septr. 1861.

"I left Toronto on Tuesday and went to Samia, stayed till Wednesday morning, and then went on to Detroit. Spent the day in Detroit, and then went on to Chicago; stayed Thursday in Chicago, and went on Friday into Illinois, over the Prairies as far as Urbano. Came back to Calumet—near to Chicago. Near Chicago I visited poor dear Ingram's drowning place. Alas! More about it hereafter—and came on thence to Detroit and this place, which I reached yesterday at 2-tired and irritated with tooth-ache, which has never left me for some days and sticks by me yet. I have travelled 1,300 miles since last Tuesday, and 3,070 in all since I landed at New York. This has necessitated travelling during eight nights out of the eighteen I have spent in this country. However, I have thereby cleared off some subsidiary work and have seen the extremes of the territory over which I have to work and plan, and by to-morrow I shall have looked at, and taken account of, most of the people I shall have to deal with. This will enable me now to go to work, and will, I hope, so much shorten my stay on 'this Continent,' as they call it. I have a hard and difficult job before me, but hope to scrape through it with credit, if not with much success. It is a very different country: and they are not only very different, but very difficult, people to manage. Socially, every one has been very civil and kind, and I have had no lack of company or advisers—the latter sometimes giving rather odd suggestions. Everyone is expecting to hear daily of a great battle near Washington, and it may be that the fate of one or other of the contending parties will be decided, for the time, at least, before I leave. At present there is great hatred and animosity, and every possible evil passion abroad. If it were not for the actual loss of *dollars* I believe they would cut each other's throats to all eternity: but the hope is that their rapacity may check their ferocity. As to any high purpose about the war—it is moonshine. It is a war for supremacy and to find out which brother shall rule the house and run away with the dying old man's goods. [Footnote: The following Resolution passed the United States House of Representatives, February 11, 1861, by a nearly unanimous vote:—

"*Resolved*—That neither the Federal Government, nor the people or Government of the non-slaveholding States, have a purpose or a constitutional right to legislate upon or interfere with slavery in any of the States of the Union.

"*Resolved*—That those persons in the North who do not subscribe to the foregoing proposition, are too insignificant in numbers and influence to excite the serious attention and alarm of any portion of the people of the Republic; and that the increase of their numbers and influence does not keep pace with the increase of the aggregate population of the Union."] I am spending to-day with Reynolds, and dine to-night with Brydges. Reynolds has a good house, but he complains of his high rent, as his house was taken in the piping times of 1858. Now rents are down one-half, and he could get as good a house for 100_l_ a year, whereas he pays 200_l_ In 1857 it was—to use a vile Yankee phrase, the literal meaning of which no one can explain, but the illustrative meaning of which is inflation—"High Felluting"— or, as the Yankees write it, "Hi Falutin"—now everything is sobered, and in many places depressed: only one house now being built in all this town of 40,000 inhabitants."

"MONTREAL,   "6 *Sep*.
1861.

"I spent Monday in Toronto and came on here on Monday night, reaching here on Tuesday afternoon. Since then I have been busy here. I have had a more satisfactory interview with the Finance Minister, and we go to Quebec together on Tuesday, after which I meet the Government, officially, and shall know before the end of next week whether they will help us, or not. I think they will do something. The management of this railway is an organized mess—I will not say, a sink of iniquity. I shall, however, know all about it before I have done with it.

"I feel tired, somehow—perhaps with travelling too hard—perhaps with too much anxiety to get on quickly with this Grand Trunk business; but, on the whole, I am very well, and have kept my spirits and nerve up to the mark, generally. I have a great task in hand, and I should like to come out of it creditably.

"There is a belief here that Jeff. Davis is dead, and, if so, it may alter the complexion of affairs in the United States. The U.S. Government have introduced passports—so one cannot leave their agitated soil without that badge of tyranny. It will not affect me, as I shall not stop long in their land—but get out of it as soon as I can.

"There is a doctor and another man to be hanged here to-morrow, for procuring abortion—the woman having died. The doctor is a Yankee, and the Finance Minister tells me that this is a common practice in the States, and carried on to an alarming extent, even amongst respectable people, and, that this, and similar, frightful practices are the cause of the degeneracy of much of the American race. He says the Canadian Government have determined to stop it in Canada, in the outset, by hanging this doctor and his employer, and so deterring the rest—and it seemed to me to be *right*. I thought once of going to see the two ruffians, expiate their crime—but I thought afterwards I would not. What a wicked world a mere money-making world becomes! true, we all require chastening by pain and misfortune and difficulty. The Americans have been spoiled by too great and sudden prosperity and too much license—not 'real liberty.' The very children, scorn obedience—in fact, there is none of the general fine 'honor of parents' we, still, find at home. As Mrs. Preston said, 'the Kentucky boys are fine generous fellows; but as to obeying *anyone*—even father or mother, after 15—*that* is out of the question.'"

"HALIFAX, NOVA SCOTIA,
"Sep. 18, 1861.

"I left Quebec last Thursday, and went by railway to Riviere de Loup. There I had a fall, and hurt my ribs. Next day I drove over the, new, Temiscouata road to the Lake, and thence took a birch bark canoe and two men and paddled down the Lake, and down the river Madawasca to Little Falls, where I arrived in a drenching storm of rain at one o'clock in the morning—having had 'perils by water.' Our canoe leaked, and we damaged its bottom in going through a rapid, and had to haul up for repairs and to bale out, for fear of sinking.

"Next day I drove to Grand Falls in a spring waggon, and then by Tobique to Woodstock, where I arrived on Sunday morning—having driven through the night.

"On Sunday drove to Canterbury, and then railed to St. Andrews, where I stayed with the able manager of the Railway.

"Monday railed and drove to Frederickton, where I had an interview with the Government of New Brunswick—then steamed down the St. John river to St. John; yesterday went by railway, St. John to Shediac, and then completed my journey, by hard travelling, driving through the night from Shediac (over the Cobequid Mountains) to Truro, where I joined the railway at 5 a.m., and came on to this place, reaching it at 12—three hours late—owing to our engine getting off the track. Here I have seen the Government, and also the Governor-General, and to-morrow I go by St. John's and Portland to Montreal, where I shall arrive on Saturday at 8 p.m., and go on to Toronto on Monday.

"I have only time to write a bare list of my doings, but will write fully by next mail. I hope to find heaps of letters at Montreal, and good news of your health and comfort."

"MONTREAL,

"*Sunday, Sept. 22, 1861.*

"I have made the tour described in my note from Halifax, and I got back here yesterday at 2 p.m., having travelled about 1,780 miles since leaving Quebec, and nearly 2,000 since I left here last Thursday week. I have spent the best part of one day and night in a canoe—two late nights on the road in the spring waggon and stage—one night, and part of another, in steamers—and the remaining five nights in bed. I am all right to-day— except my ribs—having had a good sleep. I could not consult any one with any good while travelling, but as soon as I got here I sent for Dr. Campbell, and he prescribed for me, and I am now wearing, a belladonna and irritant plaster, and a flannel bandage. He says the pleura is badly bruised, and that there is some inflammation, but that if I keep quiet, and do not catch cold, I shall soon be right. I assure you it does not affect my appetite, which is a good one—very different from home—needing substantial carrion, and no put off of slop or shadows. I am, too, as hard as a horn, and believe I could travel for a week without any great personal grief. I went to New Brunswick and Nova Scotia to see the Governments of the two Provinces, and I had favourable interviews at Frederickton and Halifax, at the latter place seeing Lord Mulgrave, who was very polite, and invited me to stay, and, if possible, also to come again. I go to Quebec on special summons, to see the Government on Tuesday.

"I am growing anxious to know what Government will do: and I do hope I shall be able to get them to propose something before I leave. Until they declare themselves, I cannot arrange to leave for home; cannot complete my plans, or do anything, in fact. It is annoying—but the negociation is serious, and I must have patience. I know, from painful experience, how, when the nerves and brain are excitable from over tension and exertion, and anxiety and constant worry and wear, little matters are magnified. But already I feel myself so much stronger in nerve and courage that I look now complacently upon much which in the last two years would have cut me to the quick.

"I have worked very hard here, and done much in a little time."

"QUEBEC,

"Septr. 26, 1861.

"I am glad to tell, and you will be glad to learn, that I have to-day got my business with the Government into a good shape, and I shall have an official and, to a fair extent, favourable, answer to my application, on Saturday next. This will enable me, I hope, to come home sooner than otherwise—and I shall, at all events, be in the position of having, to a fair extent, succeeded. The Government agree to leave the amount they have to pay for postal service to arbitration, and to consider the question of capitalizing the amount as soon as Parliament meets, and on certain conditions, which I shall have to take home and consult my principals about. This will necessitate coming out next year. My side is better, but the plaster Dr. Campbell gave me has blistered me, with little hard pustules, over a piece of my side as big as a pancake; and I have suffered three days and nights of downright misery. To-day, however, I am almost all right, and go to dine with the Governor-General and Lady Head on Saturday. On that day the deputations, got together owing to my visit to Nova Scotia and New Brunswick, come here to meet the Canadian Government about the Halifax and Quebec Railway. If this succeeds I shall have not been idle.

"I send some trees which I got on the Madawasca river, and which please plant at once. Also a box containing samples of Canadian woods, which keep till I come. They are very beautiful. I think we must give them to Mr. Glyn."